LEGAL INTERPRETATION IN INTERNATIONAL COMMERCIAL ARBITRATION

Law, Language and Communication

Series Editors
Anne Wagner, Lille University – Nord de France, Centre for Legal Research and Perspectives of Law, René Demogue Group, France and Vijay Kumar Bhatia, City University of Hong Kong

This series encourages innovative and integrated perspectives within and across the boundaries of law, language and communication, with particular emphasis on issues of communication in specialized socio-legal and professional contexts. It seeks to bring together a range of diverse yet cumulative research traditions related to these fields in order to identify and encourage interdisciplinary research.

The series welcomes proposals – both edited collections as well as single-authored monographs – emphasizing critical approaches to law, language and communication, identifying and discussing issues, proposing solutions to problems, offering analyses in areas such as legal construction, interpretation, translation and de-codification.

Legal Interpretation in International Commercial Arbitration

JOANNA JEMIELNIAK
University of Copenhagen, Denmark

Routledge
Taylor & Francis Group
LONDON AND NEW YORK

First published 2014 by Ashgate Publishing

2 Park Square, Milton Park, Abingdon, Oxfordshire OX14 4RN
52 Vanderbilt Avenue, New York, NY 10017

Routledge is an imprint of the Taylor & Francis Group, an informa business

First issued in paperback 2020

British Library Cataloguing in Publication Data
A catalogue record for this book is available from the British Library

The Library of Congress has cataloged the printed edition as follows:
Jemielniak, Joanna.
Legal interpretation in international commercial arbitration / by Joanna Jemielniak.
pages cm. -- (Law, language and communication)
Includes bibliographical references and index.
ISBN 978-1-4094-4719-1 (hardback)
1. International commercial arbitration I. Title.

K2400.J46 2013
347'.09--dc23

2013021102

ISBN 978-1-4094-4719-1 (hbk)
ISBN 978-0-367-60097-6 (pbk)

Contents

List of Acronyms ix
List of Legal Journal Abbreviations xi
Acknowledgements xv

Introduction **1**
Structure of the Book 8

PART I: ARBITRATION AS A LEGAL AND SEMIOTIC PHENOMENON

1 International Commercial Arbitration: The Reasons for Success **13**
Historical Background 13
Definitions of Arbitration 15
Arbitration and ADR Methods 16
Arbitration and Litigation 19
Current Significance of Arbitration 21

2 ICA in the Context of Theories of Legal Discourse **27**
Capturing the Phenomenon: The Search for Tools 27
Legal Positivism 31
Legal Hermeneutics 35
Legal Deconstructivism 39
Sociolinguistics 44

3 ICA and the Semiotic Web of Law **49**
Semiotics and the Discursive Concept of Culture 49
The Semiotic Web of the Law 56
The Semiotic Web of Legal Interpretation in ICA 61
The Application of Foreign Substantive Law: The Issue of Double Intermediacy 64
ICA and Discourse Analysis 67

PART II: STRUCTURAL DETERMINANTS OF LEGAL DISCOURSE IN ARBITRATION

4	**Ad Hoc and Institutional Arbitration**	**73**
	Basic Notions	73
	Ad Hoc Arbitration	73
	Institutional Arbitration	77
	The Role of Procedural Soft Law	87
	Arbitration – Scale and Trends of Development	89
5	**Processualization of Arbitration**	**93**
	Arbitration Colonized?	93
	Status of an Arbitrator	97
	Limits of Judicial Control – Expanded Review Problem	99
	Processualization of Arbitration and Competition in the Market of Arbitral Services	100
6	**Arbitration in a Multicultural Environment: Structural and Procedural Aspects**	**103**
	General Issues	103
	Civil Law and Common Law Procedural Approaches – Addressing the Differences	105
	Shari'a and the Resolution of Commercial Disputes	113

PART III: LEGAL INTERPRETATION IN THE ARBITRAL DISCOURSE: FUNCTIONAL ASPECTS

7	**Comparative Method**	**125**
	Comparative Analysis – its Concept and Role in Adjudication	125
	Comparative Analysis and the Monolocal Approach	133
	Comparative Analysis and the Pluralistic Approach	137
	Comparative Analysis and the Representation of ICA as an Autonomous Legal System	141
8	***Lex Mercatoria* in Arbitration**	**149**
	Lex Mercatoria: The Concept and its Historical Development	149
	Sources of *Lex Mercatoria*	154
	The Role of Arbitration	158
	Lex Mercatoria in Arbitration – a Historical Perspective	160
	The Dilemma of Legal Predictability	169

9 ***Amiable Composition*** **175**
Recourse to Extralegal Standards in Arbitration: *Amiable Composition* and Elements of Mediation 175
Amiable Composition and Decision-Making *Ex Aequo et Bono* 180
Amiable Composition and *Lex Mercatoria* 183
Amiable Composition and Legal Certainty 189

10 **Public Order Considerations** **193**
Public Order – Concept and Contexts 193
Ordre Public Exception and Mandatory Rules of Law 200
Arbitration and Transnational Public Policy 203

11 **ICA: A Paradigmatic Change in Legal Interpretation?** **211**

Bibliography *221*
Index *245*

List of Acronyms

AAA	American Arbitration Association
ADR	alternative (sometimes amicable) dispute resolution
AFEC (VIAC)	International Arbitral Centre of the Austrian Federal Economic Chamber
ASA	Association Suisse de l'Arbitrage/Swiss Arbitration Association
BCICAC	British Columbia International Commercial Arbitration Centre
CENTRAL	Center for Transnational Law (University of Cologne School of Law)
CIETAC	China International Economic and Trade Arbitration Commission
CISG	(UN Convention on) Contracts for the International Sale of Goods
CLS	critical legal studies
CPIL	Code on Private International Law (Switzerland)
CPR	conflict prevention and resolution
FAA	Federal Arbitration Act (US)
HKIAC	Hong Kong International Arbitration Centre
IBA	International Bar Association
ICA	international commercial arbitration
ICC	International Chamber of Commerce
ICCA	International Commission on Commercial Arbitration
IICPR	International Institute for Conflict Prevention and Resolution
INCOTERMS	International Commercial Terms
JCAA	Japan Commercial Arbitration Association
KCAB	Korean Commercial Arbitration Board
KLRCA	Kuala Lumpur Regional Centre for Arbitration (Malaysia)
LCIA	London Court of International Arbitration
OAPEC	Organization of Arab Petroleum Exporting Countries
OIC	Organization of the Islamic Conference
OPEC	Organization of Petroleum Exporting Countries
PECL	Principles of European Contract Law
RICO	Racketeer Influenced and Corrupt Organization Act (US)
SASC	South Australia Supreme Court
SCC	Stockholm Chamber of Commerce
SIAC	Singapore International Arbitration Centre
SPA	sales and purchase agreement

PIL Act	Private International Law Act (Switzerland)
UCP	Uniform Customs and Practise for Documentary Credit
UNCITRAL	United Nationals Commission on International Trade Law
UNIDROIT	International Institute for the Unification of Private Law/Institut International pour l'Unification du Droit Privé
VCLT	Vienna Convention on the Law of Treaties
VIAC	Vienna International Arbitral Centre

List of Legal Journal Abbreviations

AC	Law Reports, Appeal Cases
All ER Rep	All England Law Report Reprints
Alta L Rev	Alberta Law Review
Am J Comp L	American Journal of Comparative Law
Am J Int'l Law	American Journal of International Law
Am Rev Int'l Arb	American Review of International Arbitration
Am U Int'l L Rev	American University International Law Review
Ann de l'Inst Droit Int'l	Annuaire de Institut de Droit International
Arb	Arbitration
Arb Int'l	Arbitration International
Arch Phil Dr	Archives de philosophie du droit
Ariz J Int'l & Comp L	Arizona Journal of International and Comparative Law
Bing	Bingham's Common Pleas Reports
Boston U Int'l LJ	Boston University International Law Journal
Brook J Int'l L	Brooklyn Journal of International Law
Bus Law	Business Lawyer
Canta L Rev	Canterbury Law Review
Cardozo J Conf Res	Cardozo Journal of Conflict Resolution
Cardozo L Rev	Cardozo Law Review
Chicago J Int'l L	Chicago Journal of International Law
CLR	California Law Review
Colum J Transnat'l L	Columbia Journal of Transnational Law
Const LJ	Construction Law Journal
Dick L Rev	Dickinson Law Review
Disp Res J	Dispute Resolution Journal
EJIL	European Journal of International Law
EJLR	European Journal of Law Reform
Fordham Urb LJ	Fordham Urban Law Journal
Geo Wash L Rev	George Washington Law Review

Hast LJ	Hastings Law Journal
Hastings Int'l & Comp L Rev	Hastings International and Comparative Law Review
Harv Int'l LJ	Harvard International Law Journal
Harv Negot L Rev	Harvard Negotiation Law Review
ICC Int'l Ct Arb Bull	ICC International Court of Arbitration Bulletin
ICLQ	International and Comparative Law Quarterly
IJSL	International Journal for the Semiotics of Law
ILSA J Int'l & Comp L	ILSA Journal of International and Comparative Law
Ind LJ	Indiana Law Journal
Int'l Bus Law	International Business Lawyer
ISLJ	International Sports Law Journal
J Am Arb	Journal of American Arbitration
J Comp Legis & Int'l L	Journal of Comparative Legislation and International Law
J Droit Int'l	Journal du droit international
J Int'l Arb	Journal of International Arbitration
J Int'l Econ L	Journal of International Economic Law
J Priv Int'l L	Journal of Private International Law
JIDS	Journal of International Dispute Settlement
J Transnat'l L & Pol'y	Journal of Transnational Law and Policy
J World Inv	Journal of World Investment
L & Soc Inquiry	Law and Social Inquiry
L & Soc'y Rev	Law and Society Review
L Ed	US Supreme Court Reports, Lawyers' Edition
Lloyd's L Rep	Lloyd's Law Reports
Loy LA L Rev	Loyola of Los Angeles Law Review
Marq L Rev	Marquette Law Review
Mealey's Int'l Arb Rep	Mealey's International Arbitration Report
Melb J Int'l L	Melbourne Journal of International Law
Mich L Rev	Michigan Law Review
Nev LJ	Nevada Law Journal
New Eng L Rev	New England Law Review
NY Int'l L Rev	New York International Law Review
NYLJ	New York Law Journal
OGEL	Oil, Gas and Energy Law Intelligence
Ohio St J Disp Res	Ohio State Journal on Dispute Resolution

Pace Int'l L Rev	Pace International Law Review
Pep Dis Resol LJ	Peppardine Dispute Resolution Journal
Rev Arb	Revue de l'Arbitrage
S & L S	Social and Legal Studies
SASC	South Australia Supreme Court
St John's L Rev	Saint John's Law Review
Stock Int'l Arb Rev	Stockholm International Arbitration Review
Tul L Rev	Tulane Law Review
U Kan L Rev	University of Kansas Law Review
U Pa L Rev	University of Pennsylvania Law Review
Unif L Rev	Uniform Law Review
U Tol L Rev	University of Toledo Law Review
Va J Int'l L	Virginia Journal of International Law
Vand J Transnat'l L	Vanderbilt Journal of Transnational Law
Vict U Well L Rev	Victoria University of Wellington Law Review
WLR	Weekly Law Reports (England and Wales)
Yale LJ	Yale Law Journal

Acknowledgements

This book is the outcome of several years of research and it could not have been written without the support of a number of institutions and persons with whom I have had the pleasure of working and from whom I have learnt so much. My work would be incomplete without their advice and help.

Participation in various projects connected with the legal semiotics movement over the years has provided many invaluable opportunities to collaborate with great colleagues, to discuss my research and to compare my primary, legal perspective with various linguistic and philosophical approaches. I feel particularly indebted to Anne Wagner and Vijay Bhatia, whose work has largely helped me to explicate my own methodological assumptions in the study of arbitration.

This book is based on research conducted during my stays at (among other locations) Harvard Law School (2007 and 2011/12) and the University of California's Berkeley School of Law (2008). I would like to express my particular gratitude to Roberto Mangabeira Unger and Mark Wu from HLS and to Meir Dan-Cohen from Berkeley for all their inspiration and encouragement.

I would also like to thank the Faculty of Law, University of Copenhagen, for the support that it has extended for this project. I am also indebted to Alison Kirk, my Ashgate editor, whose highly professional and friendly approach had helped me significantly throughout the process of preparing this book for publication.

Special thanks go to my husband Dariusz, whose insight, drive and sense of humour have constantly been a source of precious energy during my various professional undertakings.

Introduction

Legal interpretation has always been one of the focal issues for legal studies. The art of understanding, explaining and applying the law has for centuries intensely engaged jurists and philosophers, practitioners and the legal academia. The linguistic turn in the twentieth century philosophy, which also strongly affected jurisprudence, further drew the attention of the commentators to the discursive aspects of functioning of the law. A variety of streams in legal theory, from positivism and analytical jurisprudence to legal hermeneutics, sociolinguistics and semiotics, approached the phenomenon of legal interpretation and inevitable tension between the Montesquieuan striving towards discovery and transmission of the original meaning of the law, conventional character of interpretative canons and directives, and creative character of legal interpretation in its meaning-making and law-making aspects. As Roberto M. Unger observes, characterizing this dilemma, addressed predominantly by a strategy of rationalizing legal analysis:

> [f]or the jurist to reject too much of the received understanding of law as mistaken, expanding the revisionary power of legal analysis, would be to upset the delicate balance between the claim to discover principles and policies already there and the willingness to impose them upon imperfect legal materials. It would be to conspire in the runaway usurpation of democratic power.[1]

New developments in philosophy and legal theory coincided with a rapid revival of arbitration as an extrajudicial method of resolution of cross-border commercial disputes. Unprecedented success of international commercial arbitration (ICA) in the past decades led to a change of its status from one of the available ways of addressing private controversies, related to trade exchange, to the default method of resolving them. It is, however, not only the vital, practical significance of ICA in commercial relations that makes it a highly compelling object of study – it is also the specific character of legal discourse realized in arbitration and determined by its unique structure. In its current, consolidated form, ICA functions through an institutionalized, private and highly competitive network of centres and expert communities, with a distinctive, evolving regional and global dynamics. This book aims at exploring the influence of this characteristic setting on legal discourse, and in particular on legal interpretation in arbitration. In the quickly changing field of commercial arbitration the ways of legal inquiry, as well as the

1 Roberto Mangabeira Unger, *What Should Legal Analysis Become?* (Verso Books 1996) 40.

relevant argumentative repertory, have been developed in a specific and innovative way. Whereas to a large extent they have evolved from methods used in domestic adjudication, in many aspects they significantly differ from them.

The volume adopts primarily the perspective of legal studies to examine the issues of legal discourse in ICA, with a focus on legal interpretation. While significantly indebted to existing jurislinguistic research on the discourse of arbitration, it retains a predominantly legal orientation. Its main objective is an examination of discursive framework of arbitral proceedings through exploring the unique status of arbitration as a legal and semiotic phenomenon. On the methodological level, it has been inspired by the streams in legal theory, which adopt the view of legal interpretation as a discursive, non-linear process and perceive the role of legal argumentation as a rhetorical device and not as a syllogistic matrix, as discussed in detail in Chapters 2 and 3. The research perspective of legal theory, with a special focus on the Peircean tradition of legal semiotics, has been adopted; consequently, it has been assumed that the law functions as a specialized system of signs, recurrently communicated, reproduced, interpreted and reinterpreted by the community of participants to the discourse. These signs should not be observed and cannot be fully analysed apart from their cultural and social context. Legal interpretation and legal argument are thus perceived as a debate between possible solutions rather than as a direct way to the target, inscribed in the corpus of the law. This perspective thus remains in opposition to linear models of legal interpretation and assumes an adoption of a dynamic approach. The resulting concept of legal interpretation, adopted in this book, is – as explained in Chapter 3 – one that perceives it as semiosis, or a process of meaning-making through chains of reactions to and reformulations of legal communications. Those processes are examined, pursuant to discourse analysis postulates, in the context of specific legal, institutional, economic and social determinants, which affect the functioning of international arbitration.

The international character of the object of study required comparative examination of the existing legal framework and case law. Arbitral awards and correlated courts' decisions were examined for the extraction of interpretive and argumentative schemes. Due to the main scope and aim of analysis adopted in this volume, the dogmatic scrutiny was (however) performed as far as it was needed for explanatory purposes in regard to ascertaining the determining factors, goals, tools, administration and effects of the processes of legal interpretation. Consequently, the offered study of case law primarily illustrates the circumstances and components of interpretive activity in ICA.

Both institutional and ad hoc forms of arbitration are considered. The volume, particularly in the analysis of structural determinants of legal discourse, concentrates however, for several reasons, primarily on institutional arbitration. First, the discourse of ICA is largely influenced by a complex interplay between major arbitration centres, affected by market competition but also to a certain extent by convergence of procedural rules and standards. A number of key issues in arbitration, observable at a macro scale (such as the rise of new regional and global leaders, and the relation between the rise of arbitration centres and general trends in international trade) as well as at the micro level (such as forum shopping in one particular case), appears in the field of institutional ICA. Finally, while quantitative data on administered arbitration are accessible and can be explored and compared, the possibility of evaluating the volume of ad hoc arbitration lies to a large extent outside the reach of available research tools.

The discussion of the structural framework of ICA and current trends in its development serves as a background for further analysis of legal interpretation, its scope, goals and methods in commercial arbitration. The focus is on those aspects of legal interpretation which are specific and characteristic to arbitration – not those that are directly transplanted from domestic adjudication. It is also argued that in those cases that rely completely on application of domestic law to the merits of the dispute, and in which interpretation might aim at being possibly close to one that is assumed would have been offered in the same case by national courts acting 'from within' the legal system to be applied, the structural context of arbitration already changes the orientation of performed legal rendition and 'internationalizes' it through a recourse to a number of different sets of modifying considerations.

The analysis of the structural framework of arbitration reveals how it forms a specific context and introduces an 'outsider' perspective on applicable domestic rules. From the institutional point of view, the fact that arbitral tribunals do not render awards in the name of any State is a critical factor in creating the distance necessary for ensuring neutrality. The often-invoked anational character of ICA is indeed not tantamount to a complete delocalization (which – as the recent example of online arbitration demonstrates – remains unattainable under the New York Convention regime, even if the components of localization can be treated as conventional constructs and not material, geographical objects).

The anational aspect of arbitration is primarily present in the fact that the tribunals do not function as a manifestation of the State in the sphere of administration of justice. As Emmanuel Gaillard points out, despite this, for many commentators the phenomenon of ICA is no longer reducible merely to a private mechanism, pragmatically oriented at the demands of handling particular cases – but can be rather perceived as a *sui generis*, transnational system, with a developed function of delivery of justice and the relevant, established self-consciousness of the arbitral community (see Chapter 7).

Besides institutional and procedural, far-reaching independence, the outsider approach to domestic law in arbitration is realized also on the personal level: the nationality and primary legal training of arbitrators is often connected with a different State from the one whose law is applicable to the merits of the dispute. In such cases (as well as in those where an arbitrator consciously adopts a universal rather than domestic approach), they do not analyse proper substantive law according to a pre-established set of hermeneutic preconceptions as to proper tools and course of legal interpretation, characteristic to this law. They might project onto applicable law interpretative patterns acquired in their own legal education.

This possibly parochial aspect of legal interpretation in ICA is, nevertheless, moderated by the demands of international trade usages, widely implemented in the regulatory framework of arbitration.

However, it is also discussed how the immense global success of arbitration to some extent undermines its ideally sought-after, cosmopolitan and expert character. The group of 'truly international', highly specialized professionals – arbitrators and counsel – is undoubtedly vigorously expanding, as are numerous opportunities for relevant training and study. However, high popular demand for arbitration has also caused many general legal practitioners to get involved in arbitral cases occasionally rather than on a regular basis. It is this group of lawyers who are likely to attempt to transplant to arbitral proceedings their interpretive habits acquired in the domestic setting – sometimes as part of a deliberate procedural strategy, but often as an automatic action. The specific challenge of accommodating divergent procedural and interpretive approaches without disturbing principle of neutrality of the arbitral forum is separately addressed in the book.

The structure and institutional framework of arbitration, as well as the profile of participating actors, create a specific setting for realizations of legal discourse. They are effected as communications about the law, uttered on a meta-level; they are an outcome of specialized processes of semiosis – and as such necessarily imply the presence of an interpretive component. Characteristic manifestations of this aspect of arbitral decision-making are the object of the proposed analysis. In performing their function, arbitrators have not only drawn from methods of legal interpretation developed in the domestic context, and reapplied them in a changed environment: the practice of arbitration has also led to the unfolding of several characteristic ways of conducting legal rendition. They range from a broad and creative use of the comparative method, acquired and readapted from the domestic repertories, to *amiable composition*, one of the key examples of discretionary powers with which the arbitrators can be vested, being historically rooted in French jurisprudence, though scarcely used in domestic practice. The book aims at exploring those characteristic features of legal inquiry and exposing their conceptual and functional gravity.

The issue of interpretative practice in arbitration can also be placed in a broader context of modern institutional design and adjudicatory practice of various transnational bodies. In the broadest sense, the postwar renaissance of commercial arbitration was concurrent with the emergence of a number of international and regional courts and tribunals, created by the means of public international law. Developments in the fields of international criminal law and justice, international human rights and international trade law in the last decades marked, in a general sense, a broadening of the multilateral forum and formed an important part of its complex economic, geostrategic, political and social environment.[2]

2 Karen J, Alter and Sophie Meunier, 'The Politics of International Regime Complexity' 7 Perspectives on Politics (2009).

In this context, arbitration remains unique as a result of private initiative; arbitral tribunals derive their powers from the will of the parties and are not endorsed by the State, which raises a risk of them being treated merely as ephemeral ventures, which, even if created and operating on the basis of steady procedural rules and connected with specific arbitral institutions, are in practice assembled on demand. This ad hoc composition of tribunals, selected by the parties for a particular case, might augment the image of international commercial arbitration as a nebula of short-lived particles, with concentrations around several main centres – as opposed to the, institutionally and personally much more solidified, adjudicating bodies of public international law, with specific corpora of case law, the developments of which can be more easily distinguished and compared.

This picture of arbitration as a multitude of specific contractual arrangements, a globally dispersed collection of free electrons, is, however, not completely accurate. Several factors determine that neither on the institutional level nor in the sphere of case law can arbitration be easily reduced to an assembly of isolated instances of dispute resolution processes. First, arbitration is currently notably institutionalized and proceduralized, even if not in a way that is directly analogical to the permanent international courts. The vast popularity of arbitration and its dominant character as a way of resolving international business controversies have led to reformulations of the original concept of 'informal justice', and the saturation of ICA with components typical of litigation can be seen as a symptom of its consolidation and autonomy, where functional, pragmatic legitimacy no longer needs to be sought.

The role of arbitration centres as regional and global hubs for resolution of cross-border commercial disputes is complex and multifaceted. Besides offering organizational and administrative support, ensuring established standards and increasing certainty and reliability as to the neutral character, course and outcome of the proceedings, arbitration centres have also been commented upon as not only fora, but also – indirectly – actors in clashes of powerful economic interests. Arbitral institutions also play a certain part in harmonization of procedural standards, with some solutions (such as, for example, the possibility of applying rules of law – and not only law – to the merits of the dispute; or the *voie directe* competence) being gradually recognized by a growing number of different centres in their rules of procedure. However, competition between arbitral institutions can be observed also on the level of procedural rules (which might attract or discourage the parties) – which is a factor evidently obstructing harmonization. The centres might also reflect, strengthen and develop local approaches to arbitration, as could have been observed in the 'American wave' in arbitration or in the growth and evolution of the East Asian centres.

On the level of case law, this consolidation of ICA, characterizing its current stage, can be seen in what has been described as *sui generis* precedent, effective not due to its formal binding force but to its persuasive authority. The current body of the new *lex mercatoria* principles has been to a large extent developed by the means of such chains of arbitral awards, leading to the formulation and integration of transnational legal concepts. This cross-fertilization of legal concepts in the case of ICA seems particularly interesting, as it takes place across the tribunals, convened ad hoc and connected with arbitral centres. Due to the extensive use of comparative analysis, it is also influenced by domestic and public international jurisprudence – as can be seen in the evolution of such principles as transnational estoppel, merged from a common law concept, the civil law principle *non concedit venire contra factum proprium*, described as a specialized emanation of the principle of protection of good faith, and estoppel as known to the public international law jurisprudence.[3]

Another key difference between permanent international courts and ICA is the role of the State. The former are formally created by the common will of States and operate on their mandate, and this 'myth of origin' is a major source of legitimacy, even if, as Ingo Venzke observes, 'the common narrative according to which international law owes its existence and normativity to the consent of its subjects'[4] is seriously challenged by what he characterizes as the lawmaking activity of judicial authorities. The original impulse for creating international courts comes from the States, which on this level assume an active role. Arbitration, on the other hand, occupies a sphere in which the States largely abstain from action, as the limits of judicial control are restricted and the grounds for refusal of recognition and enforcement of an award are, under the New York Convention, narrowed down to a limited list of predominantly procedural concerns. Moreover, as often observed, the success of specific arbitral centres has also been historically related to the possibly liberal character of the relevant domestic laws on arbitration, constituting part of the *lex fori* and securing freedom of arbitral decision-making.

The vast success of arbitration in the sphere of commercial disputes, to the effect of largely replacing domestic litigation, has also been perceived as taking over the sphere traditionally reserved to the State, as the global scale of this phenomenon has exceeded its original conceptual formulation in the exercise of private, contractual freedom. Commercial arbitrators and centres have also been sought after in disputes which did not arise from contracts between private parties. The selection of the LCIA arbitral tribunal for the resolution of public international trade disputes, arising from an agreement between the US and Canada in *Softwood Lumber* is a remarkable example of sovereign States opting for a private forum for the handling of an international trade controversy.[5]

---

3 Paul Bowden, 'L'interdiction de se contredire au détriment d'autrui (Estoppel) as a Substantive Transnational Rule in International Commercial Arbitration' in *Transnational Rules in International Commercial Arbitration* (Emmanuel Gaillard and Piero Bernardini eds, ICC 1993).

4 Ingo Venzke, *How Interpretation Makes International Law: On Semantic Change and Normative Twists* (Oxford University Press 2012).

5 *Softwood Lumber (Canada v United States of America)*, LCIA Case No. 91312; *Softwood Lumber (Canada v United States of America)*, LCIA Case No. 81010 (2011);

It is worth noting that what Venzke defines as a semantic authority in international adjudicatory practice is thus in commercial arbitration allocated quite specifically. An accumulation of the body of arbitral case law is also different from the practice of permanent international courts. The network of arbitral centres is globally dispersed, supplemented by ad hoc arbitrations, and, while offering administration of justice, it is also directly subjected to market forces and competition. Moreover, arbitrators are usually explicitly granted (also in regard to legal interpretation) broad discretionary powers, which can be further extended by the parties.

The number of cases resolved by the leading centres worldwide, as compared with caseload of the public international adjudicating bodies, is vast (see Chapter 4). They are also relatively quickly handled – and time-efficiency is one of the commonly indicated reasons for selecting arbitration as a method of dispute resolution. Another one is confidentiality, which attracts the parties, but also necessarily affects transparency of arbitration. Only a fraction of the totality of arbitral awards is being published. Furthermore, the issue of completeness of knowledge can also be raised in regard to the published arbitral case law – as S.I. Strong remarks, the false conviction that a user who has a subscription to the main ICA databases has an access to a full range of available awards, is a dangerous state of 'not knowing what one doesn't know'.[6]

This opaque character of commercial arbitration, which distinguishes it from the practice of other international adjudicating bodies,[7] combined with the multicentric, autonomous landscape of ICA, did not hamper the development of an arbitral culture of legal interpretation, including such manifestations as cross-referencing and the development of legal concepts inspired by previous awards. In categories introduced by Gilles Deleuze and Félix Guattari, what seems to make this culture specific is its rhizomatic character, with multiple directions of growth and incoming inspirations, a vast part of the rootstock remaining underground, hidden from sight, and 'ceaselessly established connections between semiotic chains, organizations of power, and circumstances'.[8]

The dynamic changes of the narratives of arbitration – from the 'creature of contract', established within the limits of contractual freedom granted by the State, and approached on the micro scale of specific transactions, to an autonomous, anational system, effectively replacing adjudicatory activity of the domestic courts – are also consistent with this metaphor. Horizontal rhizomatic structures

---

Leonila Guglya, 'The Interplay of International Dispute Resolution Mechanisms: The Softwood Lumber Controversy' 2 JIDS (2011).

6 S.I. Strong, 'Research in International Commercial Arbitration: Special Skills, Special Sources' 20 Am Rev Int'l Arb (2009) 124, 129–30.

7 Cf. Catherine A. Rogers, 'Transparency in International Commercial Arbitration' 54 U Kan L Rev (2005).

8 Gilles Deleuze and Félix Guattari, *A Thousand Plateaus: Capitalism and Schizophrenia* (Continuum International 2004), 8.

are contrasted by Deleuze and Guattari with tree-like, vertical systems, with clear limits and reflecting linear orders. The sensitivity of arbitration to the trends of the market, mobility of its actors and its evolving, legitimizing strategies, all correspond with remarks on the proliferation of rhizome-like cultures, compared to water, filling available spaces, adjusting to the shape of the basins or fissures, but also capable of erosion and reshaping them.

These aspects of arbitration define communicative situations and utterances through which legal discourse is realized. This book aims at examining them and capturing the influence they have on the sphere of legal interpretation in ICA.

Structure of the Book

The volume is comprised of three parts, gradually unfolding the issue of legal discourse and legal interpretation in international commercial arbitration: it moves from a presentation of the object of study, theoretical background and methodological approach; through an examination of structural factors conditioning legal discourse in arbitration; to an analysis of its functional aspects, focusing on sets of interpretive considerations, identified as characteristic to ICA.

The first part aims at presenting arbitration as a unique legal and semiotic phenomenon and placing it in the light of relevant streams in legal and linguistic theory. The first chapter discusses the historical evolution of ICA and traces reasons for its unprecedented, global success in the field of international commercial controversies. After World War II, arbitration has gradually advanced from being a possible method of dispute resolution with a relatively limited scope of practical application, to achieving a status of the capital way of addressing cross-border trade controversies. The chapter examines legal, social, economic and organizational factors that have determined this course of development.

Chapter 2 locates arbitration – an anational, highly prosperous, privately developed alternative to State-administered litigation – in the context of contemporary theories of legal discourse and legal interpretation. Examined in its historical development, arbitration may serve as an illustration of prevalence of discursive, dynamic, non-linear models of legal reasoning over the syllogistic, linear ones, based on the Montesquieuan assumption that the role of a judge is that of a mouth of the law, pronouncing its letter.

The third chapter explores the semiotic theory of legal discourse. It critically approaches Robert W. Benson's concept of the semiotic web of the law in order to identify and locate key determinants and agents in the functioning of legal discourse in ICA, as affecting legal interpretation. It aims at capturing the specific character of arbitral legal rendition as seen from the perspective of the Peircean tradition of semiotics. The issue of diversity and heterogeneity of interpreted rules, determining the dynamics of legal discourse in arbitration is addressed. The chapter also discusses recent developments in the field of discourse analysis in ICA, reflecting the semiotic perspective.

The second part of the book is dedicated to institutional and structural determinants of legal discourse in ICA, which affect interpretative strategies and decisions. Chapter 4, opening this part, analyses two main forms of contemporary arbitration: the ad hoc and the institutional. The context of specific requirements and challenges which they pose for the actors involved in the practice of legal interpretation is further discussed. The chapter examines the influence of the organization of arbitral proceedings on the processes of legal rendition in the 'custom-tailored' mode of arbitration, as compared with its institutional counterpart.

Chapter 5 further addresses the issue of the evolution of arbitration, and its gradual abandoning of the historically acclaimed status as a particularly flexible and informal method of dispute resolution. As some authors observe, the phenomenon described as colonization of arbitration by litigation, or its judicialization, is a symptom of its increasingly mass and standardized character. It can be thus perceived as a direct consequence of the vast global success of ICA and understood as a strategy of enhancing its legitimacy. A relationship between processualization and the 'American wave' in arbitration is explored. The phenomenon of judicialization of ICA is also discussed in the context of competition in the market for arbitration services.

The following chapter examines procedural and interpretative demands, which are to be addressed when arbitral proceedings for cases with multicultural aspects are organized. It identifies and comments on procedural methods of reconciling differences in arbitrations, in which competing approaches of common, civil and Islamic law are present. These issues are put in a historical perspective: evolution of relevant methods and approaches in arbitration is examined, for example in the context of reasons for the late reception of the New York Convention in the Islamic countries and the reluctant approach of Shari'a jurisprudence towards the new *lex mercatoria*.

Part III of the volume focuses on functional aspects of legal interpretation in the arbitral discourse, in particular on interpretative standards, methods and considerations typical to decision-making in ICA. Chapter 7 analyses the role of comparative method in the processes of legal interpretation performed in ICA. It discusses possible different ranges of use of this method in arbitral decision-making (from formulation of a rule, through a corrective and supplementary application, to its use as a shield against an argument of the other party). It also explores how the wide extent of use and variety of fulfilled functions determine the specifics of adoption of the comparative method in arbitration. The analysis is placed in the context of three representations of ICA, as offered by Emmanuel Gaillard: the traditional or monolocal; the Westphalian or decentralized; and the transnational one.

The following chapter discusses the fundamental role of arbitration in the development of the new *lex mercatoria*, or the autonomous law of international trade. The body of the New Law Merchant has been to a large extent formulated and popularized through arbitral case law. The chapter scrutinizes the double role played in this process by the ICA awards. Over the decades, arbitral tribunals have exercised interpretation of already-existing, albeit often not sufficiently precise principles; but they have also expressed the rules not explicitly formulated before, by means of what Ana M. López Rodríguez characterizes as *sui generis* precedents.

Chapter 9 examines the concept of the competences, procedural framework and scope of the powers of arbitrators acting either as *amiables compositeurs* or resolving the case *ex aequo et bono*. Exercise of both those powers requires an explicit, relevant empowerment of arbitrators by the parties. The possible scope of authorization, the ways of administering it and the consequences thereof for the interpretive practice in arbitration are objects of further discussion. The chapter also examines the topic of grounds for resolution of a case through *amiable composition*, defined as either subjective or objective standards. The issue of appearance of a bias in arbitrators acting as *amiables compositeurs* is further addressed.

The tenth chapter discusses the role of recourse to public order in arbitral decision-making in international commercial cases. This argument, generally treated as having a supplementary and modifying influence in legal interpretation, has also been used in several awards as an autonomous ground for the decision. The concepts of *ordre public interne, ordre public international* and *ordre public transnational* are considered and their applicability to arbitral decision-making is examined. The chapter also addresses the issue of distinction between the public order exception and the mandatory rules of law in the context of representation of arbitration as an anational, neutral forum.

Finally, the concluding chapter examines the role of legal interpretation in ICA in the context of arbitration being one of the fields of emergence of transnational legal order. It explores the autonomizing status of commercial arbitration and its specific, flat, rhizomatic character. The issue of finality of awards as a factor in the growing independence of ICA is explored. The representation of arbitration as a transnational legal order, independent from the influences of national systems, is confronted with the still-present, procedural, legal substantive, personal and institutional connections of legal discourse in arbitration with the domestic environment.

PART I
Arbitration as a Legal and Semiotic Phenomenon

Chapter 1
International Commercial Arbitration: The Reasons for Success

Historical Background

Arbitration has been characterized as the oldest form of dispute resolution. Its first written evidence comes from ancient Greece, where the process of private adjudication was traditionally endorsed by the recourse to deities and was frequently conducted in the sanctuaries.[1] Its intensive development in the area of trade relations was a result of the expansion of maritime commerce in the region of the Mediterranean Sea. Egyptian, Phoenician and Greek trade customs served as an autonomous basis for decisions reached in commercial controversies. In the third century BCE the customs of the sea trade, applied in arbitration, were compiled in the first Maritime Code on the Greek island of Rhodes (re-implemented in medieval Italy in the city of Pisa).[2]

In the early Middle Ages, along with the decrease of international trade exchange, commercial arbitration became a practice of secondary importance. A revival of urban life in the tenth and eleventh centuries and an awakening of commerce in the age of crusades, as well as the growing exchange with Asia, stimulated the development of financial instruments and the recourse to specialized means of dispute resolution. In medieval France, Germany, Italy and England, arbitration became a regular way of settling controversies, adopted by the guilds of craftsmen in particular areas of trade.[3] Arbitral tribunals were also regularly summoned during the fairs and it was generally recognized that the parties whose dispute had been resolved by arbitration did not have a further recourse to the courts. The development of arbitration as a method of amicable and expert dispute resolution was accompanied by the emergence of medieval *lex mercatoria* – a set of substantive, uniform customs of the international trade, applied in such cases.[4]

---

1 Marcus Niebuhr Tod, 'International Arbitration amongst the Greeks' in *International Commercial Arbitration: A Transnational Perspective* (Tibor Varady et al. eds, Thomson/West 2003) 255ff.

2 Martin Domke et al., *Domke on Commercial Arbitration (The Law and Practice of Commercial Arbitration)* (3rd edn, Thomson/West 2003).

3 Sheilagh Ogilvie, *Institutions and European Trade: Merchant Guilds, 1000–1800* (Cambridge University Press 2011) 296ff.

4 Rodolphe J.A. de Seife, 'A Plea for the Creation of Commercial Courts' Spring New Eng L Rev (1982).

The consolidation of modern nation-States and State-administered justice in the seventeenth, eighteenth and nineteenth centuries to a large extent marginalized arbitration due to the lack of judicial support for enforcing arbitration agreements. In England, traditionally functioning as a significant centre of maritime trade and arbitration, this lack of autonomy of arbitration was expressed in the doctrine of revocability of an arbitrator. It was explicitly formulated for the first time probably in 1609 in *Vynior's Case* by Lord Coke, who upheld that before issuing an award an arbitrator could be revoked by a party, as his powers are directly derivative from the will of the parties (which does not affect the binding force of the main obligation in question):

> [a]lthough William Wilde, the defendant, was bound in a bond to stand to, abide, observe, etc., the rule, etc., of arbitration, etc., yet he might countermand it, for one cannot by his act make such authority, power, or warrant not countermandable which is by the law or of its own nature countermandable.[5]

As a consequence, in the cases where an arbitration agreement was concluded, there was no assurance that it would be executed if one of the parties rejected it. On the other side, not only arbitral awards but also pending arbitral proceedings were closely controlled by the domestic courts. This policy discouraged the parties to trade controversies from seeking a relief through arbitration. It also remained in contradiction with the vital interests of the participants to international commercial relations, who sought a neutral forum.

These difficulties were largely overcome in the late nineteenth and twentieth centuries by implementation of statutory law, granting actual effectiveness to arbitral agreements.[6] The US Supreme Court recognized this turn, stating in the *Marine Transit Corporation v Dreyfus* decision that '[i]n the light of the clear intent of Congress it is our obligation to shake off the old judicial hostility to arbitration'.[7]

The change of approach, arising worldwide, HAD gradually led to a renaissance of arbitration as a method of resolving international commercial disputes in the twentieth century. As Arthur von Mehren and Eduardo Jiménez de Aréchaga observe:

> arbitration – unlike national-court adjudication – is a dispute resolution process whose venue is contingent and transitory so that the place of arbitration neither represents nor establishes a permanent geographical or governmental relationship with a given national legal system. … The days when national legal systems intervened, as England did through the case-stated system, with on-going arbitrations are largely past.[8]

5 77 ER 595 (KB 1609) 598–99.

6 English Arbitration Act of 1889; United States Arbitration Act of 1925.

7 *Marine Transit Corporation v Dreyfus*, 284 US 263, 52 S Ct 166, 76 L Ed 282 (1932).

8 Arthur von Mehren and Eduardo Jiménez de Aréchaga, 'Final Report on Arbitration between States and Foreign Enterprises' 63 Ann de l'Inst Droit Int'l (1989).

In recent decades arbitration, after regaining its anational status, has undergone an impressive revival. In the field of commercial disputes it turned out to be the most successful alternative to dispute resolution by national courts. As Gabrielle Kauffmann-Kohler remarks: '[t]he last decades of the twentieth century have seen a phenomenal boom in arbitration, with all the hazards and vagaries that come with sudden success.'[9]

This process has been accompanied by a growing institutionalization, described as a transition from an informal 'merchant's justice' towards professionalism, legalism and proceduralization.[10] As discussed in Chapter 5, this trend has also been criticized for a tendency towards excessive formalization, making ICA increasingly close to litigation.

Definitions of Arbitration

According to René David, arbitration can be defined as

> a device whereby the settlement of a question, which is of interest for two or more persons, is entrusted to one or more other persons – the arbitrator or arbitrators – who derive their powers from a private agreement, not from the authorities of a State, and who are to proceed and decide the case on the basis of such agreement.[11]

Lew, Mistelis and Kröll distinguish the following four key features of this method of dispute resolution:

- an alternative to national court;
- a private mechanism for dispute resolution;
- selected and controlled by the parties;
- final and binding determination of parties' rights and obligations.[12]

The parties' intent is indeed decisive for the selection of arbitration as a method of dispute resolution, as well as for delimitation of its passage, including such vital issues as choice of law or the rules of law applicable to the merits of the dispute, and selecting and/or designing applicable procedural rules. However, while the

9 Gabrielle Kauffmann-Kohler, 'Foreword' in William W. Park, *Arbitration of International Business Disputes: Studies in Law and Practice* (Oxford University Press 2006).

10 Christian Bühring-Uhle et al., *Arbitration and Mediation in International Business* (2nd edn, Kluwer Law International/Aspen 2006) 32.

11 René David, *Arbitration in International Trade* (Kluwer Law and Taxation Publications 1985) 5.

12 Julian D.M. Lew et al., *Comparative International Commercial Arbitration* (Kluwer Law International/Aspen 2003) 3.

powers of arbitrators are entirely derivative from the will of the parties, after the commencement of proceedings arbitrators are obligated to remain autonomous and neutral in order to provide an award independently from parties' influence.

An instrument of control over this sphere, available to the parties when reasonable doubts are raised as to the neutrality of an arbitrator, is the challenging of an arbitrator (analogical to the challenging of a judge). Whereas traditionally the decisions on challenges have remained largely unpublished, there is a recent trend towards introducing more clarity in the process, observable in (among others) the Permanent Court of Arbitration's occasional disclosure of such decisions.[13] In this context, the practice of the LCIA Court to publish challenge decisions on a regular basis,[14] introduced in 2006 and explained by transparency reasons, but also by a need to fill 'the void in guidance',[15] is a remarkable step. The component of control can also be found in the right of the parties to seek, when applicable, for a further judicial review of the already rendered award, but it is usually not relevant to arbitral proceedings still pending (unless it concerns interim awards).

Arbitration and ADR Methods

Arbitration is often discussed in the context of other methods of extrajudicial dispute resolution, known as ADR. The acronym has been traditionally elaborated as alternative dispute resolution,[16] although ICC uses it as an abbreviation for amicable dispute resolution.[17]

As the field of ADR is quickly evolving, the spectrum of techniques in use is also broadening. As a result, the lists of ADR methods proposed by different authors may vary. The following techniques can be indicated as the most common:

- conciliation (sometimes treated as a form of mediation);
- early neutral evaluation/expert determination;
- expertise-arbitrage;
- mediation;
- med-arb (mediation/arbitration);
- mini-trial;

13 Gary Born, *International Commercial Arbitration* (Wolters Kluwer Law and Business/Kluwer Law International/Aspen 2009), vol 2, 1560.

14 'LCIA to Publish Challenge Decisions' in Global Arbitration Review, 1 June 2006 (vol 1(3)), available at <http://www.globalarbitrationreview.com/journal/article/16483/lcia-publish-challenge-decisions>.

15 Geoff Nicholas and Constantine Partasides, 'LCIA Court Decisions on Challenges to Arbitrators: A Proposal to Publish' 23 Arb Int'l 9(2007).

16 See, for example, Jerome T. Barrett et al., *A History of Alternative Dispute Resolution: The Story of a Political, Cultural, and Social Movement* (Jossey-Bass 2004) xxi; Stephen J. Ware, *Alternative Dispute Resolution* (West Group 2001) 5.

17 ICC ADR Rules in force as from 1 July 2001.

- negotiation;
- neutral listener arrangements;
- non-binding arbitration;
- private judging/'rent-a-judge';
- settlement conference;
- summary jury trial.

Some authors adopt a broad definition of ADR, characterizing it as all legally permissible methods of dispute resolution besides litigation.[18] According to this view, arbitration should be qualified as one of the ADR techniques. Tom Arnold describes this inclusive approach as specific to US jurisprudence, whereas the narrower concept of ADR as an 'alternative to adjudicative processes and hence not including binding arbitration which is adjudicative' is, in his opinion, rather European.[19]

This *sensu stricto* concept of ADR assumes that these methods serve as an alternative to adjudication (both litigation and arbitration) and not to litigation only. As a consequence, arbitration is treated as a separate category, not belonging to the ADR area. This view, also adopted in this book, seems to resonate with legal practice, where, in the field of international commercial disputes, arbitration has long become a regular (if not a default) method of dispute resolution. Moreover, as Fali S. Nariman observes, international commercial arbitration, perceived initially as a more expeditious and flexible alternative to domestic courts, has become significantly formalized and rigid – a phenomenon described as colonization of arbitration practices by litigation.[20] The demarcation between two adjudicative methods of dispute resolution (litigation and arbitration) on one side and the ADR techniques on the other seems thus increasing, although hybrid services such as med-arb and arb-med are also offered by some arbitral institutions. Practical difficulties, related to their efficient application, might arise though in the context of skills required from an arbitrator who also has to be able to act as a mediator, as well as parties' willingness to fully collaborate with arb-mediator or med-arbitrator and to disclose sensitive information while facing potential adjudicative procedure before the same person afterwards.

What appears to be disputable is thus the supposed status of arbitration as 'the only ADR process that can produce binding results without a post-dispute contract'.[21] This view, when considered after adopting the *sensu stricto* definition of ADR, would result in the assumption that an essential difference between arbitration

---

18 Cf. Ware (n 16) 5.

19 Tom Arnold, *Alternative Dispute Resolution: How to Use It to your Advantage. A Vocabulary of Alternative Dispute Resolution Procedures* (American Law Institute & American Bar Association 1996) 1.

20 Fali S. Nariman, 'The Spirit of Arbitration: The Tenth Annual Goff Lecture' 16 Arb Int'l (2000) 261ff.

21 Ware (n 16) 8.

(as well as litigation) and ADR is the lack of definitively resolving mechanisms of the latter. This notion seems to be expressed by the ICC, where arbitration is offered separately from ADR services. The clarification of the acronym as amicable dispute resolution also enhances the recognition of ADR as a set of methods based on processes leading to and supporting eventual resolution of the dispute by the parties themselves: 'ADR is an amicable dispute resolution procedure based on the goodwill of the parties and the assistance of a neutral third party'.[22]

Identification of ADR as a set of non-definitive techniques, aimed at achieving settlement, might raise some reservations. Lew, Mistelis and Kröll indicate that in expert determination, expertise arbitrage and private judging, parties to a dispute may decide in advance on submitting their entire case or its selected aspects to the definitive decision by a third party.[23] Use of these methods for resolving international business disputes is, however, still limited.

An alternative classification of methods of dispute resolution, based on the subject (delivering the solution) and on the adopted approach, addresses the doubts mentioned before. It does not accentuate the oppositions (ADR *sensu largo* versus litigation; or ADR *sensu stricto* versus litigation and arbitration) but focuses on mechanisms for concluding controversies. Having adopted this perspective, Varady, Barcelo and von Mehren[24] recognize (after Thomas Franck) three approaches to dispute resolution:

- one-party approach – characterized by *power* and resulting in imposition of the will of one contestant upon the other;
- two-party approach – characterized by *compromise*, resulting in a settlement between the contestants;
- three-party approach – characterized by *impartiality*, resulting in a decision issued by a neutral person or body not involved in the controversy in question.[25]

Legally permissible methods of dispute resolution fall within the scope of the two latter categories. The third-party approach is typical for litigation and arbitration (and present also in the selected ADR techniques, mentioned below); most ADR methods are based on the two-party approach; some of them (such as med-arb) are of mixed type.

The *impartiality*-oriented mechanism distinguishes arbitration from most other methods of extrajudicial dispute resolution: in mediation or negotiations it is the decision of the parties as to what the final outcome of this process shall be. In

---

22 <http://www.iccwbo.org/court/>.

23 Lew et al. (n 12) 10ff.

24 Tibor Varady et al., *International Commercial Arbitration: A Transnational Perspective* (3rd edn, Thomson/West 2006) 1.

25 Thomas M. Franck, *The Structure of Impartiality: Examining the Riddle of One Law in a Fragmented World* (Macmillan 1968) 11–15.

arbitration, the award is rendered by a third actor, obligated to remain independent and neutral (although the issue of securing this state in a setting where the parties by definition have the right to appoint arbitrators, has been widely discussed – also in the context of such practices as interviewing prospective arbitrators by the parties' counsel[26]).

In the majority of cases, the choice of an ADR method implies a striving towards amicable dispute resolution. Some of the ADR techniques, such as mediation (described as a prototype of ADR procedures[27]) or negotiations have been in use for centuries. ADR techniques are also extensively in use in some regions of the world, as the methods meet the needs of local and regional legal cultures particularly well. Bühring-Uhle, Kirchhoff and Scherer observe that:

> [m]ost of the countries of the Far East have a tradition of using conciliation – as a separate procedure or as an integral part of arbitration – as the dominant method of dispute resolution, even in commercial matters. Conciliation has deep roots in China and an overwhelming significance for dispute resolution throughout the entire society, including business relations with foreign investors and traders.[28]

As a consequence, the adoption of mixed approaches, while more demanding from an arbitrator, might be also a more natural way of handling controversies under such circumstances, as less antagonizing the participants than pure arbitration (see for example Art. 45 of the CIETAC Rules, which offers the parties a possibility of combining 'conciliation' with arbitration (which seems to function as arb-med rather than arb-conciliation).

Arbitration and Litigation

Both arbitration and litigation are examples of application of the three-party approach in dispute resolution. In comparisons of those two methods, the following aspects of arbitration are usually exhibited:

- selection and the powers of arbitrators are directly derivative from the will of the parties; not endorsed by a State (private character);
- the case is resolved in one place (an unwelcome effect of court shopping is eliminated);
- flexibility of procedure, resulting from the will of the parties as well as

26 See, for example, Olga K. Byrne, 'A New Code of Ethics for Commercial Arbitrators: The Neutrality of Party-Appointed Arbitrators on a Tripartite Panel' 30 Fordham Urb LJ 1815(2002); Seth Lieberman, 'Something's Rotten in the State of Party-Appointed Arbitration: Healing ADR's Black Eye that is "Nonneutral Neutrals"' 5 Cardozo J Conf Res (2004).

27 Bühring-Uhle et al. (n 10) 176.

28 Ibid. 169–70.

from the use of discretionary powers by arbitrators;

- confidentiality (there are no open hearings and the publication of awards is limited: the eventual publicity of the dispute is often a result of a subsequent review of an award by a domestic court);
- cost-efficiency (no high depositions are required; an overall cost of arbitral proceedings compared with litigation might be still equivalent or higher, due to the charges for arbitrators fees and costs of institutional administration).

Preference will be thus typically given to litigation in cases where the agreement between the parties as to the choice and terms of arbitration cannot be reached. James H. Carter notices that in the cases with multiple parties to the transactions, when there is a need for consolidation of several related proceedings, or when a broader discovery is required, litigation techniques provide better developed rules of procedure,[29] although, as discussed later, this landscape is changing along with the trend towards increased processualization of arbitration.

According to the survey by Loukas Mistelis, flexibility of procedure, different from a rigid procedural framework of litigation, is the reason most commonly provided by the parties for using arbitration.[30] The popular view that elasticity of arbitral procedure is one of its most important advantages over litigation, frequently expressed by legal doctrine, was also adopted relatively early in adjudication:

> [a]rbitration may or may not be a desirable substitute for trials in courts; as to that the parties must decide in each instance. But when they have adopted it, they must be content with its informalities; they may not hedge it about with those procedural limitations which it is precisely its purpose to avoid. They must content themselves with looser approximations to the enforcement of their rights than those that the law accords them, when they resort to its machinery.[31]

These expectations, however, might be confronted with a progressing trend towards actual formalization of arbitral proceedings, particularly those administered by the institutions. Fali S. Nariman comments on this phenomenon, invoking the biblical distinction between the letter and the spirit. While the parties favouring arbitration are arguably looking for a spirit of justice,

> [t]here is far too much of the 'letter' in modern International Commercial Arbitration (ICA) as practised: there is just too much legal baggage taken on

---

29 James H. Carter, 'Dispute Resolution and International Agreements' in *International Commercial Arbitration: A Transnational Perspective* (Tibor Varady et al. eds, Thomson/West 2009) 25.

30 Loukas Mistelis, 'International Arbitration – Trends and Challenges', conference paper, Rome (2007).

31 *American Almond Products Co v Consolidated Pecan Sales* (US Court of Appeals, Second Circuit).

> board the good ship ICA – as a result, it moves slowly and ponderously … ICA has become almost indistinguishable from litigation, which it was at one time intended to supplant.[32]

This view is shared by many commentators. Vijay Bhatia refers to the phenomenon of '*arbitigation*', or 'judicialization' of arbitration and introduces the concept of colonization of arbitration by litigation.[33] The theory of arbitration as 'litigation *bis*' for resolving international commercial disputes will be discussed in detail in Chapter 5.

Current Significance of Arbitration

There is little doubt that in the area of international commercial relations the growth of arbitration turned out to be spectacular: as Ana M. López Rodríguez[34] remarks, currently as much as around 95 per cent of international commercial contracts contain an arbitration clause. Following Braekhus, she also observes that 'in the field of [international] commercial contracts the only disputes falling under national courts concern less professional milieus, which conclude their deals under homemade or obsolete contract forms.'[35] As a result, arbitration, traditionally described in the context of alternative dispute resolution methods, in the field of international commercial disputes has become the default technique applied.[36] As Pierre Lalive had noticed already in 1987: '[i]nternational arbitration is now known to be "the" ordinary and normal method of settling disputes of international trade'.[37]

Several practical reasons are usually offered to explain this phenomenon. For centuries arbitration has served as a useful tool for confidential, expertise-based and quick resolution of international commercial controversies. Its contemporary success is perceived predominantly as a direct result of its pragmatic design, well-established institutional independence, as well as recognition of arbitral awards

---

32 Nariman (n 20) 262.

33 'International Commercial Arbitration Practices: A Discourse Analytical Study. Project Background' available at <http://enweb.cityu.edu.hk/arbitrationpractice/background.html>.

34 Ana M. López Rodríguez, *Lex Mercatoria and Harmonization of Contract Law in the EU* (Djof 2003) 67.

35 Ibid.

36 Markus A. Petsche, *The Growing Autonomy of International Commercial Arbitration* (Sellier European Law Publishers 2005) 1.

37 Pierre Lalive, 'Transnational (or Truly International) Public Policy and International Arbitration' in *Comparative Arbitration Practice and Public Policy in Arbitration* (Pieter Sanders ed, Kluwer Law and Taxation Publishers 1987) 293.

worldwide, due to general acceptance of the New York Convention, currently in force in 146 States.[38]

The advantages of arbitration of international commercial disputes, forwarded in the context of its vast popularity, are mostly pragmatic. Parties to those contractual relationships, which are hardly reducible to the sphere of one legal regime, are vitally interested in finding a convenient and neutral forum for the resolution of their controversies. Its anational and professional character and the confidentiality of proceedings are commonly acknowledged as key factors of the success of arbitration as a default alternative to litigation (although it is worth emphasizing that its anationality stands to some extent at odds with the territoriality principle permeating the New York Convention regime – as has been recently articulated anew in the context of the increased use of new technological means in arbitration[39]).

A relatively high level of predictability of the results of the adjudication process is another important reason, often indicated as decisive for the global popularity of arbitration. The sentences of judicial decisions, rendered by domestic courts in international litigation, are frequently hardly foreseeable to the parties, whereas the degree of predictability associated with arbitration (especially the institutional one), is evaluated as comparatively high.[40]

Resolution of a private international dispute through adjudication involves applying the law (or rules of law) on three different levels. First, rules of procedure (in litigation – civil procedure stipulated by *lex fori*) govern the course of examination of the case. Second, conflict of laws regulations (private international law rules, belonging to domestic legal orders of particular States) are construed in order to determine the rules to be applied to the substance of the dispute. Third, *lex causae* (proper law), or the substantive regulations which have been identified on the second level, are applied to produce a decision on the merits of the controversy.[41]

A party involved in litigation (especially before a foreign court) can find the results of interpretive processes on each level hard to anticipate. Confronted with foreign procedural law in action, a party may be disoriented as to its own position, admissible evidence, the course of proceedings, etc., which will in practice result in the balance of equal footing for the contestants being impaired. Analogically, criteria provided by the domestic conflict of laws rules as connecting factors for the determination of substantive law applicable to legal relationship in question differ among the States, and thus their application

38 See <http://www.uncitral.org/uncitral/en/uncitral_texts/arbitration/NYConvention_status.html> (see under '1958 – Convention …' in the bibliography in this volume).

39 Margaret L. Moses, *The Principles and Practice of International Commercial Arbitration* (2nd edn, Cambridge University Press 2012) 63.

40 Carter (n 29) 24.

41 Arthur Taylor von Mehren and Eckart Gottschalk, *Adjudicatory Authority in Private International Law: A Comparative Study* (Martinus Nijhoff 2007).

can lead to the outcomes unexpected to the parties. Finally, substantive rules identified as relevant (*lex causae*) may affect the position of a party in a way not always easy to be pre-established, and occasionally this may be to a grave degree (as, for example, through the recognition of particular types of remedies).

Arbitration facilitates the parties to reduce the risk of such unexpected results of law application in all of the described spheres. The will of the parties is decisive not only for the commencement of arbitral proceedings and for vesting arbitrators with authority. It is also decisive in regard to the rules of procedure to be applied, as well as to the choice of substantive law to govern the relationship in question (which in litigation can be rejected if it does not meet the *lex fori* conflict of laws standards).

If the parties do not use their right to choose substantive law and/or design rules of procedure, but they decide for resolution of their dispute by a particular arbitral institution, the process will be conducted according to the institution's standard rules of procedure, available in advance to both parties. Whereas a judge is bound to apply private international law regulations belonging to *lex fori*, an arbitrator is obligated to follow it as *lex loci arbitri* to a far lesser degree. Notably, in legislations based on the UNCITRAL Model Law on International Commercial Arbitration (currently enacted in over 80 States and territories[42]), arbitrators are assigned with significant discretionary powers in ascertaining which conflict of laws standards shall be applied in order to determine proper substantive law.[43]

There is also a tendency towards shaping the authority of an arbitrator as even more far-reaching. A direct choice competence (*voie directe*), stipulated by regulations of numerous arbitral institutions, entitles an arbitrator to take a short-cut through the conflict of laws application stage. An arbitrator can instead select and apply directly such substantive rules which he or she deems to be proper.[44] A standard requirement of providing the rationale for an award (including sufficient grounds for the adopted choice of substantive law) is indicated as a practical constraint to a potential abuse of this competence.[45]

Another important issue is that arbitral proceedings are generally conducted with regard to the fact that consequences of an arbitral award will take place principally in the country where it will be enforced and not in the one where the arbitration took place. Awareness of these circumstances supports an adoption of

42 As of 30 March 2012, see <http://www.uncitral.org/uncitral/en/uncitral_texts/arbitration/1985Model_arbitration_status.html>.

43 See, for example, UNCITRAL Model Law on International Commercial Arbitration Art. 28(2); UNCITRAL Arbitration Rules Art. 33(1).

44 See, for example, ICC Arbitration Rules Art. 17.1; Arbitration Rules of the Arbitration Institute of the Stockholm Chamber of Commerce Art. 22.1; 2006 Rules of Arbitration of the International Arbitration Centre of the Austrian Federal Economic Chamber (Vienna Rules) Art. 24.2.

45 López Rodríguez (n 34) 77.

a more universal approach to shaping and interpreting rules of procedure, conflict of laws principles as well as substantive rules (including transnational and not only domestic regulations). In resolution of international commercial disputes the tendency towards avoiding national legal particularities, justified by the transnational character of the relationships in question, seems well grounded.

As a result, arbitration seems to attract parties seeking for a possibly standard and predictable treatment. It is also a way of minimizing the risk of forum shopping (competing efforts of the parties to initiate the process of resolution of their case before the body predicted to be most likely to render a favourable decision)[46] – the practice which substantially increases the level of legal uncertainty in case of a controversy. Von Mehren and Jiménez de Aréchaga observe that in order to reduce the restrictive effect of *lex loci arbitri* on arbitration, the locations for arbitral proceedings are, in practice, established mostly in the States where this form of dispute resolution is granted a broad autonomy and the possibility of court intervention in pending proceedings is minimal.[47] Consequently, the role of ICA in formulating the autonomous rules of the international trade, both procedural and substantive, is significant.[48]

The complex issue of securing impartiality and neutrality in the context of procedure itself, as well as of a person or a body authorized to decide the dispute, is another key factor, affecting the choice of method of dispute resolution. As already discussed, litigation commenced in a foreign country, representing not only a different legal system, but possibly also a different legal tradition, which can be unknown to the party, can turn out to be unreasonably burdensome. The demands of participation in proceedings conducted in a non-native (or even entirely unfamiliar) language can negatively affect actual implementation of the neutrality principle. The lack of acquaintance with foreign procedural regulations (in regard to such issues as requirements about the professional representation, admissibility of particular types of evidence, oral hearings/documentary analysis orientation of the procedure), combined with the cost and effort of finding a local counsel with adequate expertise, can also form a serious challenge to a party.

It has been also often emphasized[49] that the fact that international commercial arbitration is not endorsed by any particular State seems to facilitate both conflicting parties to seek for non-discriminatory proceedings and decision. Arbitration is

46 Andrew S. Bell, *Forum Shopping and Venue in Transnational Litigation* (Oxford University Press 2003) 275ff.

47 Von Mehren and Jiménez de Aréchaga (n 8).

48 Filip De Ly, 'Lex Mercatoria (New Law Merchant): Globalization and International Self-Regulation' 14 Diritto del Commercio Internazionale (2000); López Rodríguez (n 34) 81ff.

49 See, for example, Lew et al. (n 12); Christopher R. Drahozal and Richard W. Naimark, *Towards a Science of International Arbitration: Collected Empirical Research* (Kluwer Law International/Aspen 2005).

frequently characterized as anational, delocalized, floating or drifting,[50] which is a result of what Thomas E. Carbonneau describes as a nearly complete privatization of the international arbitral process:

> [b]y ratifying the New York Arbitration Convention, states abandon their sovereign authority over arbitration – legitimating the process with their sovereign legal authority initially, but thereafter allowing it to self-regulate. The proclaimed independence of arbitration from national law traditionally was expressed in terms of the autonomy of the procedure and the award. Progressively, anational arbitration also gained expression through a statement of substantive arbitrator autonomy: international arbitrators were alleged to have the authority to apply a nonnational arbitral commercial law to the merits of disputes.[51]

The non-national status of arbitration under the New York Convention, as already discussed, is, however, not absolute, as the domestic regimes of the place of arbitration, as well as of jurisdictions in which the recognition and enforcement of an award is sought, might materially influence the final outcome of the process of dispute resolution. As compared to domestic litigation, arbitration still offers remarkable flexibility in the sense of arbitral proceedings not being directly subordinated to procedural constraints and which mandatorily bind national courts. The professional expertise of arbitrators in addressing specific issues of international business transactions is yet another factor that might turn out to be decisive in parties' selection of arbitration rather than litigation. In cases involving parties coming from different legal systems and traditions, arbitration thus offers a convenient and reasonably neutral forum.

---

50 William W. Park, 'The Lex Loci Arbitri and International Commercial Arbitration' 32 ICLQ (1983); Filip De Ly, *International Business Law and Lex Mercatoria* (North-Holland 1992).

51 Thomas E. Carbonneau, 'The Remaking of Arbitration: Design and Destiny' in *Lex Mercatoria and Arbitration: A Discussion of the New Law Merchant* (Thomas E. Carbonneau ed, JurisNet 1998) 6.

Chapter 2
ICA in the Context of Theories of Legal Discourse

Capturing the Phenomenon: The Search for Tools

The unprecedented success of international commercial arbitration in the last decades of the twentieth century, and the characteristic features of this method of resolution of private, cross-border disputes, lead to a question of the determinants and status of legal interpretation in ICA. This chapter aims at placing arbitration – an anational, highly prosperous, privately developed alternative to State-administered litigation – in the context of contemporary theories of legal discourse and legal interpretation. When approached with regard to its historical development, arbitration may serve as an illustration of the prevalence of discursive, dynamic, non-linear models of legal reasoning over the syllogistic, linear ones, based on the Montesquieuan claim that the role of an adjudicator is to be no more than the mouth of the law.[1] However, the recent, observable trend of judicialization or colonization of arbitration by litigation (as discussed in detail in Chapter 5) calls for a renewed interest to be paid to conceptualizations of legal interpretation in arbitral decision-making.

The private character of arbitration and its significant (though certainly not absolute) level of procedural detachment from the influence of domestic legal orders; the (nowadays ubiquitous) presence of this method in the field of commercial disputes with an international element emerging worldwide; advanced global and regional institutionalization; the increasingly formalized (processualized) character of arbitral proceedings; as well as the wide discretionary powers of arbitrators in regard to determining applicable rules of law – all these factors affect the conceptual and pragmatic framework, course and tools of interpretive activity performed by commercial arbitral tribunals.

These specific features of international arbitration, distinguishing it from domestic adjudication, make an inquiry on legal interpretation in this field a task as challenging as it is captivating. This task requires an identification of relevant theoretical background, offered by jurisprudence and other disciplines, such as jurislinguistics and legal social studies, which would enable putting the phenomenon of legal interpretation in ICA in the context of contemporary theories of legal discourse and interpretation.

---

1 Charles de Secondat Montesquieu et al., *The Spirit of the Laws* (Cambridge University Press 1989).

Vijay Kumar Bhatia, Christopher Candlin and Jan Engberg capture an essential difficulty of preserving the original claim to non-ambiguity and precision of legal interpretation, extended and sought to be protected under the auspices of domestic legal systems, in the conditions of increasingly globalized areas of law and its administration – with arbitration being perhaps the most prominent of such fields. As they observe in regard to the strive towards certainty of legal language and, consequently, legal interpretation:

> There are several other factors that make this claim somewhat problematic: the legal system, the language, the socio-political and the cultural context within which a specific instance of legal discourse is embedded. One of the main issues arising from this variation is the extent to which the integrity of a specific legal genre is likely to be maintained when it crosses linguistic, socio-political, cultural or legal boundaries in the present-day global business, trade or other professional environment. These issues of diversity in construction and interpretation of legal discourse acquire a more serious importance when we see law losing its jurisdictional character in this rapidly changing corporate world of international trade and commerce.[2]

Whereas the interpretation and application of proper substantive rules to the merits of the dispute in arbitration are based largely on domestic law, the recourse to it in ICA is specific. First, it is the domestic law applied outside its usual context, by adjudicators not acting from the positions of insiders to this system in a way, in which the domestic judges perform their function. Even if arbitrators resolving a controversy are in fact primarily trained in the legal system, the rules of which they are going to apply to the merits of the dispute – which, due to the international character of the arbitral profession, as well as to the neutrality requirements governing the appointment of arbitrators, is very often unlikely – the tribunal itself is a private body, which does not act and render awards in the name of the State.

First, the bonds between the tribunal and *lex fori* (while still existing, due to the territoriality principle permeating the New York Convention, as discussed in Chapters 1 and 7) are also remarkably weaker than in case of the domestic courts, up to the point of leading many commentators to claim that arbitration is an anational or floating way of resolving disputes. The fact that *lex causae* does not necessarily have to be either the system of the forum or that of the place of anticipated enforcement (which nevertheless remain relevant due to setting aside and enforcement concerns) steers legal interpretation in ICA further away from the strictly national legal orientation and enriches it with additional, comparative components.

---

2 Vijay Kumar Bhatia et al., 'Concepts, Contexts and Procedures in Arbitration Discourse' in *Legal Discourse across Cultures and Systems* (V.K. Bhatia et al. eds, Hong Kong University Press 2008) 9.

Second, the law of particular national systems is not the only source of rules applicable to the merits of the dispute resolved by the means of international arbitration and the saturation of arbitral decision-making with international and transnational considerations (including interpretive directives and methods) is higher than in the private international cases resolved by the domestic courts. These considerations cover a wide range of interpretive issues – from substantive rules, such as the new *lex mercatoria*; through transnational public policy principles, channelling and modifying the process of application of domestic law; to particular methods of legal interpretation, originally rooted in domestic adjudication, but further developed and used with increased intensity in arbitration (as the comparative method, extensive use of which is necessarily and naturally connected with arbitral decision-making, as well as *amiable composition* and deciding *ex aequo et bono*, enjoying much more popularity in the ICA practice than their historical, national counterparts).

Third, what seems to make legal interpretation in arbitration specific is also its intrinsically international institutional and cultural setting, which puts rendition and application of the domestic legal provisions in a general context very different from that of national courts' adjudication. This includes circumstances and considerations much broader than strictly legal ones, as the functioning of arbitration adds in the field of private commercial dispute resolution an entire net of new threads to the complex fabric of international trade, economic, social and political relations. What Robert Benson characterizes as the semiotic web of the law[3] – or the context in which the legal discourse *sensu largo* functions – is in ICA very different from that of domestic courts, even when they happen to face a case of substantially the same kind.

One of the crucial factors, decisive for arbitration gaining its current position, has been the achievement of the status of a neutral forum. In case of national courts such status is augmented by the official authority of a State, which the courts represent and in the name of which they render the decisions. The character of adjudication as belonging to the States' *imperium* sphere is also emphasized by the visual and ritual aspects of court proceedings, from the judges' robes to the spatial organization of a courtroom – the parties are ever reminded about the decisive role of the State in the resolution of their controversy. As Oscar Chase and Jerome Bruner remark, in the context of American trial:

> [s]uch ceremonial features evoke deeply held values through the use of symbols appropriate to the task for that culture. As the judge is both instrumentally and symbolically the personification of state authority, it is not surprising that her activity is intensely ceremonial. Adherence to the details of the rites helps to maintain belief in the impersonal nature of the result. Otherwise

3 Robert W. Benson, 'The Semiotic Web of the Law' in *Law and Semiotics* (Roberta Kevelson ed, Plenum 1987).

> puzzling behaviors are almost entirely in the service of depersonalization and sacralization.[4]

However, it is precisely what in a domestic setting augments the position of a judge as an impartial umpire that in international commercial cases makes it problematic. The direct, official and socially accentuated connection of an adjudicator with a particular State and its legal system may be perceived as not securing sufficient neutrality in relation to parties coming from different legal orders. Additionally, if the court is acting in the name of the State of one of the parties, this party gains the advantage of relatively closer access to justice, relevant legal services, familiarity with the judicial system and court proceedings, lack of linguistic barrier, etc.

The current status of arbitration – private (not representing any State), yet institutionalized – has been indicated as supportive to its neutrality in the context of international commercial relations. As Yves Dezalay and Bryant G. Garth observe, arbitration does not need to seek legitimization through lack of formality, as a flexible, efficient and simple merchants' tool anymore. The new source of legitimacy is, as they argue, to be found in its increased processualization.[5] It seems, though, that the crucial legitimizing attribute of arbitration can be rather its neutrality, successfully advocated in both phases of development of modern ICA, as represented in arbitration literature: the renaissance of expeditiously acting, anational tribunals for business disputes and current institutions operating in proceduralized and complex case settings.

The discussion is vivid in legal doctrine as to whether arbitration currently fulfils a role exceeding that of merely offering legal services on an *a casu ad casum* basis, and has also gradually undertaken a more general function of an autonomous, transnational, institutional network, serving the needs of administration and preservation of justice (previously reserved for public courts), and performing a *de facto* judicial function.[6] Certainly, ICA has been generally successful in creating an image of a global, institutionalized system, largely independent from the States' judicial interference and what have been described as parochial legal influences. At the same time, arbitral centres are private institutions, intensely participating in the competition in the market of dispute resolution services on a global and regional scale (as further described in Chapter 5) – which is an aspect not present in the functioning of the domestic courts. This makes them more directly, organizationally and procedurally responsive to the evolving needs of international commerce, but also turns the challenge of developing standards of neutrality for cross-border cases to a more consciously undertaken one.

---

4 O. Chase and J. Bruner, *Law, Culture, and Ritual: Disputing Systems in Cross-Cultural Context* (New York University Press 2005) 119.

5 Yves Dezalay and Bryant G. Garth, 'Fussing about the Forum: Categories and Definitions as Stakes in a Professional Competition' 21 L & Soc Inquiry 285(1996) 299.

6 Cf. Emmanuel Gaillard, *Legal Theory of International Arbitration* (Martinus Nijhoff 2010) 35.

In the context of providing a functional framework for legal discourse and legal interpretation, this aspect of continuous, intentional design (instead of reproduction of institutional and procedural patterns) seems to be a highly important feature of arbitration. Conclusions on the place of proceedings, language or admissibility of particular types of evidence – predetermined in litigation – are examples of decisions to be made by an arbitral tribunal with regard to parties' intent, so as to offer the contestants a fair opportunity to present their claims and to provide equal footing for all throughout the entire procedure. Flexibility as to the determination of the language of proceedings, instantly broadening the limits of legal discourse in ICA, is one of its key features. Indeed, one of the most frequently commented-upon innovations in the 2012 CIETAC Rules, indicated as a sign of a broader international opening of the centre, has been the introduction of the competence of the tribunal to designate, in the absence of relevant parties' agreement and with regard to circumstances of the case, Chinese or any other language as the language of arbitration (Art. 71(1)) – as opposed to the 2005 version of the Rules, Art. 67(1), under which Chinese was the default language of the proceedings unless the parties explicitly stipulated otherwise.

International commercial arbitration thus forms a specific setting for the functioning of legal discourse, affecting its flow and outcomes. As a private, globalized, highly institutionalized, dispersed and competitive network that claims legitimacy through securing procedural and personal neutrality in an international context, arbitration has adopted and developed new ways of using the existing legal interpretive instrumentarium.

This unique phenomenon and its functioning on the level of legal interpretation will be further addressed in the context of various streams in modern legal theory. As argued later in this volume, the practice of international commercial arbitration can not only be explained (that is, serve as a passive object of analysis, undertaken from one of the possible theoretical perspectives) but has also consciously derived inspiration from legal theory in formulating its own regulatory framework and related jurisprudence.

Legal Positivism

This conscious approach seems particularly noticeable in the context of legal positivism, which assumes the necessary connection between the law and the will of a sovereign. Legal discourse perceived from this perspective is thus not dialogical, but rather seen as a series of communications which bear a necessary mark of formal authority; an official legitimization by the State. The attention of an interpreter is thus focused on rendition of a legal text possibly close to its authentic, encoded meaning; the Montesquieuan vision of the role of an adjudicator, rendering judgments which are no more and no less than 'a precise text of the law' (as the judges are 'only the mouth that pronounces the words of the law, inanimate beings who can moderate neither its force nor its rigour'[7]) results in a perception of the process of legal interpretation as a formalized search for legal Logos.[8]

The authentic meaning, permeating the letter of the law, has to be uncovered by an interpreter. The dominant model of legal reasoning is thus a syllogistic one, taking the form of a possibly straight path, leading to the goal: the decoded meaning, embedded in a legal text. Also the soft versions of legal positivism assume this functional orientation of legal interpretation and concentrate on the act of decoding and on overcoming possible obstacles to reaching this goal. The natural indeterminacy and openness of language is a major one: in Herbert L.A. Hart's works the opposition against 'mechanical jurisprudence' is an effect of recognition of the infinite richness of factual situations to which the rules of law apply, but also of the character of the expression of the rules, the linguistic openness of which increases the difficulty of the process of legal subsumption.[9]

Language as a vehicle for the meaning is thus an object of main inquiry and relevant logical operations. Inspiration that legal positivism has derived from analytic philosophy is its important characteristic. It has influenced further development of formal analytic jurisprudence, as well as the proposition by Hart (after John L. Austin) that legal theory be based on ordinary language philosophy. While rejecting the fiction of the possibility of an always-precise subsumption, Hart nevertheless continues the discussion on verifiability/falsifiability of performatives (which E.J. Lemmon defined as verifiable by their use[10]), including the laws. The core of Hart's longstanding polemic with Ronald Dworkin, as elaborated in an extensive Postscript to the 1994 edition of *The Concept of Law*, relates in fact to diverging concepts of legal discourse. It was Dworkin's postulate that descriptive legal theory has a primarily semantic character (as lawyers apply the category of truth to propositions of law and explain them through a recourse to meaning) that raised Hart's objections on the grounds of lack of sufficient distinction between communications external and internal to the legal system.[11] The latter, internal elements were in Hart's theory tantamount to rules (it should also be noted that Dworkin, after criticizing such an approach as limiting, eventually acknowledged the difference between Hart and himself in defining rules[12]). Hart also rejects Dworkinian arguments on legal interpretive activity as a search for the best possible solution, available on the grounds of a particular legal culture.

Analytic orientation, focus on decoding legal texts, as well as the emphasized link between the law and the State, and legitimization of rules through formal

7 Montesquieu et al. (n 1) 163.

8 Cf. Joanna Jemielniak, 'Just Interpretation: The Status of Legal Reasoning in the Continental Legal Tradition' 15 IJSL (2002) 327ff.

9 H.L.A. Hart, *The Concept of Law* (with 'Postscript' eds P. Bulloch and J. Raz) (Clarendon Press 1997) 128ff.

10 E.J. Lemmon, 'On Sentences Verifiable by their Use' 22 Analysis (1962).

11 Hart (n 9) 247.

12 Ronald Dworkin, *Taking Rights Seriously* (Harvard University Press 1978) 58–59.

authority (effected, according to Hart, through the secondary rule of recognition[13]) have significantly influenced the development of legal positivism. These features have also made the capturing of the phenomenon of international arbitration and its functioning within this paradigm a challenging task.

The embedment of law in the State and the State's endorsement validating the administration of justice, recurring motifs of positivist legal analysis, had to be reinterpreted in the context of the quickly developing network of international commercial arbitration. The entirely private character of arbitration, combined with its currently ubiquitous presence, have led some authors to question the grounds of its official myth of origin. The possibility for arbitrating has been traditionally (and along the lines of positivist legal theory) explained as a specific exercise of contractual freedom, which can be undertaken by the parties precisely and solely because of a State's initial concession in this regard. In this localized vision of international arbitration, it is enabled as an available method of dispute resolution from within particular national legal systems, as States acting in their sovereign authority may choose to allocate relevant rights to private actors.

Creation of the global legal framework for ICA, in particular the entry into force of the New York Convention, is similarly an expression of the will of the States which have decided to accede to the international regime of recognition and enforcement of arbitral awards. Consequently, private parties seeking resolution of their controversies through arbitration, and the subsequent enforcement of rendered awards, are acting with the limits set by the national legal systems.

Legal positivism thus offers a necessary, plausible explanation of the legality and legitimization of arbitration, without detriment to the traditional theory of hierarchy of sources of law of domestic as well as public international origin (as on both levels the sovereign authority of the State controls admissibility of arbitration and recognition of its effects). It seems, however, that such view, while formally correct, is also reductionist, as some important institutional and functional aspects of modern arbitration escape an analysis thus oriented. An important issue is the scale of autonomization and the unprecedented popularity of arbitration, which results in administration of justice in the entire field of international commercial contracts being (by and large) effectively outsourced to private bodies and beyond the mechanisms and institutions of the States. As a result, arbitration has been often indicated as a model example of successful legal globalization,[14] to a large extent escaping the intervening control of the State (as the grounds for refusal of enforcement of an award under The New York Convention are generally procedural, and not related to the merits of the decision). The process of gradual autonomization of international arbitration has been addressed by a number of commentators, as further described in the following chapters.

13 Hart (n 9) 147ff.

14 Cf. Gunther Teubner, 'Global Bukowina: Legal Pluralism in the World Society' in *Global Law without a State* (Gunther Teubner ed, Dartmouth 1997).

Another object of controversy is the definition of the role and limits of discretionary powers of arbitrators, noticeably wider than in the case of domestic judges (which serves as a main model and point of reference for positivist theories of adjudication). While the judges function primarily as agents of the State, arbitrators do not render the awards from the positions of insiders to a particular domestic legal system; in fact their detachment from the legal system applied to the merits of the case supports their claim to neutrality, that has to be achieved in the transnational context of the cross-border relationship between the parties. The formal requirement that arbitrators should not be of the nationality of any of the parties to a dispute, introduced by some arbitral centres (as seen, for example, in the LCIA Rules, Art. 6), considering that *lex causae* is very likely to be determined as the law of one of the parties, further augments the status of arbitrators as outsiders to the applicable legal system.

On the textual level of their interpretive activity arbitrators also act as outsiders in the sense that their application of proper substantive law is mandatorily readjusted in the light of international customs and usages of trade. The intrinsically international character of the analysed transactions thus directs legal analysis. Regard for additional, modifying elements, such as securing enforceability of an award by respecting public policy rules of the countries of anticipated enforcement, intensifies this process. Positivist orientation on the text of the law, being analysed with regard to the hierarchical structure of the sources of the law, is challenged in the process of arbitral interpretation, in which the adjudicator might face a mosaic of provisions belonging to different domestic legal systems, public policy considerations, international instruments, rules of transnational origin and established ways of interpretation of model agreements and standard contractual clauses, as well as self-validating contracts.[15]

Finally, some highly creative aspects of arbitral decision-making turned out to be hardly reconcilable with positivist model of adjudication based on linguistic inquiry of rules, enacted by the sovereign State. In particular, the key role of international commercial arbitration in formulating the principles of the new *lex mercatoria* turned out to be controversial and was claimed to be exceeding the limits of discretionary powers of the arbitrators. The autonomous status of *lex mercatoria* as law (and a valid ground for arbitral decision-making) has also been denied by different authors for several reasons. One of the most prominent is the lack of endorsement by a sovereign State authority, which has been indicated in positivist jurisprudence as a necessary condition for creation of valid legal norms.[16] *Lex mercatoria* as a set of rules of transnational, yet private origin, largely developed through arbitral case law (that is, private adjudication), might

15 Bernardo M. Cremades and Steven L. Plehn, 'The New Lex Mercatoria and the Harmonization of the Laws of International Commercial Transactions' 2 Boston U Int'l LJ (1984).

16 John Austin et al., *Lectures on Jurisprudence, or, The Philosophy of Positive Law* (3rd edn, John Murray 1869).

appear as a highly subversive concept, when approached from the perspective of the traditional hierarchy of the sources of law. This has led Gunther Teubner to characterize the phenomenon of *lex mercatoria* as double taboo-breaking in regard to the State monopoly on regulating international relations: first, as it accepts that private undertakings can be a source of valid rules without State control and authorization; and second, as *lex mercatoria* is applied (predominantly by arbitral tribunals) without formal, global recognition, and official legitimization extended by the governments.[17]

Legal Hermeneutics

An alternative concept of legal discourse is offered by legal hermeneutics. The term 'hermeneutics' has an ancient Greek etymology: an expression *hermēneutikos*, denoting a master of interpretation, derives from the words *hermeneuein* (to interpret) and *hermeneus* (interpreter). Originally practised as the art of interpretation of the Bible and theological inquiry, hermeneutics as an autonomous philosophical trend was initiated by German romantic thinkers David Friedrich Schleiermacher and Friedrich Schlegel, and continued by Wilhelm Dilthey. Dilthey formulated the theory of the specific character of the humanities, which differ from sciences in regard to both the object of study and methods of inquiry. Hermeneutics, according to this theory, is a (characteristically for the humanities) general method of interpretation of cultural objects and creations, based on the category of understanding (*Verstehen*) and divergent from the descriptively oriented methods used in science. While this method can be used for study of all cultural artefacts, for Dilthey it was applicable primarily to those that were expressed in language, in particular in writing – hence the perception of Dilthey's concept of hermeneutics as predominantly philological.[18]

An ontological concept of hermeneutics, developed by Martin Heidegger in *Sein und Zeit*,[19] where understanding is presented as not just an epistemological category, but as a way of human existence in the world, had further inspired Hans-Georg Gadamer.[20] The model of understanding presented by Gadamer is based on the concept of conversation: it is intrinsically linguistic and dialogical, and never completely controlled by just one side of the communication. The notion of a hermeneutic spiral (reformulated after Schleiermacher's and Heidegger's hermeneutic circle), describing the process of cognition as interpretation, a universal experience, in Gadamer's theory involves repetitions and recalibrations, reiterated sequences of approximations, as well as distancing and recurring

17 Teubner (n 14) 24.

18 Jerzy Stelmach, *Współczesna filozofia interpretacji prawniczej* (Wydział Prawa i Administracji Uniwersytetu Jagiellońskiego 1995) 55.

19 M. Heidegger, *Sein und Zeit* (Max Niemeyer 1977).

20 Hans-Georg Gadamer, *Truth and Method* (Continuum International 2004).

mediations between the familiar and the alien components. The Gadamerian concept of language as the essential human way of 'being in the world' is also necessarily dialogical or even polyphonic, existing as a continuous exchange with the others.

The dialogical character of understanding, according to Gadamer, refers also – if not primarily – to a text, and can be found in interpretation of legal texts as well. The text itself takes the place of an interlocutor, and the initiated dialogue realizes in the process of reading/interpretation. While this concept of understanding through a conversation relates to Hegel's dialectic and its triad of thesis-antithesis-synthesis, the outcome of the process is not the truth in Hegelian, absolute meaning. The truth for both Heidegger and Gadamer is always an existential truth, located here and now; hermeneutics thus contextualizes interpretation.

Finally, historical and cultural differences, in Gadamer's (and unlike Schleiermacher and Dilthey's) view, do not create potentially insurmountable barriers for understanding. On the contrary, they can support keen readers and help them in sifting out their conventional interpretive habits. Gadamer claims then that the text has an autonomous character and interpretation should not be limited to attempts at discovery of the presumed will of its author.

These aspects of the process of interpretation and understanding, highlighted by general hermeneutics, seem particularly relevant in the context of international commercial arbitration. An international arbitrator – unlike a domestic adjudicator – acts in the conditions of a permanent confrontation with the Gadamerian 'other' on multiple levels. He or she has to deal with the parties, frequently not only coming from different legal systems and traditions, but also from systems different from those of an arbitrator. An arbitrator faces procedural challenges in planning the proceedings so as to accommodate diverse, involved interests and to keep equal footing under the fluid circumstances of a particular case (while not relying on the fixed base of domestic procedural rules, as in litigation).

He or she also inevitably encounters the textual 'other' (or multiple 'others') in the law itself due to the demands of determining and applying substantive rules to the merits of the case; there will be norms that frequently belong to a legal system in which an adjudicator has not obtained his or her primary legal training, and which can be a combination of rules of different origin, binding force and legitimization (including, for example, the new *lex mercatoria* principles and public policy considerations of the place of anticipated enforcement). A successful fulfilment of this role requires precisely an ability to put aside one's predetermined, local interpretive lenses and to adopt a genuinely dialogical attitude in the Gadamerian sense – one that involves the apprehension and accommodation of the other.

Hermeneutics has exerted a far-reaching impact not only on the development of philosophy, but also on other disciplines, such as anthropology and sociology. As Gibson Burrell and Gareth Morgan emphasize, it has played a highly significant role in the formulation of two of the four basic research paradigms used in the modern social sciences: interpretivism and radical humanism.[21] It has also significantly influenced legal theory, being a source of inspiration for two main trends of hermeneutically oriented jurisprudence. One of them draws from Schleiermacher and Dilthey's epistemological tradition, focusing on formulating methodological postulates for the humanities and aiming at determination of the framework conditions of cognition and on interpretive canons. This current in legal theory is in consequence characterized as an epistemological trend in legal hermeneutics, oriented at *Methodenlehre*. The other one refers primarily to the ontological hermeneutics, developed by Heidegger and Gadamer, and, as Jerzy Stelmach and Bartosz Brożek remark, aspires to functioning as an autonomous philosophy of legal interpretation.[22]

On the grounds of the epistemologically oriented legal hermeneutics, Emilio Betti rejects the Heideggerian vision of the hermeneutic circle as a model of cognition and claims that its mixture of subjective and objective elements inevitably leads to ignoring both: a complete otherness and an autonomous logic of the text. Betti advocates a concept of objective understanding of a text, by postulating a reconstruction of the identity, conceptual world and culture of its author in an act of interpretation. In the legal context, he consequently favours a rendition aimed at an objective discovery of the intentions of the lawmaker.[23] The assumption that understanding is possible as such a reconstructive discovery of an objectively existing meaning was refused by Gadamer (who got involved in a polemic with Betti, accusing him of deep methodological inconsistency by pointing to his psychologism and, contrarily to his official stance, a radical subjectivism).[24] A claim of an objective character of legal interpretation has also been abandoned by further commentators, perceiving legal hermeneutics primarily as a *Methodenlehre*: Karl Larenz and Josef Esser. For the latter, legal interpretation has a fully creative character, guided by the purpose of the process of application of law, which determines the limits of pre-understanding of a legal text for an interpreter.[25]

Legal hermeneutics has been explicitly supplemented by ontological arguments by Arthur Kaufmann, who perceives interpretive activity as an act of creation of law (as he observes that the law always has a time- and context-specific historical character). Approached from this perspective, legal text, as well as the ideas of equity and justice, leading the interpreter, function merely as potentialities, possibilities of the law, to be realized through particular acts of

---

21 Cf. G. Burrell and G. Morgan, *Social Paradigms and Organizational Analysis: Elements of the Sociology of Corporate Life* (Heinemann Educational 1979).

22 Jerzy Stelmach and Bartosz Brozek, *Methods of Legal Reasoning* (Springer 2006) 175ff.

23 Emilio Betti, *Allgemeine Auslegungslehre als Methodik der Geisteswissenschaften* (Mohr-Siebeck 1967).

24 Gadamer (n 20) 511ff.

25 Cf. Monika Frommel, *Die Rezeption der Hermeneutik bei Karl Larenz und Josef Esser* (Rolf Gremer 1981).

interpretation. Furthermore, the law itself has for Kaufmann a quintessentially analogical character;[26] it is a

> correspondence between *is* and *ought*, between legal norm and the case in point. It is only when *Sein* and *Sollen*, a specific life relationship and one or more norms, are brought into correspondence that law can be made concrete, that law becomes actual. This correspondence between *is* and *ought* means, however, that the knowledge, application and securing of law are based on a fundamentally analogical basis.[27]

The law, analysed from a hermeneutic perspective, is at the same time a linguistic phenomenon, as the understanding – a result of the interpretive process – is achieved in linguistic categories. For Kaufmann, understanding of the law, expressed through language, is both a way of conducting interpretation and a form of existence of the law itself, an ontological category.[28]

A possible applicability of concepts proposed by hermeneutic legal theory to the institutional and procedural architecture, as well as the functioning of international commercial arbitration, seems extensive, even if not necessarily leading to unambiguous results, due to a complex and multifaceted character of this stream of jurisprudence. On the grounds of the epistemological and method-oriented branch of legal hermeneutics, with the emphasis put on the process of legal interpretation as a creative activity, significant original relevant developments in the arbitral practice can be found in such its aspects as adjudication based on and formulating *lex mercatoria*, or *amiable composition* and decision-making *ex aequo et bono*.

The key issue of the proper definition of limits of discretionary powers of arbitrators rendering awards under circumstances of this kind, has been addressed with much attention by arbitration specialists. It can be arguably further theoretically approached in the categories proposed by legal hermeneutic *Methodenlehre*, aimed at capturing the phenomenon of legal interpretation as a creative, yet restricted activity, directed by its reconstructive character and the goal of the process. Moreover, the practice of arbitration seems to add yet another layer to the hermeneutic theory of legal interpretation, as the reconstruction of the meaning of norms, as applicable to the case in question, frequently involves necessary references to a meta-level set of considerations, if the case cannot be completely encapsulated within the

26 Arthur Kaufmann, *Analogie und 'Natur der Sache': zugleich ein Beitrag zur Lehre von Typus* (Decker & Müller 1982).

27 Giuseppe Zaccaria, 'Analogy as Legal Reasoning. The Hermeneutic Foundation of the Analogical Procedure' in *Legal Knowledge and Analogy. Fragments of Legal Epistemology, Hermeneutics and Linguistics* (Patrick Nerhot ed, Kluwer Academic 1991) 43.

28 Cf. Arthur Kaufmann, 'Die Sprache als hermeneutischer Horizont der Geschichtlichkeit des Rechts' in *Rechtsphilosophie im Wandel: Stationem eines Weges* (Athenäum Verlag 1972).

limits of a particular national legal system. Even if basically resolved on the ground of domestic rules, with a limited actual recourse to additional, modifying considerations such as usages of international trade (although their deliberation is mandatory and functions as a procedural standard among arbitral institutions), an arbitral case shall still be decided with a regard to enforcement concerns, including the public policy of the State (or States) of the anticipated enforcement. As a result, a possibility of application of a syllogistic model of legal interpretation is in the arbitration practice – and very much in accord with the hermeneutic postulates (which contest validity of its use already in a context of a single legal system) – highly restricted, if not virtually impossible.

Also in the ontological perspective, international commercial arbitration can be approached through legal hermeneutic arguments. The multiplicity and diversity of sources of rules applicable to the dispute, as well as the heterogeneous character of considerations which an interpreter faces, determine his or her task, as well as the outcome of the interpretive process. In the hermeneutic spirit, legal interpretation (but also, more broadly speaking, the very functioning of the law) in arbitration can be thus perceived dialogically, as a constant interplay of rules, considerations, policies and modifiers. If the law is to be understood, as Kaufmann proposes, as an actualization of a relationship between being and what ought to be, functioning of this relational concept in international arbitration can be identified, perhaps even in a version more prominent than in domestic litigation.

The saturation of mechanisms of arbitral decision-making with different forms of recourse (mandatory, optional, or available upon authorization by the parties) to standards transcending the limits of a single domestic legal system, makes the possible substantive base for an award a potentially complex creature. An actual influence of arbitrators on ascertaining what *ought* to be is of course delimited differently in different cases – due to the parties' intent, procedural rules governing resolution of a particular dispute and the arbitrators' preferences. It is the range of available options, though, that is notable, and that potentially allows for a significant presence of discretionary, and even creative components in legal interpretation. The fact that the determination of the substantive grounds for the decision usually takes place through a conflict of laws analysis, but – if arbitrators are authorized so – can also be performed in an unmediated way through a *voie directe* competence, further enhances its status as a specific realization of an ongoing legal discourse.

Legal Deconstructivism

An alternative theory of legal discourse, represented in contemporary jurisprudence, is offered by legal deconstructivism and inspired by the general philosophy of deconstruction, as proposed by Jacques Derrida. Derrida recognizes (and subjects to criticism) a basic, logocentric orientation of Western philosophy since antiquity, grounded in Hellenic as well as Judaic thought. Logos as a rudimentary order of the world might have been defined differently over time: as a presocratic principle, the infinite intellect of God, or Husserl's reason as 'the logos which is produced in history'.[29] At the same time, Derrida remarks that the Western thought has not only developed as a logocentric but also a phonocentric array of systems, assuming after Aristotle that the spoken word is a symbol of the 'affections of the soul'[30] (or, as Talmy Givón observes, that '*language somehow mirrors thought, and thought, in turn, some external reality*'[31]).

As the voice is a natural form of expression of the soul, phonocentrism is an aspect of logocentrism, as the script is merely an attempt at translation of what has already been translated onto the 'affections of the soul' and further into spoken language, thus inevitably distant from the original. A contrariety between speech and writing, as well as the original and the derivative, are just examples of the essential cultural practice of meaning-making (with signified–signifier, intelligible–sensible, active–passive being further ones), which, as Derrida claims, is based not on a concurrence of the opposites, but on an adversarial practice of allocating primacy to one of them, and hierarchical subordination of the other. Creation of meaning is in this approach a violent act, and an overturning of the established hierarchy enables an interpreter to deconstruct the opposition and uncover its previously unexposed, disregarded or neglected aspects and their interplay.[32] Deconstruction as an interpretive practice is then not aimed at obliterating the differences – as they are necessary for creation of meaning – but rather at their unfolding and exposure without the constraining corset of pre-established, conceptual hierarchies.

A significant part of Derrida's work is dedicated to the rehabilitation and emancipation of script, perceived by Western thinkers from Socrates to de Saussure as derivative and inferior in relation to speech. He also undertakes a polemic with Claude Lévi-Strauss, who, after Rousseau, perceives writing as a disease, a means of institutionalized violence destroying primitive cultures, with the law being its primary instrument: 'Everyone must be able to read so that the government can say: Ignorance of the law is no excuse.'[33] Derrida comments on this stance by stating that Lévi-Strauss not only represents a nostalgia for an archaic ethic, idealizing non-literate cultures, but also manipulates the concept of the law:

> [w]hat is going to be called enslavement can equally legitimately be called liberation … The idea of law and positive right, although it is difficult to think

29 Jacques Derrida, '"Genesis and Structure" and Phenomenology' in *Writing and Difference* (2nd edn, Routledge 2001) 208.

30 Aristotle, *'Categories' and 'De interpretatione'* (J.L. Ackrill tr and ed, Clarendon Press 1963).

31 Talmy Givón, 'Isomorphism in the Grammatical Code' in *Iconicity in Language* (Raffaele Simone ed, J. Benjamins 1995) 47.

32 Jacques Derrida, *Positions* (Alan Bass tr, University of Chicago Press 1981) 41ff.

33 Claude Lévi-Strauss, *Tristes tropiques* (Penguin 1997) 300.

> them in their formality – where it is so general that ignorance of the law is no defense – before the possibility of writing, is determined by Lévi-Strauss as a constraint and enslavement. Political power can only be the custodian of an unjust power. A classical and coherent thesis, but here advanced as self-evident, without opening the least bit of critical dialogue with the holders of the other thesis, according to which the generality of the law is on the contrary the condition of the liberty in the city.[34]

The law is thus treated not only an essentially written, linguistic phenomenon. It is also, as Derrida suggests, legitimized as such not only within the grammatological approach, but, as a special type of system, in the traditional logocentric perspective as well ('The legislator is a writer. And the judge a reader'[35]). This exceptional status of the law, as Derrida remarks, was explicated already by Plato, who, despite his general deep mistrust in script and other mimetic techniques, nevertheless approves the written character of the laws as a guarantee of their certainty and unchangeable status: 'The immutable, petrified identity of writing is not simply added to the signified law or prescribed rule like a mute, stupid simulacrum: it assures the law's permanence and identity with the vigilance of a guardian.'[36]

Deconstruction as a method of interpretation, exposing the constant interplay between texts and unveiling its hidden, unofficial or suppressed elements, has also been adopted by legal theory. The beginnings of this trend are often connected with the development of the critical legal studies (CLS) movement in the 1970s and 1980s in the US.[37] The CLS scholars started using deconstructivist techniques in legal analysis, examining rhetorical figures and tropes and their relations with the dominant logic of the text. A deconstructivist interpreter can thus discover consonances, tensions and even contradictions between the argumentative and the rhetorical side of a legal text.[38] By unveiling the use of topical and rhetorical components, often treated in an official legal discourse as secondary or even marginal, he or she demonstrates their actual significance in legal reasoning.

These methods were used by the CLS commentators as instruments of critique directed against established legal and social structures, presented as rational in theory (as the liberal principle of the rule of law), but functioning in practice as a façade, or even oppressively.[39] An ideologically directed use of legal deconstruction as a

34 Jacques Derrida, *Of Grammatology* (John Hopkins University Press 1998) 131.

35 Jacques Derrida, 'Plato's Pharmacy' in *Dissemination* (2004) 115–116.

36 Ibid. 115.

37 Cf. Roberta Kevelson, 'Introduction to the First Round Table on Law and Semiotics' in *Law and Semiotics* (Roberta Kevelson ed, Plenum 1987).

38 Cf. Jack M. Balkin, 'Tradition, Betrayal, and the Politics of Deconstruction' 11 Cardozo L Rev (1989).

39 Gary Peller, 'The Metaphysics of American Law' CLR (1985) 1175ff.

means of unmasking the ostensibly neutral use of law and other social institutions for exercise of power was also adopted by British critical theory.[40]

This normatively engaged form of legal deconstruction, developed by the CLS movement, was an object of a critique, formulated by Pierre Schlag[41] and Jack M. Balkin.[42] They claimed that such a use of deconstruction as a weapon is instrumental and inconsistent with its original, philosophical concept – as Derrida insisted on not reducing deconstruction to a set of interpretive techniques. In opposition to the politically committed version of legal deconstruction, Balkin formulates its alternative theory as a modern variety of rhetoric.[43] He claims that due to its philosophical foundations (in particular, the antihumanistic concept of a subject – an interpreter – functioning always as a social construct), as well as to its pragmatic aspect (offering a set of analytic tools), deconstruction can not have a normative character in itself. Like classical rhetoric tools, it is a neutral instrument that can be used for both noble and evil purposes.

The applicability of theory – or, rather, theories – of legal deconstruction to the study of international commercial arbitration seems potentially wide, albeit not without reservations. The concept of legal discourse as a constant, textual interplay, completely socially constructed (including identity of the interpreters), seems to possibly capture well a contractual provenience of arbitration and the fact that it has proliferated like a Deleuze and Guattari rhizome:[44] as an alternative to the hierarchical, State-rationed administration of justice, which had initially just filled empty spaces in the fabric of international commercial dispute resolution until reaching the point when it has overgrown the original default option of domestic litigation. The efforts and struggles of the parties and their counsel in navigating this institutionalized, yet flat, global network of arbitral centres and rules of procedure can be potentially well recognized within this paradigm.

A possible difficulty might lie in a strongly textual orientation of deconstruction, at least in its Derridian version, engaged in uncovering the hidden aspects and backstage life of the official discourse. The arbitral interpretive and adjudicatory practice, as discussed in Chapters 7 to 10, can go beyond, and occasionally reverse, the predominantly textual character or legal inquiry, known from domestic litigation. Areas of expanded discretionary powers of arbitrators, such as *lex mercatoria*-based adjudication or *amiable composition*, as well as an option of

---

40 Cf. Peter Goodrich, *Languages of Law: From Logics of Memory to Nomadic Masks* (Weidenfeld & Nicolson 1990); Costas Douzinas et al., *Postmodern Jurisprudence: The Law of Text in the Texts of Law* (Routledge 1991).

41 Pierre Schlag, '"Le Hors de Texte, C'est Moi": The Politics of Form and the Domestication of Deconstruction' 11 Cardozo L Rev (1990).

42 Balkin (n 38).

43 Jack M. Balkin, 'Being Just with Deconstruction' 3 S & L S (1994); Jack M. Balkin, 'Deconstruction's Legal Career' 27 Cardozo L Rev (2005).

44 Gilles Deleuze and Félix Guattari, *A Thousand Plateaus: Capitalism and Schizophrenia* (Continuum International 2004) 3ff.

hybrid proceedings (such as arb-med, highly popular in certain contexts, notably in Chinese arbitration[45]) might serve as examples for a possible adjustment and reformulation of the concept of textuality in legal discourse.

Another important feature of arbitration, which makes research on its textual side a challenge, is its opaque character: the proceedings are generally confidential (and the discreet character of arbitration is frequently indicated as one of its significant advantages for commercial parties); only a small fraction of awards is published (and usually in a manner that is not freely accessible); the identity of the parties is often not disclosed, etc. This issue can be possibly addressed through the exploration of the links between deconstruction and psychoanalysis, and their joint interest in uncovering what is hidden and unexpressed, staying under the external surface. While social transparency is one of the important aspects of the official discourse of the judiciary practice (observable for instance in the conduct of proceedings, as well as standard publication of the decisions), its undisclosed facets can be perceived as its shadow[46] – a repressed, unofficial side.

The (to a large extent) impenetrable character of arbitration seems to locate it in a different position: the practice of arbitration occupies rather the domain of a shadow; neither arbitral centres nor the parties seeking resolution of their disputes appear to be interested in increased transparency. The *a casu ad casum* appointment of arbitrators is yet another example of the transient, fluid character of arbitration in comparison to fixed structures of the domestic (and public international) courts. Autonomy of arbitration, observable in (among other places) the very limited judicial control over arbitral decision-making, largely restricted to procedural issues under the New York Convention regime, increases its status as a sphere of discretion, in multiple meanings of the word. The reversal of proportions in the use of litigation and arbitration for the resolution of international commercial disputes is in this context a highly interesting turn of events, demonstrating an elevation of what used to be alternative, marginal and subsidiary to the level of the default method of addressing cross-border, commercial controversies.

Finally, the experience of the use of deconstruction for the study of the relationships of power and hierarchy, as well as political influences in legal decision-making, popularized by the CLS scholars, can be revived in the context of arbitration. Instances of exercise of economic influence in the relations between the parties; the problem of power in forum shopping and competition between the arbitral centres; or the question of arbitrators' appointments and the tension between their obligation to remain neutral and not act as an advocate to a party who selected them; and practices such as organizing interviews with prospective

---

45 Simon Greenberg et al., *International Commercial Arbitration: An Asia–Pacific Perspective* (Cambridge University Press 2010) 334.

46 Cf. Carl Gustav Jung, *The Archetypes and the Collective Unconscious* (R.F.C. Hull tr, Princeton University Press 1980).

arbitrators, sometimes described as 'beauty contests',[47] are among the examples of specific issues which can be analysed with the help of such instruments.

Even if it is not easily susceptible to transformation into a practical toolbox for an arbitrator, it can be argued that the philosophy of deconstruction can offer a fresh perspective and inspiration for the theory of arbitration, operating on a meta-level. It can be thus possibly developed as a research perspective, helpful in attempts to explain specific aspects of the phenomenon of international commercial arbitration, its discursive forms and functioning. It might also offer a conceptual basis for capturing the historical point of gaining momentum by the globally fragmented, privatized, competitive and relatively flat structure (or, rather, a mosaic of structures) of arbitration, created in the times when grand narratives were seen as replaced by multiple small ones, remaining in mutual interactions and a dialogue.[48]

Sociolinguistics

The study of the social aspects of linguistic communication has been developed since the last century as one of research perspectives, allowing for a formulation of an autonomous theory of discourse. One of its specialized subfields, legal sociolinguistics, focuses on communications performed as acts of legal discourse.

The conflict between the two trends of analytic philosophy mentioned above – the reconstructionist (logical, formal) and the descriptionist one (oriented at non-formal analysis and the study of ordinary language, inspired by late works of Wittgenstein) – heavily affected the evolution of philosophy of language in the twentieth century.[49] As Tomasz Gizbert-Studnicki remarks, a quick development of linguistic studies, observable since the 1950s, made it possible for the linguists to propose an independent stance in this discussion.[50] A striving towards a formulation of a general theory of ordinary language, and a constatation that the existing philosophical tools do not enable an accomplishment of this task, gave a decisive impulse to these efforts.

This trend in linguistics marks a notable change of its focus. Already Ferdinand de Saussure in his *Course in General Linguistics*,[51] published in 1916, distinguished

47 Gerald Aksen, 'The Tribunal's Appointment' in *The Leading Arbitrators' Guide to International Arbitration* (Lawrence W. Newman and Richard D. Hill eds, Juris 2008) 35–36.

48 Jean-Francois Lyotard, *The Postmodern Condition: A Report on Knowledge* (Geoff Bennington and Brian Massumi tr, University of Minnesota Press 1984) 37ff.

49 Jan Wolenski, 'Carnap's Metaphilosophy' in *Language, Truth and Knowledge: Contributions to the Philosophy of Rudolf Carnap* (Thomas Bonk ed, Springer 2003) 29.

50 Tomasz Gizbert-Studnicki, *Język prawny z perspektywy socjolingwistycznej* (Państwowe Wydawnictwo Naukowe, Oddział w Krakowie 1986) 23.

51 Ferdinand de Saussure, *Course in General Linguistics* (Baskin Wade tr, Columbia University Press 2011).

between two aspects of language (*langage*) – *langue*, where the language functions as a system with an organized, cognizable structure; and *parole*, which is realized in specific, oral acts of use, often chaotic or incorrect. For de Saussure it was *langue* that was treated as the proper object of research for internal linguistics, while the linguistics of *parole*, characterized as external, and including such branches as historical linguistics and geographic study of languages, was treated as a rather secondary field.

In the following decades, the research of linguists representing the descripionist approach tended to exclude the issues of social functioning of language from its main focus even further, as in case of Bloomfield's *Language*[52] or Hjelmslev's theory of glossematics.[53] Even the breakthrough in modern linguistics, brought by the publication of *Syntactic Structures* by Noam Chomsky in 1957, was initially not connected to any significant changes in this regard.[54] A limitation of research perspective to the analysis of 'ideal speaker–listener', postulated by Chomsky, originally resulted in marginalization, or even exclusion, of those issues that were related to the *parole* concretizations. The views of Chomsky in this regard have undergone a significant evolution though, explicitly articulated in his polemics with Saul Kripke on the normative aspect of language. The confrontation between post-Wittgensteinian conventionalism, represented by Kripke,[55] and Chomsky's late vision of communication as involving primarily the individual potential of the participant[56] can also be seen in a broader light as a dispute between two major streams of contemporary linguistics, as well as an indication of its gradual embrace of social aspects of functioning of language.

The critical impulse for the development of external linguistics in the Saussurean sense, including sociolinguistics, was a result of broader, multidisciplinary developments. Research initiatives on the functioning of social structures, undertaken in the 1960s by sociologists, anthropologists and psychologists, related to linguistic phenomena as well – and the constitution of sociolinguistics as a separate branch can be perceived as a response of linguistic studies to these attempts, driven by the striving towards building reliable empirical foundations for theoretical inquiry.[57] The accompanying reorientation of general linguistics turned out to be so deep as to famously lead William Labov, one of the pioneers of studies

52 Leonard Bloomfield, *Language* (Holt, Rinehart & Winston 1933).

53 Louis Hjelmslev and Hans Jørgen Uldall, *Outline of Glossematics: A Study in the Methodology of the Humanities with Special Reference to Linguistics* (2nd edn, Nordisk Sprog- og Kulturforlag 1967).

54 Noam Chomsky, *Syntactic Structures* (de Gruyter Mouton 2002).

55 Saul Aaron Kripke, *Wittgenstein on Rules and Private Language: An Elementary Exposition* (Harvard University Press 1982).

56 Noam Chomsky, *Knowledge of Language: Its Nature, Origin, and Use* (Praeger 1986).

57 David M. Smith and Roger W. Shuy, *Sociolinguistics in Cross-Cultural Analysis* (Georgetown University Press 1972) 2.

on social functioning of language, to continuously express objections against the use of the term 'sociolinguistics' – as, in his view, pursuing any linguistic analysis without regard to its social aspects, would be ungrounded.[58]

Sociolinguistics has been defined as a systematic study of how social factors influence the use of language; how the diversification of languages reflects the diversification of societies; and how the acts of linguistic communication, understood as social interactions, are being performed.[59] Its main object of interest is thus close to pragmatics (as further discussed in the following chapter), while in the methodological sphere sociolinguistics has remained close to anthropological and ethnographic studies.[60]

The language of the law has been one of the objects of study within the paradigm of applied sociolinguistics. As Tomasz Gizbert-Studnicki postulated in his 1986 book on legal language from the sociolinguistic perspective,[61] the analysis of components of the sociolinguistic situation, proposed by Hymes (after Jakobson), can be adapted to the study of legal communication. For Hymes, in his gradually modified proposal, the theorization of communication and message approached from the anthropological perspective involves the presence of such elements as (1) a code or codes; (2) participants – with the reservation that an addressor and an addressee might be the same person; (3) an event created by the transmission of the message; (4) a channel or channels of communication; (5) a social context; (6) form of the message; and (7) a topic[62] (which in Gizbert-Studnicki's theory is redefined as a topical or thematic field, or as a field of social praxis, in the framework of which a specific act of *parole* functions[63]).

Gizbert-Studnicki also reduces the number of considered components of the situation of legal communication to the addressor, the addressee, the channel, the thematic field and the context, and he further subjects them to a detailed analysis. He emphasizes the conventional character of the legislator as an addressor of the legal text and examines the sociolinguistic situation, the object of which is a legal instrument, as a situation with a message that is non-directed (at a specific addressee or a group of addressees), and expressed in a formal stylistic variety of natural language. The discussion on the channel of communication focuses on the

58 William Labov, *Sociolinguistic Patterns* (University of Pennsylvania Press 1972) xiii.

59 Gizbert-Studnicki (n 50) 30–31.

60 Cf. Dell H. Hymes, *Foundations in Sociolinguistics: An Ethnographic Approach* (University of Pennsylvania Press 1974); Edwin Ardener, *Social Anthropology and Language* (Routledge 2004); John J. Gumperz and Jenny Cook-Gumperz, 'Studying Language, Culture, and Society: Sociolinguistics or Linguistic Anthropology?' 12 Journal of Sociolinguistics (2008).

61 Gizbert-Studnicki (n 50).

62 Cf. Dell H. Hymes, 'Ethnography of Speaking' in *Readings in the Sociology of Language* (Joshua A. Fishman ed, de Gruyter 1968); Hymes (n 60) 13.

63 Gizbert-Studnicki (n 50) 73.

specific status of a legal communiqué as a written text, with its graphical, syntactic and lexical particularities.

The social context, in turn, is defined as a common knowledge of participants of the sociolinguistic situation, which enables them to achieve an actual understanding. For Gizbert-Studnicki it is tantamount to a legal culture within which legal texts function. Specific interpretive paradigms are indicated as an important aspect of legal cultures. They seem to be understood rather 'softly' than as sets of absolutely applicable rules, which resembles Balkin and Levinson's concept of legal canons – the forms of reasoning difficult to be avoided in the course of legal interpretation, yet diversified in type and depth.[64]

One of the rudimentary assumptions of legal sociolinguistics is the thesis that the processes of communication are essentially constituted by instances of *parole* as the concretizations of the use of language. The law, according to this approach, operates through the communiqués of normative instruments and their perception, intermediated by lawyers (as Anne Wagner remarks, there are three basic groups of social actors that create legal discourse: lawmakers, judges and legal practitioners[65]). The law is thus perceived as an intrinsically discursive phenomenon, and the legal discourse is defined as predominantly professional. While currently widely shared by different streams of legal theory, the focus on the discursive character of the law and its ushering into the spotlight can certainly be associated with the developments of legal sociolinguistics.

The possibilities of application of sociolinguistic analysis to research on arbitration are broad. In particular, the pioneering works of Vijay Bhatia, Christopher Candlin and Maurizio Gotti[66] should be mentioned in this regard. In Candlin and Bhatia's extensive studies on legal discourses of arbitration, the conceptualizations of social context reappear, adapted to the specific environment of ICA. The sociolinguistic perspective thus helps one to grasp the characteristic features of arbitral proceedings and legal interpretation in a context of professional roles of their actors, as contrasted with the practice of domestic litigation.

As Patrizia Anesa demonstrates on an example of informal examination of witnesses,

> The construction of this communicative event is necessarily embedded in specific discourse practices and power relationships ... The oft-repeated presumption that arbitrators are granted the power to determine most aspects of an examination holds true to some extent, especially in comparison with litigative procedures; however the scope for procedural practices that are not widely accepted and

64 Jack M. Balkin and Sanford Levinson, 'Legal Canons: An Introduction' in *Legal Canons* (Jack M. Balkin and Sanford Levinson eds, New York University Press 2000) 15–24.

65 Anne Wagner, 'Introduction: The (Ab)use of Language in Legal Discourse' 15 IJSL (2002).

66 Cf., for example, V.K. Bhatia et al., *Discourse and Practice in International Commercial Arbitration: Issues, Challenges and Prospects* (Ashgate 2012).

> commonly used is considerably limited by the need to comply with standardized practices and routines.[67]

The analysis of relations between communication and power, and their connection with assumed procedural roles, is perceived as critical, 'as professional and communicative roles play a fundamental function in the development of arbitration discourse'.[68]

As a consequence of the adoption of the sociolinguistic approach, significant issues are thus exposed, such as the large (albeit not unrestricted) scope of the discretionary powers of arbitrators; the unique character of particular proceedings, resulting from an exercise of those powers, meant to enable a possibly flexible accommodation of needs of the parties; or concretizations of legal discourse in specific instances of oral communication throughout the proceedings at their different stages, as well as connected power relations.

---

67 Patrizia Anesa, 'Language and Power in Arbitration Proceedings: Insights into Theory and Practice' in *Discourse and Practice in International Commercial Arbitration: Issues, Challenges and Prospects* (V.K. Bhatia et al. eds, Ashgate 2012) 109–110.

68 Ibid. 110.

Chapter 3
ICA and the Semiotic Web of Law

Semiotics and the Discursive Concept of Culture

As discussed in the previous chapter, the concepts of legal discourse, proposed by legal theory and related disciplines, are diverse, and their application to studies on legal interpretation in international commercial arbitration (ICA) can be performed on different levels. The notion of legal discourse, as well as the consequences of its adoption for the theory of legal interpretation, have also been an object of interest of yet another discipline – legal semiotics. Developed as a separate field since the 1970s, the semiotics of law aims at capturing legal discourse in its semantic, structural and functional dimensions, combining the methods of philosophy of language and linguistics with those of social and legal studies. It has been advanced as one of the subfields of the general semiotics, or the general systematic study of signs and sign processes.[1]

The semiotic approach seems to be well suited for an analysis of the highly dynamic phenomenon of commercial arbitration. Such features of arbitration as its extensive reliance on national law, however removed from its original domestic context on several different levels; the still-existing procedural flexibility; the significant role of written submissions; the notable procedural and institutional autonomy (leading some commentators to postulating that ICA has become an emancipated transnational system); its far-reaching confidentiality, including very limited publicization of awards; and the participation of specific groups of actors (highly specialized, expert arbitrators and counsel, but also general practitioners, who get increasingly involved due to the universal popularity of this method of dispute resolution) – all these characteristic facets can be successfully theoretically addressed from this perspective.

The term 'semiotics' stems from Greek *semeiotikòs* (related to signs, aware of signs) and is defined after Charles Peirce as a general theory of sign. In 1938 Charles W. Morris in his work *Foundations of the Theory of Signs*[2] suggested the division of semiotics into three subdisciplines: semantics, syntactics and pragmatics. Of those fields, semantics has been characterized as the study of relations between the signs and the objects which they denote, oriented at interpretation of signs as well as of sentences and linguistic expressions. Depending on the adopted

---

1 Charles Sanders Peirce, 'Logic, considered as Semeiotic' Manuscript L75 (1902).

2 Charles W. Morris, *Foundations of the Theory of Signs* (University of Chicago Press 1938).

definition of meaning, semantics can be described as the theory of meaning or the theory of signifying.[3]

The second subdiscipline of semiotics, as indicated by Morris, is syntactics (the study of syntax, or signs organized in structures, as well as the rules governing such organization). The third one, pragmatics, focuses on the utility of the sign and text, and analyses possibilities of their specific application, with regard to the context of a particular utterance. Semiotics is often perceived as a part of philosophy, rhetoric or linguistics. In accordance with the Peircean tradition, and after Roberta Kevelson, it is assumed here that this field is generally autonomous, as it constitutes in itself a separate method of scientific inquiry, not appropriated from a methodological repertory characteristic to any other, specific discipline.[4] It should also be noted that, while semiotics is indeed a study of signs and texts (utterances, expressions), the semiotic concept of a text is, as Umberto Eco remarks, wider than the purely linguistic definition.[5] It is thus applicable also to non-literary and non-verbal texts (theatre, cinematography, painting).

Eco further distinguishes between semiotic theories of the first and second generation (emphasizing that the distinction is a logical, not a chronological one – hence classification of Peirce as an author representing the second generation). What he defines as the first generation is a set of theories, which express scepticism in regard to attempts at the successful establishment of the linguistics of the code, and focus on the study of language as a structured system preceding its actualizations in discourse instead. The first generation is described in terms of encyclopaedic competence, which assumes a possibility of such an ideal, descriptively and structurally complete analysis of language/code, which enables a theoretical anticipation of all its acts of use in specific situations and contexts.[6]

Theories of the second generation, according to Eco, shift their focus onto seeking channels connecting such structural examination of language/code with the study of discourses and texts as its specific realizations. The analysis is thus supplemented by explorations of the theory of rules of generation and interpretation of such discursive actualizations and enriched with the discussion of the pragmatic aspects of the texts. The authors representing the second generation indicate that the meaning of a sentence, of a complete text, and of all its potential realizations, cannot be reduced to semantic and lexical categories (which would lead to a thesis that the meaning is initially and definitively encoded in the text). The study

3 Cf. Willard Van Orman Quine, *Word and Object* (MIT Press 1964).

4 Roberta Kevelson, 'Introduction to the First Round Table on Law and Semiotics' in *Law and Semiotics* (Roberta Kevelson ed, Plenum 1987) 8.

5 Umberto Eco, *The Role of the Reader: Explorations in the Semiotics of Texts* (Indiana University Press 1979) 14.

6 Umberto Eco, *Lector in fabula. Współdziałanie w interpretacji tekstów narracyjnych* (Piotr Salwa tr, Państwowy Instytut Wydawniczy 1994) 17–18.

of signs, their structures and functioning in this approach is thus compared to a creation of a thesaurus rather than an encyclopaedia.[7]

It seems worth noticing that – not on the level of the method of inquiry, which might be semiotic or not – but on the level of assumptions as to the legal language, adopted and shared explicitly or tacitly, this dispute is present in legal theory as well. It significantly affects the concept of legal interpretation and its perception as a logocentric and Montesquieuan process, or rather a dynamic, discursive and creative one.

The semiotics of law had evolved as a separate subfield of general semiotics in the 1970s, to a large extent due to the pioneering efforts of Roberta Kevelson. The drive towards defining the limits of this research perspective was continued in the following decade, and had been manifest in the activity of such fora as the Center for Semiotic Research in Law, Government and Economics at Pennsylvania State University. In 1987, on the occasion of the First International Round Table on Law and Semiotics, Kevelson observed that legal semiotics, rather than establishing one, solidified model of scientific inquiry, draws primarily from two important and distinct sources of inspiration: the works of Algirdas Greimas and Charles Peirce.[8] Jan M. Broekman and Larry Catà Backer reach a similar conclusion, observing that the significance of Peirce's thought for legal semiotics, while vast, is not the only influence in this field. Broekman and Catà Backer call him – along with Greimas and Jacques Lacan – one of the godfathers of semiotics as a general discipline, and of legal semiotics as its specialized field.[9] They also note that neither of these founding fathers had a systematic knowledge of the law; nevertheless, their impact on legal theory has been decisive: without them '*nobody could ever have developed the idea of a semiotics of law or legal semiotics*'.[10]

The influence of Peirce, as Kevelson remarks, turned out to be particularly rich and multifaceted, and affected legal theory in two main ways. The first was an adoption of the semiotic method and its instruments in the form proposed by Peirce for the purposes of analysis of the language of the law. The second was the impact of Peircean philosophical pragmatism onto legal realism in its American, but also its Scandinavian version, as well as on the critical legal studies (CLS) authors, sometimes characterized as the successors and continuers of the 1930s realism's legacy in US legal theory.[11]

It can be noticed that – in regard to the proposed concept of semiotic inquiry – Peirce's theory bears remarkable differences from that proposed by Ferdinand de Saussure. For the latter, the object of semiotic studies is generally limited to

---

7 Ibid. 17–18.

8 Kevelson (n 4).

9 Jan M. Broekman and Larry Catà Backer, *Lawyers Making Meaning* (Springer 2013) 33, 83.

10 Ibid. 33.

11 Cf. Mark V. Tushnet, 'Perspectives on Critical Legal Studies' 52 Geo Wash L Rev (1983) 239ff.

linguistic communication, while Peirce includes non-verbal and natural signs in the scope of analysis. The term 'sign' was explicated by Peirce repeatedly – as Robert Marty notes, 76 different definitions of it can be found in his writings.[12] His classification of signs is also more detailed than that of de Saussure. Finally, while for de Saussure the sign represents an object (a correlate), Pierce introduces an additional component: an interpretant, which is an effect produced by the sign in the mind of an interpreter, or a 'mediating representation'.[13]

An interpretant, the semiotic response to a sign, which can take a mental or physical form, might also become a sign itself. Peirce further remarks on the chain of references, produced in the process of interpreting the sign:

> [e]very reference to a correlate, then, conjoins to the substance the conception of a reference to an interpretant; and this is, therefore, the next conception in order in passing from being to substance.
>
> Reference to an interpretant cannot be prescinded from reference to a correlate; but the latter can be prescinded from the former.[14]

Whereas de Saussure perceives the main task of semiotics (semiology) as the research of signs and their structures (in a primarily linguistic setting), for Peirce semiotics is oriented at the study of semiosis, the process of interpretation of a sign and creation of meaning; it thus widely includes pragmatic, functional and dynamic elements.[15]

Semiosis is also for Peirce a potentially never-ending process (which is a concept resembling the hermeneutic theory of spiralling interpretation, which might be stopped by a decision of an interpreter, but can be possibly continued *ad infinitum*). In de Saussure's model semiosis is an intellectual journey between two worlds: that of signs and that of designated objects, reflected in a dual nature of a sign, based on the signifier–signified distinction.[16] For Peirce a sign is always contemplated as a part of an immensely complex and dynamic structure, in which it always remains in shifting relationships with other signs, as well as being an object of continuous paraphrases and reformulations in the process of semiosis.[17]

12 Robert Marty, *76 Definitions of the Sign by Charles Sanders Peirce Collected and Analyzed by Robert Marty*, Department of Mathematics, University of Perpignan, France.

13 Charles Sanders Peirce, 'On a New List of Categories' 7 Proceedings of the American Academy of Arts and Sciences (1868) sec 9.

14 Ibid. sec 9.

15 The term 'semiosis' was borrowed by Peirce from an Epicurean philosopher, Philodemus; cf. G. Deledalle, *Charles S. Peirce's Philosophy of Signs: Essays in Comparative Semiotics* (Indiana University Press 2000) 80.

16 Ferdinand de Saussure, *Course in General Linguistics* (Columbia University Press 2011) 67ff.

17 Cf. Tomasz Komendziński, *Znak i jego ciągłość: semiotyka CS Peirce'a między precepcją i recepcją* (Wydawnictwo Uniwersytetu Mikołaja Kopernika 1996).

Peirce thus breaks with the Aristotelian (and logocentric) tradition of perceiving reproduction of signs through the syllogistic principle of a 'mark of a mark' (*nota notae est nota rei ipsius*), which assumes that the predicate of the predicate is the predicate of the subject[18]). Peirce, and the semiotic methodology inspired by his works, adopts the view that

> a mark of a mark is not a 're-mark' but an Interpretant, or new potential subject. Peirce's transformation of the principle of the mark will be seen to coincide with the revaluation of the principle of the 'authority of the precedent' in pragmatic approaches to the law, as in Legal Realism, according to Holmes, Frank and Llewellyn.[19]

Besides the main channels indicated by Kevelson, through which Peirce's thought has penetrated modern legal theory, other, less direct or less explored links can also be identified. The influence of Peirce's concept of semiosis on the later development of structuralist theories (including also their post-structuralist phase, which has led to the formulation of the postulates of deconstruction as an interpretive approach – as described in the preceding chapter) had been very far-reaching. It has thus affected legal theory not only directly, but also through inspirations derived from those trends. It seem also worth noting that, as Max Fisch observes, it was precisely the legal system and its specific structure that led the author of the 'Lectures on Pragmatism' to the formulation of a prototypical general theory of signs. As Fisch indicates, a remarkable part of Peirce's abundant works, relating to the law (also in the form of indirect references), and so far remaining in the shadow, is still awaiting its proper 'discovery', publication and systematic study.[20]

The reasons for the lasting popularity of Peirce's concept of semiotics and its further adoption by different, specific disciplines can be arguably sought not only in the broad formulation of its scope (exceeding the limits of linguistic inquiry and inspired, but not restrained by Peirce's own logical orientation). They can also be traced in the corresponding, inclusive formulation of the methodological postulates regarding semiotic inquiry. Peirce himself perceived semiotics as an overarching theory of processes of cognition and meaning-making. As Kevelson observes:

> [s]emiotics is that 'science of sciences' which inquires into all processes of inquiry, and which seeks to discover processes of discovery. Peirce held that Semiotics was to be the method of methods ... Rather *[than rely on fixed*

18 Cf. Aristotle, *The Categories* (E.M. Edghill tr, Kessinger 2004) 3, 4.

19 Roberta Kevelson, *Charles S. Peirce's Method of Methods* (John Benjamins 1987) 8.

20 Max H. Fisch, 'Introduction to Writings of Charles S. Peirce' in *Writings of Charles S. Peirce: A Chronological Edition* (M.H. Fisch and C. Kloesel eds, Indiana University Press 1982–2000).

> *definitions – JJ]* semiotic method wants to show how the sign grows, as a living reality.[21]

The semiotic method of methods should be then – according to Peirce's later works – able to draw from the methodological repertories of different scientific disciplines, but also to formulate its own, general principles, universal in character. This concept of semiotics remains open in the sense that its principles can be themselves an object of critique (in accordance with the basic assumption of the potentially never-ending character of the process of semiosis). Semiotics is thus, in Peirce's view, both a method and an object of revision, reinterpretation and autotransformation.

This key assumption in the Peircean semiotic research perspective is then the open character of the systems of signs and of the potentially continuous and self-reproducing sequences of interpretations of signs[22] – which are nevertheless not arbitrary and unconstrained, but guided by the character and teleological orientation of their objects.[23] This principle has also been applied to legal texts, produced and operating in specific legal systems. A triadic nature of semiosis, described by Peirce as a relationship between the sign, its object and an interpretant, has been adopted in the studies on law; as Anne Wagner, Wouter Werner and Deborah Cao remark: 'in the same fashion, legal semiotics has emphasized the dynamic character of legal concepts and stressed the importance of interpretation and the construction of meaning.'[24]

As a consequence, the semiotic perspective contradicts the classical positivist claim of a closed character of the system of law and opposes Jeremy Bentham's argument that it should be freed from internal inconsistencies and contrarieties.[25] Not only does legal semiotics perceive this postulate as unachievable, but also as remaining in conflict with the intrinsic character of the legal system as an evolving, self-directing and open structure. Its inconsistencies and flaws are also treated as signs, which require particular attention and enhanced interpretive efforts of legal practitioners, but are still not necessarily fully surmountable.[26]

---

21 Kevelson (n 19) ix.

22 Kelly A. Parker, *The Continuity of Peirce's Thought* (Vanderbilt University Press 1998) 149.

23 *Charles Sanders Peirce, Collected Papers (Vols 1–8)* (C. Hartshorne, P. Weiss and A.W. Burks eds, Harvard University Press 1931–35), vol 8, 191.

24 Anne Wagner et al., *Interpretation, Law and the Construction of Meaning: Collected Papers on Legal Interpretation in Theory, Adjudication and Political Practice* (Springer 2006) xi.

25 Jeremy Bentham, *'A Fragment on Government' and 'An Introduction to the Principles of Morals and Legislation'* (Blackwell 1967).

26 Cf. Roberta Kevelson, 'Legitimizing "Repugnancy" in Law: Peirce and Contradiction' 1 Law and Semiotics (1988).

As Umberto Eco,[27] inspired by Peirce, observes, the unfolding, continuous processes of semiosis are performed due to existing and multiplying interconnections between signs, which correspond to the totality of human culture, accumulate it and transform it through subsequent interpretations and reinterpretations. The essence of these processes is creation of meaning; as Clifford Geertz famously observes:

> [t]he concept of culture I espouse … is essentially a semiotic one. Believing, with Max Weber, that man is an animal suspended in webs of significance he himself has spun, I take culture to be those webs, and the analysis of it to be therefore not an experimental science in search of law, but an interpretive one in search of meaning. It is explication I am after, construing social expressions on their surface enigmatical.[28]

Such a perspective thus assumes that the culture (including legal culture) has a performative, and not ostensive character; it is not discovered, but socially constructed by the actors.[29] The complete, cultural universe of semiosis is compared by Eco to a labyrinth[30] without a centre or a network in which it is potentially possible to reach any point starting from any other. A user – a reader of texts which are objects to semiosis – is yet in practice incapable of comprehending all those relations and available paths and determined in his or her choices by the cultural proximity of available options, but also by personal curiosity, educational background and mental faculties, as well as chance and eventuality – arguably analogically to the limitations described by Richard Rorty through a category of a final vocabulary, larger or smaller subsets of which might be shared with other users, but which remains unique to every person.[31]

A selection of a path through a particular sequence of signs can (although it does not necessarily have to) be consistent with one indicated by the text itself. Many interpretive avenues are customarily preferred and frequented by readers (which can be applied, among other things, to specialized canons and directives of legal interpretation; while it is possible to read a normative instrument as a literary work, it is not commonly practised, etc.). As a consequence of such conceptualization of semiosis as an individual (even if conventional and repeatable) journey through a sequence of signs, resulting in production and attribution of meanings, Eco proposes a model of this process with a reader placed in the centre.

27 Umberto Eco, *A Theory of Semiotics* (Indiana University Press 1979) 71ff.

28 Clifford Geertz, 'Thick Description: Toward an Interpretive Theory of Culture' in *The Interpretation of Cultures* (Basic Books 1977) 5.

29 Dariusz Jemielniak, 'Kultura – odkrywana czy konstruowana?' 2 Master of Business Administration (2002).

30 Umberto Eco, *Semiotics and the Philosophy of Language* (Indiana University Press 1986) 2.

31 Richard Rorty, *Contingency, Irony, and Solidarity* (Cambridge University Press 1989) 73ff.

The Semiotic Web of the Law

This proposal, influenced by Peircean tradition of semiotics, has served in turn as a point of reference for Robert W. Benson, who offers a model of semiosis/interpretation adapted specifically to communications performed within the legal system (and thus oriented at revealing its particularities). At the same time, in accordance with the basic concept of an open character of any cultural stream of adoptions and transformations of signs, Benson's representation of legal semiosis aims at displaying links of such communications with an environment. His model is thus intended to be a reconstruction of a general conceptualization put forward by Eco, reformulated for the purposes of the specialized legal analysis.[32]

In the process of attributing meanings to the law, as proposed by Benson, again the reader takes a central position. His or her interpretive decisions are yet directed by different sets of factors of diversified origin and force of conventional influence. The reader is never abstract and transparent, but always contextual and specific – and in this sense he or she forms a Gadamerian type of a subject (see Chapter 2), capable of comprehending the present by means of the ways of perception and cognition inherited from the past.[33] This is not tantamount to an unreflective reproduction of past renditions; Benson explicitly acknowledges, after David Hoy, that Gadamer himself does not advocate following the tradition as a normative postulate. An interpretation may well be subversive, innovative and its path non-obvious; rather, Gadamerian hermeneutics is invoked for its exposure of the role of a specific cultural setting in realizing the background and initial determinants of a particular process of semiosis.

Benson's model, originally presented in 1987, and later developed in an article on the semiotics of international law published in 1989,[34] is presented by the author as a post-structuralist one. It thus opposes the heritage of positivism in the theory of legal interpretation, as well as rejects the linguistic structuralist tradition stemming from the works of de Saussure:

> Structuralist semiotics, in my view, tend to be static, mechanical systems based, at bottom, on claims to universal structures of the human mind which either do not exist at all, or if they exist are so deep and so minimal that they have only feeble influence on the cultural superstructure. Structuralist legal semiotics becomes merely a neo-positivist exercise of analyzing law as an autonomous system of coded norms. It suffers the fatal irrelevance of ignoring historical and social context.[35]

32 Robert W. Benson, 'The Semiotic Web of the Law' in *Law and Semiotics* (Roberta Kevelson ed, Plenum 1987).

33 Ibid. 48.

34 Robert W. Benson, 'The Semiotics of International Law: Interpretation of the ABM Treaty' 2 IJSL (1989).

35 Ibid. 258.

In its pragmatic and contextual orientation, Benson's proposal thus joins what is characterized by Eco as the semiotic theories of second generation, largely influenced by Peirce. The landscape of semiosis, characterized by Eco as labyrinthine, rhizome-like and encyclopaedic, is renamed by Benson, after Thomas A. Sebeok, a semiotic web[36] – a multilayered network of signs.

The reader (understood broadly, in accordance with the Peircean tradition, as any individual creating the meaning through semiosis[37]), who is the focal point of the model, is influenced by four groups of factors, labelled by Benson as follows: the text; the source of the text; other readers; and normative lenses.[38] The last category in the later version of the model has been further reformulated as a heterogeneous set of historical, cultural and sociological circumstances, psychological lenses and value lenses.[39] All these parts of the web, further analysed by Benson in detail, reflect the, according to him typical, recurrent considerations, acknowledged or ignored by a specific Anglo-American professional legal reader (a judge or a legal practitioner) in a particular process of legal interpretation. They also delineate the conventional scope of the available signs through which this process might pass; their eventual selection and the final production of meaning being a matter of choice of a concrete interpreter.

Each of these sets is treated very broadly and comprises heterogeneous components; for instance the category of 'text' includes the body of relevant instruments, as well as linguistic rules and canons of construction, legislative history, previous judicial, administrative and practical interpretations, related case law, but also such typical considerations (known as conventional interpretive directives) as the purpose, reason, nature and equity (also silence and disregarded text). The 'source of text' category contains institutionally and procedurally oriented elements (such as the intent of different stakeholders: legislature, key legislators, groups of interest, framers, ratifiers, citizens, individual authors, etc.), as well as general and axiological ones (the nature of law, human nature, God, history, social and economic conditions, etc.).[40]

In the following category of 'other readers' Benson does not distinguish between *sensu stricto* insiders (authors of utterances, not just their passive addressees) and outsiders to the legal discourse. 'Other readers', potentially influencing the interpreter, are thus professional participants of the system (judges, legislators, jury members, legal practitioners, as well as expert commentators such as law professors), but so is virtually any author of communications about the law (citizens, librarians, philosophers, journalists, anthropologists, doctors,

36 Thomas A. Sebeok, 'The Semiotic Web: A Chronicle of Prejudices' 2 Bulletin of Literary Semiotics (1975) 1ff.

37 Benson (n 34) 260.

38 Benson (n 32) 44.

39 Benson (n 34) 262.

40 Ibid. 263.

etc.).[41] Finally, in the original version of his model, Benson lists under 'normative lenses' a number of (again, quite highly diversified as to their scope, solidification and impact) streams in legal theory, including positivism, realism, CLS, law and economics, Marxism, humanism, feminism, theology and machismo.[42] In the revised version he replaces this list with a conglomerate combination of (generally indicated) historical, cultural and sociological circumstances, psychological lenses and value lenses (which is a much broader and more varied set of considerations).[43] In the lack of a more detailed explanation, they can be possibly interpreted as different factors determining an individual *Weltanschauung* of the reader.

It is the holistic, overarching character of Benson's model that seems to be particularly calling for further development and clarifications. It deliberately abandons the reductionist linguistic concepts of legal discourse, which focus on its character as a set of acts of communication in a specialized register of natural language, accomplished between specific types of subjects. It is also an attempt to grasp the whole net of official and unofficial factors, those formally recognized, or even recommended, as well as those suppressed beyond the limits of conventionally admitted considerations, affecting interpretive choices of a reader, in their phenomenological plenitude.

As a consequence, it also blurs the borders of the legal system as a specific cultural setting for the realizations of legal discourse – and does not distinguish it sharply from the social environment. It also notably adopts a concept of legal discourse in a very broad sense, including not only normative utterances – the realizations of the law itself – but also all kinds of meta-communications. In fact, various elements from intra- and meta-levels are, as indicated above, freely mixed in the categories proposed by Benson. The normative component, so strongly emphasized by the theories of legal discourse *sensu stricto*, remains thus unexposed. As Gérard Cornu observes:

> [l]egal discourse is the operationalization of language, through words at the service of law. One must differentiate between the two elements that make up the definition. Legal discourse is, at the same time, an act of linguistics and an act of law.[44]

Even if the concept of legal discourse in such a strict sense is not adopted, it is still possible to distinguish between the two levels of its social functioning. Such an approach is also forwarded by Cornu himself, who remarks that besides performative communiqués of the law, the utterances supporting realization of the

41 Benson (n 32) 49.

42 Ibid. 49.

43 Benson (n 34) 262.

44 Gérard Cornu, *Linguistique juridique* (2nd edn, Montchrestien 2000) 211. After Evandro Menezes De Carvalho, *Semiotics of International Law: Trade and Translation* (Springer 2010) xix–xx, fn 31.

law (its construction, explication, application, etc.) form a part of the generally understood legal discourse. Purposive orientation of such acts of communication (aimed either at lawmaking or at application of the law and its support) is thus a key feature of legal discourse.[45]

In Benson's model this characteristic normative dimension of legal discourse, as well as purposive character of its utterances, is however not clearly present. This might be a result of the antipositivistic stance of its author. Nevertheless, the general character of this representation makes it uncertain why the reader is defined as a lawyer or a judge 'in actual practice'[46] if the kaleidoscope of components of the web does not differentiate between the conventional character of his or her role and the position of any other reader of a legal text, unrestrained by any conventional and purposive considerations in the performed construction of meaning.

Benson remarks that Eco's concept of semiosis is too unspecific for the requirements of the analysis of legal discourse. It seems though that an explicit supplementation of the model of the semiotic web of the law, as proposed by Benson, with Eco's observations on the role of the reader in case of relatively closed texts (such as legal utterances) would in fact make the former more precise and would help to unveil the intrinsically purposive character of legal discourse (in both the strict and the broad sense). Closed texts are defined as those that 'apparently aim at pulling the reader along the predetermined path'.[47] However, as Eco further remarks '[t]hose texts that obsessively aim at arousing a precise response on the part of more or less precise empirical readers … are in fact open to any possible "aberrant" decoding.'[48] Arguably, such reading, performed against the paths of possible rendition encoded in a closed, legal text itself – as its pragmatic, applied purpose is socially, conventionally and institutionally fixed – would be, however, a usage of text rather than its interpretation within the scope of specialized legal discourse.

The relatively stiff predetermination of ways of performing legal interpretation, and the conventional character of occasions on which it is being offered, as well as of outcomes of such processes (judicial decisions, legal opinions), forming subsequent links in the universe of available signs of legal discourse, is hardly disputable. As Hugues Rabault observes in his work on the limits of judicial interpretation: '[t]he law is a system which displays an extreme mistrust in an interpreter, and which guards itself against his subjectiveness by the use of a formal organization of signs.'[49] This, however, still does not undermine the basic, semiotic assumption of a creative character of interpretation, including legal interpretation, being customarily exercised in a highly regulated environment. The

45 Cornu (n 44) 214.

46 Benson (n 34) 261.

47 Eco (n 5) 8.

48 Ibid. 8.

49 Hugues Rabault, *Granice wykładni sędziowskiej* (B. Janicka tr, Wydawnictwo Naukowe Scholar 1997) 200 [this extract tr by JJ].

quintessence of semiosis is the production of meanings; in the ongoing theoretical dispute on the status of legal interpretation as a process of either discovery and retransmission or creation of the law, legal semiotics offers arguments for the latter stance. The highly conventional and formal character of the process does not lead to a complete control over the results and their full predictability and repetitiveness. It seems rather analogical to the traditional, medieval practice of the writing of icons: fulfilment of all the intricate rules and requirements of tradition does not yet make it possible to entirely foresee the final appearance of the painting (which might eventually turn out to be a masterpiece, but also an artistic failure, or a non-distinctive work of a reasonably skilled craftsperson).

In regard to legal interpretation, Peircean semiotics of law can be thus classified as belonging to the set of streams in legal theory acknowledging a dynamic character of the interpretive process.[50] It opposes the still-prominent Montesquieuan tradition of treating legal interpretation as a basically logocentric activity, grounded in the assumption of a supreme, absolute value of the original. The meaning of a legal text, according to this latter approach, exists objectively, and the main task of a reader is to discover (not develop) it, and to further pass it on in a possibly unchanged state: legal interpretation has to serve the role of a transparent vehicle for the safe delivery of the pre-existent meaning to the audience. The group of theories, according to which an interpreter has to act as 'the mouth of the Law', comprises not only the textualist trends, characterized by Rabault as exegetic.[51] It seems that also those intentionalist theories, which presuppose a possibility of uncovering (and not construing) the genuine will of the lawmaker can also be considered as representative of this perspective.

Another level of analysis seeks to distinguish between the approaches to interpretive activity as creative/reproductive (which is not tantamount to the distinction between the creative and reproductive character of the outcome of the interpretive process, as described above). The dynamic theories of legal interpretation indeed presume that both interpretive activity itself *and* its result are creative. However, even contemporary logocentric theories do not deny the existence of some creative aspects of legal interpretation, usually identified as the necessity of undertaking choices based on values in seeking the fulfilment of general norms and in resolving conflicts between principles of the law.[52] The logocentric theories are also often associated with a procedural, step-by-step approach, determined by the order and hierarchy of interpretive directives, and with the syllogistic model of interpretation. In the doctrine of public international

---

50 William N. Eskridge et al., *Legislation and Statutory Interpretation* (Foundation Press 2000) 211ff.

51 Hugues Rabault, *L'interprétation des normes: l'objectivité de la méthode herméneutique* (Harmattan 1997) 10.

52 Cf. Zygmunt Ziembiński, *Szkice z metodologii szczegółowych nauk prawnych* (Państwowe Wydawnictwo Naukowe 1983); Jerzy Wróblewski, 'Pragmatyczna jasność prawa' 4 Państwo i Prawo (1988).

law they found their counterpart in what Laura Nielsen in her analysis of Art. 31.1 of the Vienna Convention on the Law of Treaties (the VCLT) characterizes as a sequentialist approach, contrasted with a holistic one.[53]

The semiotic perspective also acknowledges that the primary text of the law (legal instrument), being an object of legal interpretation, is closed and addressed at a precisely defined model reader, expected to perform the process of legal rendition in a specific, conventional way. The open components of such text can, however, be identified and might emerge in the body of the text for different reasons. They may arise without a specific intent of the lawmaker, as a result of the general indeterminacy and vagueness of certain expressions of common language, a variety of which is the legal language. They might also, as mentioned above, be used by design, in the form of general clauses (*Generalklauseln*) and other expressions leaving the decision as to the actual and specific scope of application of the rule to the discretion of the court. Finally, they can be an effect of an inaccuracy or an error of the lawmaker, which might arise on the semantic and lexical, as well as on the syntactic, level.

A possible model of the semiotic web of the law, placing the reader in the centre of the process of legal interpretation, and taking into consideration its textual, conventional, formal and institutional restrictions, would be a response to those concerns. Semiosis is always a contextually located process; an outcome, as well as a mechanism of generating artefacts of a specific culture. The coexistence and co-functioning of multiple domestic legal systems can be thus represented as distinct, but interwoven networks. This aspect is also not exposed in Benson's analysis, which focuses on the American perspective – the construct of a semiotic web(s) of the law seems, however, highly adequate for illustrating interconnections between various national orders, manifest also in the arbitral discourse.

While distinct, they are not isolated, but linked on different levels: from the general educational background of national lawmakers and adjudicators, who might be sharing similar readings and conceptual (philosophical, social, economic) categories; through applications of a comparative approach, noticeable in legal doctrine as well as in adjudicatory practice; to the presence of harmonized rules and sets of rules of different origin (international and regional) permeating domestic legal systems. This corresponds with the semiotic representation of the entirety of culture as an overarching network, connecting multiple subsets of signs, or a labyrinth in which it is possible, through a long enough sequence of signs, to reach any point from any other.

The Semiotic Web of Legal Interpretation in ICA

The practice of international commercial arbitration, as further discussed in the following chapters, has brought a new dynamics to this interplay, by contributing

53 Laura Nielsen, *The WTO, Animals, and PPMs* (Martinus Nijhoff 2007) 200–01.

to the development of new substantive connections and by broadening the range of paths through which the interpretive solutions might be reached. The functioning of legal interpretation in arbitration can be envisioned not as a map of a labyrinth but rather as a multidimensional and multiplanar model, with its segments representing different domestic legal systems with their specific requirements and internal interpretive traditions, but also with the private level of arbitral rules of procedure, a separate set of considerations introduced by the public international law instruments (most notably by the New York Convention), and the transnational layer of the new *lex mercatoria*.

Whereas the majority of arbitral cases are resolved through an application of the substantive rules of a domestic legal system determined as *lex causae*, the process cannot be exercised mechanically. First, the determination of proper law requires a relevant conflict of laws analysis, unless the *voie directe* competence has been granted and exercised. The conflict of laws rules themselves are, however, – unlike in the private international law cases resolved by the domestic courts – not predetermined by *lex fori*, but, in the absence of the relevant parties' choice, selected by the arbitrators within their discretionary powers.[54] The conflict of laws analysis in arbitration thus relies on a more flexible framework than in domestic litigation and is not meant to be carried on 'from within' a specific national legal system.

Second, an admissible outcome of such analysis is, as a standard, not restricted to substantive law of a given State, but can also include the rules of law deemed by the arbitrators to be proper. Such a formulation of provisions on the grounds for an award, adopted by major global arbitral institutions, has been widely described as opening the door for applying the new *lex mercatoria* principles (as described in Chapter 8), as the concept of the rules of law is logically broader than that of the law. Even if relatively rarely treated as an autonomous ground for an award, the New Law Merchant might help to redirect interpretation of proper domestic law if in its 'pure' version it would lead to unreasonably parochial effects, irreconcilable with the international character of the disputed transaction. Notably exceptional in this regard is Art. 35.1 of the UNCITRAL Rules, which obligates the arbitral tribunal to respect the parties' choice of relevant rules of law, but, failing such selection by the parties, it entitles the tribunal to determine applicable law (not rules of law) which it deems appropriate.

The 2012 CIETAC Rules are even more strict in this regard – as Art. 47.2 provides:

> Where the parties have agreed on the law as it applies to the merits of their dispute, the parties' agreement shall prevail. In the absence of such an agreement or where such agreement is in conflict with a mandatory provision of the law, the arbitral tribunal shall determine the law as it applies to the merits of the dispute.

54 Cf., for example, AAA Rules, Art. 28.1; CIETAC Rules, Art. 47; ICC Rules, Art. 21; LCIA Rules, Art. 14.2; Stockholm Rules, Art. 22; UNCITRAL Rules, Art. 35; VIAC Rules Art. 24.

The range of available options is thus limited to the determination of proper domestic law. This seems consistent with the rather reluctant approach of the CIETAC arbitrators towards applying *lex mercatoria*, even in its gap-filling role, as demonstrated by Chi Manjiao in an analysis of references to UNIDROIT Principles in CIETAC case law.[55] While the CIETAC Rules also do not allow for *amiable composition* (and might seem to express a clear preference for domestic law-based awards), they also provide an opening for hybrid, arb-med proceedings (indeed quite frequently used in practice) through Art. 45 (see Chapter 9).

Third, the application of proper domestic law is not performed 'from within' this very system and arbitral tribunals do not render awards in the name of a State, as the domestic courts do. Moreover, the legal system determined as applicable law is often not the system in which the arbitrators have been primarily educated. The adopted approach to interpretation of domestic rules determined as applicable substantive law can thus take one of three possible forms. The arbitrators (as well as the parties' counsel) might attempt to undertake their interpretive tasks in an authentic way, consistent with canons of legal interpretation internal and characteristic to the applied system (which might be difficult if they are themselves not insiders to this system). They can also aim at international (or transnational) interpretation of the domestic law, for instance by employing comparative analysis or by filtering *lex causae* through the *lex mercatoria* considerations. Finally, they can – often in an unreflective way – construe applicable rules of a specific domestic legal system as they would their own. In other words, they can project interpretive canons and directives acquired in the process of their primary legal education onto the rules, which possibly belong to a different system.

The – usually mandatory – recourse to international customs and usages of trade, required by the rules of procedure, adds to legal interpretation of substantive law the level of considerations related to the intrinsically international character of the analysed contractual relationship. A comparative approach is also often assumed, and its specific use in arbitration has been indicated as a key factor in the development of the new *lex mercatoria* (even leading some authors to expressing the thesis that the New Law Merchant is in fact a method of arbitral adjudication based on comparative inquiry – cf. Chapter 8).

Fourth, the regards of recognition and enforcement, as regulated by the New York Convention, require arbitrators to adopt a perspective exceeding, on the level of substantive rules, the limits of a single legal system. In particular, considerations of *ordre public* rules of the place in which the enforcement of an award is likely to be sought affect interpretive processes in arbitration.

Fifth, the recourse to public transnational order (understood as a national or as an autonomous transnational concept) has been reappearing in the arbitral practice

55 Chi Manjiao, 'Application of the UNIDROIT Principles in China: Successes, Shortcomings and Implications' 15 Unif L Rev (2010); see also Chi Manjiao, 'The Iceberg Beneath the Water': The Hidden Discrimination against the Lex Mercatoria in Chinese Arbitration' 7 J Priv Int'l L (2011).

and discussed by legal scholars in the context of both – the place of arbitration, as well as the place of anticipated enforcement. As further examined in Chapter 10, the notion of *ordre public* and its implications for arbitral decision-making are to be approached carefully and not treated as tantamount to the doctrine of mandatory rules of law.

Sixth, the possibility of authorizing arbitrators to act as *amiables compositeurs* exposes legal interpretation in ICA to increased influence of extralegal considerations and broadens the scope of adjudicative choices based on values, as compared with their restrictive delineation in domestic litigation, exercised within a specific national legal system. It is worth emphasizing that *amiable composition* and arbitration *ex aequo et bono* are not contradictory to and do not exclude exercise of legal interpretation. Rather, they allow an adjudicator to resign from strict application of proper law in the form to which its rigorous legal interpretation would lead (see Chapter 9).

Legal interpretation in ICA thus resembles juggling with many balls of different size and weight. The semiotic model of reading as a process of discovery/creation of meaning, further adapted to this specific version of legal rendition, seems thus to capture well its multifaceted character. It also seems particularly fit for apprehending another characteristic feature of arbitration, which distinguishes it from domestic litigation and affects the processes of legal interpretation: the linguistic diversity present in different forms and on various stages of arbitration, which has to be accommodated without negatively affecting the neutrality of the proceedings, the equal footing for the contesting parties, and the substantive quality of an award.

The Application of Foreign Substantive Law: The Issue of Double Intermediacy

Besides legal concerns related to the interplay of different domestic systems and rules of different origin, force and scope of regulation, another characteristic feature of legal interpretation in international arbitration is the fact that the law, determined to be *lex causae*, is construed and applied not necessarily in its original linguistic version, but often in translation into a language known to the arbitrators. These additional, intermediate aspects of languages in which the proper law is originally expressed, in which it is being accessed (through translation), in which interpretive activity is being undertaken, in which the proceedings are being held and in which award is being rendered – which may be at least in some of these aspects different – add a whole new dimension to the complexity of tasks performed by an interpreter.

Some components forming this potentially mosaic linguistic situation can also be found in international cases resolved by the domestic courts – for example, in the application to the merits of the case of foreign law, available in translation; or the aid of an official interpreter assisting a party or a witness who is not familiar with the language of the proceedings. Nevertheless it should be noted that the language of the proceedings is predetermined; it is also the native language of the judges, and the language in which they conduct the analysis of proper substantive law (even if this law is accessed in its original in another language or through a translation). In domestic litigation the applicable law on the levels of rules of procedure and of private international law is also expressed in the language of the court; and finally, courts' decisions, rendered in the name of the State, are naturally formulated in the language of that State.

UNCITRAL Model Law (and legislations patterned after it) addresses the issue of linguistic uncertainty in regard to arbitral proceedings, procedural acts, evidence, awards and other statements by the arbitral tribunal – elements that affect the process of legal interpretation:

> Article 22. Language
> (1) The parties are free to agree on the language or languages to be used in the arbitral proceedings. Failing such agreement, the arbitral tribunal shall determine the language or languages to be used in the proceedings. This agreement or determination, unless otherwise specified therein, shall apply to any written statement by a party, any hearing and any award, decision or other communication by the arbitral tribunal.
> (2) The arbitral tribunal may order that any documentary evidence shall be accompanied by a translation into the language or languages agreed upon by the parties or determined by the arbitral tribunal.

The problem of access to, and proper interpretation of, foreign substantive law, be it in the original linguistic version or in translation, is, however, left largely unregulated by domestic legislation on arbitration. It is also at least partially shifted onto the parties, who might be obliged to produce relevant evidence for their claims, including the proof of applicable law.

As Gabrielle Kaufmann-Kohler explicates,[56] the two traditions formed in this regard by the domestic courts (the continental approach, shared also by the US Federal Rules of Civil Procedure, of treating foreign law as law, which either can or shall be accessed and examined *ex officio*; and the English tradition of treating foreign law as a fact, to be proven by the parties) should be distinguished from and not attempted to be directly transferred to the arbitral practice.

In regard to arbitration, Kaufmann-Kohler demonstrates on the example of the Swiss PIL Act (silent on this issue) that the courts addressing the question of whether arbitrators are free to choose the method of determination of the content of applicable law, answered it positively, without indicating a necessity for consulting the parties. Considering the issue of possible limits of their discretion in this

56 Gabrielle Kaufmann-Kohler, 'The Governing Law: Fact or Law?' – A Transnational Rule on Establishing its Contents' in *Best Practices in International Arbitration*, ASA Special Series no. 26 (Markus Wirth ed, ASA Swiss Arbitration Association 2006) 2ff.

regard, she notes that '[e]xcept for limits arising out of a possible agreement of the parties and the requirement that the arbitral tribunal must consult with the parties on the application of an unexpected legal rule, there appear to be no limits.'[57]

She also observes that in the arbitral practice the general expectation is for the parties to offer evidence as to the contents of applicable law,[58] with such an approach being consistent with the practical requirements of decision-making in a cross-cultural and transnational legal environment. A strict 'law-as-a-fact' approach might, however, turn out to be inappropriate under specific circumstances (such as a possible expert competence of an arbitrator in the field of law being an object of the counsel's opinion). As a consequence, a compromising transnational solution is being proposed, inspired by the formulation of Rule 44.1 of the US Federal Rules of Civil Procedure:

> The parties shall establish the contents of the law applicable to the merits. The arbitral tribunal shall have the power, but not the obligation, to conduct its own research to establish such contents. If it makes use of such power, the tribunal shall give the parties an opportunity to comment on the result of the tribunal's research.
>
> If the contents of the applicable law are not established with respect to a specific issue, the arbitral tribunal is empowered to apply to such issue any rule of law which it deems appropriate.[59]

Proper substantive law, to be interpreted and applied by the tribunal, is thus likely to be an object of a double, linguistic and legal intermediacy, resulting from the indirect access to it gained through translation, and being an effect of a possible (and frequent in practice) reliance on submissions on its contents, offered by the parties and their counsel.

The Platonic logocentric ideal of preservation of an original, as well as its Montesquieuan adaptation for the realm of legal interpretation, is thus particularly difficult to defend in the sphere of international commercial arbitration. Unlike a judge, an arbitrator is not potentially exercising the function of 'the mouth of the law' in the sense of pronouncing it to the parties and to society through publicly available decisions. He or she is rather acting as an umpire in a rhetorical competition on the determination of the content and meaning of the applicable law. It is thus likely in practice that the award is based on the representation of applicable law, persuasively forwarded by one party and not contested successfully by the other.

It should be noted that the rhetorical character of judicial decision-making has been widely disputed by theorists contesting the syllogistic model of legal reasoning as a straight path to the absolute meaning. The character of legal

57 Ibid. 5.
58 Ibid. 6.
59 Ibid. 6.

interpretation as a discursive contest of varied versions of rendition of applicable law is of course not new in legal theory. As Pierre Schlag argues, the violence of judging lies precisely in these acts of selection: '[j]udges arrive at their decisions by killing off rival conceptions of law'.[60] Such an approach is close to the semiotic vision of an interpretive process as navigation through different interpretants (which, in case of legal interpretation, is not free, but instructed by interpretive canons and directives, and which is a purposive activity; in other words, it has to end with an establishment of the version applied to the merits of the case). *Iura novit curia* and proper construing of the rules, is an object of fierce intellectual competition – possibly externalized in communications from the parties and their counsel, but also exercised within the discretion of the judge as an interpreter.

In arbitration, the rhetorical character of legal interpretation is further increased by the fact that this competition does not affect just the sphere of interpretation of the already known law, but also the knowledge of the law itself. In other words, even if in domestic litigation precise determination of what rules are applicable to the merits of the dispute can also be an object of controversy, in arbitration it is so practically by definition. The violence of arbitrating would be thus the killing off of the rival representations of the applicable rules first, so as to continue killing off their opposing renditions.

Legal interpretation in arbitration is exercised in a transnational environment – though not in an anational vacuum. As discussed in detail above, the New York Convention regime upholds the principle of localization of an award; regard to recognition and enforcement issues introduces specific considerations of the substantive law of the place of arbitration and of the place of anticipated enforcement to the conducted analysis; law applicable to the merits of the case is usually domestic law as chosen by the parties or determined by the arbitral tribunal. However, many factors increase the non-obvious, non-automatic character of legal interpretation: these include procedural autonomy; the private institutional setting; the heterogeneity of sources of law to be considered; the status as well as the personal qualifications of arbitrators (who are not necessarily expert in the rules of a particular national system to be applied, and who, unlike judges, are selected by the parties themselves and for the resolution of a specific case); and the regard to the cross-border character of the case, observable (for example) in a recourse to international trade usages and customs and a gap-filling function of the *lex mercatoria*. Even if its object is primarily the domestic law, it is applied in a transnational environment, not within the context of a national legal system.

ICA and Discourse Analysis

The specific, structural, conventional, institutional, procedural and personal framework of arbitration has made it a target of interest for researchers embracing

60 Pierre Schlag, 'Clerks in the Maze' 91 Mich L Rev (1993) 2053.

the semiotic paradigm – either as a main research perspective or as part of a broader agenda of discourse analysis. The latter addresses reality as socially constructed through a variety of discourses and defines its main task as an epistemological one: an examination of the relationship between discourse and reality.[61]

Michel Foucault postulates that discourses are no longer to be approached as

> groups of signs (signifying elements referring to contents or representations) but as practices that systematically form the objects of which they speak. Of course discourses are composed of signs; but what they do is more than use these signs to designate things. It is this more that renders them irreducible to the language (*langue*) and to speech. It is this 'more' that we must reveal and describe.[62]

The main centre of gravity of inquiry is thus being shifted from the analysis of signification and the perspective of an individual reader onto the social functioning of the processes of meaning-making through the textual communication in a broad sense. While indeed indebted to semiotics (partly due to the concept of semiosis as an always contextual and historically located process of meaning-making), discourse analysis is thus not reducible to its pragmatic aspect.

Ian Parker forwards the view that a discourse is a coherent system of statements which constructs an object, emphasizing such its aspects as (among other things) self-reflexivity, interdiscursive cross-referencing, historical embedment, support to institutions, reproduction of power relations and ideological effects.[63] Nelson Phillips and Cynthia Hardy further explore this creative mechanism, defining discourse as:

> An interrelated set of texts, and the practices of their production, dissemination and reception, that brings an object into being … In other words, social reality is produced and made real through discourses, and social interactions cannot be fully understood without reference to the discourses that give them meaning.[64]

The definition of a text as a 'discursive unit' is broad and encompasses different forms of communications: oral, written, expressed through visual representations, artefacts, behaviour, symbols, etc.[65] It is thus not limited to linguistic objects and is closely related to the Peircean concept of a sign.

Parker also notes, though not without reservations, the affinity between the so-defined discourse and the concept of an interpretative repertoire, offered by

---

61 Nelson Phillips and Cynthia Hardy, *Discourse Analysis: Investigating Processes of Social Construction* (Sage 2002) 3.

62 Michel Foucault, *Archaeology of Knowledge* (Routledge 2002) 54.

63 Ian Parker, *Discourse Dynamics: Critical Analysis for Social and Individual Psychology* (Taylor & Frances/Routledge 1992) 5ff.

64 Phillips and Hardy (n 61) 3.

65 Parker (n 63) 7; Phillips and Hardy (n 61) 4.

Jonathan Potter and Margaret Wetherell, and related to recurrent and limited systems of terms, stylistic and grammatical structures, applied in reference to particular phenomena, and frequently focused around specific metaphors and figures of speech.[66] This aspect of functioning of the highly conventional legal discourses seems particularly interesting in international arbitration, which – as demonstrated in the following chapters – changes the context for and further transforms the already-existing domestic interpretative repertories.

Consequently, the concept of legal interpretation adopted in this book is thus one that combines its representation as semiosis – a process of creation of meaning through sequences of reactions to and reformulations of legal communications – with an apprehension of its recurring, typical components, determined by legal, institutional, economic and social factors which affect the functioning of international commercial arbitration (and is thus consistent with the discourse analysis postulates).

Linguistic aspects of the functioning of arbitration, studied from the discourse analysis perspective, were the object of pioneering, long-term international studies conducted by Vijay Kumar Bhatia, Christopher Candlin and Maurizio Gotti. The projects were dedicated to the issue of integrity in the legally and linguistically fragmented realm of ICA – first, the generic integrity of its legal discourse, and second, the integrity of arbitration practice, scrutinized at the intersections of law and language.[67]

One of the important findings is the application of the general theory of identities employed by the participants in a professional discourse, which has led to a delineation of the specific identities of the actors engaged in the practice of ICA. Bensonian notions of an interpreter and the set of 'other readers', presented as a list of authors of (any) utterances of the law and about the law – both insiders and outsiders to the lawmaking and adjudication process – are thus replaced by a more precise categorization of discourse participants. Such an approach, besides providing an opportunity for efficient allocation and comparison of the discursive situation of particular participants (and not just 'labelling' them by their professional function), also allows for tracing the cases of multiple identities assumed by the same person.

Bhatia, Candlin and Gotti's research reveals that the dynamics of arbitral proceedings is significantly influenced by:

> strong and marked contestations based on various kinds of identities … which can be narrowed down to professional, disciplinary, jurisdictional and individual, because of the involvement of two rather different though overlapping juridical practices (litigation and arbitration), two or more disciplinary concerns (legal,

66 Jonathan Potter and Margaret Wetherell, *Discourse and Social Psychology: Beyond Attitudes and Behaviour* (Sage 1987) 149.

67 V.K. Bhatia et al., *Discourse and Practice in International Commercial Arbitration: Issues, Challenges and Prospects* (Ashgate 2012) 4–5.

> commercial and other content areas of disputes), at least two jurisdictions (common law and civil law), and at least two main categories of participants, viz. specialist (lawyers) and lay (witnesses).[68]

Research focus is thus clearly on legal discourse as professional discourse, exercised in the formal setting of dispute resolution, and does not include actors who are not participating in arbitral proceedings and may be authors of indirectly relevant utterances on the meta-level (as some of the actors listed by Benson).

A similar approach, concentrating on the professional character of legal discourse (understood *sensu stricto*) is also adopted in this book. As its main topic is legal interpretation, the character of examined materials and communications is predominantly written and prepared by specialist participants. Such materializations of the arbitral discourse, which are oriented at establishing the facts (as the hearings) or at organizational matters remain thus outside the central scope of discussion. The high relevance of possible tensions, resulting from clashes of identities indicated by Bhatia, Candlin and Gotti, and their impact on the overall course of proceedings, are however fully acknowledged. The following chapters address these concerns and explore them in the context of multilevel competition in the field of ICA and its frequently cross-cultural character.

68 Ibid. 304.

PART II
Structural Determinants of Legal Discourse in Arbitration

Chapter 4
Ad Hoc and Institutional Arbitration

Basic Notions

As discussed in Chapter 1, the decision of the parties to select arbitration as a method of resolution of their dispute is affected by different kinds of considerations. A further choice to be made is a decision on type of arbitration best serving the interests of the parties.

Two types of arbitration – ad hoc and institutional (administered) – can be distinguished on the basis of the method of their respective administration. In the latter, proceedings are managed by an established institution, and routinely pursuant to that institution's pre-existent rules of procedure. Such an agency can specialize solely in offering arbitration services or it can propose them among other functions performed within its scope of activity.

In ad hoc arbitration no such allocation of administrative authority takes place and the parties are exercising their right to devise and determine the rules of procedure on their own. They can achieve that either by contractually designing a set of rules for a specific purpose of a particular arbitration, or by opting for already-existing rules of procedure (such as the UNCITRAL Arbitration Rules), or by transferring the rights to regulate the procedure upon the arbitral tribunal.

Ad Hoc Arbitration

General Characteristics

While examining the advantages of ad hoc arbitration, Alan Redfern remarks that if a dedicated and successful cooperation between the parties and their counsel over a task of formulating specific rules of procedure is accomplished, 'the difference between an ad hoc arbitration and an institutional arbitration is like the difference between a tailor-made suit and one which is bought off the peg.'[1] This potential for modelling the procedure in order to accommodate the individual needs of the parties and specific demands of a particular case is the most commonly emphasized

1 As quoted in Gerald Aksen, 'Ad Hoc Versus Institutional Arbitration' 2 ICC Bulletin (1991) 9.

benefit of ad hoc arbitration. The level of control which the parties keep over the course of proceedings is in this form particularly high.[2]

Financial efficiency and expedition of the proceedings are also invoked as the factors endorsing the choice of ad hoc arbitration. The parties selecting this form for their dispute resolution avoid the risk of delays resulting from the fulfilment of internal administrative standards of arbitral institutions, where the wheels of justice might turn at a slower pace.

It is also worth observing that the argument that ad hoc proceedings are more economical than the ones organized by an arbitral institution might not always be accurate. Gerald Aksen notices that the costs saved by opting for ad hoc arbitration are

> those of administering agency itself, but not the usually far larger legal and arbitrators' fees. Moreover, since most international institutions are now facing substantial competition from other arbitral bodies, transnational businesses are enjoying the benefit of lower and more reasonable fees.[3]

The introduction of capped fees for administration of proceedings by many arbitral institutions reflects such effort towards overcoming the negative image of overpriced services. The eventual overall cost of ad hoc arbitration is in practice a result of the negotiation skills of specific parties (as well as arbitrators) and is consequently much more difficult to estimate. Its relative efficiency depends also on which arbitral institutions are being compared; that is, the services of those organizations which the parties would take into account as an alternative to ad hoc proceedings.

Another possible factor is an occasional inability of the parties to reach a common decision as to the arbitral institution which should resolve their case. Under such circumstances, ad hoc arbitration might turn out to be the only compromise the parties are able to achieve.

Finally, arbitral institutions frequently provide their own internal mechanisms of review of the issued awards. For the parties demanding a particularly expeditious resolution of their controversy this may lead to unwelcome, obstructing effects. The choice of the ad hoc form of arbitration enables them to avoid undesirable delays. However, as Thomas J. Stipanowich observes, the advantages of arbitration can also, under certain circumstances, be perceived as its weak points.[4] This argument is relevant in the context of specific features of ad hoc arbitration as well. The lack of easily accessible institutional control may also work to the disadvantage of the parties, increasing the risk of rendering flawed decisions. The parties, dissatisfied with an award will be left with the possible (but also, under the New York Convention provisions, remarkably limited) recourse to the domestic court.

2 Julian D.M. Lew et al., *Comparative International Commercial Arbitration* (Kluwer Law International/Aspen 2003) 35.

3 Aksen (n 1) 11.

4 Thomas J. Stipanowich, 'Rethinking American Arbitration' 63 Ind LJ (1988) 432ff.

UNCITRAL Arbitration Rules and Ad Hoc Arbitration

The main risk connected with choosing this form of arbitration seems to be that of 'reinventing the wheel'[5] through recurrent efforts of the parties and their counsel to draft rules of procedure and solve problems already successfully managed before. An opportunity to have a controversy resolved according to the indeed 'tailor-made' procedural standards seems decisive for only a fraction of all parties involved in international commercial disputes. In most cases time and effectiveness are the factors particularly compelling to the parties potentially interested in ad hoc arbitration.

As a consequence, introduction of 'ready-made' sets of rules of procedure, suitable for the needs of ad hoc decision-making, turned out to be a successful initiative. Adoption by UNCITRAL on 28 April 1976 of the UNCITRAL Arbitration Rules has been indicated as a breakthrough in this regard. The UNCITRAL Rules have become an instrument fit for ad hoc arbitrations as well as for administered ones. Still, as it is a common practice of arbitral institutions to issue their own procedural regulations, the significance of the UNCITRAL Arbitration Rules is very much that of a document upon which the parties may easily agree in the absence of institutional support.

In drafting the UNCITRAL Rules, the expert committee collaborated extensively with arbitral institutions. A formal cooperation was also established between UNCITRAL and a private organization, the International Commission on Commercial Arbitration (ICCA). The subsequent influence of UNCITRAL's work on procedural regulation of arbitral institutions, though evident, is rather indirect: Howard M. Holtzmann remarks that

> most modern institutional rules resonate with strong echoes of the UNCITRAL Rules, and some, indeed, include key provisions identical to the UNCITRAL text. Further, some new arbitration centers adopt the UNCITRAL text as their institutional rules.[6]

Additionally, many arbitral institutions

> allow the parties to opt for UNCITRAL Rules instead of their own arbitration rules, and still offer full administration services. Those institutions include, inter alia, American Arbitration Association ('AAA'), London Court of International Arbitration, Stockholm Chamber of Commerce, Arbitral Center of the Federal Economic Chamber of Austria in Vienna ... Support from several other institutions is limited to serving as the appointing authority: e.g, the International

5 James K. Hoenig, 'The Pros and Cons of Administered Arbitration' 49 Disp Res J (1994).

6 Howard M. Holtzmann, 'Recent Work on Dispute Resolution by the United Nations Commission on International Trade Law' 5 ILSA J Int'l & Comp L (1999) 425–26.

> Chamber of Commerce ('ICC'), the Netherlands Arbitration Institute, and Zurich Chamber of Commerce.[7]

The functional success of the UNCITRAL Arbitration Rules can also be seen in the fact of their use for the resolution of controversies falling outside their intended primary scope of application, such as investment treaty cases. Paul D. Friedland and Lucy Martinez point out that besides the ad hoc resolved commercial cases, the UNCITRAL Rules have been used for numerous arbitrations under bilateral or multilateral investment treaties, as well as preferential trade and investment agreements,[8] including cases resolved by the Iran–US Claims Tribunal and investor–government disputes under NAFTA.

They have also been used as a default set of rules of procedure by some permanent arbitral institutions, including, notably, the Hong Kong International Arbitration Centre (HKIAC). They were adopted as the default rules of procedure for international arbitrations administered by HKIAC with the intention to support parties who 'seek the formality and convenience of an administered arbitration while maintaining the flexibility afforded by the UNCITRAL Arbitration Rules (Rules)'.[9] They were applied until the issuance of the Centre's own HKIAC Administered Arbitration Rules in September 2008 (and are still recommended by this Centre for ad hoc arbitrations[10]). While the intended, primary function of UNCITRAL Arbitration Rules, as adopted in 1976, was to provide an effective instrument for ad hoc commercial arbitrations, its widespread reception, also outside its main scope of application, confirms the practical utility of this instrument.

The UNCITRAL Arbitration Rules are the most successful example of a standard procedural regulation serving the purposes of ad hoc arbitrations. Several private institutions, such as the International Institute for Conflict Prevention and Resolution, have followed this route by drafting their own rules of procedure for ad hoc cases. The first version of Rules for Non-Administered Arbitration (the CPR Rules – originally Rules and Commentary for Non-Traditional Arbitration for Business Disputes) was adopted in 1989. They were principally aimed at application in domestic ad hoc arbitrations, although their use in international disputes has not been excluded. In 1992 the separate CPR Rules for Non-Administered Arbitration of International Disputes (the CPR International Rules)

---

7 William K. Slate II et al., 'UNCITRAL (United Nations Commission on International Trade Law). Its Workings in International Arbitration and a New Model Conciliation Law' 6 Cardozo J Conf Res 1 (Fall 2004) 79.

8 Paul D. Friedland and Lucy Martinez, 'The UNCITRAL Arbitration Rules: A Commentary. By David D. Caron, Lee M. Caplan, and Matti Pellonpää. Book Review' 101 Am J Int'l L (2007) 519.

9 Susan Block-Lieb and Terence C. Halliday, 'Incrementalisms in Global Lawmaking' 32 Brook J Int'l L (2007).

10 <http://hkiac.org/index.php/en/aribtration-rules-a-guidelines>.

and the Commentary were introduced and subsequently amended (with the most recent version being in force since 2007[11]).

As explicated in the Commentary to the CPR International Rules, also in the cases involving persons or business enterprises of different nationalities or located in different countries, as well as contracts with a foreign element, '[w]here parties have provided for CPR arbitration generally, without specifically identifying which CPR arbitration rules shall apply, the general CPR Rules for Non-Administered Arbitration (the "Rules") shall apply.'[12]

One of the most important solutions, adopted in the CPR International Rules and not finding a direct counterpart in the general Rules, is their suitability for multi-party disputes. Thus, the CPR International Rules seem particularly adequate for complex, international ad hoc arbitrations. They also provide an example of a trend towards developing arbitral rules of procedure meant to be adjusted to the demands of more compound cases, previously better accommodated by litigation.

The same tendency can be found in the recent version of the UNCITRAL Arbitration Rules, which underwent a major process of revision in 2006 to 2010. The outcome of its process – the 2010 edition – contains new (and much awaited) provisions on, among other things, multi-party proceedings, joinder (but, remarkably, not consolidation) and liability, as well as a number of procedural modifications, including reviewed mechanisms for introduction of interim measures. The resulting, amended version of the UNCITRAL Rules thus seems suitable for application in the conditions that have changed over the first thirty years of use of this instrument. Whether the adopted changes will help in broadening the range of ad hoc arbitration from a method considered to be 'suitable for experienced parties only'[13] to a wider spectrum of cases remains be proven.

Institutional Arbitration

According to Hans Smit, the most frequently mentioned advantages of administered arbitration are the following:

> (1) it provides procedures for selection of the arbitrators; (2) it provides rules of procedure for conducting the arbitration; (3) it may provide, at least to some extent, rules for deciding the merits of the dispute; (4) it may provide facilities

11 <http://www.cpradr.org/Resources/ALLCPRArticles/tabid/265/ID/610/2007-CPR-Rules-for-Non-Administered-Arbitration-of-International-Disputes.aspx>.

12 2007 Commentary to CPR Rules for Non-Administered Arbitration of International Disputes, General Commentary (Types of Disputes), available at <http://www.cpradr.org/Resources/ALLCPRArticles/tabid/265/ID/610/2007-CPR-Rules-for-Non-Administered-Arbitration-of-International-Disputes.aspx>.

13 Jan Paulsson and Georgios Petrochilos (eds), *Revision of the UNCITRAL Arbitration Rules. A Report* (informal report 2006) 5.

> for the arbitrators, such as hearing rooms and administrative assistance; and (5) it may provide a measure of supervision over the arbitrators.[14]

These factors and their actual significance in arbitration will be further discussed in turn in this chapter.

Of the four elements listed by Smit, the availability of pre-existing procedural mechanisms has already been mentioned as an important consideration, affecting the choice of a particular form of dispute resolution. The personal selection of arbitrators (or selection of the procedure of their appointment, including their possible assignment by a third party), as well as designing individually modelled rules of procedure, both require a cooperation of the parties much closer than is needed in case of a simple agreement upon a choice of a particular arbitral institution.

In fact the decision on having a dispute arbitrated ad hoc or institutionally is a consequence of balancing the values and goals which both parties would like to achieve. It also depends upon the actual readiness of the parties to collaborate in the efforts towards resolution of their controversy and the practical feasibility of such cooperation. The objectives, frequently appearing as contradictory or requiring a decision on giving a clear preference to one of them, are time effectiveness and absence of unnecessary institutional burdens on one hand and a guarantee of procedural accuracy, clarity and control on the other.

As demonstrated above, time- and cost-efficiency are most commonly mentioned as most significant benefits of ad hoc arbitration. The possibility of designing 'custom-tailored' rules of procedure for a particular case seems appealing, yet applicable to a rather limited extent to highly specialized contracts and by parties fully conscious of their procedural demands and expectations. Establishment of an entirely new set of rules of procedure may be also time-consuming and requires a consensus by the parties, often difficult to achieve in the circumstances of an already open controversy. These obstacles can be overcome by choosing already-existing rules of procedure, appropriate for non-administered arbitration, and accepted by the parties either as a whole or with agreed upon modifications.

From this perspective, institutional arbitration may seem as an unnecessary formalization of a flexible mechanism of dispute resolution. This can be distinctly observed in larger cases (which have been defined by the AAA as involving claims of at least $500,000[15]), where the lack of flexibility often seriously affects the speed of dispute resolution. The decisions by the parties to choose an ad hoc form

14 Hans Smit, 'The Future of International Commercial Arbitration: A Single Transnational Institution?' 1986 Colum J Transnat'l L (1986) 15.

15 American Arbitration Association, Supplementary Procedures for Large, Complex Commercial Disputes (1 February 1993. Amended and effective 15 September 2005) 2005 #36.

of arbitration can be thus interpreted as directly resulting from a need for omitting an additional level of redundant structure and rigidity.[16]

Many arbitral institutions have reacted to these reservations by granting a broader discretionary power to arbitrators in regard to the determination of applicable rules of procedure. According to the LCIA Rules (Article 14.2):

> Unless otherwise agreed by the parties under Article 14.1, the Arbitral Tribunal shall have the widest discretion to discharge its duties allowed under such law(s) or rules of law as the Arbitral Tribunal may determine to be applicable; and at all times the parties shall do everything necessary for the fair, efficient and expeditious conduct of the arbitration.

Analogical powers have been vested in the Arbitral Tribunal by virtue of Art. 15 of the ICC Rules of Arbitration.

It is worth remarking that the increasingly popular *voie directe* competence, regarding the determination of substantive rules to be applied to the merits of a dispute, finds its procedural counterpart in recent regulations issued by several arbitral institutions. According to Art. 20.1 of the 2006 VIAC Rules of Arbitration and Conciliation (Vienna Rules), the sole arbitrator (arbitral tribunal) may conduct the arbitration proceedings at his (its) absolute discretion, with the regard to the principle of equal treatment of the parties and the right to be heard being ensured at every stage of the proceedings. Correspondingly, Art. 19 (1) of the 2007 Stockholm Chamber of Commerce Arbitration Rules (SCC Rules) provides that, subject to these rules and any agreement between the parties, the Arbitral Tribunal may conduct the arbitration in such manner as it considers appropriate.

The 2008 HKIAC Administered Arbitration Rules (Art. 14.1) offer a more stringent version of this competence, stating that the tribunal shall adopt suitable procedures so as to avoid unnecessary delay or expenses, provided that equal treatment of the parties is ensured, and the parties are given reasonable opportunity to present their case (see also the provision of Art. 33.1 of the CIETAC Rules, notably modified by introduction of oral hearings as a default option under Art. 33.2). Similarly, an arbitral tribunal resolving the case under the 2008 AAA International Arbitration Rules, may, according to Art. 16, conduct the arbitration in whatever manner it considers appropriate, provided that the parties are treated with equality and that each party has the right to be heard and is given a fair opportunity to present its case. It is also obliged to proceed with a view to expediting the resolution of the dispute. In 1996 AAA has established the International Centre for Dispute Resolution, entrusted with exclusive administration of all of the AAA's international matters.

---

16 George H. Friedman, 'Is Administered Arbitration Still Needed?' C976 American Law Institute – American Bar Association Continuing Legal Education. ALI-ABA Course of Study (1994) 317.

Moreover, at AAA the implementation of the Supplementary Procedures for Large, Complex Commercial Disputes was oriented at fulfilling the demands of the parties in such cases, regarding the expertise criteria as well as efficiency requirements. George H. Friedman characterizes the foundations of this AAA programme as:

> (1) the selection of arbitrators that satisfy rigorous criteria to insure that the panel is an extremely select one, and the training, orientation and coordination of those arbitrators in a manner designed to facilitate the Program; (2) the establishment of new procedures for the administration of those cases that elect to be included in the Program; (3) the flexibility of those parameters so that parties may more speedily and efficiently resolve their disputes; and (4) administration of large, complex cases by trained, senior AAA staff.[17]

On the other hand, the recent tendency towards increasing institutional arbitration's similarity to litigation (for example, by endorsing discovery, dispositive motions, provisional relief and reasoned awards[18]) can be perceived as an answer to the often complex and advanced demands of the parties involved in international trade disputes.

Another advantage of institutional arbitration, presented by Smit, is the suggested accessibility of specific substantive rules, applicable to the merits of the dispute. It can be assumed that such rules, supposedly either non-available or hardly available before the domestic court, belong to the sphere of the new *lex mercatoria* or are discovered as a result of an exercise of *amiable composition* competences by the arbitral tribunal. These two methods of adjudication can be indeed characterized as typical for arbitration and not employed by most national courts. While the scope of their availability marks a difference between litigation and arbitration, the statement that they also distinguish institutional arbitration from the non-administered one, seems controversial.

In ad hoc arbitration the limits of discretionary power of arbitrators are defined by domestic regulations of *lex loci arbitri*, without the additional layer of specification provided by the rules of arbitral institutions. In the cases where parties did not secure specific rules of procedure for the controversy in question, national law on international arbitration is the primary source of the rights and duties of an arbitrator. In those legal systems where the standards set on this issue by the UNCITRAL Model Law have been implemented, the possibility of deciding a case on a basis of *lex mercatoria* or *ex aequo et bono* has not been excluded:

17 Ibid. 317.

18 Cf. Richard Chernick and Rufus Rhoades, 'How to Conduct a Complex Financial Arbitration: A Rapidly Evolving Process' 1440 Securities Arbitration 2004, Corporate Law and Practice Course Handbook Series (Practising Law Institute 2004) 455.

Article 28. Rules applicable to substance of dispute

(1) The arbitral tribunal shall decide the dispute in accordance with such rules of law as are chosen by the parties as applicable to the substance of the dispute. Any designation of the law or legal system of a given State shall be construed, unless otherwise expressed, as directly referring to the substantive law of that State and not to its conflict of laws rules.
(2) Failing any designation by the parties, the arbitral tribunal shall apply the law determined by the conflict of laws rules which it considers applicable.
(3) The arbitral tribunal shall decide *ex aequo et bono* or as *amiable compositeur* only if the parties have expressly authorized it to do so.
(4) In all cases, the arbitral tribunal shall decide in accordance with the terms of the contract and shall take into account the usages of the trade applicable to the transaction.[19]

Art. 28 (1) of the Model Law requires respecting parties' choice of rules of law (and not only the law – thus validating possible selection of *lex mercatoria.* In the absence of such consensus, according to Art. 28 (2), the tribunal's scope of finding is limited to the (national) law, to be determined by the use of applicable conflict of laws rules. Still, *lex mercatoria* as a body of usages of the international trade can be applied, to a modifying effect, by virtue of Art. 28 (4) and only its application as a sole ground for an award seems precluded.

Possibility of deciding the case *ex aequo et bono* or via *amiable composition* is limited to the cases where the parties have explicitly delegated such powers to the arbitral tribunal. Formulation of Art. 28 (3) is directly analogous to the solutions adopted as a standard by arbitral institutions.

The provisions of UNCITRAL Model Law regarding possibility of the *lex mercatoria* application seem rather cautious in determining the limits of discretionary powers of the arbitral tribunal when compared with private institutional regulations. There is neither a *voie directe* competence granted nor possibility of application of *lex mercatoria* as a sole source of rules to be applied to the merits of the dispute. A possibility of recourse to *lex mercatoria* is indirectly stipulated by Art. 28 (4), but to a limited extent. In this sense, institutional arbitration indeed enables *lex mercatoria* application to a much broader extent, as the proper rules of law (and not only law) can also be determined by the tribunal as *lex causae* in the absence of parties' choice.

The parties preferring non-administered arbitration and definitely interested in having their dispute resolved according to the New Law Merchant rules shall therefore expressly state their choice. It seems also worth noticing that the rather conservative delimitation of powers of the arbitrators by the UNCITRAL

19 Stipanowich (n 4).

Model Law is a result of a carefully and slowly developed compromise.[20] The very method of work on this instrument – through extended expert consultations and consensus – can be, however, perceived as one of the reasons for its success and subsequent implementation by numerous legislations, as it turned out to be acceptable in different legal systems.

Art. 28 has not been amended during the major update of the UNCITRAL Model Law in 2006 and has been maintained in the original form adopted in 1985. After over twenty years it may seem traditional, but it is worth recalling the opinion of Joachim Bonell, expressed during one of the preparatory meetings for this provision, that most of the national laws on arbitration then extant did not address the problem of the law applicable to the substance of the dispute at all.[21]

Finally, if substantive rules specific to arbitration are to be understood as arbitral case law, again, their attribution to administered arbitration only seems ungrounded. In the ongoing dispute regarding the nature of the New Law Merchant, its development by the means of arbitral awards (discovering and explicating usages and customs of international trade) has been widely discussed. Although lacking the formal binding force of a precedent, these awards have directly led to the expansion and consolidation of the body of *lex mercatoria*, due to the persuasiveness of presented lines of reasoning.[22] Nevertheless, this arbitral case law is also available in ad hoc arbitration. National acts on international commercial arbitration, modelled in accordance with the UNCITRAL standard, as examined above, do not exclude the possibility of the New Law Merchant application, even if they do not authorize arbitrators to use it as the only substantive regulation to decide the case. The unfolding corpus of *lex mercatoria* is generally available not only to institutional arbitrators, but to all interested persons, thanks to such initiatives as the Trans-Lex Database created by the CENTRAL unit at the University of Cologne School of Law.

The development of the New Law Merchant through case law has been by far a result of institutional arbitration, as most of the published awards (including those subsequently serving as patterns for the following decisions) were rendered under the auspices of arbitral institutions. There are also extensive procedural possibilities for application of the New Law Merchant in administered arbitration. Still, there are no substantive or procedural reasons to state that *lex mercatoria* in the form of arbitral case law is unavailable to ad hoc arbitrators.

The significance of the next factor, presented by Smit as typical for administered arbitration, seems rather undisputed though. Availability of the necessary facilities and organizational assistance offered by arbitral institutions is

---

20 William. D. Smith, 'Price Quadruples for Iranian Crude Oil at Auction' *New York Times* (12 December 1973).

21 Glen H. Spencer, 'Administered vs. Non-Administered Arbitration' 54 Disp Res J (1999) 42.

22 Ana M. López Rodríguez, *Lex Mercatoria and Harmonization of Contract Law in the EU* (Djof 2003) 82.

of much convenience for the parties, who would expend much time in managing these issues on their own. Securing appropriate scheduling, administrative support and a neutral location for the hearing are examples of activities that must be undertaken in a preparatory phase of arbitration. The assistance of a professional case manager, provided by an arbitral institution, can be of significant help in this regard, while also protecting the neutrality of the forum:

> [i]n private arbitration, parties may speak directly with the neutral ex parte on 'procedural' matters. Such an ex parte communication with an arbitrator on what starts off as (for example) scheduling matters can easily segue into prejudicial substantive discussions since the line between procedure and substance is often unclear. Communicating through a case manager, and thus avoiding the reality or even the appearance of improper ex parte communication, eliminates a possible basis for subsequent bias claims and helps to assure that the parties know they have had a truly fair 'day in court.' Managers also control the exchange of briefs, correspondence and documents, making certain that the parties do in fact communicate with each other.[23]

While ad hoc arbitration may be perceived as an economic option in purely financial terms, individual efforts by the parties to make the necessary arrangements are time-consuming and in a general overview may turn out not to be as effective. As Glen H. Spencer observes, the perception of institutional arbitration as cost-excessive

> most likely stems from the fact that fees for arbitration services are sometimes charged up front. Again, it should be noted that parties do not avoid the need for administration if an ad hoc system is selected; it only means that they either pay the arbitrator or the attorneys and their staff to administer the process instead of paying the administrative agency.[24]

The parties bear the financial burden of organizing the proceedings, no matter whether they are administered privately or by an institution. Financial transparency of services, when offered by the latter and available in advance, combined with the time-efficiency factor, may be an argument for choosing institutional arbitration in a particular case.

The use of new technologies in arbitration is often separately regulated and scrutinized by the institutions in order to provide equal access to them by both parties; the absence of such regulations in ad hoc arbitration may be a source of controversies; for example, regarding the admissibility of a suggestion by the tribunal for a set of respective protocols.[25]

---

23 Hoenig (n 5) 62.

24 Spencer (n 21) 49.

25 Thomas D. Halket, 'The Use of Technology in Arbitration: Ensuring the Future is Available to Both Parties' 81 St John's L Rev (2007) 290ff; also ibid. note 80.

It should also be noted that organizational obstacles can be overcome by the parties not interested in institutional arbitration by choosing the third option: limited administration of their case. Spencer defines this form of arbitration as providing services for selected aspects of procedural arbitration by an independent administering agency.[26] It allows the parties to control the extent to which they want to involve an arbitral institution and spares their time which would have been dedicated to unassisted organization of the proceedings.

The last component indicated by Smit, an institutional supervision over the arbitrators, can be interpreted as both an advantage of administered arbitration and its weakness. An additional layer of institutional oversight can be perceived by the parties as a guarantee for a proper conduct of the proceedings and correctness of an award. On the other hand it can also be recognized as an unnecessary formal extension of the proceedings, hampering their expeditious conduct. Among arbitral institutions, the ICC can be noted as one with particularly far-reaching administrative and procedural quality control. Winston Stromberg describes this institutional involvement of the ICC into individual arbitrations as 'intimate', emphasizing the supervisory role of the ICC Court – an administrative body overseeing the proceedings.[27] Besides organizational and procedural control, the ICC Court also provides preliminary review of awards, including formal as well as substantive matters. These extensive quality-assurance standards of the ICC are, according to Coe, the factor that 'may explain the infrequency with which national courts have set aside ICC awards'.[28]

The problem of substantive control over the awards is directly related to the issue of the finality of awards. As avoidance of unnecessary formalities and lengthiness of litigation is a classical reason for the choice of arbitration, the scope of possible judicial review is, in most countries actively participating in the international economic exchange, decidedly limited.[29] The New York Convention on the Recognition and Enforcement of Foreign Arbitral Awards (the 'New York Convention') in Art. V enumerates the reasons for refusal of recognition and enforcement of the award. They are meant to secure a minimum level of due process in procedural and substantive aspects. The exceptions stipulated by Art. V practically do not authorize the court to a substantive review of the award, besides the criterion of public policy of the country of enforcement, specified in Art. V.2 (b). The list can be extended in particular countries – member States to the New York Convention, encompassing manifest

26 Spencer (n 21) 43.

27 Winston Stromberg, 'Avoiding the Full Court Press: International Commercial Arbitration and Other Global Alternative Dispute Resolution Processes (III)' 40 Loy LA L Rev (2007) 1353.

28 Jack J. Coe, *International Commercial Arbitration: American Principles and Practice in a Global Context* (Transnational Publishers 1997) 209.

29 Kenneth M. Curtin, 'An Examination of Contractual Expansion and Limitation of Judicial Review of Arbitral Awards' 15 Ohio St J Disp Res (2000) 339ff.

disregard of the law in an award as a reason for refusal of its recognition and enforcement.

These limits of judicial control over arbitral awards, aimed at increasing the efficiency of arbitration, enlarge the burden of responsibility of the arbitrators for the correctness of an award. Thus, availability of private instruments of control over the arbitral decision-making is an issue of highest practical importance.

The mechanism of awards supervision, introduced by the ICC, is one of possible solutions of this kind. According to Art. 27 of the ICC Rules, preliminary scrutiny of an award by the Court is mandatory. The tribunal resolving a case is obliged to submit a draft of the award to the Court, which may lay down modifications regarding its form, as well as formulate suggestions as to its substance.

The evolution of substantive self-control over arbitral awards had been influenced by judicial distrust in arbitral decision-making, which severely limited the scope of possible correction of an erroneous arbitral award. This view found its expression in a common law doctrine of *functus officio* ('task performed'), characterized as a 'shorthand term for common-law doctrine barring arbitrator from revisiting merits of award once it has issued'.[30] The insistence upon the finality of an award was rooted in a general assumption that arbitrators may yield to the outside pressure and influence, articulated after the rendering of an award.

The *functus officio* reasoning has been contradicted by the institutional practice of arbitration and by the commentators who reflected that the development of arbitration, its current highly professional profile, and the pragmatic reasons for securing quality of arbitral decision-making do not leave sufficient space for the continuation of the doctrine of limited trust in arbitrators.[31] There are also no legal grounds which would exclude the right of the parties to authorize an arbitral tribunal to review its own award within the scope of their general contractual freedom.[32]

Accordingly, numerous arbitral institutions implemented relevant mechanisms of internal control, allowing for bifurcation of the proceedings (splitting them into separate stages of liability and damages determination). Bifurcation of arbitral proceedings may be admitted either explicitly (as in Art. 16.3 of the CPR Rules) or through providing for interim, interlocutory or partial awards in cases where the tribunal will find it recommendable (see for example Art. 2 (iii) of the ICC Rules; Art. 32.1 of the UNCITRAL Arbitration Rules and, remarkably, Art. 21.2 of the new CIETAC Rules, being a much-awaited amendment).

---

30 *Office and Professional Employees Intern. Union, Local No. 471 v Brownsville General Hosp.* (US Court of Appeals, Third Circuit).

31 James M. Gaitis, 'Reexamining Finality: How to Revise Institutional Practice Rules to Allow for Reconsideration of Reasoned Arbitration Awards' 23 Alternatives to the High Cost of Litigation 7(2005) 113ff.

32 See Ian R. Macneil et al., *Federal Arbitration Law: Agreements, Awards, and Remedies under the Federal Arbitration Act* (Little, Brown 1994) § 37.6.4.2.

Analogically, in some institutions omissions of claims and counterclaims presented to the arbitral tribunal, but not covered by the final award, can be corrected by an issuance of an additional award (see for example Art. 42 of the Stockholm Rules, Art. 27.3 of the LCIA Rules and Art. 52 of the CIETAC Rules).

It is worth noticing that CPR also provides the parties with an opportunity of seeking internal recourse from the controversial award. Introduction of appellate panels within arbitral agencies is an important step in the development of administered arbitration as it results in adding an optional, supplementary stage of dispute resolution within the framework of private adjudication. By adopting the CPR Arbitration Appeal Procedure,[33] the Institute created an additional mechanism for a correction of an erroneous decision. The grounds for rendering an appellate award are enumerated in Rule 8.2:

> Rule 8. The Decision
>
> ...
>
> 8.2 If the Tribunal hears the Appeal, it may issue an Appellate Award modifying or setting aside the Original Award, but only on the following grounds:
> a. That the Original Award (i) contains material and prejudicial errors of law of such a nature that it does not rest upon any appropriate legal basis, or (ii) is based upon factual findings clearly unsupported by the record; or
> b. That the Original Award is subject to one or more of the grounds set forth in Section

The choice of arbitration with a possible, private appellation might be an attractive option for those parties who are immune to the 'limited allure of finality'.[34] This might be of importance in controversies of complex character and involving excessive claims, where the parties are particularly careful to avoid the risk of an aberrant, yet final decision.

On the other hand, in some institutions the tendency towards securing the finality of an award has led to introducing separate provisions, obligating the parties to waive their right to seek for a recourse within the limits of mandatory law. According to Art. 26.9 of the LCIA Rules:

> [a]ll awards shall be final and binding on the parties. By agreeing to arbitration under these Rules, the parties undertake to carry out any award immediately and without any delay (subject only to Article 27); and the parties also waive irrevocably their right to any form of appeal, review or recourse to any state court or other judicial authority, insofar as such waiver may be validly made.

---

33 CPR Arbitration Appeal Procedure, available at <http://www.cpradr.org/arb_appeal_procedure.asp?M=9.2.3.3>.

34 William H. Knull III and Noah D. Rubins, 'Betting the Farm on International Arbitration: Is It Time to Offer an Appeal Option?' 11 Am Rev Int'l Arb (2000) 536.

The advanced character of the procedural rules of arbitral institutions results in the adoption of, often complex, mechanisms and instruments, facilitating resolution of large and compound cases, as well as control over the administrative and substantive aspects of the process of adjudication. As a consequence, the level of predictability of the procedure and final results is relatively high and can be considered by the parties as a significant argument in favour of administered arbitration. Moreover, selection of a specific arbitral institution by the parties can be interpreted as a decision to subscribe to a certain organizational culture, or what Marek Zirk-Sadowski characterizes as 'good judicial governance', gaining particular importance in the conditions of plurality and heterogeneity of normative orders.[35]

The Role of Procedural Soft Law

The discussion of administered and ad hoc arbitration, concentrating on procedural issues, should be placed in the context of a growing body of additional, non-binding, procedural instruments, described as the 'soft law' of arbitration.

According to William W. Park, arbitral 'hard law' encompasses the national regulations and international treaties and conventions ratified by the State where arbitration takes place, as well as the rules of arbitral institutions. The current development of international commercial arbitration has also led to the emergence of procedural 'soft law', which Park describes as

> guidelines of professional groups and non-governmental organizations, related to evidence, conflicts of interest, ethics and the organization of arbitral proceedings. Frequently these procedural standards build on the lore of international dispute resolution as memorialized in articles, treatises and learned symposium papers.[36]

The proposed characterization of institutional rules of procedure as 'hard law' seems to some extent controversial in the light of classical theories of the sources of law. Nevertheless, after the parties have consented to adopt them for the resolution of their dispute, by virtue of the contract the rules form a binding source of obligations. This attribute of binding force is missing in the area of procedural soft law. Professional as well as institutional guidelines and internal codes are effective mostly by virtue of informal authority. Their significance is, however, growing, as they are generally intended to serve as tools of practical guidance, sets

---

35 Marek Zirk-Sadowski, 'European Judicial Governance and Legal Philosophy' in *Between Complexity of Law and Lack of Order. Philosophy of Law in the Era of Globalization* (Bartosz Wojciechowski et al. eds, Toruń 2009) 336ff.

36 William W. Park, 'The Procedural Soft Law of International Arbitration' in *Pervasive Problems in International Arbitration* (Loukas A. Mistelis and Julian D.M. Lew eds, Kluwer Law International 2006) 141.

of organized and detailed suggestions as to the issues not covered by the rules of procedure of particular arbitral institutions.

The 1996 UNCITRAL Notes on Organizing Arbitral Proceedings (the UNCITRAL Notes) are presumably the most popular instrument of this kind, prepared after wide consultations with experts from various legal systems, as well as diverse arbitration bodies and professional associations. As stated in the Introduction:

> 1. The purpose of the Notes is to assist arbitration practitioners by listing and briefly describing questions on which appropriately timed decisions on organizing arbitral proceedings may be useful. The text, prepared with a particular view to international arbitrations, may be used whether or not the arbitration is administered by an arbitral institution.[37]

The UNCITRAL Notes contain a practical 'checklist' of issues for possible consideration in organizing arbitral proceedings, along with annotations. It is explicitly stated that the character of the Notes is not binding and that the arbitral tribunal resolving a case may use them at its discretion and in accordance with the arbitration rules upon which the parties have agreed.

The 2004 International Bar Association Guidelines on Conflicts of Interest in International Arbitration (the IBA Guidelines) are also worth mentioning in this context as an example of proposing precise categorizations for the fields traditionally reserved to arbitral discretion. They introduce lists of reasons for challenging an arbitrator due to an assumed threat to his or her impartiality. These reasons have been classified, according to their gravity, in the form of red, orange or green lists.

The red list enumerates situations raising justified doubts as to the arbitrators' neutrality. It is divided into two parts: the first one encompasses non-waivable cases (such as an arbitrator being a legal representative of a party); the second covers waivable ones (to be overcome if both parties expressly agreed to do so; for example, an arbitrator being a lawyer in the same firm as the legal counsel to one of the parties). The orange list enumerates situations in which an arbitrator is obligated to disclose information to the parties (such as the fact that an arbitrator has within the last three years served as a counsel for one of the parties) and the parties are deemed to have accepted an arbitrator if, after disclosure, no timely objection was made. Finally, the green list enumerates the cases where no disclosure to the parties is required as, according to IBA, no actual conflict of interest exists (such as the arbitrator's law firm having acted against one of the parties on an unrelated matter without the personal involvement of the arbitrator). The lists are declared to be non-exhaustive.

The practical significance of the growing volume and increasingly detailed procedural soft law of international arbitration is a matter of a dispute. Park

---

37 UNCITRAL Notes on Organizing Arbitral Proceedings (*UNCITRAL Yearbook* vol XXVII 1996, pt 1), paras 11 to 54.

characterizes this dilemma as a result of a disjunction between official rhetoric (emphasizing flexibility and arbitral discretion as the very cornerstones of arbitration) and reality (which calls for regulatory enhancement of the occasionally too vague procedural framework).[38] His postulate that an optimal soft law should offer guidance for managing typical and recurring problems without imposing unnecessary rigidity on the process seems thus fully legitimate.

Arbitration – Scale and Trends of Development

Ad Hoc Arbitrations

The evaluation of the exact numbers of performed arbitrations of both kinds can be only roughly estimated due to the deficiency of global statistical data. The private character and confidentiality of arbitration, while often indicated as its important advantages, result in highly limited accessibility of research material in general: Alan Redfern and Martin Hunter[39] compare the study on the practice of international commercial arbitration to peering into the dark. As discussed above, only a small fraction of all rendered awards are published, and many of them only because of their subsequent history of being reviewed before national courts.

This extended privacy of arbitration also affects the availability of quantitative data on the numbers of arbitral proceedings conducted annually. Whereas the activity of arbitral institutions worldwide can be traced, albeit with only approximate accuracy, the actual number of ad hoc arbitrations is by and large uncertain. As Richard W. Naimark notes, the calculations of the global numbers of ad hoc arbitrations extend between 'just a few' and 'far more … than all the arbitral institutions put together'.[40] The actual practical significance of this form of arbitration remains thus particularly difficult to judge.

Institutional Arbitrations

The scale of growth of the number of institutional arbitrations worldwide is by far easier to identify. Available data provides evidence of an unprecedented expansion of this form of dispute resolution in the recent years. Only in the decade 1993 to 2003

> the number of international arbitration proceedings administered by leading institutions almost doubled. During that same period, the international

38 Park (n 36) 147.

39 Alan Redfern and Martin Hunter, *Law and Practice of International Commercial Arbitration* (2nd edn, Sweet & Maxwell 1991) xv.

40 Richard W. Naimark, 'Building a Fact-Based Global Database: The Countdown' 20 J Int'l Arb (2003) 105, 106.

> arbitration caseload of the American Arbitration Association (AAA) more than tripled, prompting the AAA to announce in 2002 that it had 'become the largest international commercial arbitral institution in the world'.[41]

Statistics published by the Hong Kong International Arbitration Centre present the case load of twelve globally renowned arbitral institutions, as shown in Table 4.1.

According to these statistics, the number of arbitrations administered just by the 12 examined institutions reached the level of approximately 2,500 cases resolved annually. The data also captures the widely discussed phenomenon of a rapid rise of CIETAC's activity in recent years (with the reservation that about one third of its reported annual caseload is characterized as foreign-related;[42] recent dispute about the status of the Shanghai and Shenzhen subcommissions might also affect the number of cases resolved under the auspices of CIETAC). HKIAC remains another outstanding regional and global centre; the issue of a possible impact of CIETAC's expansion (observable, amongst other things, in the evolution of its rules of procedure and in the opening of a branch in Hong Kong in September 2012) on the position of HKIAC will be certainly observed in the upcoming years with much attention.

Another East Asian arbitration hub of quickly growing significance is Singapore, traditionally perceived as one of the main regional competitors of CIETAC,[43] which has already assumed a globally renown position (reporting in 2012 a record caseload of 235 new filings, which the centre itself characterized as marking its '*coming of age*').[44] Singaporean flexibility and ability for quick reaction through adopting changes to both domestic legislation on arbitration (as seen in the International Arbitration Act amendments passed on 9 April 2012) and SIAC procedural rules (including the 2013 revision) further facilitate its strategic positioning for the resolution of commercial disputes.

It is also worth noting that the 2005 report on trends in third-party dispute resolution prepared for Fulbright and Jaworski shows a decided preference for institutional arbitration over non-administered ones in two major common law jurisdictions. The survey was conducted among 354 corporate general counsel in the US and the UK, nearly two-thirds of whom expressed a clear predilection towards the administered form of arbitration. Two main reasons for this preference, indicated by the respondents, were the overall satisfaction with the process and the

---

41 Christopher R. Drahozal, 'New Experiences of International Arbitration in the United States' 54 Am J Comp L (2006) 233.

42 Lukas Steinberg and Chen Yun, *New CIETAC Rules to Internationalize China Arbitration, July 2012* (R&P China Lawyers 2012) 1.

43 Jingzhou Tao, *Arbitration Law and Practice in China* (2nd edn, Kluwer Law International/Aspen 2008) 24 fn 62.

44 'SIAC Comes of Age with the Record Case Filings' (19 February 2013), available at <http://www.siac.org.sg/index.php?option=com_contentandview=articleandid=420:siac-comes-of-age-with-the-record-case-fillingsandcatid=1:latest-newsandItemid=50>.

Table 4.1 International Arbitration Cases Received – Compilation by HKIAC

	1998	1999	2000	2001	2002	2003	2004	2005	2006	2007	2008	2009	2010
AAA	387	453	510	649	672	646	614	580	N/A	621	703*	836*	888
CIETAC	645	609	543	731*	684*	709*	850*	979*	981*	1,118*	1230	1482	1352
HKIAC	240	257	298	307	320	287**	280	281	394	448	602	746	624
ICC	466	529	541	566*	593*	580*	561*	521*	593*	599*	663*	817	793
JCAA	14	12	10	17	9	14	21	11	11	15	12	N/A	26
KCAB	59	40	40	65	47	38	46	53	47	59	47*	78*	52
KLRCA	7	10	11	1	2	4	19	30	37	40	47	N/A	N/A
LCIA	70*	56*	81*	71*	88*	104*	87*	118*	133*	137*	213*	232*	237*
SIAC	67	67	83	99	114	100	48*	45*	65*	70	71*	114	140*
SCC	92	104	73	74	55	82	50	56	141	84	176	215	197
BCICAC	49*	60*	88*	88*	71*	76*	84*	77*	76*	82*	N/A	N/A	N/A
AFEC	100	100	100	100	33	45	50	55	N/A	40	51	N/A	N/A

Source: after <http://www.hkiac.org>, last accessed April 2012.

* The statistics include domestic as well as international arbitrations.

** As a result of Severe Acute Respiratory Syndrome, the caseload for 2003 was down compared to 2002.

N/A – not available.

rules and higher level of familiarity with 'that type' of arbitration. The research was characterized as probably the only study of this kind, including the data from these two countries. It also pointed to the American Arbitration Association's International Arbitration Rules as the most preferred international arbitration rules among examined companies with gross revenues under $100 million and companies with gross revenues of $1 billion.[45]

What seems to be worth noting, though, is the geographically focused character of these findings, combined with the fact that in the years following the survey, ICA has been exposed to significant new developments. It would be most interesting to further access broader data of this kind, including counsel beyond targeted common law jurisdictions and expanding the scope of review, so as to cover large, non-Western, arbitral centres as well.

45 'Corporate Counsel Prefer AAA Rules, Fulbright Survey Finds' 60 Disp Res J (2005–06).

Chapter 5
Processualization of Arbitration

Arbitration Colonized?

As discussed in the preceding chapter, arbitration has an established tradition of being presented as an expertise-based, efficient and informal method of dispute resolution. The representation of arbitration as a particularly flexible technique has, however, recently been repeatedly called into question. As some authors observe, the phenomenon described as colonization of arbitration by litigation,[1] or its judicialization,[2] is a symptom of its increasingly mass and standardized character.

The vast expansion of global trade in the last decades and the resulting growth in the number of international commercial controversies have augmented the development and competition in the sphere of arbitral services. According to much-discussed estimations, as indicated *supra*, over 90 per cent of international commercial contracts concluded worldwide contain arbitration clauses.[3] As already mentioned, the status of arbitration as the regular and dominant method of resolution of international commercial disputes has been currently widely acknowledged.

In the opinion of Dezalay and Garth, the growing formalization and institutionalization of arbitration should be perceived as an adaptation strategy, enhancing legitimization of this form of dispute resolution in the circumstances where it is applied on a mass scale:

> [t]he legitimacy of international commercial arbitration is no longer built on the fact that arbitration is informal and close to the needs of business; rather legitimacy now comes more from a recognition that arbitration is formal and close to the kind of resolution that would be produced through litigation.[4]

---

1 Fali S. Nariman, 'The Spirit of Arbitration: The Tenth Annual Goff Lecture' 16 Arb Int'l (2000) 261.

2 See Charles Nelson Brower, 'Introduction' in *International Arbitration in the Twenty-First Century: Towards 'Judicialization' and Uniformity?: Twelfth Sokol Colloquium* (Richard B. Lillich and Charles Nelson Brower eds, Transnational International 1994) ix.

3 See A.J. van den Berg et al., *Arbitragerecht* (W.E.J. Tjeenk Willink 1988) 134; Ana M. López Rodríguez, *Lex Mercatoria and Harmonization of Contract Law in the EU* (Djof 2003) 67.

4 Yves Dezalay and Bryant G. Garth, *Dealing in Virtue: International Commercial Arbitration and the Construction of a Transnational Legal Order* (University of Chicago Press 1996) 299, quoted by Christopher R. Drahozal, 'Commercial Norms, Commercial Codes, and International Commercial Arbitration' 33 Vand J Transnat'l L (2000) 96.

The commentators further identify the procedure, which ICA is supposed to be following, as US-style, adversarial litigation. This thesis seems to be at present somewhat controversial. Its applicability is limited – as discussed in detail in this volume, the evolution of arbitral practice regarding intercultural disputes reflects a conciliatory turn and the efforts towards finding a common procedural ground have become a common *modus operandi*. For similar reasons the sometimes-offered argument of 'Americanization' of the arbitral process seems – as discussed in detail later – not to be completely accurate.

The question of legitimacy achieved through formalization, however, remains relevant. International commercial arbitration, the method of dispute resolution of an intrinsically private character, indeed lacks external authority to support the awards, as opposed to judicial decisions, rendered in the name of and endorsed by the State. Standardization of arbitral procedure can be thus interpreted as a means of helping to overcome this difficulty and enhancing predictability and stability of decision-making, performed at a mass scale.

However, in the opinion of some commentators this evolution of arbitration towards extended formality of procedure should not be assessed as advantageous, as it stands in contradiction with rudimentary principles and the very nature of this method of dispute resolution. This sceptical view has been enhanced by the use of such expressions as 'arbitigation'[5] or 'colonization of arbitration by litigation'.[6] Still, the recognition of the existence of this phenomenon does not necessarily require taking a stance in a dispute as to its negative or positive character and as to whether the parties to international commercial relations have lost or rather benefited from it. As Christopher Drahozal observes, the parties discontented with the formality of international commercial arbitration can always opt for a less rigid form of dispute resolution,[7] choosing from a plethora of available ADR techniques.

Moreover, the effect of the accompanying decrease of time-efficiency in proceduralized arbitration can be seen not only as a consequence of the demands of handling large, complex disputes. It can be interpreted as a cultural emanation of the already-established independent standing of ICA, consistent with the functioning of time as a symbolic currency in knowledge work, including legal professional roles (it is the processes and solutions in which a significant amount of dedicated time and attention is socially valued, and not merely those outcomes that have been achieved fast).[8]

5 Gerold Herrmann, 'Does the World Need Additional Uniform Legislation on Arbitration?' in *Arbitration Insights: Twenty Years of the Annual Lecture of the School of International Arbitration* (Julian D.M. Lew and Loukas A. Mistelis eds, Kluwer Law International 2007) 241.

6 Nariman (n 1) 261.

7 Drahozal (n 4) 96.

8 Dariusz Jemielniak, 'Time as Symbolic Currency in Knowledge Work' 19 Information and Organization (2009).

Dezalay and Garth perceive the tendency towards judicialization and standardization of arbitral proceedings as a consequence of the striving for legitimacy, but also as a direct result of the high competitiveness of modern arbitration practice. Almost three decades ago Jacques Werner remarked that:

> [b]eing today recognized for what it is, namely a service industry, international arbitration has become a field of intense competition: competition between the arbitration sites, between the arbitral institutions, between counsel, between arbitrators, and even between the periodicals on international arbitration.[9]

Dezalay and Garth supplement this list with another area of competition present in arbitration – a rivalry of national approaches, which they denominate, after Charny and Trachtman, as 'regulatory competition'.[10]

The antagonistic concept of a permanent contention between legal traditions in international commercial arbitration advocated by the same authors in *Dealing in Virtue* has, however, been disputed since the mid-1990s when it was introduced. As examined above, the regulatory framework of international commercial arbitration has indeed been historically frequently shaped in the conditions of cultural differences or even collisions. Such confrontations have also been present in the practice of arbitration, in the sphere of decisions left to the discretion of arbitrators. Still, a remarkable evolution of arbitration can be observed, oriented at reconciling and achieving consensus in regard to the expectations of the parties representing different cultural and legal backgrounds. Elena V. Helmer remarks that so far

> international commercial arbitration has not become 'Americanized'; nor has it become 'Civilized.' Arbitration is opting for the middle ground and tends to encompass the best of both legal traditions ... There are, and always will be, disputes in which parties lean towards one or the other legal tradition. It can be attributed to the parties' and their attorneys' backgrounds, the bargaining power of one of the parties, the composition of the arbitral tribunal, or some other factors. Strong American influence, as well as strong Continental influence, on arbitration will continue. Thanks to both of them, as well as other influences, arbitration is moving ahead because positive development normally does not occur without struggle.[11]

---

9 Jacques Werner, 'Competition within the Arbitration Industry' June J Int'l Arb (1985) 5.

10 Yves Dezalay and Bryant Garth, 'Merchants of Law as Moral Entrepreneurs: Constructing International Justice from the Competition for Transnational Business Disputes' 29 L & Soc'y Rev (1995) 30.

11 Elena V. Helmer, 'International Commercial Arbitration: Americanized, "Civilized," or Harmonized?' 19 Ohio St J Disp Res (2003) 66–67.

In Helmer's opinion, domination of American procedural approach, suggested by some commentators, would be in fact disastrous for the practice of arbitration in the long run – as the parties coming from other legal traditions would lose interest in choosing this form of dispute resolution:

> [t]he transnational character of arbitration is one of its principal advantages in comparison to litigation before national courts. If arbitration turns into U.S.-style 'off-shore litigation,' the incentive to arbitrate international disputes will diminish or even go away.[12]

The supposed connection between judicialization and Americanization of ICA, implied by Dezalay and Garth[13] as well as other authors,[14] seems therefore somewhat controversial, arguably partially due to new regional and global trends of development in arbitration, as discussed in Chapter 4. The competition of national approaches in arbitration is undeniable and probably unavoidable. However, the thesis, that US-style procedural standards for litigation might become a worldwide pattern for domestic legislation on arbitration as well as for the rules of arbitral institutions and for the arbitral practice, seems highly disputable.

The regulatory framework of international commercial arbitration is, as Drahozal puts it, an outcome of interjurisdictional competition for arbitration business.[15] In the opinions of several commentators, its processualization has been generated primarily by the will to avoid the resolution of controversies by the domestic courts of the State of the other party. Charles N. Brower perceives this factor as decisive for the choice of ICA, overshadowing in practice its other benefits:

> [i]nternational arbitration is thus in large measure a substitute for national court litigation. It has the additional advantage of enabling the parties also to determine the rules of law applicable to their relations and thus to avoid even further any national straitjacket.[16]

Whereas the intention to avoid 'hometown justice'[17] is a powerful incentive for the parties to opt for arbitration of their controversies instead of litigation, the demands for predictability of awards and expeditiousness of procedure are other

12 Ibid. 67.

13 Dezalay and Garth (n 10) 27.

14 Lawrence W. Newman, 'International Arbitration – Unfinished Business' April NYLJ 1(2001) 3.

15 Drahozal (n 15) 83.

16 Brower (n 2) x.

17 William W. Park, 'Arbitration Avoids "Hometown Justice" Overseas (The NLJ Corporation Counsel Report of Multinational Corporations Dispute Resolutions)' May National Law Journal (1998).

key factors in the selection of method and place for dispute resolution,[18] enhancing the trend towards standardization and formalization of arbitral practice.

There are several spheres in which the tendency towards processualization[19] of international arbitration can be observed. The most evident one is the domain of institutional regulations where the aggregation of increasingly intricate rules and variations of procedure has been undeniably taking place in the recent decades. The status of a (general) international commercial arbitrator has also been indicated as bearing more and more resemblance to the position of a domestic judge. Another important aspect of colonization of arbitration by litigation is the expanding volume of judicial intervention and control over arbitrations.[20] The scope of this control has been recently an object of a dispute, as the problem of validity of contracting for expanded judicial review by business entities has arisen.

Status of an Arbitrator

It is usually the area of the arbitral rules of procedure, where the effort towards providing certainty through introducing increasingly detailed regulations has been interpreted as a threat to original flexibility of arbitral procedure.

It is, however, interesting to note that, in a partially correlated process, the position of an arbitrator seems to be showing an increasing resemblance to the status of a domestic judge, drifting quite far away from the original concept of commercial arbitration as justice measured out by participants' peers. On the other hand, the universalizing approach to legal interpretation (exceeding the restrictions of formalistic adjudication and admitting purposive analysis of substantive, applicable law in comparative context, as well as acknowledging modifying influence of such soft standards as course of dealing and usages of trade),[21] naturally present in general commercial arbitration, is also gradually embraced by the domestic courts (in particular in cases involving application of transnational rules), yet rather not followed in the interpretive practice of specialized arbitration.

Drahozal compares the functions of different decision-makers in resolving international commercial disputes and observes that the tasks and responsibilities of a general arbitrator are in several aspects closer to those of a domestic judge than

---

18 Kazuo Iwasaki, 'Selection of Situs: Criteria and Priorities' 2 Arb Int'l 57 (1986) 57.

19 Pierre Lalive, 'The Internationalisation of International Arbitration: Some Observations' in *The Internationalisation of International Arbitration: The LCIA Centenary Conference* (Martin Hunter et al. eds, Graham Trotman/Martinus Nijhoff 1995) 54.

20 Brower (n 2) ix.

21 Joanna Jemielniak and Przemysław Mikłaszewicz, 'Capturing the Change: Universalising Tendencies in Legal Interpretation' in *Interpretation of Law in the Global World: From Particularism to a Universal Approach* (Joanna Jemielniak and Przemysław Mikłaszewicz eds, Springer 2010) 1ff.

a specialist arbitrator in trade association arbitrations.[22] This seems to be a direct consequence of the historical evolution of arbitration. Its original character as a dispute resolution process organized and performed by the merchants for themselves has been preserved in arbitration services offered by trade associations for specific branches of industry, but not in the rules of procedure of general arbitral institutions.

At its early stages, arbitration was understood as 'justice by peers', administered by persons involved in the same type of commercial activity as the parties to a controversy. Thus, arbitrators already possessed specialized knowledge as to the practical aspects of the case and did not have the need for expertise-seeking consultations in this regard.[23] Rapid expansion of international trade and the accompanying development of arbitration after World War II have largely put an end to these habits. Businesspeople, interested in settlement of their disputes by the means of general arbitration, find them resolved not by other members of the international *societas mercatorum*, but either by practising business lawyers or by legal scholars.[24] This difference can also be observed on the level of formalization of procedure, which remains significantly lower in specialized arbitration than in the general, 'judicialized' one.

On the other hand, as Lisa Bernstein demonstrates (examining the practice of the US National Grain and Feed Association), arbitrators in cases resolved under the auspices of trade associations tend to demonstrate a much more formalistic approach than do the domestic judges in commercial cases. In particular, specialized arbitrators give a decided priority to the contractual provisions and written trade rules of the association, and do not allow for a modifying effect of such considerations as course of dealing, course of performance and usages of trade in interpretation of the contract and applicable substantive law.[25]

Drahozal explains this discrepancy, stating that:

> [a]rbitrators in international commercial arbitrations, like public court judges, tend to be generalists in substantive legal knowledge but specialists in legal procedure. International arbitrators are ordinarily lawyers or academics rather than persons engaged in the same business as the parties to the arbitration.

Thus, although general arbitrators might as a rule possess higher expertise in the field of international business law than average domestic judges, they no longer have a substantive knowledge as to the technical aspects of the business transactions in question. The vast expansion of ICA means that, while arbitral services are performed on a mass scale, the range of issues and subject matters submitted for

22 Drahozal (n 4) 83.

23 Jacques Werner, 'The Trade Explosion and Some Likely Effects on International Arbitration' June J Int'l Arb (1997) 10.

24 Ibid. 11.

25 Lisa Bernstein, 'Merchant Law in a Merchant Court: Rethinking the Code's Search for Immanent Business Norms' May U Pa L Rev (1996) 1769–70.

a decision is particularly broad (unlike in arbitration offered by trade associations, which have kept their specialized character). The resulting professional orientation of international commercial arbitrators towards general legal proficiency, and not specialized experience in a relevant branch of trade, is analogous to the functional profile of a judge sitting in a domestic court, and has been identified as a noticeable parallel development in modern arbitration and litigation.[26]

Limits of Judicial Control – Expanded Review Problem

Some authors associate the notion of judicialization of arbitration with the recent, observable tendency for contractual stipulation by the parties for expanded judicial review. The parties voluntarily admit the potential control by the courts over the award to be broader than is specified by the mandatory provisions of the law.[27] In such cases the parties are by choice giving a precedence to legal accuracy and strictness over the finality of an award and time-efficiency of the procedure. Such strategy can be explained as resulting from the concerns of the parties that their dispute might be settled on a basis of too general and uncertain standards, such as *lex mercatoria* or equity. A contractual introduction of expanded, substantive judicial review might be treated as a remedy for what the parties perceive as an excessive arbitrariness of a decision.[28]

This trend emerged in the US, raising questions as to the limits to parties' freedom to contract, the constitutionality of the right to expanded judicial reviews of arbitral awards besides the reasons provided by the Federal Arbitration Act (FAA), and the admissibility of such a solution, which in practice undermines the concept of arbitration as a method of offering final decisions to the disputes.[29] The grounds for a judicial *vacatur* (annulment) of an award are listed in section 10 of the FAA, and they have been supplemented over the years by case law with such common law grounds as manifest disregard of the law and violations of public policy.[30] Consequently, the advocates of the right to agreements for extended judicial control argue that the list provided in section 10 is not exhaustive, so there are also no impediments to the acknowledgement of the right to expanded judicial review, including *de novo* review.[31]

---

26 Drahozal (n 4) 97.

27 Sarah Rudolph Cole, 'Managerial Litigants? The Overlooked Problem of Party Autonomy in Dispute Resolution' 51 Hast LJ (2000) 1240–41.

28 Edward J. Brunet and Charles B. Craver, *Alternative Dispute Resolution: The Advocate's Perspective* (Michie 1997) 427.

29 Ilya Enkishev, 'Above the Law: Practical and Philosophical Implications of Contracting for Expanded Judicial Review' 3 J Am Arb (2004) 63.

30 Thomas E. Carbonneau, *Cases and Materials on the Law and Practice of Arbitration* (rev 2nd edn, Juris Publishing 2003) 82.

31 See Enkishev (n 29) 68.

The body of rulings on this issue is equivocal, as the opinions of federal appellate courts differ as to the acknowledgment or denial of existence of such a right. The beginnings of this debate are associated with the US Supreme Court's decision in *Volt Information Sciences Inc v Board of Trustees of Leland Stanford Junior University*. The Court recognized that the enforcement of agreements to arbitrate under the rules different from those provided by the FAA is not contradictory to this act, as 'such a result would be quite inimical to the FAA's primary purpose of ensuring that private agreements to arbitrate are enforced according to their terms'.[32] Priority was thus given, perhaps somewhat unexpectedly, to the party autonomy principle over the provisions of statutory law, apparently treated in this context as *ius dispositivum*. Whereas party autonomy has always been by definition treated as a foundation of the arbitral process, the question that still remains open is whether the introduction of expanded judicial review will not erode this process by undermining its autonomy. It is also worth noting that the practice of contractual stipulation for expanded review remains in contradiction with an opposite trend towards parties' waiving their right of seeking recourse to the domestic court (standard, for example, under the LCIA regulations), described in the third section of Chapter 3.

Processualization of Arbitration and Competition in the Market of Arbitral Services

The aspect of competition in international commercial arbitration, affecting formalization of its procedural regulations, is also worth consideration. As Richard Reuben observes, the practice of arbitration is to a large extent regulated by market forces.[33] As discussed above, the selection of this method of dispute resolution, its particular (ad hoc or institutional) version, and, in case of administered arbitration, of arbitral institution, is by definition dependant upon the will of the parties. Further aspects of ICA, determined by parties' decisions include procedural rules, composition of the tribunal and empowerment of arbitrators to act as *amiable compositeurs* or decide the case *ex aequo at bono*.

As a consequence, as Jacques Werner observes:

> [b]eing today recognized for what it is, namely a service industry, international arbitration has become a field of intense competition: competition between the arbitration sites, between the arbitral institutions, between counsel, between arbitrators, and even between the periodicals on international arbitration.

---

32 *Volt Information Sciences Inc v Board of Trustees of Leland Stanford Junior University*, 468 (Supreme Court of the United States).

33 Richard C. Reuben, 'Process Purity and Innovation: A Response to Professors Stempel, Cole, and Drahozal' 8 Nev LJ (2007) 294.

Dezalay and Garth add to this list an aspect of contest between divergent national approaches, characterized, after Charny and Trachtman, as 'regulatory competition'.[34] This concept seems quite far-reaching. On the level of domestic arbitration laws there are indeed still differences, regarding such issues as the scope of judicial review (which, as discussed above, in some countries may include addressing legal errors or scrutinizing the award's consistency with public policy[35]). The liberal character of national procedural frameworks has also been traditionally indicated as supportive for the development of arbitral centres. This picture, however, seems to have somewhat changed in recent decades, along with an increased level of general consistency, achieved across different domestic jurisdictions, due to now virtually universally ratified New York Convention, reproduction of the UNCITRAL Model Law standards, and the emergence of new, regionally and globally significant centres. Undoubtedly, certain jurisdictions (like Singapore) seem to be reacting particularly quickly in their legislative initiatives to new developments in arbitration, but an arbitration-friendly domestic setting seems to have become by far a standard rather than an exception. As further discussed in Chapter 6, the regulatory competition, mentioned by Dezalay and Garth, seems not to take the form of a suggested clash of procedural approaches on the level of particular rules of procedure, as these are accommodated in the activity of arbitral institutions. It is rather observable in the (sometimes very energetic) support extended by the States by the means of legislation, so as to enhance attractiveness of their arbitral venues (visible, for example, in the Singaporean policy, including recent amendments to the International Arbitration Act passed on 9 April 2012 – which might be interpreted as a reaction to the developments at CIETAC, but which has also been analysed in the context of the Hong Kong's 2011 Arbitration Ordinance and the underlying rivalry between SIAC and HKIAC[36]).

This convergence effect is also observable on the level of the rules of procedure of arbitral institutions. Proliferation of provisions addressing similar issues (such as *voie directe*, multiparty proceedings or joinder) takes place through rules revisions across different centres. The detailed, adopted solutions still differ, which affects the competition between the rules, as observed by Drahozal.[37] Not only are preferences of the parties and their counsel necessarily directing them towards particular courses of proceedings, but the procedural choices of the parties also

---

34 Dezalay and Garth (n 10) 30.

35 William Park, 'Why Courts Review Arbitral Awards' in *Recht der internationalen Wirtschaft und Streiterledigung im 21. Jahrhundert – Festschrift für Karl-Heinz Böckstiegel* (R. Briner, L.Y. Fortier, K.P. Berger and J. Bredow eds, Carl Heymanns 2001) 595.

36 Darius Chan and Wilmer Hale, 'Singapore's International Arbitration Act 2012 vs Hong Kong's Arbitration Ordinance 2011' Kluwer Arbitration Blog, 5 April 2012, available at <http://kluwerarbitrationblog.com/blog/2012/04/05/singapore%E2%80%99s-international-arbitration-act-2012-vs-hong-kong%E2%80%99s-arbitration-ordinance-2011/>.

37 Drahozal (n 4) 101.

affect the determination of substantive law to be applied to the merits of the dispute. Such considerations as costs and the scope of administrative assistance are also strongly present in the process of forum and rules selection. The characterization of international lawyers as 'transaction cost engineers'[38] is thus compelling, even if it affects only some of the counsel involved in arbitration cases. A side effect of ubiquity of international commercial arbitration is that general practitioners are more and more commonly faced with the challenge of providing legal services for arbitral cases. This seems to have significant consequences for multicultural cases: whereas truly international lawyers can very expertly manage diverging procedural requirements, and are not necessarily attached to their own legal tradition if their client would rather benefit from reaching to another, those counsel for whom arbitral cases are not their main specialty might be more inclined to transferring their habits and expectations acquired in domestic litigation onto the arbitral forum.

38 Ronald Gilson, 'Value Creation by Business Lawyers: Legal Skills and Asset Pricing' 94 Yale LJ (1984) 239, 243.

Chapter 6
Arbitration in a Multicultural Environment: Structural and Procedural Aspects

General Issues

Resolution of international commercial disputes raises particular challenges due to the fact that the conflicted parties frequently come not only from different legal systems, but also from diverse legal traditions. Their legal relationship may prove difficult to be evaluated without a bias towards one of the possible, competing interpretive approaches (bringing an additional layer of consideration to the issue of determining proper substantive law). Moreover, as already discussed, the arbitral tribunal is also usually granted wide discretionary authority in determining relevant standards of procedure. Choice of such standards, typical to one legal tradition rather than to the other, is not just a purely technical matter. Arbitral decision-making in a multicultural environment turns out to be a particularly sensitive issue when considered from the perspective of achieving neutrality and impartiality of both an arbitrator and the proceedings.

In describing the ideal of a fair and neutral arbitration forum, the concept of 'ideal speech conditions' developed by Jürgen Habermas[1] is frequently invoked as a theoretical basis for the moves towards involvement of practices of democratic discourse into dispute resolution. As Carrie Menkel-Meadow observes, the theory of extrajudicial dispute resolution has fruitfully employed the thought of Habermas and his successors, who developed the ideas of deliberative democracy[2] and democratic discourse,[3] as well as suggested a call for a greater participation of individuals and for mitigating the impact of policy issues on the resolution of private controversies.

Recognition of the practical importance of an unbiased and responsive attitude of an arbitrator towards the parties representing different legal backgrounds has led William K. Slate II, President and CEO of the American Arbitration Association, to the formulation of a *credo* for multicultural arbitration:

---

1 Jürgen Habermas, *The Theory of Communicative Action* (Thomas McCarthy tr, Beacon Press 1984) 305–07.

2 James Bohman, *Public Deliberation: Pluralism, Complexity, and Democracy* (MIT Press 1996).

3 Mark Kingwell, *A Civil Tongue: Justice, Dialogue, and the Politics of Pluralism* (Pennsylvania State University Press 1995).

> A 'legal culture' is the product of the fundamental values of society as reflected in its history, language and views about social justice. We in the international arbitration community should undertake the responsibility for understanding these values and how they could affect the quality of the process from the viewpoint of the parties. We need to recognize cultural prejudices and be sensitive to cultural traditions lest we unintentionally offend our real and would-be friends. At the same time, we need to pay attention to culturally induced personal behaviors of our own that could be perceived in an unflattering light.[4]

One of the currently widely discussed problems is the suggested transnational universality of arbitral mechanisms. It is visible not only in the field of procedural regulations, but also in the sphere of substantive norms, affecting arbitral decision-making. It can be seen, for example, in the practice of arbitral application of the new *lex mercatoria*, classically defined by Berthold Goldman as an 'arrière-plan' – an underlying set of principles of every award in international commercial arbitration.[5] This view, assuming a uniform character of transnational commercial customs, has also met with opposition as reducing the New Law Merchant to the rules and ideas characteristic to the Western legal traditions.[6] An introduction of the concepts of 'macro' and 'micro' *lex mercatoria* has been forwarded so as to address these controversies. Analogically, as Abul F.M. Maniruzzaman observes, traditional international law can also be described as fundamentally Europocentric.[7] He invokes a classic John Westlake's remark that for the statement of existence of customary law 'it is enough to show that the general consensus of opinion within the limits of European civilization is in favour of the rule'.[8] This concept of the Westernized Law Merchant has been subsequently challenged by the efforts of international community to achieve universal (although not necessarily uniform) rules, acceptable as a 'common core' of different legal systems or the sets of minimal standards, satisfactory for parties coming from various legal traditions.

The vast popularity of international commercial arbitration in recent decades has been accompanied by a phenomenon described by Slate as 'the growing impact of international norms on arbitration practices'.[9] The norms include not only 'hard' international law instruments (such as the Vienna Convention) but also usages and customs of the international trade, recognized as the new *lex mercatoria*. Moreover, even in the lack of explicit choice by the parties of a particular *lex*

4 William K. Slate II, 'Culture Connection in International Commercial Arbitration. A Speech delivered on 18 May 2004, at the 17th ICCA Conference in Beijing, China' Aug–Oct 2004 Disp Res J (2004).

5 Berthold Goldman, 'Frontiers du droit et "lex mercatoria"' 9 Arch Phil Dr (1964) 183.

6 Abul F.M. Maniruzzaman, 'The Lex Mercatoria and International Contracts: A Challenge For International Commercial Arbitration?' 14 Am U Int'l L Rev (1999) 690ff.

7 Ibid.

8 John Westlake, *International Law* (Cambridge University Press 1904) 16.

9 Slate (n 4).

mercatoria codification (such as the UNIDROIT Principles of International Commercial Contracts), international trade customs and practices are nevertheless regarded as guided by the standard procedural provisions of arbitral institutions, requiring arbitrators to take into account relevant trade usages. Their significance can be thus characterized as at least supplementary and modifying the adopted interpretation of the substantive domestic law governing the case.

The relation between ICA and the new *lex mercatoria* is reciprocal and arbitration has largely contributed to consolidation of the body of the New Law Merchant, not long ago criticized for its nebulous and elusive character.[10] It has played a major role in what Klaus Peter Berger describes as a creeping codification of transnational commercial law.[11] A standard recourse to usages of the international trade in processes of arbitral interpretation, combined with a frequent, extensive use of comparative inquiry, has led some authors[12] so far as to identify *lex mercatoria* itself as a characteristically arbitral method of adjudication.[13]

According to this theory, while the autonomous character of the New Law Merchant would have still been accepted, it would not be treated as a substantive legal system, but as a procedural creation. These differences in conceptualizing the new *lex mercatoria* as either a set of substantive transnational rules or rather as a specific method of arbitral adjudication notwithstanding, the link between the New Law Merchant and arbitration remains substantial, as further discussed in Chapter 8.

Civil Law and Common Law Procedural Approaches – Addressing the Differences

The problem of procedural differences between continental and common law systems, potentially leading to serious misconstructions as to the conduct of arbitral proceedings, has been frequently considered.[14] While legal systems based

10 Cf. Georges Delaume, 'The Proper Law of State Contracts and the Lex Mercatoria: A Reappraisal' 3 ICSID Review – Foreign Investment Law Journal (1988) 79; A.F.M. Maniruzzaman, 'Choice of Law in International Contracts – Some Fundamental Conflict of Laws Issues' 16 J Int'l Arb (1999) 151.

11 Klaus Peter Berger and Center for Transnational Law, *The Creeping Codification of the New Lex Mercatoria* (2nd edn, Kluwer Law International/Aspen 2010) 3.

12 Emmanuel Gaillard, 'Thirty Years of Lex Mercatoria: Towards the Selective Application of Transnational Rules' 10 ICSID Review (1995) 12; Emmanuel Gaillard, 'Transnational Law: A Legal System or a Method of Decision Making?' 17 Arb Int'l (2001); Ana M. López Rodríguez, *Lex Mercatoria and Harmonization of Contract Law in the EU* (Djof 2003) 109ff.

13 Gaillard (n 12 1995) 224.

14 See, for example, Christian Borris, 'The Reconciliation of Conflicts Between Common Law and Civil Law Principles in the Arbitration Process' in *Conflicting Legal Cultures in Commercial Arbitration: Old Issues and New Trends* (Stefan N. Frommel and

on the common law tradition prevail in majority of the English-speaking countries, the civil law systems prevalent in continental Europe have been adopted in all of Latin America, as well as most of Asia and Africa.[15]

The existence of significant differences between those legal traditions as to the commencement of proceedings and their conduct in resolution of private disputes can hardly be seen as controversial. The practical importance of these dissimilarities in arbitration is, however, a matter of discussion. It is frequently emphasized that, in a highly professionalized field of international commercial arbitration, it is an ordinary and legitimized requirement to expect from legal counsel to the parties a relevant openness to different procedural solutions, even when they differ from the counsel's domestic standards. In administered arbitration the rules of arbitral institutions are also known in advance to the parties and to their advocates.

The evolution of the rules of procedure of major arbitral institutions mirrors, as Elena V. Helmer observes, harmonization processes taking place in ICA.[16] This phenomenon is also described as homogenization of the civil law and common law procedural standards, or, as Hans Smit puts it, as a hybrid that is drawn from both systems by the efforts of arbitral tribunals. As a result, a counsel cannot expect the procedure to directly replicate the patterns known from either of these legal traditions.[17] Eric Bergsten perceives this evolution as a change of the traditional European 'Grand Old Men's' model of arbitration, based on document discovery, under the influence of American participants within the last fifty years; he uses a metaphor of immigrants, who adapt to the new country, but whose new country is also changing under their influence.[18]

It would be a far-reaching oversimplification, though, to assume that the nationally gained professional training will always necessarily determine a preference of a party's counsel for the standards of procedure he or she was primarily trained in (presumably, his or her own legal system). As Lew and Shore remark, it is rather a matter of a pragmatic calculation in regard to a particular dispute:

> [t]he approach of most experienced advocates and arbitrators is rather more case-driven than ideological. Depending on the strength of a case or of a particular witness or of a single document, common law lawyers may well be comfortable

Barry Alexander K. Rider eds, Kluwer Law International 1999); Julian D.M. Lew and Laurence Shore, 'International Commercial Arbitration: Harmonizing Cultural Differences' 54 Disp Res J (1999).

15 Siegfried H. Elsing and John M. Townsend, 'Bridging the Common Law–Civil Law Divide in Arbitration' 670 International Business Litigation and Arbitration (Practising Law Institute 2002) 637.

16 Elena V. Helmer, 'International Commercial Arbitration: Americanized, "Civilized," or Harmonized?' 19 Ohio St J Disp Res 49.

17 Vladimir uro Degan, *Sources of International Law* (Martinus Nijhoff/Kluwer Law International 1997) 88.

18 Eric Bergsten, 'The Americanization of International Arbitration' 18 Pace Int'l L Rev (2006) 300–301.

in seeking limited cross-examination, no discovery, and lengthy witness statements. Depending on the nature of a particular case, civil law lawyers may seek a procedure in which oral submissions are extensive.

As long as pragmatism prevails, and the 'Western canon' of literature is a staple of a lawyer's education, the harmonization of cultural differences in international arbitral practice should proceed with relative ease.[19]

Whereas a wide discretional power as to the detailed organization of the proceedings is usually granted to the arbitral tribunal, it is also an already well-established practice that a compromising *modus operandi* can be proposed to the parties coming from a common law legal system (especially from the US) on one side and from a continental one on the other. Siegfried H. Elsing and John M. Townsend observe that it is an increasingly popular habit of international arbitrators to promote compromising procedural solutions instead of choosing standards characteristic to one or the other party's legal systems.[20]

This practice of procedural convergence is present at virtually all stages of the arbitral process. As Elsing and Townsend demonstrate, it affects even the issues traditionally described as bones of contention between conflicting parties coming from the common law and civil law legal traditions. Under such circumstances, the required formulation of the claim, as seen for example in the ICC arbitral practice, is set up somewhere between American standards of laconism and continental expectations to have the details of the claim fully developed already at this initial stage of the proceedings. One of the possible, practical tests for qualification of the statement of claim as sufficient is that it would provide an arbitrator in an ICC arbitration with the information and attached documentation adequate for a preparation of the 'terms of reference'[21] for the case.

Consequently, if formal demands regarding the claim statement exceed those expressed in American litigation, the standards of admissible document discovery shall also be set up accordingly. Between the opposite poles of American liberal discovery and civil law canons of limited elicitation of documents, a consensus can be achieved, as

[m]ost civil lawyers and arbitrators now accept that it is reasonable to permit a party to obtain some documents from its adversary, as long as the process is not called 'discovery' (a term which, to most civil lawyers, resonates with all of the positive associations of bubonic plague) and does not permit an adversary to 'fish' for documents that it does not have some reason to believe to exist.[22]

---

19 Lew and Shore (n 3) 38.

20 Elsing and Townsend (n 15) 637ff.

21 See <http://www.iccwbo.org/court/arbitration/id4091/index.html>.

22 Elsing and Townsend (n 15) 639–40.

In the 2010 IBA Rules on the Taking of Evidence in International Arbitration (the IBA Rules of Evidence; a revised version of the 1999 IBA Rules on the Taking of Evidence in International Commercial Arbitration), such a compromising stance is sought. A party may submit a 'Request to Produce' specific documents from the other party. In order to be supported by the arbitral tribunal, a Request shall meet formal requirements, according to which:

> Article 3
>
> …
>
> 3. A Request to Produce shall contain:
>
> (a) (i) a description of each requested Document sufficient to identify it, or
>
> (ii) a description in sufficient detail (including subject matter) of a narrow and specific requested category of Documents that are reasonably believed to exist; in the case of Documents maintained in electronic form, the requesting Party may, or the Arbitral Tribunal may order that it shall be required to, identify specific files, search terms, individuals or other means of searching for such Documents in an efficient and economical manner;
>
> (b) a statement as to how the Documents requested are relevant to the case and material to its outcome; and
>
> (c) (i) a statement that the Documents requested are not in the possession, custody or control of the requesting Party or a statement of the reasons why it would be unreasonably burdensome for the requesting Party to produce such Documents, and
>
> (ii) a statement of the reasons why the requesting Party assumes the Documents requested are in the possession, custody or control of another Party.[23]

Another of the most commonly emphasized differences between the Anglo-American and the continental types of civil procedure is the role of a judge. In the common law-based adversarial model, the activity of a judge is mostly limited to a general supervision of the course of proceedings, as well as the fact- and law-finding, while it is the contesting parties and their counsel who are directly involved in the unfolding of the controversy before the court.

In civil law jurisdictions, the inquisitorial (investigative) model of procedure requires the active participation of a judge, who has to determine the details of the case and applicable law, while personally participating in questioning the witnesses and the experts. A party or a counsel who wants a witness to be asked a particular question must present this question to the court, which will ask it. Live direct examination of a witness is thus relatively restricted.[24]

As often emphasized, the practice of arbitration, borrowing from this approach, may turn out to be particularly demanding for the counsel trained in the Anglo-

---

23 René David, *L'arbitrage dans le commerce international* (Economica 1982).

24 Urs Martin Laeuchli, 'Civil and Common Law: Contrast and Synthesis in International Arbitration' 62 Disp Res J (2007) 83.

American legal tradition of extensive cross-examination. He or she may not be (at least initially) fully prepared for participation in proceedings based largely on documentary findings, and for oral hearings to be provided only to a limited extent. Analogically, the self-authenticating status of written evidence, characteristic to the civil law procedural regulations, may turn out to be surprising for a person coming from a common law jurisdiction.

There is indeed an established tradition of common law counsel promoting cross-examination in multicultural arbitral proceedings, as documented for example in the practice of the Iran–US Claims Tribunal. Still, in the controversies involving civil law adversaries, the limits of admissibility of witness testimony are rather strict. It is frequently required of a party to submit in advance the testimony of its witnesses in writing to the arbitral tribunal. Whereas model instruments, as well as rules of arbitral institutions and agencies, generally leave the decision on organizing a hearing to the discretion of the tribunal, the traces of civil law or common law influences can be found in what is suggested as the default options for the arbitrators.

In the UNCITRAL Model Law, the standard of respecting the will of the parties regarding a hearing has been adopted. According to Art. 24(1), unless the parties have agreed otherwise, the arbitral tribunal shall decide whether to hold oral hearings or whether the proceedings shall be conducted on the basis of documents and other materials. The tribunal shall also hold hearings upon a request by a party, unless both parties have previously decided that there shall be no hearings. A similar formulation can be found in Art. 15.2 of the UNCITRAL Rules: unless any party has requested oral hearings at any stage of the proceedings, the arbitral tribunal is free to decide whether they will be held.

Analogically, according to Art. 20.6 of the ICC Rules, the arbitral tribunal may decide the case solely on the basis of documents submitted by the parties unless any of the parties requests a hearing. The HKIAC Administered Arbitration Rules provide (Art. 14.2) for holding hearings if the arbitral tribunal so determines or if either party so requests. Art. 27(1) of the Stockholm Rules stipulates that a hearing will be held if requested by a party, or deemed appropriate by the Arbitral Tribunal. Also, pursuant to Art. 20.3 of the Vienna Rules, oral hearings shall take place at the request of one party or if the sole arbitrator or arbitral tribunal considers it necessary. Correspondingly, Art 19.1 of the LCIA Rules stipulates that any party has the right to effectively demand an oral hearing on the merits of the dispute, unless the parties have explicitly agreed in writing on documents-only arbitration.

On the other hand, the CIETAC Arbitration Rules offer in this regard a solution with hearings as a default option:

> Art. 33.2
> The arbitral tribunal shall hold oral hearings when examining the case. However, the arbitral tribunal may examine the case on the basis of documents only if the parties so agree and the arbitral tribunal consents or the arbitral tribunal deems that oral hearings are unnecessary and the parties so agree.

Moreover, the conduct of hearings is an object of further clarification, as pursuant to Art. 33.3, unless otherwise indicated by the parties, the arbitral tribunal may adopt either an inquisitorial or an adversarial approach in hearing the case, with regard to the circumstances of the case. Whereas under the other, discussed sets of rules of procedure this competence was also implicitly granted within the general limits of discretionary powers of the arbitrators, its direct formulation in the CIETAC Rules seems to emphasize the flexible character of the powers of the tribunal – and to subscribe in this regard to the general tendency described in this chapter.

Not surprisingly, the 'pro-hearings' approach has also been expressed in the IBA Rules of Evidence, where a submission of a written witness statement is supposed to be followed by an oral testimony of this witness at an evidentiary hearing, unless the parties explicitly agree otherwise. Also, the consequences of the witness's absence at a hearing are more far-reaching than in the more 'continentally fashioned' regulations:

> Art. 4.8
> If a witness who has submitted a Witness Statement does not appear without a valid reason for testimony at an Evidentiary Hearing, except by agreement of the Parties, the Arbitral Tribunal shall disregard that Witness Statement unless, in exceptional circumstances, the Arbitral Tribunal determines otherwise.

Furthermore, in the AAA International Rules a distinctively common law-based model of procedure has been implemented. Orality of proceedings is stipulated here as a self-evident form of conducting arbitration (see Art. 20). Also, it is left to the discretion of the tribunal whether any written statements will be required from the parties besides the initial statements of claims and counterclaims and statements of defence (although the submission of witnesses' evidence in the form of signed, written statements is also admitted (Art. 20.5).

In the regulations discussed above, influenced by the continental legal tradition, the self-authenticating status of documentary evidence is – on the contrary – generally acknowledged and the submission of a witness's testimony in writing may be considered sufficient. It is also interesting to observe that the Rules of the London Court of International Arbitration leave the evaluation of the pre-submitted written witness statement in a case when the witness failed to attend the oral hearing without good cause to the discretion of the arbitral tribunal (see Art. 20.4 of the LCIA Rules).

It can be noted that pragmatic reasons, such as cost- and time-efficiency, have been frequently raised against the organization of extensive hearings in arbitration. While acting within the limits of their discretionary powers, arbitrators seem also to have worked out a possible compromising stance:

> [a]rbitrators will commonly, especially if prompted by common-law lawyers, allow very abbreviated live direct testimony when the witness appears at the

> hearing, in order to avoid the tribunal's first live impression of a witness being produced by hostile questioning, but such testimony is normally (except for experts) kept to 15 to 30 minutes.[25]

The differences between the Anglo-American and continental procedural approach are visible also in the position of experts in the proceedings. The counsel trained in common law generally assume that the parties will find their own experts to highlight the contestable facts and their testimonies form a part of the overall adversarial dispute. From this perspective the experts are perceived as a 'specialized form of witness'.[26] By contrast, in the civil law tradition it is also (and, in some cases, exclusively) the tribunal who appoints an expert, whose role is to serve as a supposedly neutral authority, and who should not be involved on any side of the controversy.

The efforts towards arching both approaches in arbitration have resulted in a rather liberal admissibility of expert appointment by the tribunal, as well as by the parties. Analogically to the witness statements, expert testimony is also generally allowed to be submitted in writing as well as orally at the hearing. The parties are also granted the right to question experts (including those appointed by the tribunal) at the hearings. This compromising practice is often characterized as an important example of successful convergence or 'blending' processes in arbitration.[27]

It is also interesting to observe that in the IBA Rules of Evidence (Art. 5.4) a separate procedure for converging the opinions of the experts, inspired by English tradition, has been adopted. The aim of this practice is to minimize the costs and time of oral examination. The experts appointed by the parties, who have submitted Expert Reports on the same or related issues, may be ordered by the arbitral tribunal to meet in order to attempt to work out an agreement of opinions on those issues on which they have differed. If such an agreement is reached, they should submit it to the tribunal, while the remaining contended matters shall be resolved at the hearings.

Another important source of possible procedural misunderstandings is the way in which legal argument is developed by the counsel. Formal pleadings, submitted by civil lawyers, are supposed to serve as a basic structure, outlining the points of offered reasoning which are to be elaborated at the hearing. In the civil law-style proceedings, the submitted documents of pleading do not usually cite case law among the sources of law and authoritative opinions. On the other hand, the briefs offered by common law lawyers are not supposed to be exhaustive and they may differ in their content from issues selected by the counsel to be further developed during the oral argument and in reaction to the inquiries by the tribunal.

In arbitration a liberal approach is usually adopted in setting up requirements regarding the style of introducing legal argument by counsel. As Elsing and

25 Elsing and Townsend (n 15) 643.

26 Degan (n 17) 86.

27 Helmer (n 16) 54.

Townsend observe, most arbitrators will accept recapitulations of legal argument in writing, be it pleadings or briefs. They are also usually inclined to approve the delivery of an oral argument in a form which suits the parties best.[28] The admissibility of presentation and the binding force of legal precedent will, however, be evaluated on a ground of substantive law applicable to the merits of the arbitrated controversy.

Further examples of possible differences between national standards are such issues as producing the proof of substantive applicable law (achieved through research by the judge or secured by the parties) or the costs of the procedure (with the European standard of the losing party paying the costs).[29]

As demonstrated above, flexibility of procedure in international commercial arbitration might serve as a tool in the process of bridging the civil law and the common law standards for particular cases. According to Pierre Lalive, there can be observed a 'definite evolution towards the "internationalisation" of general principles of procedure, and it is no longer possible to oppose ... common law and civil law types of arbitration.'[30] Instead of imposing solutions typical to one or the other system, this pragmatic approach of international arbitrators has led to the development 'in action' of procedural mechanisms intermediating between these two legal traditions. It has also promoted a consensual mode in coping with the needs of the parties and a liberal stance in regard to formal requirements (as seen in the example of written statements of legal argument).

Additionally, the suggested common law/civil law opposition in arbitration seems not to precisely reflect the conventional national areas of influence of both traditions. The tension between competing concepts of arbitral procedure were, as already mentioned, occasionally described in the categories of attempts towards the 'Americanization' of arbitration.[31] As regards the actual procedural weight of the hearings, a remarkable scope of discretion is, however, generally left to the arbitrators. Furthermore, new developments in East Asia, including the rise of regional leaders into global significance, reflected in the revision of procedural rules by CIETAC in 2012 and SIAC in 2013 (but also affected by the 2012 Shanghai and Shenzen CIETAC subcommissions' breakaway), bring new and powerful dynamics into the current procedural landscape of institutional arbitration.

---

28 Elsing and Townsend (n 15) 646.

29 Lew and Shore (n 3) 36ff.

30 Pierre Lalive, 'The Internationalisation of International Arbitration: Some Observations' in *The Internationalisation of International Arbitration: The LCIA Centenary Conference* (Martin Hunter et al. eds, Graham Trotman/Martinus Nijhoff 1995) 56.

31 Stephen Bond, the Secretary General of the International Court of Arbitration of ICC, after Nicolas C. Ulmer, 'A Comment on "The Americanization" of International Arbitration?' 16 Mealey's Int'l Arb Rep 24(2001) 24.

Shari'a and the Resolution of Commercial Disputes

As discussed above, a substantial degree of harmonization has been successfully achieved in procedural matters in commercial arbitration as regards the common law and the civil law influences. Although a major share of international trade controversies is indeed resolved within the area of prevalence of those two legal traditions, the rate of transnational commercial cases involving Shari'a law is growing.

Arbitration has a long-established tradition as a favoured method of dispute resolution in the Islamic world, in accordance with the doctrine of Allah being the ultimate arbitrator. In the sphere of commercial relations, amicable means (mediation and arbitration) are the forms of dispute resolution customarily preferred over adversarial litigation.[32] Historically, the Prophet Muhammad was actively involved in promoting arbitration, following an established, pre-Muslim, Arabian practice.[33] Charles N. Brower and Jeremy K. Sharpe remind us that the Treaty (the Charter) of Medina, concluded between Muslims, non-Muslim Arabs and Jews of the city of Medina in 622 CE, provided that this form of resolving controversies should be used for any disputes.[34] Muhammad also acted personally as an arbitrator in the dispute between the tribes of Banu Qurayza and Banu Nadir during his stay in Medina.[35] This custom was followed by the Muslim leaders and one of the best known historical examples in this regard took place in the controversy between the Prophet's son-in-law, Ali ibn Abi Talib, and the governor of Syria Muawiyah, who refused to acknowledge Ali's appointment as a caliph. Repeated attempts at arbitration in this succession conflict ended in vain as Ali did not acknowledge the decision issued in favour of his rival. The controversy evolved into a military clash and eventually served as one of the reasons for the split between Sunni and Shia factions of Islam.[36] Also, the concept of *ijma* (consensus), developed by Islamic jurisprudence, is often associated with arbitration as a form of dispute resolution, traditionally practised in the Muslim world.[37]

The popularity of arbitration as a method of dispute resolution in the Islamic world has also affected the sphere of commercial controversies where at least

32 See Salah Al-Hejailan, 'Mediation as a Means for Amicable Settlement of Disputes in Arab Countries' WIPO Conference on Meditation, available at <http://www.arbiter.wipo.int/events/conferences/1996/hejailan.html> (1996).

33 Mohammed Abu-Nimer, *Nonviolence and Peace Building in Islam: Theory and Practice* (University Press of Florida 2003) 247.

34 Charles N. Brower and Jeremy K. Sharpe, 'International Arbitration and the Islamic World: The Third Phase' 97 Am J Int'l L (2003) 643.

35 'Abd al-Malik Ibn Hisham and Muhammad Ibn Ishaq, *The Life of Muhammad: A Translation of Ishāq's 'Sīrat Rasūl Allāh'* (Alfred Guillaume tr, Oxford University Press 1955) 267–68.

36 Brower and Sharpe (n 34) 643.

37 Abd al-Hamid Ahdab, *Arbitration with the Arab Countries* (2nd edn, Kluwer Law International 1999) 13.

one party represents the Muslim legal tradition. As a result of a flourishing trade exchange in the Persian Gulf region, by 1900 Bahrain enjoyed a status of an international centre for arbitration of commercial disputes, attracting Islamic as well as European merchants.[38] However, Brower and Sharpe compare the modern phase of evolution of international arbitration (after World War II) involving participation of the Islamic world in this form of dispute resolution to a 'roller coaster' experience.[39] Although strongly embedded in the Muslim tradition, arbitration methods applied to international commercial and investment controversies (concerning predominantly petroleum trade) were used with recurrent scepticism in this period.

In the history of arbitration of trade disputes between Islamic and Western parties since 1945, three phases have been distinguished:

> [e]ach phase reflects precisely the power equation in place at the time between Islamic states that are sources of petroleum and the foreign developers and off-takers of those resources. Each is also bound up with closely related developments in, and developing nations' broader attempts to shape, international law relating to compensation for expropriation. Finally, each marks the evolution of the relationship between the domestic law of Islamic states and international law.[40]

The first phase, lasting from the end of World War II until the 1970s, is interpreted as a period of a factual domination of the Western parties in arbitrations, conducted mostly on the basis of long-term (usually concluded for more than fifty years) oil concession contracts. As these agreements materially favoured Western standards (also through the recourse to *lex mercatoria*), they have been compared with the system of 'Capitulations' in the former Ottoman empire, where extraterritorial jurisdictions were granted to the European consuls over the nationals of their States in particular regions of the empire. It is interesting to observe that the same arbitral awards from this period, including references to universal commercial practices, which inspired Western scholars to the formulation of the new *lex mercatoria* doctrine, were interpreted in the categories of a post-colonial subjection policy. The perception of a famous series of New Law Merchant-based decisions in the 'oil cases', dating from the much-publicized *Abu Dhabi* award,[41] has been a matter of deep differences in perception by the Western and Islamic public opinion.

The second phase is identified by Brower and Sharpe with the actions of the Organization of Petroleum Exporting Countries (OPEC) turning the tables on international investors in the region and ending the long period of lowering the prices of crude oil. This period lasted through the 1970s to early 1980, and found

38 Hassan Ali Radhi, 'State Courts and Arbitration in the Gulf Cooperation Council (GCC) Countries' 3 ICC Int'l Ct Arb Bull (1992) 57.

39 Brower and Sharpe (n 34) 643.

40 Ibid.

41 *Petroleum Development (Trucial Coast) Ltd v Sheikh of Abu Dhabi*, 247.

its expression in the policy of using petroleum as an 'economic weapon'.[42] In 1973 the Arab States of OPEC (assembled in the subgroup the Organization of Arab Petroleum Exporting Countries – OAPEC) imposed oil embargoes against the US, the States of Western Europe and the Republic of South Africa, which supported Israel in its conflict with the Arab countries. The consequence of the resulting radical rise in oil prices (which quadrupled by 1974[43]) was an unprecedented growth in the economic and geopolitical significance of the OPEC countries. It has also led to a restructuring of the legal framework, regulating the issues of exploration, exploitation and distribution of petroleum – no longer protecting one-sidedly the interests of the international oil corporations with Western capital.[44] The main reason for this was the fact that

> [m]any developing states felt that they could not abide by this legal system, in whose creation they had not participated and whose values were felt to be inconsistent with their own cultural and legal traditions ... This new era saw such states repudiate contractual obligations, renegotiate or nationalize oil concessions, and reject arbitrations invoked by Western contracting partners.[45]

It is also worth noting that in only a few Islamic States at that time the existing legislative framework enabled an active participation in the quickly expanding international arbitration, as neither international conventions nor domestic acts on arbitration had been adopted so far. Also, the stance taken by the courts reviewing the awards was often exerting a hampering effect on recognition and enforcement of arbitral decisions.[46]

The third phase of presence of Islamic States in the modern system of international commercial arbitration is connected with a process of gradually overcoming these obstacles. Increasing participation in the global network of international commercial arbitration by Islamic States, marked by accessions to the New York Convention regime, can be symbolically associated with two events: the inauguration of the Iran–United States Claims Tribunal in 1981 and with the *Kuwait v AMINOIL* case.[47] In this arbitration, in which Kuwait was fully and actively engaged as a party, a decision favourable to this State was rendered (as

42 Daniel Yergin, *The Prize: The Epic Quest for Oil, Money, and Power* (Simon & Schuster 1991) 597.

43 William D. Smith, 'Price Quadruples for Iranian Crude Oil at Auction' *New York Times* (12 December 1973).

44 W. Michael Reisman, 'International Arbitration and Sovereignty' 18 Arb Int'l 231(2002) 233.

45 Brower and Sharpe (n 34) 645–46.

46 Abdul Hamid El-Ahdab, 'Enforcement of Arbitral Awards in the Arab Countries' 11 Arb Int'l (1995).

47 *Government of Kuwait v American Independent Oil Company (AMINOIL)*, Award of 24 March 1982, 976.

opposed to the line of reasoning formerly adopted in the awards, including three remarkable expropriation cases in which the Libyan government was involved against three companies: *BP*,[48] *TOPCO*[49] and *LIAMCO*[50]).

The majority of the 59 States belonging to the Organization of the Islamic Conference (OIC), as well as most of the 22 countries who are members of the League of Arab States, have thus far ratified the New York Convention, the decisive international instrument for securing recognition and enforcement of foreign arbitral awards.[51] Numerous Islamic States have also adopted 'arbitration-friendly' domestic legislation, frequently based on the UNCITRAL Model Law or inspired by laws enacted in other countries (such as the French Law of Arbitration of 1981, which served as a basis for the Lebanon, Qatar and Algeria arbitration laws[52]).

The reception of this new approach towards arbitration as a method of resolution of international commercial disputes has helped to manage many practical, procedural problems, resulting from various regional limitations present in the Islamic States. Examples of such issues are: limitations to party autonomy in determining substantive and procedural law to govern the dispute;[53] rules restricting the freedom of appointment of arbitrators (including the requirements that all of them shall be Muslim men[54]); or expanded exclusions of particular subject matters from under arbitration (such as controversies regarding foreign trade or where state enterprises were involved[55]).

The change of attitude towards international arbitration can be associated with the fact that in the preparation of UNCITRAL Model Law the experts from the countries of Shari'a legal tradition took an active part, along with the specialists coming from the civil law and common law States. In the opinion of Susan Block-Lieb and Terence C. Halliday, the cooperative approach has been thus adopted mutually by the international community too, no longer concentrating on the values shared by countries representing only the Western legal traditions (or the economically powerful States of the North as opposed to the developing countries).[56] The comparison of reception of the two acts crucial for arbitration and

48 *British Petroleum Co (Libya) Ltd (BP) v Government of the Libyan Arab Republic*, Award of 10 October 1973.

49 *Texaco Overseas Petroleum Company and California Asiatic Oil Company (TOPCO) v The Government of The Libyan Arab Republic*, Award of 19 January 1977.

50 *Libyan American Oil Company (LIAMCO) v Government of The Libyan Arab Republic*, Award of 12 April 1977.

51 Mark Wakim, 'Public Policy Concerns regarding Enforcement of Foreign International Arbitral Awards in the Middle East' 21 NY Int'l L Rev (2008) 2.

52 Brower and Sharpe (n 34) 650.

53 Samir Saleh, *Commercial Arbitration in the Arab Middle East: A Study in Shari'a and Statute Law* (Graham & Trotman/ICC 1984) 282 and 310.

54 Ibid. 297.

55 Ahdab (n 37) 561ff.

56 Susan Block-Lieb and Terence C. Halliday, 'Incrementalisms in Global Lawmaking' 32 Brook J Int'l L (2007) 899.

created under the auspices of the United Nations – the 1958 New York Convention and the 1985 UNCITRAL Model Law – may serve as an illustration of this process (with regard to the basic difference in scope of the two instruments, as the Convention concerns any foreign arbitration, whereas the UNCITRAL Model Law applies to international commercial arbitration only and does not differentiate between domestic and foreign awards).

The apparent reluctance of less developed and developing nations in Asia, Latin America and Africa to adopt the New York Convention was a matter of discussion at the international forum. As the Special Rapporteur to UNCITRAL, Ion Nestor indicated in his report in 1972 that the reason for this policy of abstention was 'the mutual distrust between both private and governmental undertakings belonging to countries with differing forms of economic organization or differing levels of development.'[57] The Model Law, on the other hand, was welcomed by the developing nations with much less scepticism – mostly due to the flexibility of this instrument. Implementation of this soft law instrument has been possible with local adjustments, meeting cultural, social and legal requirements, whereas the rigid structure of New York Convention left virtually no space for regional variations.[58]

The political and economic emancipation and advancement of numerous Islamic countries in the second phase of their involvement in international arbitration have materially helped in their undertaking of an active and cooperative stance. Furthermore, the introduction of national laws based on the UNCITRAL Model Law has arguably triggered a new wave of accessions to the New York Convention, vitally enhancing the global network of countries participating in the system of ICA (the total number of the parties to the Convention has exceeded 140 in the recent years).[59]

In the contemporary, third phase, the promotion of arbitration as a means of commercial dispute resolution in the Middle East has also been locally initiated, through such ventures as the meetings of the Saudi Chamber of Commerce and Industry and the Gulf Chambers of Commerce, held in order to endorse the development of arbitration in the region.[60] Another indicator of growing popularity of this mechanism of resolving trade controversies has been a formation and expansion of new arbitral centres in the region.

Some agencies of this kind have been created as a result of transnational cooperation, such as the Cairo Regional Centre for International Commercial

57 Ion Nestor, *Problems concerning the Application and Interpretation of Existing Multilateral Conventions on International Commercial Arbitration and Related Matters: Report by Ion Nestor (Romania), Special Rapporteur* (A/CN.9/64) (UNCITRAL 1972) 233.

58 Kenneth T. Ungar, 'The Enforcement of Arbitral Awards under UNCITRAL's Model Law on International Commercial Arbitration' 25 Colum J Transnat'l L (1987) 734ff.

59 Block-Lieb and Halliday (n 56) 877.

60 'Efforts to Increase Use of Arbitration in Middle East' August World Arbitration and Mediation Report (1998) 212.

Arbitration established by the African-Asian Legal Consultative Committee; the Arab Centre for Commercial Arbitration in Rabat, founded by virtue of the 1987 Amman Arab Convention on Commercial Arbitration (although the fact that all proceedings administered by this institution have to be conducted in Arabic restrains its extraregional influence); or the Arab Association for International Arbitration, created in 1991, and its Arbitration Center in Beirut.[61]

Almas Khan suggests that the growth of economic exchange between the Islamic and non-Islamic countries, combined with the existence of remarkable differences between Western and Islamic legal canons, has led to a domination of Shari'a as a preferred substantive legal system to govern the disputes resolved by the means of arbitration:

> international arbitration provisions in business contracts with at least one Muslim party have often stipulated that Islamic law governs all disputes arising from the contract. As international trade has flourished, and as Islamic banks have grown at an annual rate of 5 to 15 percent per year (with a total of $200 billion invested in shariah-compliant financial institutions as of 2002), the number of international arbitrations involving Islamic law has burgeoned dramatically ... International Islamic arbitration centers have fostered this progression by certifying arbitrators, encouraging parties to use arbitration, providing information about the process, and helping to formulate uniform laws.[62]

Arbitral procedure involving a Muslim party would thus not only require reaching decisions on intercultural procedural issues, but it will also likely lead to application of substantive Islamic law. The most notable differences concerning business activity and trade regulations between the Shari'a requirements and the Western legal traditions concern the issues of interest, profit and available remedies. As Saeed observes, in the traditional Islamic jurisprudence the gathering of interest and usury (*riba*), as well as gaining excessive profits, are prohibited.[63] Moreover, contractual clauses based upon a speculation or a condition (a future, uncertain event, on the existence or non-existence of which the accomplishment, the modification or the rescission of an obligation depends) are considered void – hence an arbitrator resolving a dispute on a basis of Islamic law will not award anticipated profits in a case regarding breach of contract.[64] The possibilities of awarding specific performance are relatively broad in the Shari'a tradition, and remarkably closer to the concept adopted by civil law than to specific performance as an equitable remedy of common law jurisdictions. It is also worth mentioning

61 Brower and Sharpe (n 34) 654.

62 Almas Khan, 'The Interaction between Shariah and International Law in Arbitration' 6 Chicago J Int'l L (2006) 798–99.

63 Abdullah Saeed, *Islamic Banking and Interest: A Study of the Prohibition of Riba and its Contemporary Interpretation* (Brill 1996) 41ff.

64 Khan (n 62) 799.

that in several Muslim countries, such as Iran and Morocco, the existing statutory private law regulations have been directly inspired by the French civil law model.[65]

The wide recourse of substantive commercial rules of Shari'a to a dispute involving an Islamic party might be perceived as a significant constraint to the parties' freedom. Nevertheless, procedural standards present in the Islamic tradition of arbitration, compared with Western regulations, allow for a flexible and adjustable organization of the proceedings.

First, the limits of authority of arbitrators are less strictly defined and their discretionary powers in the Islamic legal culture are particularly far-reaching. As Syed Khalid Rashid observes, a traditional Muslim arbitrator (*hakam*) is not strictly bound by any rules of procedure or evidence. If the parties are given an opportunity to be heard in the presence of each other, and the award is disclosed with a rationale, it is considered to be a sufficiently fair arbitration as regards the matters of procedure.[66]

Analogically, the power of an arbitrator to act as *amiable compositeur* or to decide the case *ex aequo et bono* is assumed to be a default competence attributed to this function, and not one that must be explicitly agreed upon by the parties. According to Islamic jurisprudence, an arbitrator is generally *ex definitione* entitled to decide a case on a basis of fairness, equity and public policy grounds, insofar as it would not violate any Shari'a principle or an applicable customary rule.[67]

There are several characteristics of Islamic arbitration which are conducive to a material acceleration of proceedings. Simplicity and informality of procedure in Shari'a based arbitration affects the rules on evidence, which have also traditionally been kept at a minimum level (for example, there is no presupposed distinction between the value of parole and written evidence). The parties are already obligated to appoint their arbitrator by name at the moment of concluding the arbitration agreement. This requirement helps to eliminate parties' obstruction practices in commencement of the proceedings; nevertheless it can be also hampering in those cases where an arbitrator agreed upon by the parties turns out to be unavailable. It is also possible for the parties to agree upon the time limits of arbitration. If such a contractually stipulated deadline for rendering an award cannot be met by an arbitrator, the proceedings will be automatically terminated.[68]

One of the most important and burdensome procedural particularities of the traditional Islamic approach to arbitration is that in the latter each party was acknowledged to reserve the right to withdraw from already commenced

---

65 Fatima Akaddaf, 'Application of the United Nations Convention on Contracts for the International Sale of Goods (CISG) to Arab Islamic Countries: Is the CISG Compatible with Islamic Law Principles?' Spring Pace Int'l L Rev (2001) 35–38.

66 Syed Khalid Rashid, 'Alternative Dispute Resolution in the Context of Islamic Law' 8 Vindobona Journal of International Commercial Law and Arbitration (2004) 108.

67 Ibid. 107.

68 See ibid. 109–10.

proceedings until the award was rendered.[69] According to this concept (referring also to Arabian tribal customs), arbitration is not perceived as an adjudicatory method of dispute resolution, but as a technique close to conciliation. However, as Zeyad Alqurashi remarks, this interpretation of Shari'a has been recently rejected by Muslim scholars:

> The modern trend in Islamic law is to consider the arbitration agreement binding upon the parties once it has been entered into. Parties would also be bound by the decision of the arbitrator(s). Authorities on the subject proved that this view is the direct application of the general principles in Islamic Law. It is the direct application of the Koran when it states '... and fulfil every agreement, for every engagement...'. This meaning was stressed by the Prophet Mohamed in a famous Saying; he said, 'Believers should honour their engagements ...'. It may be concluded that the view that receives mostly full approval and application in the legal profession is that arbitration agreements are binding and no party is permitted to withdraw from any agreement he concluded with others by his own free and valid will.[70]

This new construction of Shari'a principles is consistent with the Western concept of arbitration being irrevocable once validly commenced. It has thus led to a significant increase of stability to the relations between non-Muslim parties seeking resolution of their controversies with Islamic contractors.

In the opinion of Rashid, the relative procedural simplicity of Islamic arbitration can be perceived as its major advantage in comparison with increasingly formalized, rigid and time-consuming Western forms of international commercial arbitration.[71] Shari'a-based arbitration can be thus recognized as preserving the essential features of arbitration which originally made it a successful alternative to overly formalized litigation in the sphere of international commercial disputes. Scarcity of procedural requirements, besides general standards of fairness, can be however interpreted as threatening, because of too much power being left to the discretion of an arbitrator. Nevertheless, the flexibility and openness of Islamic rules of arbitration enable achievement of a consensus on procedural standards adopted for a multicultural case. The fast growth of trade exchange between Muslim and non-Muslim countries in the recent decades, the active accession of Islamic States to the international legal framework of arbitration and the accompanying development of arbitral practices are the factors that indicate that such consents are being achieved on an increasingly regular basis.

***

69 S.H. Amin, *Commercial Arbitration in Islamic and Iranian Law* (Vahid Publications 1988).

70 Zeyad Alqurashi, 'Arbitration Under the Islamic Sharia' 1 OGEL (2003).

71 Rashid (n 66) 109.

International commercial arbitration is not only already the dominant method of resolving international commercial disputes – it is also becoming increasingly popular in the States which either decided to accede to the New York Convention regime relatively late, like the Islamic countries and Brazil or, although being early signatories of the convention (like India), had long remained reserved in interpretation of its provisions. ICA, which has always been a forum for the meeting of different legal cultures in commercial cases, has also been in the last decades witnessing such powerful trends as the 'Americanization' wave and growth of East Asian arbitral centres.

The evolution of the procedural framework and practices of ICA, observable in successful accommodation of these phenomena, reveals a significant scope for adaptability of arbitration in the multicultural context. This feature arguably also suggests that the antagonistic concept of arbitration as a place of cultural clash is not necessarily completely adequate on a procedural level. The growth of global popularity of ICA and the increasing number of new parties at the arbitral fora raise a further question about the significance of these trends for legal profession. There is undoubtedly an already well-established and expanding class of commercial arbitration specialists, who are cosmopolitan in a sense that their procedural strategies in handling a case are not predetermined by their primary legal background. These counsel are able to act fluently and effectively as 'transaction cost engineers' while planning the case on all levels – from forum selection, through conflict of laws considerations, to substantive, as well as procedural aspects.

However, the ubiquity of arbitration in international commercial cases causes growing numbers of general practitioners to be occasionally involved, with a tendency for transferring their domestic litigation procedural habits onto the arbitral forum. In cases of this kind, the rules of procedure, as described above, are to be used in an adaptive and reconciliatory manner, with regard to circumstances of the case, and to offer proper opportunity to the parties to have their arguments presented and the neutrality of the forum to be secured.

Interpretative methods, canons and sets of considerations, the exercise of which has developed in a way specific to arbitration, applied in particular cases in so established a setting, are an object of analysis in the following part of the book.

PART III
Legal Interpretation in the Arbitral Discourse: Functional Aspects

Chapter 7
Comparative Method

Comparative Analysis – its Concept and Role in Adjudication

As S.I. Strong emphasizes in his study on research skills in international arbitration, the competences needed for construing legally exhaustive and persuasive argumentation in this field necessarily require the adoption of a comparative perspective.[1] The essentially international nature of the arbitral process, combined with its increasingly cross-cultural character, as discussed in Chapter 6, inevitably places a comparative approach at the very core of methods applied by arbitration practitioners:

> the best written submission in this area of law adopts a purposeful blend of common-law and civil-law techniques. Any advocate who is unaware of how lawyers from different systems view legal authority will be unable to craft arguments that demonstrate the kind of sophistication and complexity that re the hallmarks of a good international practitioner.[2]

This particular, very fundamental need for comparative expertise and sensitivity in ICA is combined with notably high entry barriers in terms of training materials. It has been pointed out that the restricted access to resources (arbitral awards, but also commentaries and articles authored by leading experts) might effectively hamper the development and proliferation of skills in the discipline at a pace that would be consistent with the unprecedented global growth of ICA in the last decades.[3]

As already discussed, this results in practitioners occasionally transferring their habits from litigation, whilst not always fully adequate in the arbitration context (as, without guidance, beginners in this area of legal practice are not just unfamiliar with their content, but often not even cognizant of the existence of relevant materials). This is highly unfortunate, as the differences between the practice of ICA and those of both litigation and domestic arbitration are substantial (as Jan Paulsson famously observed, 'international arbitration is not arbitration'[4]).

---

1 S.I. Strong, 'Research in International Commercial Arbitration: Special Skills, Special Sources' 20 Am Rev Int'l Arb (2009).

2 Ibid. 121.

3 E. Jolivet, 'Access to Information and Awards' 22 Arb Int'l (2010) 266.

4 Jan Paulsson, 'International Arbitration is not Arbitration' 4 Stock Int'l Arb Rev (2008).

In Strong's opinion this deepening dissonance has already led ICA to a critical moment of its evolution, as many skills and competences connected with its practice are endangered.[5]

The comparative method is strongly present on all three levels of application of law (and other binding rules) in international arbitration. Whereas a familiarity with comparative aspects of arbitral procedure and conflict of laws belongs undoubtedly to the key competences of an arbitration practitioner (and remains the centre of attention for some authors[6]), it stays outside the main scope of this book, which focuses on interpretation of the substantive rules of law in ICA.

Using the examples of Aristotle's research for *Politics*, Solon's drafting of Athenian laws and the decemvirs' preparation of the Roman Twelve Tablets, René David and John E. C. Brierley demonstrate that '[t]here have always been studies of foreign laws and recourse to comparison in legal scholarship. The comparison of laws, at least in their geographical diversity, is as old as the science of law itself.'[7] The need for comparative inquiry in both historical and synchronic aspects has always been present in legal studies. In fact, the historical orientation of legal research was the original perspective of modern comparative jurisprudence, influenced by Montesquieu, known as the 'father of comparative law'.[8] It is worth noting that in the arbitration literature the term 'comparative interpretation' seems to be generally used in a rather narrow sense, to describe the study of similar norms, provisions, instruments and institutions across legal systems, using a contemporary perspective as the point of reference. If comparative legal interpretation *sensu largo* includes diachronic, as well as synchronic inquiry, in ICA it is the latter that is widely in use.

Another important feature of comparative law is its still often advocated, essentially functional rather than substantive character: it is described as a method of study and research or a technique and not as a branch of law[9] (Harold Cooke Gutteridge even characterizes the term 'comparative law' as 'an unfortunate but generally accepted label for the comparative method of legal study and research'[10]). This concept has a long and well-established tradition in legal theory: as Frederick Pollock famously argued at the 1900 International Congress of Comparative Law in Paris, comparative law is nothing more than the introduction of comparative

---

5 Strong (n 1) 124.

6 See J. Epstein, 'The Use of Comparative Law in Commercial International Arbitration and Commercial Mediation' 75 Tul L Rev (2000) 915ff.

7 R. David and J.E.C. Brierley, *Major Legal Systems in the World Today: An Introduction to the Comparative Study of Law* (Free Press 1978) 3.

8 Ibid. 4.

9 A. Watson, *Legal Transplants: An Approach to Comparative Law* (University of Georgia Press 1993) 1.

10 H.C. Gutteridge, *Comparative Law: An Introduction to the Comparative Method of Legal Study and Research* (Cambridge University Press Archive 1971) ix.

method into law ('*droit comparé n'est pas une science propre, mais n'est que l'introduction de la méthode comparée dans le droit*'[11]).

More recently, Konstantinos D. Kerameus notes the two trends in defining comparative law: as an autonomous (or quasi-autonomous) branch of law and as an auxiliary method used in legal research and reasoning, and he observes that the latter is the dominant one.[12] Thus understood, and traditionally described as close to disciplines such as the sociology of law or legal history, comparative law also enriches the interpretive competences and perspectives of a legal practitioner in a domestic setting. Kerameus observes, though, that comparative law remains a distinctively legal discipline, without a direct recourse to a wider theory of an extralegal field, such as general sociology, history or philosophy.[13]

Adrian Vermeule describes the comparative method, along with direct experiment, as one of the (too rarely used) rational options available for judges faced with the necessity of making interpretive choices in cases of informational uncertainty and limited capacity of processing the accessed data, as they are bound by procedural time frames.[14] Historically, the development of this field of law has been closely connected with the establishment and solidification of modern nation States since the sixteenth century, 'as a means of understanding (the taxonomic function) and ameliorating national law',[15] so as to secure its better drafting, organization and understanding. As Gutteridge emphasizes: 'for the most part applied comparative law has a practical aim in view, such as law reform or the unification of divergent laws, and it is this form of comparative research which is the most vigorous and fertile in output.'[16]

Comparative analysis had been thus traditionally perceived as an instrument of improvement of the domestic law. As a result, it was applied in legislative and doctrinal initiatives rather than in legal practice[17] (although its essential usefulness for academic inquiry and for judicial interpretation, with its perspective of leading to a '*droit commun de l'humanité civilisée*' was emphasized as early as 1900 at the International Congress of Comparative Law in Paris[18]). In Glenn's view, such limited perception of comparative inquiry, staying primarily in the service of national legal policy, is no longer compatible with the changing role of States and

11 *Congrès international de droit comparé tenu à Paris du 31 juillet au 4 août 1900: procès-verbaux des séances et documents* vol 1 (LGDJ 1905) 60.

12 K.D. Kerameus, 'Comparative Law and Comparative Lawyers: Opening Remarks' 75 Tul L Rev (2000) 866.

13 Ibid. 867.

14 A. Vermeule, *Judging under Uncertainty: An Institutional Theory of Legal Interpretation* (Harvard University Press 2006) 159.

15 H. Glenn, 'Comparative Law and Legal Practice: On Removing the Borders' 75 Tul L Rev (2000) 979.

16 Gutteridge (n 10) 9.

17 Glenn (n 15) 979–80.

18 D.S. Clark, 'Nothing New in 2000 – Comparative Law in 1900 and Today' 75 Tul L Rev (2000) 875–76.

global legal practice, which includes a growing number of transnational initiatives. The processes of global and regional harmonization of law and their impact on legal interpretation, as well as the increasing transfer of States' authority in the legal sphere onto transnational institutions (including the creation and broadening of space for private initiatives, such as ICA), have in recent decades accompanied the rapid growth in cross-border economic exchange worldwide.[19] Along with internationalization of law firms and augmented mobility in the legal profession, it has resulted in a proliferation of the comparative approach and its wide use in legal practice. International arbitration is, according to Glenn, a striking example of a wide implementation of the reformulated comparative method – being no longer instrumental to the parochial interests of a particular domestic system and exercised only by a narrow group of specialists, but enabling a large number of practitioners to move beyond these limitations.

As Mads Andenas and Duncan Fairgrieve argue, the recent, observable growth of the significance of the comparative method in the practice of domestic courts (as exemplified primarily in the UK context) has already resulted in a variety of outcomes, from overturning authority in domestic context to developing the principles of domestic law and, notably, in the application of European and international law.[20] While concluding that '[c]omparative law is no longer an impractical academic discipline',[21] they also note that the wide expansion of the discipline has been attained at the cost of a loss of consistency, and they call for an accompanying development of legal scholarship.[22]

Moreover, whereas the recent growth of transnational legal initiatives in the spheres of lawmaking and dispute resolution is hardly disputable, the 'decline of the state'[23] seems still to have been announced all too early. As Judd Epstein observes, despite the relatively diminishing significance of State-enacted private law and the increasing role of non-State actors in this area (which leads to the wide applicability of the comparative method in legal practice): 'the death knell for national law is premature. National law and the national law of others remain prime concerns for the practitioner.'[24]

This caveat remains adequate on the level of procedural decisions (on which Epstein concentrates), as well as in the sphere of conflict of laws considerations

---

19 Joanna Jemielniak and Przemyslaw Mikłaszewicz, 'Capturing the Change: Universalising Tendencies in Legal Interpretation' in *Interpretation of Law in the Global World: From Particularism to a Universal Approach* (Joanna Jemielniak and Przemyslaw Mikłaszewicz eds, Springer 2010).

20 Horatia Muir Watt, 'Further Terrains for Subversive Comparison: The Field of Global Governance and the Public/Private Divide' in *Methods of Comparative Law* (Pier Monateri ed, Edward Elgar 2012).

21 Ibid. 59.

22 Ibid. 59–60.

23 M. Van Creveld, *The Rise and Decline of the State* (Cambridge University Press 1999).

24 Epstein (n 6) 914.

and application of proper substantive law in ICA. While Glenn's diagnosis of the unprecedentedly high use of the comparative method in legal practice (and notably in the arbitral one) is accurate, his suggestion that it will result in the creation of an amalgam of legal traditions seems too far-reaching. The defining and unifying power of the comparative method (or its appearance) in international arbitration has also been discussed by the critics of ICA as a neoliberal, market-based system of 'private justice', founded on what Horatia Muir Watt describes as the 'myth of a global legal grammar'.[25] Correspondingly, comparative law and the comparative method in arbitration (as well as in litigation) can be thus perceived as powerful means of legitimization.[26]

In fact, the application of comparative analysis in ICA, besides contributing to the development of the new *lex mercatoria* (or the autonomous, uniform law of the international trade transactions, as discussed in detail in the subsequent chapter) is more diversified and nuanced. It has also undoubtedly already effectively become part of the 'advocacy tool kit'[27] of an arbitration counsel. The outstanding status of ICA in this regard has been acknowledged: 'international arbitrations are a teeming petri dish for the practice of comparative law. Nowhere is this practice more active than in the advocacy to international tribunals.'[28]

The indispensable character of comparative analysis in arbitral practice has indeed been emphasized very early – Pierre Lalive perceives training and experience in its use as an essential professional attribute of an arbitrator.[29] He also observes that 'the arbitrator of today must show proof of a comparative or comparatist mind, open to legal pluralism, to various cultures and various political and social systems.'[30]

Frédéric Gilles Sourgens, adopting the perspective of an ICA counsel, observes that the comparative method in regard to substantive law in arbitration may be used in three basic ways: to present law foreign to the arbitrators in a way persuasive and favourable to his or her case; as an instrument enabling gap-filling in the main proper law of the dispute; and as a means for discovery of general principles of law or usages of the international trade (in other words, the new *lex mercatoria*).[31]

Whereas the comparative method can be very successfully employed for formulation of the principles of the New Law Merchant (and has, in fact, played a critical role in their consolidation through arbitral case law), *lex mercatoria* itself and its function in international arbitration is still not tantamount to a particular

25 Watt (n 20) 273.

26 Pier Giuseppe Monateri, 'Introduction' in *Methods of Comparative Law* (Pier Giuseppe Monateri ed, Edward Elgar 2012) 1.

27 F.G. Sourgens, 'Comparative Law as Rhetoric: An Analysis of the Use of Comparative Law in International Arbitration' 8 Pep Dis Resol LJ (2007) 2.

28 Ibid. 1.

29 Pierre Lalive, 'International Arbitration – Teaching and Research' in *Contemporary Problems in International Arbitration* (Julian D.M. Lew ed, Martinus Nijhoff 1987) 16.

30 Pierre Lalive, 'Enforcing Awards' in *Sixty Years of ICC Arbitration: A Look at the Future* (ICC Publishing 1984) 350.

31 Sourgens (n 27).

use of this type of legal analysis. The adoption of comparative method and the role of *lex mercatoria* in arbitration are certainly close and interconnected. While some authors advocate the concept of the New Law Merchant as a specific method of arbitral adjudication, this pragmatic yet reductionist view seems to leave significant aspects of this legal phenomenon outside the scope of scrutiny. This issue is discussed in detail in the following chapter.

The other two ways of using the comparative method in arbitration can be, with some modifications, found in arbitral decision-making, and not only in the argumentation before the tribunals, prepared by the counsel. In particular, in regard to the first discussed form, Sourgens focuses on its persuasive and rhetorical aspect, which makes his study primarily specific to the practice of parties' counsel before the arbitral tribunal, and not to the tribunal's activity *per se*. If, however, the first type of application of the comparative method in ICA was to be understood more broadly – as a use of comparative analysis as a lens for achieving a more 'international' interpretation of the proper, domestic law of the case (without the necessary orientation on the clients' interests) – it can be found in arbitral decision-making itself as well. The formulation of the second, gap-filling function of comparative analysis in arbitration does not require a similar, conceptual readjustment (although it naturally can be, and is used in practice by the counsel for pragmatic and persuasive reasons).

While discussing the input of parties' counsel into the process of comparative legal analysis before the arbitral tribunal and the decidedly intellectual character of the arguments, Sourgens claims that the arbitration proceedings tend to be, on the average, '*more precise and reasoned*'[32] than litigation due to a number of reasons. The specialized expertise of the panel and the limited orality of the proceedings (which leads to the perfection of arguments over the series of exchanges of written documents) are highlighted as crucial in this regard. On the other hand, as the comparative method is used as a tool for the 'internationalization' of interpretation of domestic law and making the construction of its rules more befitting the intentions of the parties, the question to be raised is that of limits to such activity. The extremes, to be possibly avoided, are the execution of the assumed parties' intent to the point of contradiction with the mandatory provisions of the applicable law and hollowing of legal concepts on one side; and a wooden rendition of national rules by purely national interpretive standards, disregarding the cross-border character of the analysed transaction on the other.

The reefs to be steered away from are also legal 'false friends' – legal concepts which seem to have direct counterparts in other legal systems, but which cannot be treated as freely exchangeable. A classic example would be the various concepts of domestic contract laws, addressing the issue of unforeseeable changed circumstances (such as *Unmöglichkeit*, frustration and *force majeure*,[33]

32 Ibid. 10.

33 A. Puelinckx, 'Frustration, Hardship, Force Majeure, Imprévision, Wegfall der Geschäftsgrundlage, Unmöglichkeit, Changed Circumstances' 3 J Int'l Arb 47 (1986).

as well as the *rebus sic stantibus* clauses[34]), the application of each leading to different practical outcomes. The challenges of legal interpretation in this sphere are thus connected with what Anne Lise Kjaer characterizes, in the example of the EU law, as recontextualization of concepts on a legal and on a linguistic level.[35]

In the context of arbitral decision-making, a practical limitation to the modifying use of comparative method in interpretation of domestic legal concepts lies also in the actual familiarity of particular arbitrators with the legal system determined as proper substantive law. Whereas it is arguably

> not atypical that a tribunal would have at least one member from the jurisdiction of the applicable law. In those cases, counsel must take care that the language used is not only accessible to the arbitrators that are foreign to the applicable law, but also that counsel's use of language remains plausible within the context of the original normative discourse.[36]

In this context, the procedural solution introducing limitations on the arbitrators' nationality (as seen, for example, in the LCIA Rules, Art. 6) should be noted. Whereas arbitration rules, under which the case is being resolved, might prohibit appointment of an arbitrator of the same nationality as any of the parties, it should also be taken into account that the proper substantive law very frequently turns out to be the law of one of the parties. Such a combination will be also present in all cases where, despite the lack of relevant formal limitations, the appointed arbitrators are of a nationality and/or primary educational background different from the domestic legal system determined to be the proper law.

While increasing the neutrality of the forum, this results in a diminished embedment of the tribunal in the national legal system governing the case and the production of a complete world of interconnected legal rules, concepts and interpretive standards. Arbitral interpretation of applicable law in such cases will be thus performed from an outsider's perspective, with all the positive and negative consequences of assuming such an approach. According to Rene David, 'arbitration will hardly be regarded by a party as a suitable way of solving the case if it is to be administered by an arbitrator who is imbued with the ways of thinking and the prejudices of another culture.'[37] Such detachment of an arbitrator from the legal system to be applied to the merits of the case bears, however, a risk of misplacing legal concepts with their assumed counterparts, stemmed in systems with which the arbitrator is acquainted.

---

34 I. Schwenzer, 'Force Majeure and Hardship in International Sales Contracts' 39 Vict U Well L Rev (2008) 710ff.

35 Anne Lise Kjaer, 'Recontextualization of Concepts in European Legal Discourse' in *Dialogue and Rhetoric* (Edda Weigand ed, Benjamins 2008).

36 Sourgens (n 27) 16.

37 After Lalive (n 29) 16.

Another danger is an increased susceptibility to the rhetorical efforts of counsel, offering their arguments in line with the preferred rendition most favourable to the client. As Sourgens observes, the use of the comparative method in the ICA advocacy is threefold. First, it might be performed through seeking a common denominator for legal concepts to be applied with similar concepts present in legal orders with which the arbitrators are directly familiar, as well as a relevant presentation of the argument in so-discovered 'common legal language' with which the arbitrators will supposedly find themselves familiar.[38] Whereas application of such an approach can be traced and might be helpful and clarifying not just in the counsel' practice but also arbitral interpretation, the underlying persuasive and rhetorical orientation of the latter serves as a *caveat* for accepting these kinds of arguments, when presented by the counsel, at face value.

A second, and perhaps less subtle option is the use of analogy for explanation of foreign legal concepts, available in particular on those occasions where the proper substantive law has not been applied to such a type of case before, or where the law is silent or underdeveloped on the matter in question. While similarly, generally practical in arbitral interpretation, it can also be to some extent manipulated in the ICA advocacy. Sourgens notes that, if used cautiously by the counsel, comparative analogy might create a desired effect of establishing a comfort zone for arbitrators not acquainted with the legal system in question, by explaining the unknown through the familiar.[39]

Third, comparative analysis might be used by the ICA counsel not as a positive strategy, but as a shield, to turn aside the arguments of the opposing side. This can be achieved in regard to an offered, comparative interpretation (to be discredited as inaccurate). In such cases, the negative argument

> will focus on the differences between the proposed interpretation and the 'true' meaning of the applicable law … [A]t the extreme one could rely on the techniques used by comparative law scholars that see each legal system as a specific answer to problems immanent only within the legal culture of the applicable law. At the other extreme one could simply attack a point as an ill-founded comparison in this specific instance leaving the door open for other, better-formed comparisons.[40]

Another rhetorical variation is the deflection of an argument, which is not itself based on comparative inquiry (but it is being demonstrated that such an inquiry should be arguably taken into account). In both versions, the use of the comparative method for possible rebuttal of arguments on rendition of the substantive applicable law seems very closely connected with the antagonistic character of arbitral procedure and with the practice of ICA advocacy. Its relevance to arbitral

38 Sourgens (n 27) 12ff.

39 Ibid. 18.

40 Ibid. 19.

decision-making is much less direct: while possibly present in arbitral reasoning (either thanks to the parties' pleadings or to the arbitrators' own examination of the law of the case), this kind of comparative counter-argument is rarely explicitly expressed in the issued awards.

Significance ascribed to the use of the comparative method in ICA seems also closely connected to the representation (or self-representation) of arbitration, in the sense proposed by Emmanuel Gaillard,[41] as it is adopted (openly or impliedly) by arbitrators resolving a particular case. According to Gaillard, there are currently three dominant conceptualizations of ICA in legal scholarship: one that perceives arbitration as merely an emanation of a national legal order (analogically to private international law understood as part of a given domestic legal system); a pluralistic, multilocal representation, which bases validity of an award not just on the legal order of the seat of arbitration, but on all systems which are predisposed to potentially recognize it; and a theory of ICA as an autonomous, arbitral legal order, where the authority of international arbitrators is not executed on behalf of any State, but is a *sui generis*, transnational administration of justice.[42]

These representations have been formulated primarily in a context of procedural framework of ICA and the resulting institutional status and adjudicating authority of the tribunals. However, the assumption of a particular representation of arbitration might result in a different approach adopted towards the use and rank of the comparative method. This issue is further explored below.

Comparative Analysis and the Monolocal Approach

In the first of the analysed representations, the arbitral tribunals are treated as a specialized type of domestic court and the position of an arbitrator is perceived analogically to that of a domestic judge. The rudimentary differences in the limits of discretionary powers are approached as secondary, as in both roles the status of an adjudicator is fully dependant upon the original will of the domestic lawmaker, who allows for such an institutional construct. As pointed out by Francis A. Mann:

> [i]s not every activity occurring on the territory of a State necessarily subject to its jurisdiction? Is it not for such State to say whether and in what manner arbitrators are assimilated to judges and, like them, subject to the law? Various States may give various answers to the question, but that each of them has the right to, and does, answer it according to its own discretion cannot be doubted.[43]

41 Emmanuel Gaillard and Hague Academy of International Law, *Aspects philosophiques du droit de l'arbitrage international* (Libraire Hachette 2008).

42 Emmanuel Gaillard, *Legal Theory of International Arbitration* (Martinus Nijhoff 2010) 15ff.

43 Francis A. Mann, 'Lex Facit Arbitrum' in *International Arbitration, Liber Amicorum for Martin Domke* (Pieter Sanders ed, Martinus Nijhoff 1967) 162.

While formulated in what can be seen as an earlier stage of development of international arbitration, this view is still supported by contemporary authors,[44] who further Mann's argument that the selection of the seat of arbitration is generally not left to chance or physical convenience, but is a deliberate act of subscription by the parties to a particular legal order.[45] As a consequence, the law governing arbitration is, according to this theory, necessarily and exclusively the law of the seat of the tribunal. Whereas such a solution certainly promotes predictability of the results, due to fixed localization of control over the awards, Gaillard observes that it might also lead to injustice when

> a single law, irrespective of its degree of conservatism and the manner in which domestic courts decide to apply it, is entitled to govern an arbitration for the sole reason that it happens to be that of the country where the arbitration is taking or has taken place.[46]

Such a monolocal representation of arbitration affects primarily its procedural embedment; it is, however, closely connected with the classic doctrine of private international law, which seeks to resolve cases with an international component from within a particular domestic legal order (and the application of foreign substantive law to the merits of the case is possible due to a mandate granted by the sovereign and lawmaker of the *lex fori*). The assumption that, as a result of such an approach, there is no room left in arbitral decision-making for a comparative inquiry, would be an oversimplification. Rather, as the role of an arbitrator is understood as analogous to that of a domestic judge, consequently also his or her application of the comparative method would be similarly restricted, as in the case of judicial interpretation (unless authorized otherwise by the law of arbitration).

In the context of application of foreign law by domestic courts and the accompanying role of comparative legal research, two approaches have been distinguished in private international law studies: a universalist and a unilateralist one. According to the former, dominant in civil law countries (with notable case law deviations in France and Italy), foreign substantive law, determined as proper law governing the case, should be treated as law and construed accordingly. In the unilateralist perspective, represented in common law jurisdictions (with the US courts assuming a position more moderate than the English ones), foreign law tends to be treated as a fact, its application being dependant upon the intent and evidentiary efforts by the parties.[47] The adoption of one of those perspectives bears far-reaching consequences for the judicial interpretation of law. As Jacob Dolinger

44 See Gaillard (n 42) 15.

45 R. Goode, 'The Role of the Lex Loci Arbitri in International Commercial Arbitration' 17 Arb Int'l (2001) 32.

46 Gaillard (n 42) 24.

47 Jacob Dolinger, 'Application, Proof, and Interpretation of Foreign Law: A Comparative Study in Private International Law' 12 Ariz J Int'l & Comp L (1995) 225ff.

observes, the unilateralist theory, formulated in the seventeenth- and eighteenth-century case law in England, has sought application of foreign law without losing the controlling power of *lex fori* and has seen the foreign norms through the 'lenses of one's own jurisdictional sovereignty'.[48]

As a consequence, the role of an adjudicator is perceived as constrained by his or her domestic perspective:

> [t]he only law applied by the judge is the lex fori, the only rights enforced by him are those created by the lex fori. But owing to the foreign element in the case, the foreign law is a fact that must be taken in consideration. What the judge attempts to do is to create and to enforce a right as nearly as possible similar to that which would have been created by the foreign court had it been seised of a similar case purely domestic in character.[49]

The burden of proof of the content of foreign law under this approach lies on the parties and is provable by experts to a jury, with the limited or excluded review by the appellate court.[50] The comparative component in this approach is thus hardly present, and might be (usually unintentionally) expressed through reducing foreign legal concepts to the known denominator of their counterparts in *lex fori* and its legal context.

The universalist perspective, following the nineteenth-century doctrine of Tobias Asser, assumes that foreign law shall be applied by a judge when found proper, even if the parties themselves do not make a reference to it.[51] In the sphere of legal interpretation, the adoption of the universalist approach results in a preserving application of foreign law, including a maintenance of its own interpretive canons and directives. This generally requires the domestic judge to assume what decision would be reached by the foreign court in an identical case. When strictly performed, it might, however, also occasionally lead to the judge being 'more papal than the pope' – because, as Dolinger observes (after Batiffol), there is an

> important distinction between the judge's role when applying his own national law and when applying foreign law. In the former case he is free to create or change the interpretation that has been given to his law whenever it appears

48 Ibid. 255.

49 G.C. Cheshire and P.M. North, *Cheshire's Private International Law* (Butterworths 1970) 9. Dolinger also notes the American authors Cramton, Currie and Kay as being highly critical towards this reconstructive approach ('Can you imagine a more burdensome, inconvenient, or absurd method of ascertaining foreign law?') – see Dolinger (n 47) 258 fn 164.

50 After Ehrenzweig, see Dolinger (n 47) 258.

51 T.M.C. Asser and Alphonse Pierre Octave Rivier, *Éléments de droit international privé ou du conflit des lois* (A. Rousseau 1884) 226.

> to him that his interpretation will make better justice; whereas in the latter case, the foreign law is the one which is effectively adjudicated abroad, and he has no competence to judge its value and take the initiative of a different interpretation.[52]

Of these two approaches, applicability of the unilateralist theory in the ICA context seems very limited for several reasons. First, the role of *lex fori* (*lex loci arbitri*) is much looser and less direct than it is in litigation and the course of arbitral proceedings is governed by the institutional rules (or by other rules selected by the parties) in the first place. Whereas these rules are of course mandated only so far as the *lex fori* allows, in general the scope of domestic intervention in ICA is rather minimal. Second, arbitration is by definition not just a specialized emanation of a particular national legal order, but a form of dispute resolution (and an institutional apparatus) meant to offer a neutral forum for private international controversies. In this sense, as discussed above in Chapter 1, it might be characterized as anational or floating. Arbitral awards are not issued in a name of a particular State, lack the formal endorsement of judicial decisions and are only occasionally sought to be enforced in the place of arbitration (while it is largely the enforcement considerations that still make the territoriality principle under the New York Convention regime so practically significant). Arbitrators do not operate within the fixed and constant *lex fori* systemic and institutional background to such an extent as the domestic judges do.

Third, the connection between *lex loci arbitri* and the arbitrators themselves is very frequently not dominant, as the tribunal might very well be composed of persons not primarily trained in this legal system. The unilateralist application of foreign law, as seen through the lenses of *lex loci arbitri* would be thus a functionally artificial concept, as *lex loci arbitri* itself in such cases is foreign to the arbitrators. Finally, the goal of such exercise would be dubious in the context of the classical unilateralist rationale, as the legal system providing *lex loci arbitri* might very well not have any interest either in the merits or in the outcome and enforcement of the dispute.

In the monolocal representation of ICA, it is the universalistic domestic approach to application of foreign law that seems more practical and, arguably, more proper. However, it still has observable drawbacks and limitations when considered from the arbitral perspective.

The main advantage of this approach seems to be its orientation on preserving the authenticity and purity of interpretation of the domestic law as embedded in a particular legal system. The unilateralist interpretation aims not just at invoking the letter of foreign law in an isolated manner, but at capturing its meaning in the original, national legal context (including the relevant domestic interpretive directives). Even in the context of litigation, application of such an originalist approach might in practice easily turn out to be highly challenging for the court

52 Dolinger (n 47) 240.

though, for cognitive as well as organizational reasons. Its applicability in a pure form to cases with an international component (and thus characterized as not being reducible to the limits of a single legal system) can be a matter for a separate discussion.

In arbitration, the petrifying undertone of this type of interpretation may be additionally seen as inconsistent with the basic orientation of ICA, meant to be sensitive to international character of the resolved cases. This orientation is observable, for example, in the mandatory recourse to be had by the arbitrators to usages and customs of international trade as principles modifying the interpretation and preventing it from remaining one-sided or overly parochial.

Comparative Analysis and the Pluralistic Approach

The second representation of ICA, discussed by Gaillard, is based on the plurality of national legal orders. According to this approach, the *lex fori* (*lex loci arbitri*) no longer enjoys a special status in regard to the arbitration and validity of an award. Rather, the awards gain legitimization from all legal orders potentially inclined to recognize them. Gaillard characterizes this representation as essentially decentralized, as opposed to the centralizing, monolocal approach, focusing strongly on the law of the seat. This change of perspective, described as a Copernican revolution,[53] results, in his view, from the difference in selecting the focal point for analysis: whereas the monolocal representation concentrates on the starting point of arbitration, the pluralistic one is oriented rather at the final outcome.

As a consequence:

> [i]n this conception, one may readily observe that 'arbitrators have no forum' or, rather, that the world, not a specific State – be it that of the seat – is their forum. The award is no longer considered to be specifically 'Colombian' or 'English'. Its 'international' nature prevails over the idea that it is exclusively rooted in the law of the seat based on an anthropomorphic approach of attributing a nationality to awards.[54]

Gaillard also argues, after Pierre Mayer, that the multicentric, pluralistic representation of international arbitration is not inconsistent with legal positivistic postulates, as the effectiveness of an award and the framework conditions for its enforcement are an outcome of the States' sovereign decisions. The critique of this concept as disconnected from domestic legal orders is thus unfounded.[55]

53 Emmanuel Gaillard, 'Souveraineté et autonomie: réflexions sur les représentations de l'arbitrage international' 134 J Droit Int'l 4(2007) 1173.

54 Gaillard (n 42) 25.

55 Ibid. 26–27.

Such a 'Westphalian' concept of arbitration seems to be well-grounded in the New York Convention regime, even though in the terminology adopted by the convention the term 'international award' (suggested by the ICC) has not been introduced, and the traditional notion of 'foreign award', as previously used by the 1927 Geneva Convention, has been kept. Still, as Gaillard points out, the intention to diminish the role of the law of the seat permeates the New York Convention's provisions. Precedence given to the parties' will over the rules of *lex loci arbitri* can be observed in regard to the arbitration agreement (Art. V(1)(a)), as well as the composition of the tribunal and the conduct of the proceedings (Art. V(1)(d)). References to *lex loci arbitri* in these provisions are offered in terms of 'the law of the country where the arbitration took place' (Art. V(1)(a)) and 'the law of the country where the award is made' (Art. V(1)(d)), which Redfern characterizes explicitly as used in a synonymous manner.[56] A practical consequence of such formulation of these provisions is that these issues are not an object of scrutiny in the light of the law of the seat in other countries in which the enforcement is sought.[57]

Whereas the idea that the recognition or enforcement of an international arbitral award does not lie within the sphere of sovereign authority of a single State can hardly be seen as controversial, the discussed above interpretation of the New York Convention as giving clear precedence to the parties' agreement can be also presented in a more evolutionary manner. Alan Redfern refers to the instruments preceding the enactment of the convention so as to demonstrate that their underlying philosophy of the seat of arbitration had not been departed from; on the contrary, a continuity of development of this concept can be seen. While invoking the unambiguously dualistic reference made by the Geneva *Protocol on Arbitration Clauses* of *1923* ('The arbitral procedure, including the constitution of the arbitral tribunal, shall be governed by the will of the parties and by the law of the country in whose territory the arbitration takes place'[58]), Redfern further argues that the territorial link between the place of arbitration and the law of arbitration has been sustained in the New York Convention, as well as in the UNCITRAL *Model Law* on International Commercial Arbitration. He still notices that the practical role of *lex arbitri* has been shifted to the background and it is 'increasingly likely to be supportive of the arbitral process and to intervene in that process as little as possible'.[59]

Roy Goode, frequently expressing his sceptical view of the concept of anational arbitration, notices that

---

56 Alan Redfern and Martin Hunter, *Law and Practice of International Commercial Arbitration* (Sweet & Maxwell 2004) 84.

57 Gaillard (n 42) 30.

58 Protocol on Arbitration Clauses Signed at a Meeting of the Assembly of the League Of Nations Held on the Twenty-Fourth Day of September, Nineteen Hundred and Twenty-Three (1923 Geneva Protocol on Arbitration Clauses), section 2.

59 Redfern and Hunter (n 56) 84.

> [o]ne of the more remarkable features of the territoriality/party autonomy debate is that the protagonists on both sides invoke the New York Convention to support their position: the territorialists on the ground that numerous provisions of the Convention explicitly recognize the role of the *lex loci arbitri*; the advocates of party autonomy and the statelessness of awards, on the ground that Article VII plainly establishes the right of enforcement states to allow enforcement of a foreign award which complies with their domestic law, despite its annulment by the court of origin, where that annulment is not a ground under the domestic law for refusal of recognition of the award. One thing seems clear, and that is that the New York Convention recognizes the important role of the *lex loci arbitri*; and while Article VII allows the *lex loci arbitri* to be bypassed, it certainly provides no warrant for the concept of a stateless award. On the contrary, it is strongly arguable that a stateless award would be not enforceable under the Convention.[60]

The vision of arbitration as completely anational and delocalized is indeed inconsistent with the territoriality principle, as present in the New York Convention. This issue has also been recently discussed in the context of online arbitration[61] – where, even if the *locus arbitri* functions as a purely conventional construct, it is still required and understood not as a geographical location, but as embedment of an award in a particular legal system precisely because of the New York Convention requirements. This limitation, however, does not automatically result in a special role ascribed to the substantive *lex loci arbitri* in the process of deciding the merits of the dispute. The wording of Art. VII seems also to offer arguments for the proponents of the Westphalian representation of arbitration.

The consequences of adoption of the Westphalian model of international arbitration on the arbitrators' approach to comparative analysis seem consistent with the pluralistic orientation of this representation. As discussed above, the accent is put on the loosened link between arbitration and the law of its seat; it is also emphasized that arbitrators are not bound by a mandatory recourse to it in a manner comparable to the position of domestic judges. This affects comparative aspects of legal interpretation in arbitral decision-making in several ways.

The arbitrators, as opposed to the judges, do not render the awards in the name of a particular State. This factor, combined with the, already-discussed, relative detachment of arbitration from the legal order of its place makes the arbitrators less inclined to reduce comparative analysis to the application of foreign law seen through the lenses of the national legal system of the seat and readjusted to local standards.

The fact that the arbitrators are very frequently of a nationality other than the place of arbitration (or, at least, not primarily trained in its legal system) additionally, remarkably contributes to this state of affairs. The perception and interpretation of

60 Goode (n 45) 22.

61 Cf. Rafal Morek, 'The Regulatory Framework for Online Dispute Resolution: A Critical View' 38 U Tol L Rev (2006).

proper substantive law, in numerous cases where it is a system different from the law of the place of arbitration, is thus not naturally performed from the perspective of an insider to *lex loci arbitri* (as the latter can be as foreign to the arbitrator as the proper law is; moreover, it is also possible that an arbitrator will be primarily familiar with the proper law and not with *lex arbitri*). This in practice further weakens the embedment of legal analysis in the context of *lex loci arbitri* and affects the scarcity (if not virtual non-existence) of modifying application of the argument of domestic public order of *lex arbitri* in arbitration. On the other hand, the possibility of recourse to *ordre public* and national public policy of *lex contractus* has been widely discussed and – while its scope in arbitration remains disputed – practised.[62]

Pierre Mayer, firmly following the delocalized vision of international arbitration, commented on this difference, observing that

> [o]ne might note that national court judges have always drawn a sharp distinction between the mandatory rules of the *lex fori* and the mandatory rules of foreign law. Judges are quite ready – how could they not be? – to apply their own country's mandatory rules of law, that is to say *lex fori*, even if it is not the law governing the contract ...
>
> Such a distinction is clearly not to be made by arbitrators, because they do not have a forum. They are not faced with domestic mandatory rules as opposed to foreign mandatory rules, but simply with mandatory rules external to *lex contractus*. There can be thus no half measure. For this reason, the arbitrator's position is more favourable to an objective weighing of the interests that militate in favour of applying the mandatory rules and the *lex contractus*, respectively: he views all laws as being of equal dignity.[63]

The doctrinal discussion of the delocalized vision of ICA and its consequences for admissible influence of *lex fori* and the law of the presumed place of enforcement of an award on arbitration was accompanied in the 1980s by several seminal decisions. In the decision of the US Supreme Court in *Mitsubishi Motors Corp v Soler Chrysler-Plymouth Inc*, the dispute concerned enforceability of the arbitration clause. The petitioner, a Japanese automobile manufacturer, sought arbitration in the US in a dispute on non-payment for stored vehicles with the respondent, a Puerto Rico-based corporation acting as an automobile dealer. The respondent refused to arbitrate, claiming that the merits of the controversy involved US antitrust laws as mandatory rules, and upholding that foreign arbitrators at the Japan Commercial Arbitration Association are unlikely to be familiar with the relevant antitrust provisions and not prepared for their competent construction.

---

62 H. Arfazadeh, 'In the Shadow of the Unruly Horse: International Arbitration and the Public Policy Exception' 13 Am Rev Int'l Arb (2002) 43ff.

63 Pierre Mayer, 'Mandatory Rules of Law in International Arbitration' 2 Arb Int'l (1986) 282–83.

The rationale behind the respondent's argumentation was thus a suggestion of a *de facto* evasive character of the arbitration clause, aimed at avoiding the application of the US mandatory rules. A question that follows this argument is thus whether the parties can, through the selection of a place of arbitration, manipulate the scope of application of mandatory rules forming a part of *lex contractus*, to the merits of their dispute. The answer in practice seems positive – such anticipatory calculation might well be a part of an, admittedly rather sophisticated, forum shopping strategy. As a consequence, an issue decided by the court in *Mitsubishi* was thus one of admissibility of a preventive intervention of the court of the place of enforcement of an award, based on an anticipated risk of misconstruction of the rules of the place of enforcement, made in the place of arbitration (misapplication of foreign law).

Roy Goode argues that it is the protection of the parties' legitimate expectations which serves as an elementary principle of the conflict of laws, as well as the primary reason for which the domestic courts are willing to apply foreign law to the merits of the case.[64] Disregard to the parties' explicit or indirect choice of a particular domestic law would result in frustration of the parties' reasonable expectations as to the nature of their legal relationship and scope of their mutual rights and obligations. It would also lead to unpredictability of the result of the dispute and legal uncertainty.

Comparative Analysis and the Representation of ICA as an Autonomous Legal System

The third available representation of international arbitration, defined by Gaillard, as one of ICA understood as an autonomous legal system, opens space for further possible theorization of the role of comparative analysis in legal decision-making. As opposed to the former two representations, it does not legitimize arbitration through a recourse to a national legal order or orders (of the seat or also of enforcement of an award). It rather perceives arbitration as a *sui generis*, intrinsically transnational phenomenon, functioning due to a consensus among the States rather than to the 'isolated will of a given sovereign to accept the existence of this private means of dispute resolution'.[65]

From this perspective the monistic concept of arbitration, based on its primary association with the single legal system of the seat, is characterized as 'increasingly anachronistic'.[66] The Westphalian alternative is, however, equally unsatisfactory, as far as the point of view of the arbitrators is assumed. The pluralistic model offers a sufficient theoretical grounding for validity of arbitration, when it is being assessed from the perspective of an insider of one of the legal systems in

64 Goode (n 45) 30–31.
65 Gaillard (n 42) 35.
66 Ibid. 36.

question (which takes place in particular, as Gaillard argues, in all those cases where the courts' action or assistance is called for, as in attempted commencement of court proceedings despite the arbitration agreement, in undertaking measures reinforcing arbitration, as well as when recognition and enforcement of an award is being sought). For the arbitrators, however, acting as outsiders to those systems (and, indeed, bound not to express an *a priori* preference to one of them), adoption of this representation results in facing a patchwork of competing and occasionally conflicting orders. When approached from the arbitrators' stance, the Westphalian representation turns out to be, at least potentially, dangerously unstable and impractical:

> [w]hen confronted with conflicting views of several legal orders in relation to a given arbitration – one holds the arbitration agreement to be valid, the other considers it void; one claims that the arbitrators lack the required impartiality while the other allows the procedure to continue – the arbitrators cannot simply take account of the plurality of positions. They must make their own determination, either by choosing among the conflicting positions pursuant to a choice of law methodology – with the correlating disadvantage of reducing an inherently international situation into a domestic one, as the choice of law method does – or by resorting to the direct application of substantive rules, which is more likely to take into account the international nature of the situation and the plurality of legal orders that have expressed their views on what they consider to constitute an arbitration worthy of legal protection.[67]

The resulting postulated assumption of the concept of international arbitration as an autonomous legal order finds strong support in its distinct and well-established institutional framework: a network of private centres including highly developed, global leaders and multiple smaller and local organizations. This firmament of international arbitration also encompasses short-lived flashes of ad hoc arbitration, exercised without a formal, administrative support. The general lack of judicial intervention and control over the merits of the awards augments institutional independence of arbitration. In this aspect, the theory of ICA as an autonomous order is coherent with postulates of the institutionalist stream in legal theory. As Henrik Palmer Olsen and Stuart Toddington observe:

> [l]aw … consists not only of rules and decisions, but also of a framework of institutions providing a structure that forms the conditions of its workable existence and acceptance … The *architecture of justice* therefore, refers to the art and technique of a form of institutional design.[68]

67 Ibid. 36–37.

68 Henrik Palmer Olsen and Stuart Toddington, *Architectures of Justice: Legal Theory and the Idea of Institutional Design* (Ashgate 2007) 1.

The distinctive legal network of arbitral institutions worldwide, stably anchored in the New York Convention regime, can be acknowledged as an expression of an emancipated status of ICA. Its practical significance, which has largely led to substituting domestic litigation with arbitration in the field of disputes arisen out of international commercial contracts, is yet another argument in favour of this conceptualization.

Nevertheless, an adoption of the representation of ICA as an autonomous legal order raises two basic questions. The first relates to the source of authority of the arbitrators to perform the described above process of selection of applicable rules from the available range – if they are no longer acting 'from within' a particular legal system. Gaillard invokes in this regard an idea of a collective, 'normative activity of the community of States' (as opposed to the Westphalian multiplicity of coexisting, individual approaches of particular States) – and the concept of such concerted activity of States, developed by legal doctrine since the 1990s, resembles the arguably equally conventional construct of *societas mercatorum*, standing behind the creation of the new *lex mercatoria*.

The second question connected with the transnational, autonomous vision of arbitration is one of the limits of such order. The arbitral activity described above – one of selecting legal standards of reference on an *a casu ad casum* basis – is apparently not limited to substantive law (or rules of law), to which the *voie directe* competence might apply. Gaillard characterizes procedural aspects of arbitration (such as the issue of impartiality of the arbitrators) as susceptible, according to the discussed model, to the same kind of operations – although the suggested recourse to the conflict of laws methodology, traditionally used for finding proper substantive law, might be misleading in this regard.

The rationale offered for recognition and exercising this competence is particularly important in the context of the discussed role of comparative analysis in arbitration, which, according to this representation, seems to find a very broad application. The path to determination of proper substantive law (either through the conflict of laws rules or through *voie directe*, with the latter praised for its higher relevance to cases exceeding the limits of a single domestic legal order) is being apparently extended to the procedural side of arbitration. As a result, such self-legitimizing practice might leave an impression of a bootstrap argument: the discretionary powers of arbitrators related to determination of *lex causae* are generally well-defined in relevant procedural rules and hardly controversial. Analogous competences in regard to shaping arbitral procedure, though, while often liberally granted (where the arbitrators might conduct the proceedings in a way they deem appropriate), do not have to be necessarily considered as detached from influence of any domestic legal system.

Redfern and Hunter address the issue of this, occasionally presented, procedural/substantive theoretical combination by connecting it to the dispute over the delocalized, anational or floating character of arbitration. They observe that the original discussion, vivid in legal theory in the 1980s, referred to delocalization of arbitration in the sense of its procedural release from under the control of *legis loci arbitri*, but over time it had started being extended to substantive issues in arbitration as well:

> [s]omewhat confusingly, the term is now sometimes used to indicate not only detachment from the lex arbitri but also the replacement of a national law governing the substance of the dispute by general principles or some other non-national concept.[69]

Historically, this tendency to blend procedural and substantive aspects in arguments for application of anational rules in international arbitration can be explained through parallel developments of the delocalization doctrine in ICA and the evolution of the new *lex mercatoria* (discussed in detail in the following chapter). Even if they were occasionally (and somewhat optimistically) announced to be intrinsically interconnected, as two sides of the same coin, there is still a strong sense of conceptual and legal separateness of these issues in the arbitral practice. Albert van den Berg describes the difference as

> one of procedure versus substance: the 'anational' award (and hence the 'denationalized' arbitration) concerns the procedural framework of international arbitration; in contrast, concepts such as Lex mercatoria relate to the substance of what is to be decided by the arbitral tribunal.[70]

Consequently, it has been remarked that in arbitration the possible lack of acceptance for delocalization of procedure is not automatically tantamount to analogical lack of recognition for delocalized substantive rules, which can be applied in the form of general principles, *lex mercatoria* or 'international law *per se*'.[71]

On the other hand, the trans- or supranational approach described by Gaillard, based on comparative analysis and hand-picking of relevant rules in both spheres (procedural and that of substantive law) is claimed to reflect the professional sense of adjudicatory independence. This self-defining consciousness is characterized as the 'international arbitrators' strong perception that they do not administer justice on behalf of any given State, but that they nonetheless play a judicial role for the benefit of the international community.'[72]

The question still seems to be open as whether the undisputed and colossal institutional and professional emancipation of international arbitration in the decades after the Second World War does present a sufficient legal ground for

69 Redfern and Hunter (n 56) 90 fn 68.

70 A.J. van den Berg, 'Consolidated Commentary on New York Convention (109 I. Arbitral Award: A-National Award)' *Yearbook Commercial Arbitration* vol XXVII (A.J. van den Berg ed, ICCA 2003) 576.

71 Stephen J. Toope, *Mixed International Arbitration* (Cambridge University Press/ Grotius Publications 1990) 19.

72 Gaillard (n 42) 35.

characterizing arbitration as a completely autonomous legal order, independent from domestic systems. A necessary component of such autonomy, as defined in reference to different concepts of a legal order, reviewed by Jean-Baptiste Racine,[73] is systemic self-sustainability, or the ability to produce and legitimize sources of law for itself, without external endorsement. Such a definition of autonomy of a legal order is also consistent with the Teubnerean concept of a self-reproductive, self referential, autopoietic legal system,[74] inspired by Luhmann's systems theory.

The grounds for stating the systemic autonomy of international arbitration have been initially (though rather untypically), sought in anational, natural law,[75] to further give way to transnational conceptualizations. The latter, based on the majoritarian principle (rather than on a fictitious, unanimous international consensus), are meant to reflect the changing dynamics of national laws and international legal practices better than the traditional conflict of laws method, which might lead to an application of rules exceptional and isolated on a global scale.[76] Such an approach can be arguably interpreted as an attempt to overcome the classic paradox of comparative legal analysis, described as torn between possibly conflicting, universalizing and particularizing tendencies, natural versus positive law or, as Miller and Zumbansen argue, function's abstraction versus embedment in the context.[77]

The study and search for such dominant, global trends in current lawmaking which affect commercial transactions (including for example, as Gaillard points out, regulations on combating bribery or protection of the natural environment) necessarily requires comparative examination. As a result, within this model of ICA, the comparative method is considered to lie at the very core of the interpretive activity of international arbitrators.[78] Rather than aiming at replacing the national orders with a new, universal one, it reaches out to them to seek for repeated patterns: 'the entire philosophy of transnational rules consists in avoiding the situation where solutions that are not sufficiently grounded in comparative law prevail over views that are more generally accepted by the international community.'[79] This approach still seems to predominantly take into account substantive aspects of arbitral application of law, only further (or additionally)

73 Jean-Baptiste Racine, 'Réflexions sur l'autonomie de l'arbitrage commercial international' 3 Rev Arb 305 (2005).

74 Gunther Teubner, *Autopoietic Law: A New Approach to Law and Society* (Walter de Gruyter 1988) 221ff.

75 René David, 'Droit naturel et arbitrage' in *Natural Law and World Law: Essays to Commemorate the Sixtieth Birthday of Kotaro Tanaka* (Yuhikatu 1954).

76 Gaillard (n 42) 48–51.

77 Russell A. Miller and Peer Zumbansen, 'Introduction – Comparative Law as Transnational Law' in *Comparative Law as Transnational Law: A Decade of the German Law Journal* (Russell A. Miller and Peer Zumbansen eds, Oxford University Press 2011), p. 7

78 Emmanuel Gaillard, 'Du bon usage du droit comparé dans l'arbitrage international' 2 Rev Arb (2005).

79 Gaillard (n 42) 50.

radiating onto the sphere of procedural issues. It is also worth emphasizing that in international commercial arbitration the two main aspects of application of law, present in domestic litigation, the procedural and the substantive (understood as *lex causae*) are further split and supplemented by considerations regarding: the law governing the capacity of the parties to conclude an arbitration agreement; the law governing the arbitration agreement and its performance; *lex arbitri* defined as the law governing the existence and proceedings of the arbitral tribunal; the law or rules of law identified as proper *lex contractus* (or *lex causae*); and the law (or, in case of multiple possible locations, laws) governing the recognition and enforcement of the award.[80] This list can be further broadened by the relevant conflict of laws rules.

When treated inclusively and as a complete concept of arbitration, a consistent adoption of its autonomous representation would result in the potential implementation of the comparative method on all these levels of determination and application of law in arbitral proceedings. It should be, however, remarked that – while the modern standard is to allow the parties and arbitrators the widest possible freedom in selecting or drafting the procedural rules for the resolution of their dispute, without facing national courts' intervention – the validity of this very competence is in the end dependant upon proper authorization, provided for by the law of the place of arbitration. While the autonomous standing of international arbitration is still a matter of a debate, there are definitely strong symptoms of what Julian M. Lew characterizes as an increasing emergence of ICA as a *sui iuris* institution, emancipated and irreducible to a mere fulfilment of a mandate granted by specific domestic legal orders.[81]

The comparative method can be thus broadly applied in accordance with all three theoretical representations of ICA. An adoption of a specific approach to arbitration – be it the monolocal, Westphalian or autonomous – exposes particular aspects and consequences of the use of comparative method in exercised legal interpretation. A variety of possible uses for comparative analysis – from providing resources for legal analogy (or rebuttal thereof) to harmonizing interpretation reflects its practicality in the arbitral context. In particular, the last type of application of the comparative method can be seen as a tool for creative input of arbitral decision-making to international jurisprudence. Harmonizing interpretation with a transnational component has been described as a mutual adjustment of statutory interpretation exercised within the legal orders of the involved States in the practice of the domestic courts.[82] What international commercial arbitration further offers is a harmonizing effect in legal interpretation, exercised by means of comparative analysis, and achieved from the outside of approached legal systems,

---

80 Redfern and Hunter (n 56) 78.

81 Julian D.M. Lew, 'Determination of Applicable Substantive Law' 25 Int'l Bus Law (1997).

82 D. Neil MacCormick and Robert S. Summers, *Interpreting Statutes: A Comparative Study* (Ashgate 1991) 330–31.

hence providing a more delocalized, transnational perspective. This effect has been strongly present in ICA practice: as Gabrielle Kaufmann-Kohler notes, 'arbitrators have an inclination to "transnationalise" the rules they apply'.[83]

Demands, which the use of comparative analysis in arbitration poses, also reveal its distinct, hybrid character. They disclose connections (on a professional, cultural and contextual, as well as a legal level) of the arbitral decision-making with the transnational legal setting, as well as with domestic legal orders. Commercial arbitration is not a purely anational and floating legal construct – it is still anchored in the domestic systems in a way that can be characterized as rather transitive than uprooted;[84] extensive use of tools of comparative interpretation reflects this specific *modus operandi*.

83 Gabrielle Kaufmann-Kohler, 'Arbitral Precedent: Dream, Necessity or Excuse?' 23 Arb Int'l (2007) 364.

84 Pierre Bourdieu, 'Foreword' in *Dealing in Virtue: International Commercial Arbitration and the Construction of a Transnational Legal Order* (Yves Dezalay and Bryant G. Garth eds, University of Chicago Press 1996) vii–viii.

Chapter 8
Lex Mercatoria in Arbitration

Lex Mercatoria: The Concept and its Historical Development

The discussion of specific interpretative repertory in ICA would definitely be incomplete without an analysis of the role of the new *lex mercatoria* in arbitral decision-making (and, arguably even more significantly, the critical impact of arbitral case law on the formulation, consolidation and – as some authors would assert – creation of the rules of the New Law Merchant). The relationship between those two spheres has been differently characterized by the commentators – from a perception of their link as necessary and inevitable, through its conceptualization as a pragmatic bond, reinstated if appropriate on an *a casu ad casum* basis, to scepticism in regard to the practical significance of the New Law Merchant.

Application of the *lex mercatoria* principles in arbitral decision-making, seen from the historical perspective, demonstrates how both spheres have been affected by the interaction. The body of the New Law Merchant has been substantially unfolded and expanded by arbitral case law. At the same time, the recurring recourse to *lex mercatoria* influenced interpretive canons in ICA and their formal framework, expressed in the rules of procedure of particular centres. This unique link, while certainly not omnipresent in the arbitral practice, is nevertheless significant and its evolution marks the growing autonomy of both spheres of transnational regulation of modern commerce: the substantive and the procedural.

Lex mercatoria, described as a global law without a State[1] is a set of rules, created by private participants in the cross-border commercial exchange, governing their transactions on a general or specialized (specific to a branch of commerce) level, and observed in a uniform way on a global, or at least regional scale. Whereas the modern *lex mercatoria* can be characterized as the most mature and solidified area of transnational rules, which has also become an inspiration for other fields, such as *lex sportiva*,[2] its status as an independent legal system has been disputed, predominantly from the positions of legal positivism and the traditional theory of the sources of law.[3] The key component and necessary

1 Gunther Teubner, *Global Law without a State* (Dartmouth 1997).

2 Cf. Boris Kolev, 'Lex Sportiva and Lex Mercatoria' 1 ISLJ (2008).

3 Cf. Thomas Carbonneau, 'The Remaking of Arbitration: Design and Destiny' in *Lex Mercatoria and Arbitration* (Thomas Carbonneau ed, Juris 1990); Richard B. Lillich and Charles N. Brower, *International Arbitration in the Twenty-first Century: Towards 'Judicialization' and Uniformity?: Twelfth Sokol Colloquium* (Transnational Publishers 1994).

condition of legitimacy of legal rules according to those approaches – the official origin of the law, which is seen as a direct expression of the sovereign will of the State[4] – is missing or, at best, blurred, if the recourse to international customs is adopted as a legitimizing strategy. *Lex mercatoria* is a transnational construct of private origin. As a result, the dispute about the autonomous status of the New Law Merchant, particularly vivid in the legal doctrine of the late 1980s and 1990s, is still far from being resolved.[5] Its acknowledgement is, however, increasingly frequently advocated from the positions detaching the concept of the law from the sphere of sovereign authority of a State, and encompassing instead a plurality of coexisting orders, functioning rather as normative networks than homogenous, exhaustive and hierarchically complete systems.[6]

As a consequence, the application of *lex mercatoria* principles to the merits of a dispute in arbitral decision-making had been originally least controversial when it resulted from the explicit will of the parties and could have been treated as a specific exercise of the freedom of contract. The selection of such rules, even if their status as law was uncertain, could still have been recognized as a manifestation of the parties' contractual freedom. An often-indicated reason for such choice has been the intent of the parties to minimize the risk of legal uncertainty, resulting from the selection of the domestic law, not fully known to at least one of the contractors, or, even more so, its determination by the arbitral tribunal in the absence of a relevant indication by the parties.

Another ground for selection of uniform transnational rules instead of national law is a possible inadequacy of the latter and its primarily domestic orientation, undesirable in relation to fundamentally international transactions. As Ana M. López Rodríguez remarks, those two aspects reappear in different theories of *lex mercatoria* as their common denominator, which is:

> the affirmation that traditional private international law techniques provide an uncertain legal framework for international transactions, that domestic law does not respond to the changing needs of international contract law and that, in consequence, substantive law solutions that emerge from the practice and respond to the interests of businessmen are preferable.[7]

---

4 Cf. John Austin et al., *Lectures on Jurisprudence, or, The Philosophy of Positive Law* (3rd edn, John Murray 1869); H.L.A. Hart, *The Concept of Law* (with 'Postscript' ed. by P. Bulloch and J. Raz, Clarendon Press 1997).

5 Gralf-Peter Calliess, 'Reflexive Transnational Law: The Privatisation of Civil Law and the Civilisation of Private Law' 23 Zeitschrift für Rechtssoziologie (2002).

6 André de Albuquerque Cavalcanti Abbud, 'Fifty Years in Five? The Brazilian Approach to the New York Convention', in Interpretation of Law in the Global World: From Particularism to a Universal Approach (Joanna Jemielniak and Przemyslaw Miklaszewicz eds, Springer 2010) 174–75.

7 Ana M. López Rodríguez, *Lex Mercatoria and Harmonization of Contract Law in the EU* (Djof 2003) 85 fn 3.

Such justification mirrors the rationales frequently offered for selection of arbitration instead of litigation before domestic courts by parties to international contracts (see Chapter 1). As in the case of arbitration clauses, a preference is given to a system perceived as more neutral (as it is not directly connected with any given State) and more specialized (thus better befitting the particularities of cross-border contracting). This analogy requires, however, a careful delineation of the borders between those two phenomena. The difference is, as Albert van den Berg observes,

> one of procedure versus substance: the 'anational' award (and hence the 'denationalized' arbitration) concerns the procedural framework of international arbitration; in contrast, concepts such as *Lex mercatoria* relate to the substance of what is to be decided by the arbitral tribunal.[8]

In the absence of relevant indication by the parties themselves, *lex mercatoria* has also been increasingly invoked as rules of law applicable to the merits of the dispute, on the ground of its determination as such, exercised by an arbitral tribunal or a domestic court.[9]

The legitimacy of *lex mercatoria* as a set of rules lacking the official State endorsement has been sought in its functioning as customs observed by the international community of commercial actors. Instead of States, the subjects involved in creating its body are merchants, or, rather, a number of different 'merchant communities', engaged in international transactions. Taken together, they act as a global *societas mercatorum* – a society of merchants – which is an operative legal fiction, comparable to such notions as 'a lawmaker' or 'an international community of states'. Even though the concept of *societas mercatorum* denotes in fact a set of different groups without a uniform, formal bond, it has been argued that its internal heterogeneity is not that distant from an organization of a society within a nation State, which also encloses diversified social groups.[10]

This bottom-up, self-regulatory activity[11] of the international business community has been characterized by Teubner as 'double taboo-breaking'. It undermines the nation-States' law-making monopoly, outside the traditional mechanisms of State control and endorsement. It also successfully functions and is

8 Albert Jan van den Berg, 'Consolidated Commentary on New York Convention (109 I. Arbitral Award: A-National Award)' *Yearbook Commercial Arbitration* vol XXVIII (ICCA 2003), 576.

9 López Rodríguez (n 7) 112–43.

10 Berthold Goldman, 'Lex Mercatoria' 3 Forum internationale (1983) 23.

11 Filip De Ly, 'Lex Mercatoria (New Law Merchant): Globalisation and International Self-Regulation' in *Rules and Networks: The Legal Culture of Global Business Transactions* (Richard Appelbaum et al. eds, Hart 2001) 159.

being applied without an official authorization by the States concerned.[12] Filip De Ly shares this stance, stating, in reference to empirical data offered by Freyhold and Gessner, that

> [i]nternational business law traditionally was based on a paradigm of control by government regulation consisting of national rules. In an international setting, conflict rules had to determine which national rules had to be applied. These conflict rules are also to a large extent of national origin … This whole process of national rules of jurisdiction, national conflict rules and national substantive rules nationalises international adjudication … [I]n practice one notes that often and in many countries a homeward trend may be noticed in the adjudication of international business disputes.[13]

De Ly presents a nuanced view in regard to the status of harmonized instruments of international business law in this context.[14] The outcomes of unification efforts by intergovernmental or transnational bodies (such as UNIDROIT and UNCITRAL) are, as he observes, diversified, and do not necessarily subvert the traditional doctrine of States' control.

There are both 'hard law' instruments, such as international conventions, as well as 'soft' ones, such as model laws, which acquire binding force through the mechanisms of States' authorization (ratification, implementation into the domestic order). There is, however, a plethora of forms of regulatory harmonization, such as model contracts and contractual clauses, private codifications and guidelines, the proliferation of which has been indicated as a symptom of loss of the monopoly of the States in this sphere. De Ly also notes instances of a more subtle, indirect influence of harmonized instruments beyond the States' control, in cases in which their provisions are applied not due to their formal binding force, but because of sheer persuasive authority.

In regard to *lex mercatoria*, this specific origin – private, but frequently official, institutionalized, and not befitting the traditional mechanisms of States-endorsed law-making, is expressed in its common characterization as transnational law. As opposed to international law, created between the nations, the prefix 'trans-', as Gralf-Peter Calliess remarks, indicates an activity reaching 'across, beyond, through' boundaries of the States.[15] The modern Law Merchant, as an outcome of concerted endeavours and practices adopted voluntarily by private participants to international commerce, has also been described as a revival of former, similar

---

12 Teubner (n 1) 8.

13 De Ly (n 11) 159.

14 Ibid. 160.

15 Calliess (n 5) 186.

concepts, such as the Phoenician, Egyptian and Greek trade customs,[16] Roman *ius gentium*,[17] and particularly the medieval European *lex mercatoria*.[18]

This last set of rules, recognized uniformly across Europe in major market cities, was adopted by merchants and applied by their own, specialized commercial tribunals, which allowed them to avoid legal uncertainty resulting from fragmentation of laws in feudal Europe, as well as to overcome limitations on transfers of capital and transmissibility of property, and escape the arbitrariness of decisions of local lords.[19] A. Claire Cutler observes that

> [w]hat is distinctive about medieval law merchant order is the essential self-regulatory nature of the merchant community in both law-creation (subjects and sources) and dispute resolution. This in turn reflects the more general autonomy of the merchant class from the feudal class system: the law merchant order occupied a space external to the local political economy and feudal mode of production. Even more importantly, the law merchant created property rights and entitlements that were more consistent with property relations that would later be associated with capitalism.[20]

This set of trade customs and the accompanying functioning of independent merchants' tribunals, started in the eleventh century, survived until the end of the Middle Ages and the start of the early modern era, and was suppressed by the consolidation of nation States, which assumed centralized control over law-making processes and commercial exchange. Its specific character as a private legal arrangement for commercial matters, surpassing the parochialisms of local laws, not only marks a period of an early, selective legal globalization (or, rather, regionalization) of trade regulations. It has also been described as a predecessor to contemporary processes of grass-root harmonization of rules governing international commercial exchange. Recurring contractual references to uniform customs of international trade after World War II, which was the first phase of the development of the New Law Merchant, were thus interpreted as a 'resuscitation' of 'a venerable old lady' – a revival of a specific concept of law-making well known to European practice.[21]

---

16 Grady Miller, *The Legal and Economic Basis of International Trade* (Quorum Books 1996).

17 Goldman (n 10) 3.

18 Klaus Peter Berger, 'The New Law Merchant and the Global Market Place – A Twenty-First Century View of Transnational Commercial Law' in *The Practice of Transnational Law* (Klaus Peter Berger ed, Kluwer Law International 2001) 3.

19 Harold J. Berman and Colin Kaufman, 'Law of International Commercial Transactions (Lex Mercatoria)' 19 Harv Int'l LJ (1978).

20 A. Claire Cutler, *Private Power and Global Authority: Transnational Merchant Law in the Global Political Economy* (Cambridge University Press 2003) 110–11.

21 Goldman (n 11) 3.

The renewed postwar interest in international trade customs which sought to bind participants to the cross-border exchange beyond the level of domestic laws was as much a result of commercial developments and progressing globalization of trade as it was an academic undertaking. In 1956 Berthold Goldman famously invoked an example of the Suez Canal Company as an intrinsically international undertaking, consciously planned as not belonging exclusively to either Egyptian, British or French legal domain. The rapidly increasing volume of global trade, the expanding number of participants and the new regional dynamics in the following decades affected the growing recourse to international trade customs in private transactions. The forms of such recourse are further discussed below.

Sources of *Lex Mercatoria*

In the discussion about the (medieval and modern) *lex mercatoria*, its origins as spontaneously emergent mercantile customs have been usually emphasized. The customary character of the New Law Merchant has also been frequently invoked as a key argument supporting the thesis about the autonomous character of this regulatory order.[22] While application of *lex mercatoria* in arbitral decision-making has been indeed often legitimized in this way, starting from the 1950s,[23] the legal and commercial practice, as well as representations of the New Law Merchant formulated subsequently by legal theory, offer currently a more diversified conceptual repertoire.

Among the new sources of *lex mercatoria* (or, alternatively, sources of knowledge thereof – if a reductionist perspective, limiting it to international trade customs, was to be adopted), the key role of international commercial arbitration has been widely recognized. Horacio A. Grigera Naón, commenting on modern theories which advocate the New Law Merchant, points out that they

> strongly express the place of international commercial arbitration as regards its inception, effectiveness and development. International arbitration becomes practically an independent source of law as autonomous arbitrators decide on the meaning and interpretation of contractual transactions submitted to them and on the existence, content, scope and application of usages, general legal principles and customs which might have a decisive impact on the final outcome of the dispute as they determine it. Through their action, a body of principles and rules belonging to an anational merchant community which claims a sociological and juridical existence independent from State communities establishes its existence,

---

22 Julian D.M. Lew, *Applicable Law in International Commercial Arbitration. A Study in Commercial Arbitration Awards* (Oceana Publications/Sijthoff & Noordhoff 1978).

23 Joanna Jemielniak, 'Legitimization Arguments in the Lex Mercatoria Cases' 18 IJSL (2005) 203.

> validity and effective application without State support as an unexpected derivation of the maxim 'Qui eligit iud[i]cem, eligit ius'.[24]

While the critical influence of arbitral case law on the progress and expansion of the New Law Merchant certainly goes beyond the positivist law-making framework, possibly 'saved' through a stricter adherence to a legal fiction of uniformly acknowledged, global merchants' customs, it also – perhaps paradoxically – refutes another traditional argument of the rules of the new *lex mercatoria* as being too vague and undetermined to be efficiently applied.[25]

The increasingly definite and specific set of principles, characterized as the New Law Merchant, has influenced national legal systems: as De Ly remarks, in such areas as arbitration laws, the domestic regulatory regimes have been affected by the popularity of transnational sources of substantive rules.[26] For Gunther Teubner the actual significance of international commercial customs *sensu stricto* is secondary, as the spontaneous harmonization effect is achieved predominantly by the means of contractual practice (with repeated, standardized patterns) and arbitral case law.[27] However, a mediating view that general conditions, standard terms and model contracts can be at least to some extent a formal expression of international customs (and not merely their replacement or source) can also be put forward.

Model clauses and standard contracts as tools of legal convergence for international business transactions have also been undervalued by the proponents of positivist approaches, as purely private endeavours. They have been treated as individual (even if to some extent concerted) exercises of party autonomy – based on isolated, pragmatic, *a casu ad casum* decisions of the parties, and not as contributions to the emergence of some regulatory order.[28] The limitations of this way of proliferation of contractual standards have also been indicated by the promoters of harmonization. As Michael Joachim Bonell points out when discussing the origins of the UNIDROIT project of comparative restatement of contract law (the three editions of which he coordinated), model contracts and clauses endorsed by private enterprises and trade associations suffer from a 'legitimacy deficit'

> in the sense that, even where they do succeed in becoming generally accepted within the respective trade sectors, they may come into conflict with the basic

24 Horacio A. Grigera Naón, *Choice-of-Law Problems in International Commercial Arbitration* (Mohr Siebeck 1992) 31.

25 Richard J. Howarth, 'Lex Mercatoria: Can General Principles of Law Govern International Commercial Contracts' 10 Canta L Rev (2004).

26 Filip De Ly, *International Business Law and Lex Mercatoria* (North-Holland 1992) 249–52.

27 Gunther Teubner, 'Global Bukowina: Legal Pluralism in the World Society' in *Global Law without a State* (Gunther Teubner ed, Dartmouth 1997) 15.

28 De Ly (n 11) 160–61.

> principles and values adopted by domestic legislators and anyhow fail to meet the 'democracy' test, i.e. are not the result of a balancing of conflicting interests typical of legislative process.[29]

Bonell further argues that even those model clauses and contracts which are an outcome of works by truly transnational non-governmental organizations, such as the ICC's INCOTERMS and Uniform Customs and Practice for Documentary Credit (UCP), do not fully escape criticism based on legitimacy grounds and require a validating recourse to some external regulatory order:

> [i]ndeed, these instruments, though on account of their origin more balanced in content, still presuppose a more general regulatory system to refer to for the purpose of settling the questions they do not expressly address and to establish the conditions and limits of their validity.[30]

These issues, as well as the still-existing indeterminacy of some areas of the *lex mercatoria*, accompanied by the pressing needs of commercial practice, were subsequently addressed by a number of codifying initiatives. The advancing expression and systematization of the New Law Merchant principles in arbitral case law have been gradually supplemented by a wave of transnational, non-legislative, soft, restatement-type codifications, initiated since the 1980s. Two of them can be characterized as particularly prominent. Publication of the first edition of the UNIDROIT Principles of International Commercial Contracts in 1994 was perceived as a turning point in the process of consolidation of the body of *lex mercatoria*.[31] In 1995, this initiative was followed by an issuance of a regional instrument – the first part of the Principles of European Contract Law (PECL), drafted by the Commission on European Contract Law (with the second part published in 1999 and the third in 2002).

The UNIDROIT drafters were aware of the challenges of proposing a soft instrument, drafted outside the sphere of control, but also outside the authorization of States. As the Governing Council of UNIDROIT noted in the Introduction to the 1994 edition, it was 'fully conscious of the fact that the Principles, which do not involve the endorsement of Governments, are not a binding instrument and that in consequence their acceptance will depend upon their persuasive authority.'[32]

While not formally subscribing to the New Law Merchant doctrine (and, as seen above, expressing their reservations in this regard), the authors of the

---

29 Michael Joachim Bonell, *An International Restatement of Contract Law: The UNIDROIT Principles of International Commercial Contracts* (Martinus Nijhoff 2009) 18–19.

30 Ibid. 19–20.

31 Michael Joachim Bonell, 'Do We Need a Global Commercial Code' 106 Dick L Rev (2001) 97.

32 UNIDROIT Principles of International Commercial Contracts (International Institute for the Unification of Private Law (UNIDROIT 1994) viii.

UNIDROIT Principles, as well as those of PECL, nevertheless provided that these instruments may be applied when the parties agree that their contract shall be governed by 'general principles of law', 'the *lex mercatoria*' or the like.[33] For Joseph Lookofsky this lack of explicit reference to the role of this instrument as a persuasive source of internationally accepted principles of contract law (which he sees as its essential function) is notable.[34]

According to Berger, while both those restatements adopt a deliberately cautious stance and

> intentionally refrain from any statement concerning the existence of a transnational economic law as an independent legal order, both projects have at least indirect connection with the lex mercatoria doctrine. They furnish proof that transnational contract law is open to a new and innovative method of codification.[35]

Berger further suggests that the New Law Merchant (*sensu largo*) is a field in which two significant, contradictory tendencies can be observed. On one side, the criticism of the *lex mercatoria*'s nebulous constitution and insufficiently certain content can be seen as the driving force of the transnational codification undertakings. On the other, it is often the relative openness and flexibility of the New Law Merchant principles which can be perceived as its major advantage. The quickly changing demands of international commerce do not necessarily call for precise, detailed and closed rules, but rather for general and adaptive ones, which can be further developed and explicated in adjudication.

The successful accomplishments and continued codification efforts certainly significantly contributed to transnational law reaching the mature stage, and facilitated the move of the gravity centre in the discussion on the New Law Merchant from '*lex mercatoria*: yes or no?' to '*lex mercatoria*: when and how?'.[36] The growing significance of the UNIDROIT Principles (often cautiously referred to as a project not creating or introducing, but affirming '*concepts already in the lex mercatoria*'[37]) in arbitration practice has also been acknowledged. This instrument, characterized by Yves Fortier as the 'new new *lex mercatoria*', has been praised as providing the much-needed practical certainty and order to this

33 UNIDROIT Principles 1994, 2004 and 2010, preamble; Principles of European Contract Law, Art. 1:101 (3)(a).

34 Joseph Lookofsky, 'The Limits of Commercial Contract Freedom: Under the UNIDROIT Restatement and Danish Law' 46 Am J Comp L (1998) 486.

35 Klaus Peter Berger, *The Creeping Codification of the Lex Mercatoria* (Kluwer Law International 1999) 4.

36 Felix Dasser, *Internationale Schiedsgerichte und lex mercatoria: Rechtsvergleichender Beitrag zur Diskussion ber ein nicht-staatliches Handelsrecht* (Schulthess 1989) 296.

37 Charles Molineaux, 'Applicable Law in Arbitration' 1 Journal of World Investment (2000) 130.

area, but has also been frequently criticized for being overly general and blurred.[38] Along with PECL, the UNIDROIT Principles, which can be treated as a verifiable point of reference in cases requiring application of transnational rules, have also become increasingly referred to by the domestic courts. As Mads Bryde Andersen demonstrates on the example of Nordic countries, in some States a recourse to those instruments comes very naturally, being consistent with regional legal culture (such as the Scandinavian pragmatic approach to contract law).[39]

However, in recognition of the variety of the *lex mercatoria* sources (supplemented with comparative legal analysis, separate from arbitral awards – which might lead to conceptual objections regarding the criteria of distinction), a method of codification alternative to that exercised by UNIDROIT drafters has also been proposed. Instead of a transnational restatement, heavily based on comparative analysis of contract law regimes, Klaus Peter Berger forwards a project of a looser, less integrated 'creeping codification'.[40] The proposed outcome resembles rather a thesaurus-like set of principles than a homogenous, uniform legal instrument. Berger envisions this undertaking as an open-ended list of principles, extracted from diverse sources of the New Law Merchant and accompanied by relevant descriptive and explanatory notes. As opposed to instruments such as UNIDROIT Principles and PECL, 'creeping codification' is 'intended to avoid the "static element" characteristic of other approaches and to provide the openness and flexibility required in order to take account of the rapid development of international trade and commerce.'[41] The flexible, expanding character of this project will thus, Berger argues, make it less rigid than the methodologically strict, unifying codifications, and help to keep track of changing contractual and arbitral practice related to international commercial transactions.[42] The 'creeping codification' method has been applied by Berger in the creation and operations of the CENTRAL Transnational Database, established to serve as a platform for the development of the growing list of the *lex mercatoria* principles.[43]

The Role of Arbitration

The progressing consolidation of the new *lex mercatoria* has been largely achieved thanks to arbitral case law, through which the principles of the New Law Merchant

---

38 L. Yves Fortier, 'The New, New Lex Mercatoria, or, Back to the Future' 17 Arb Int'l (2001).

39 Mads Bryde Andersen, 'Pragmatism in Nordic Contract Law' in *Unification and Harmonization of International Commercial Law* (Morten M. Fogt ed, Kluwer Law International 2012) 202.

40 Berger (n 35).

41 Ibid. 192.

42 Ibid. 6.

43 Klaus Peter Berger, 'Lex Mercatoria Online: The CENTRAL Transnational Law Database at www. tldb. de' 18 Arb Int'l (2002).

have been explored, expressed and unfolded. This has been happening practically from the beginning of the *lex mercatoria* revival in the 'oil cases' in the 1950s and 1960s. The undisputed key role of arbitration in ascertaining and expanding the content of general commercial customs has led some commentators to proposing a theory that the New Law Merchant is not an autonomous order, consisting of substantive rules, but rather a method of adjudication, characteristic to arbitral decision-making.

According to this perspective, as Emmanuel Gaillard argues, what makes arbitral decision-making, invoking *lex mercatoria*, characteristic is the specific use of comparative method with a purposive orientation – so as to deduce what the most universally accepted rule, available as a ground for the decision, would be. *Lex mercatoria*, so approached, would then function as an outcome of distillation from relevant rules of all legal orders potentially involved in particular cases.[44] This theory rejects the representations of *lex mercatoria* as a system of rules belonging neither to the domestic orders nor to the realm of public international law. It also in practice abandons the concept of *societas mercatorum* as the source of its legitimization.

This 'functional approach', as Gaillard remarks, enables arbitrators to always identify a rule applicable to any claim forwarded by the parties – which is its advantage in comparison with lists of principles.[45] It seems, however, that it also reduces the phenomenon of the New Law Merchant, to a large extent shaped by multiplicity and heterogeneity of its sources, to an operative ICA technique. It is also worth noticing, that the comparative analysis has been a cornerstone of the UNIDROIT Principles drafting process (and also a point of their – and other restatements' – critique for offering merely 'comparative snapshots'[46]). As emphasized in the Introduction to the 1994 edition, in the intention of the authors:

> [f]or the most part the UNIDROIT Principles reflect concepts to be found in many, if not all, legal systems. Since however the Principles are intended to provide a system of rules especially tailored to the needs of international commercial transactions, they also embody what are perceived to be the best solutions, even if still not yet generally adopted.[47]

As already mentioned above, the usefulness of the UNIDROIT Principles in cases involving application of the new *lex mercatoria* has also already been recognized in the growing body of arbitral awards.[48]

---

44 Emmanuel Gaillard, 'Thirty Years of Lex Mercatoria: Towards the Selective Application of Transnational Rules' 10 ICSID Review (1995).

45 Emmanuel Gaillard, 'Transnational Law: A Legal System or a Method of Decision Making?' 17 Arb Int'l (2001) 62.

46 Berger (n 35) 208.

47 UNIDROIT Principles of International Commercial Contracts (International Institute for the Unification of Private Law (UNIDROIT 2004) xv.

48 Molineaux (n 37).

This multiplicity, heterogeneity and complex interconnections between different sources of *lex mercatoria* have been an object of vivid discussion. First, the very status of all the non-customary expressions of the Law Merchant as its sources has been undermined. The *sensu stricto* definition of *lex mercatoria* would thus require referencing them as merely sources of knowledge of the *lex mercatoria* – and not sources *thereof*. If such a reductionist was not adopted, the inclusion of specific types of sources into the body of the New Law Merchant still remains disputable. As Calliess remarks in the context of the discussion on *lex mercatoria* as the most prominent example of transnational law, besides sources purely transnational, not directly endorsed by the States, some commentators also qualify as part of the New Law Merchant public international law instruments (such as the CISG) and supranational European law, as the EU and EC treaties and EC regulations (but not the EC directives which require domestic implementation).[49] While criticized as a flaw of the *lex mercatoria*, augmenting its already fuzzy character, this diversity of sources, as well as the relative openness and plasticity of some of them, has also been perceived as its strength, enabling its flexible operations and adaptability to the quickly evolving demands of international trade.

Lex Mercatoria in Arbitration – a Historical Perspective

Arbitrators resolving cases which require application of transnational principles face not only the issue of their proper identification and construction, but also finding adequate justification for such application. This is particularly visible in the situations where application of the New Law Merchant is not a result of choice by the parties, but is determined by the tribunal itself. The multiplicity of its sources, reflecting the variety of directions in which it develops, makes this task additionally demanding. Space for application of the *lex mercatoria* principles has been, however, recently relatively liberally provided by the regulatory framework of arbitration, with some notable exceptions, such as the CIETAC Rules. This state has been achieved as a result of several decades of application of transnational rules on contractual relationships in arbitral decision-making and the evolution of arbitral case law in this regard is worth consideration.

The beginnings of the recent *lex mercatoria* revival can be sought in the postwar contractual practice which emerged in the agreements on Western investments in the countries of the Persian Gulf, concluded with local partners for the extracting and distribution of oil. Parties to such contracts, aiming at avoiding an engagement of the Shari'a-based laws and judicial systems of the place of performance, opted instead for arbitration as a method of dispute resolution and for uniform principles of international commerce as the substantive rules governing the contract – with the latter being, at least at first, not directly indicated. Such pioneering attempts were made already in 1951:

---

49 Horn, after Calliess (n 5) 3.

> Art. 17 of the oil concession agreements between Petroleum Development Ltd. and the Sheikh of Abu Dhabi established that 'the Ruler and the Company both declare that they intend to execute this Agreement in a spirit of good intentions and integrity and to interpret it in a reasonable manner [...]'. When a dispute arose, it was held in an ad hoc award that 'the terms of this Clause invite, indeed prescribe the application of principles rooted in the good sense and common practice of the generality of civilized nations, a sort of "modern law of nature"'.[50]

Application of the *lex mercatoria* principles by arbitral tribunals in such cases was thus based on the assumed recognition of the choice by the parties – even if such choice was not explicitly formulated. It was also in this period frequently augmented by axiological arguments. In the quite extensive repertory invoked as grounds for such references, values can be identified as appealing to the sense of universality (justice, equity, properness) but also to properties shared not commonly but exclusively (as being categorized as 'civilized'). Another axiological strategy is an occasional legitimization through local and specific values (the welfare of trade in a certain region or area of industry).[51]

In *Petroleum Development Ltd v Sheikh of Abu Dhabi*,[52] the ad hoc tribunal treated the contractual clause, setting an intended standard of performance as goodwill and integrity and calling for reasonable interpretation, as a sufficient ground for determining that the common reason required the application of principles shared by 'civilized nations'. Analogically, in the *Sapphire International Petroleums v NIOC*[53] ad hoc award, the tribunal invoked reason and acknowledgment of the rules applied by 'civilized nations' as key arguments. It is worth noting that the same experience of *lex mercatoria*-based case law in the 1950s and 1960s, which has led part of the Western legal doctrine to welcome the re-emergence of the universal merchants' law, in the view of Islamic commentators has led the local parties to a deep mistrust towards what has been perceived as a neocolonial approach, seeking enforcement of values which were one-sidedly preferred. It has also been indicated as contributing to the reluctant stance and late accession of the Islamic States to the New York Convention regime (see Chapter 6).

From the 1970s, references to values, if they appear in *lex mercatoria*-based awards, seem exceptional and are used rather indirectly and in a supportive role. The arbitrators' avoidance in *Norsolor* to justify their decision on awarding equitable damages by an express recourse to equity is quite illustrative in this regard. Instead, they invoked the principle of good faith, legitimized comparatively and belonging to the common core of legal systems, as the main ground for the

50 López Rodríguez (n 7) 113.

51 Jemielniak (n 23) 201.

52 *Petroleum Development Ltd v Sheikh of Abu Dhabi* Ad Hoc Award, International Law Reports 18 (1951).

53 *Sapphire International Petroleums v NIOC*, International Law Reports 35 (1967).

award.[54] It can also be assumed that the frequent recourse to values at the earlier stage of development of the *lex mercatoria*-based case law was one of the factors that induced the recurring critique of application of the New Law Merchant in arbitration as hardly distinguishable from equity (see below).

A recourse to the *lex mercatoria* rules on the basis of explicit choice made by the parties seems to have been the most common and least controversial ground for its application. Its recognition by international instruments, national laws on arbitration and rules of procedure of arbitral institutions has been readily welcomed by many commentators, as,

> [u]nless they are vested with the powers of amiable composition, arbitrators are generally considered to be bound by the substantive rules contractually designated by the parties. In selecting such substantive rules, the parties may refer to a national law or laws or to anational rules.[55]

The consequences of a disregard for the parties' choice and the issue of supplementary or corrective role of the *lex mercatoria* were an object of analysis in *Chromalloy Aeroservices v the Arab Republic of Egypt*.[56] An Egyptian court decided to set aside an award due to what it acknowledged as a disregard by an arbitral tribunal for the explicit intent of the parties. The vacated award, invoking the New Law Merchant principles, was nevertheless successfully enforced by a US District Court, which did not find sufficient grounds for refusal of enforcement and stated that '*as a matter of US law, the award is proper*'. It also rejected an argument of international comity, through which the recognition of an Egyptian judgment was sought, by stating that giving effect to this decision would contravene the 'US public policy in favour of final and binding arbitration'.[57]

The arguments of the *lex mercatoria*-based adjudication being nothing more than *amiable composition*, but exercised without specific authorization, had also been recurrently raised, particularly in the years preceding solidification of the New Law Merchant through codifications. In the already-mentioned *Pabalk Ticaret Limited Sirketi v Norsolor SA* the ICC arbitrators faced the problem of inability to determine

54 *Pabalk Ticaret Limited Sirketi v Norsolor SA* ICC Award No. 3131 of 26 October 1979, in *Yearbook Commercial Arbitration* vol IX (P. Sanders ed, Kluwer Law International 1984) 109, 110.

55 Guillermo Aguillar Alvarez, 'To What Extent Do Arbitrators in International Cases Disregard the Bag and Baggage of National Systems?' in *International Dispute Resolution: Towards an International Arbitration Culture*, ICCA Congress Series 8 (Seoul 1996) (A.J. van den Berg ed, Kluwer Law International 1996).

56 *Chromalloy Aeroservices Inc v The Arab Republic of Egypt* (District Court of District of Columbia, July 1996) in *Yearbook Commercial Arbitration* vol XII (A.J. van den Berg ed, Kluwer Law International 1997).

57 Cf. also Claudia Alfons, *Recognition and Enforcement of Annulled Foreign Arbitral Awards: An Analysis of the Legal Framework and Its Interpretation in Case Law and Literature* (Peter Lang 2010) 93.

the will of the parties in regard to proper substantive law. They thus decided to apply *lex mercatoria*, instead of any domestic rules, to the merits of the dispute. As a consequence, a recourse to the Austrian court was sought by Norsolor. The court of the first instance shared the opinion that '[t]he arbitrators, who were not entitled to act as "amiables compositeurs", did not apply French or Turkish law but, referring to "the principle of good faith which inspires the international lex mercatoria", awarded damages on the basis of equity.'[58] The Vienna Court of Appeal shared this opinion, and upheld that by applying *lex mercatoria*, characterized as '*world law of questionable validity*' ('*ein Weltrecht von fraglicher Geltung*'[59]), to the merits of the dispute, the arbitrators exceeded their discretionary powers. The Supreme Court, however, did not share this stance and decided that '[a]ccording to the opinion of this Court the application of equity (*die Anwendung billigen Ermessens*) by the arbitral tribunal without special authorization of the parties does not involve a transgression of its competence.'[60] While acknowledging the validity of the arbitral award, the Supreme Court thus avoided assuming a conclusive position on the issue of status of the New Law Merchant as an autonomous legal order, even though – as Werner Melis postulated – '*it would have been desirable*'.[61]

The use of equity arguments might no longer be needed to such an extent to support the *lex mercatoria*-based arbitral decision-making, as the regulatory framework of arbitral institutions and domestic laws on arbitration, including legislation based on UNCITRAL Model Law, frequently allows for its application through the recognition of the rules of law (and not only law) as standards which the tribunal might determine as appropriate. Such formulation has been generally interpreted as an opening of the 'front door' to applying non-national rules, even if their status as an '*established and autonomous system of law*' is being disputed.[62] *Amiable composition* authorization is thus not technically necessary (or desired) as a loophole for application of the New Law Merchant to a particular case. The distinction between the two methods has also been formulated as based on the character of the applied standards (external and pre-established in case of *lex mercatoria*; internal and individualized in *amiable composition*).

Opinions about the difference between those two methods being too blurred are, however, still voiced. As Pierre Mayer remarks,

> [c]onscientious arbitrators will obviously do their utmost to ensure that their decision is made in accordance with the law governing their contract. Their

58 Oberster Gerichtshof (Supreme Court), 18 November 1982, in *Yearbook Commercial Arbitration* vol IX (P. Sanders ed, Kluwer Law International 1984) 159.

59 Werner Melis, 'Note to the Austrian Supreme Court Decision' in *Yearbook Commercial Arbitration* vol IX (P. Sanders ed, Kluwer Law International 1984), 160.

60 Ibid. 160.

61 Ibid. 163.

62 Alan Redfern and Martin Hunter, *Law and Practice of International Commercial Arbitration* (Sweet & Maxwell 2004) 118.

> professional conscience will demand no less; and they will not decide *ex aequo et bono* without the express authorisation of the parties. But if the law governing the contract consists of those rules or principles which the arbitrators consider most appropriate, and which may conveniently be labelled as part of the *lex mercatoria*, those arbitrators are in effect free to decide in accordance with what they consider to be just and equitable, whilst purporting to decide in accordance with legal rules.[63]

This issue is further addressed in the following chapter.

It is worth noting that the situation addressed by the arbitrators, and later on by the courts in Norsolor – of the application of the *lex mercatoria* rules as a sole ground for the resolution of the case – is relatively rare. Transnational principles are rather invoked along with the rules of the domestic legal order, determined as *lex causae*. According to Marc Blessing, such hybrid references are becoming an increasingly common contractual practice, reflecting explicit preferences of the parties.[64] Determination of proper law as a combination of domestic rules and *lex mercatoria* principles might also be an effect of exercise of discretionary powers by the arbitral tribunal in the absence of relevant choice by the parties.

Alan Redfern's remarks that the proper substantive law in arbitration may not necessarily be a domestic law, but also international law, a mix of national and international rules, or even an assemblage of rules of law known as international trade law, transnational law, the 'modern law merchant' (the so-called *lex mercatoria*) or by some other convenient title',[65] can be supplemented by an observation that a recourse to a combination of domestic law and *lex mercatoria* is also practised. It is possible as well to apply as proper substantive law an international legal instrument, supplemented by domestic law and *lex mercatoria* rules, as in the Award No. 97/2002, rendered by the International Arbitration Court of the Chamber of Commerce and Industry of the Russian Federation.[66]

Notably, in section 3.2 of the award (*Applicable law*) the Arbitration Court decided that the case should be resolved on the basis of the CISG, with the gap-filling role ascribed to the domestic civil law only ('*[i]ssues not settled in the CISG or only partially settled in the CISG should be governed by the Russian Federation Civil Code*'[67]). However, in the final part of the award the Court, while considering the issue of the wronged party contributing to the damage, besides

---

63 Pierre Mayer, 'The UNIDROIT Principles in Contemporary Contract Practice' in *ICC Bulletin Special Supplement: UNIDROIT Principles of International Commercial Contracts – Reflections on their Use in International Arbitration* (2002) 111.

64 Marc Blessing, 'Choice of Substantive Law in International Arbitration' 14 J Int'l Arb (1997).

65 Redfern and Hunter (n 62) 2.

66 Arbitral Award No. 97/2002, International Arbitration Court of the Chamber of Commerce and Industry of the Russian Federation.

67 Ibid. sec 3.2.

those two sources invoked also the UNIDROIT Principles: '[w]hen evaluating the actions of the [Buyer], based on Articles 74 and 77 CISG, the Tribunal took into account the provisions of the UNIDROIT Principles of international commercial contracts'.[68]

It subsequently used a sole legitimization argument based on the merits and scope of regulation ('[The UNIDROIT Principles] set forth the general rules for international commercial contracts'[69]), but did not discuss either the formal status of the Principles or their relation to the CISG. It also did not use the term '*lex mercatoria*'. Such strategy seems emblematic: a transnational instrument is naturally included in the legal analysis of an international transaction, but it is done discreetly and carefully, without adopting a stance as to its status and hierarchical position in relation to other sources of applicable rules.

This cautious approach can be seen not only as a way to avoid the dispute on the status of *lex mercatoria* as the law, which in the discussed case was not addressed through the, now recurrent in the rules of procedure of arbitral institutions, '*rules of law*' formulation. The arbitrators applied the arbitration law of the Russian Federation, which directed them to application to the substance of the dispute of law (and not rules thereof), to be determined on the basis of conflict of laws rules, the tribunal deemed appropriate. The arbitrators also impliedly introduced the UNIDROIT Principles as an instrument, the function of which in this case was channelling legal interpretation of the officially invoked sources of the law.

The activity of arbitrators applying *lex mercatoria* in addition to domestic (or domestic and international) rules, particularly in the absence of choice by the parties and based on their own decision, has been an object of a critique. Arguments of legal indeterminacy and unpredictability of results in such cases were met with an equally energetic response by Blessing:

> [w]e have heard criticisms from numerous scholars taking the view that such a dual reference would only complicate matters, would provide uncertainty and thus should rather be avoided, giving preference to one clear national legal system to prevail. However, those scholars have either never had a single arbitration to adjudicate where these issues were at the heart of the dispute, or else they have not learned to realize that local or national perceptions and laws are often shortsighted, engineered under a purely local focus and do not deserve to be of an authoritative nature in a large international context.[70]

Arbitrators who are to apply a combination of *lex mercatoria* with other types of rules face the issue of defining the main function of transnational law in this context. In particular, they have to assume the stance as to whether *lex mercatoria* rules are to be used in a supplementary (gap-filling) role, or to modify and

68 Ibid. sec 3.4.
69 Ibid. sec 3.4.
70 Blessing (n 64) 42.

correct the course of interpretation of the domestic law. The door for corrective application of the *lex mercatoria* principles has been additionally opened by an implementation of explicit provisions on a mandatory recourse to trade usages in arbitral decision-making to the UNCITRAL Model Law (Art. 28 (4)) and to some rules of procedure (see, for example, UNCITRAL Rules, Art. 35.3; ICC Rules, Art. 21.2; AAA International Arbitration Rules, Art. 28.2). Notably, the 2012 CIETAC Rules did not bring a significant change in this regard – the rules applicable to the merits of the dispute are still defined as the law (and not rules of law – Art. 47.2), and no separate recourse to trade usages is specified. Adoption of such a solution is consistent with what Chi Manjiao characterizes as a reluctant approach of the Chinese arbitration practice towards application of transnational rules.[71]

In establishing the balance between domestic and transnational rules, the scope of their application might also be defined as subject-matter-related. Such an approach was adopted in the Iran–US Claims Tribunal *Partial Award of 14 July 1987 in Cases Nos. 74 76 81 150 (311-74/76/81/150-3)*.[72] The parties sought resolution of several controversies based on a 1973 sales and purchase agreement (SPA), binding a consortium of oil companies running an onshore oil enterprise in Iran. The Consortium initiated arbitral proceedings against the Government of the Islamic Republic of Iran and the National Iranian Oil Company (respondents). As the parties did not select the law governing their contract and any disputes resulting thereof, the Tribunal resolving the case, had to determine it

> by taking into consideration all circumstances that it deems relevant. In view of the international character of the SPA, concluded between a State, a State agency and a number of major foreign companies, of the magnitude of the interests involved, of the complex set of rights and obligations which it established, and of the link created between this Agreement and the sharing of oil industry benefits throughout the Persian Gulf Countries, the Tribunal does not consider it appropriate that such an Agreement be governed by the law of one Party.[73]

In effect, the Tribunal decided that the proper law for interpretative matters was Iranian law, whereas to all the remaining issues the '*general principles of commercial and international law*' shall be applied.

It is also interesting to trace the rationales supporting the Tribunal's decision on applying *lex mercatoria* in this case. It starts with a procedural argument of

71 Cf. Chi Manjiao, 'The Iceberg Beneath the Water': The Hidden Discrimination against the Lex Mercatoria in Chinese Arbitration' 7 J Priv Int'l L (2011); Chi Manjiao, 'Are We Paper Tigers – The Limited Procedural Power of Arbitrators under Chinese Law' J Disp Res (2011).

72 Iran–US Claims Tribunal Partial Award of 14 July 1987 in Cases Nos 74, 76, 81, 150 (311–74/76/81/150-3) in *Yearbook Commercial Arbitration* vol XIII (A.J. van den Berg ed, Kluwer Law International 1988).

73 Ibid. 292.

discretionary power to identify the circumstances affecting the determination of proper law. The Tribunal further exposes several specific aspects of the analysed contractual relationship (its international nature, its highly complex character, the diversity of represented interests). Interestingly, it also uses an argument of regional trade policy and welfare, as well as of the interests of transnational oil industry. This openly liberal approach to application of the *lex mercatoria* standards contrasts with the previously analysed reasoning of the International Arbitration Court of the Chamber of Commerce and Industry of the Russian Federation.

The growing popularity of the recourse to *lex mercatoria* can also be observed in those still-rare cases where the arbitrators decided to apply it despite the explicitly expressed will of the parties indicating otherwise. The ICC Award No. 8873/1997[74] is a remarkable example of such an interpretive decision, where the strict and express choice of domestic law, provided for by the parties, was rejected by the arbitrators, who chose to apply transnational rules instead. A construction agreement in question between a Spanish and a French party explicitly stipulated that 'the contract was to be entirely governed by Spanish law, to the exclusion of any other law'. The respondent upheld that the Spanish law allows for application of trade usages only supplementarily, in regard to those issues on which the relevant domestic legislation is silent. The claimant offered a counterargument that the provisions of the contract and trade usages should be the primary point of reference in accordance with the ICC Rules of Arbitration, forming the procedural framework for the case.

The arbitral tribunal shared the latter view, claiming that

> arbitrators are not bound by the strict rules of national law to determine whether and to which extent trade usages are applicable, eventually, overriding the dispositive rules of the applicable law. In particular, Art. VII Geneva Convention has established an internationally uniform principle, which applies instead of national rules on the matter. This principle recognizes [that] arbitrators [do have] a broad margin of decision to determine the role which usages shall be given.[75]

It also further reasoned, on the basis of the 1961 European Convention on International Commercial Arbitration, that any transnational principle they determine to be relevant can be applied as long as it does not contradict the mandatory rules of proper domestic law. The scope of discretionary powers of arbitrators have been thus defined as remarkably extensive. A similar stance has been adopted by an ICC tribunal in Award No. 7518/1994.[76] Even though the parties designated Portuguese law as the only one applicable to their disputes, the tribunal invoked usages of trade, and specifically the *pacta sunt servanda* principle, so as to give precedence to the

74 ICC Award No. 8873/1997, 500ff.

75 English translation after López Rodríguez (n 73) 125.

76 ICC Award No. 7518/1994 in *Collection of ICC Arbitral Awards, 1996–2000* § 4 (J.-J. Arnaldez ed, Kluwer Law International 2003) 516.

terms of the contract over the domestic provisions, as long as the agreement did not contradict the mandatory rules of Portuguese law. Such awards can be perceived as exceeding the limits of supplementary or even corrective use of *lex mercatoria* in relation to the domestic law, and reaching directly to the transnational rules as the primary ground of the adjudicative decision.

Arbitrators, deciding to invoke *lex mercatoria*, besides procedural grounds, have also been employing different substantive arguments to support their decision. An intrinsically international character of the analysed commercial agreement, and transnational rules as an adequate legal response to the demands of cross-border trade exchange (as opposed to the, sometimes unnecessarily parochial, national rules) are among such repeatedly offered rationales. In the ICC arbitral Award No. 3131/1979 in *Norsolor* the arbitrators decided that,

> [f]aced with the difficulty of choosing a national law the application of which is sufficiently compelling, the Tribunal considered that it was appropriate, given the international nature of the agreement, to leave aside any compelling reference to a specific legislation, be it Turkish or French, and to apply the international *lex mercatoria*.[77]

The tribunal argued that one of the key *lex mercatoria* rules is the principle of good faith, that 'must preside the formation and the performance of contracts', and that furthermore 'required conduct which can be linked to the general principle of responsibility'.[78]

As López Rodríguez points out, closeness of the *lex mercatoria* to the complex and specific requirements of international commerce was, among others, also conclusive for the II Civil Chamber of the Zurich Court of Appeal,[79] which acknowledged a bank guarantee in an international transaction to be an institution of the practice of international trade, thus belonging to a supranational *lex mercatoria*. As a consequence, it assumed that it should be interpreted in the context of the needs of international trade.

Other types of arguments supporting the recourse to the *lex mercatoria* principles include the recognition of a common commercial practice (sometimes augmented by reference to its confirmation in judicial decision-making[80]) and the

---

77 *Pabalk Ticaret Limited Sirketi v Norsolor SA*, ICC Award No. 3131 of 26 October 1979, in *Yearbook Commercial Arbitration* vol IX (P. Sanders ed, Kluwer Law International 1984) 109, 110.

78 Ibid. 110.

79 López Rodríguez (n 7) 134.

80 Cf., for example, *Compania Valenciana de Cementos Portland SA v Primary Coal Inc*, Cour de Cassation [Supreme Court] 22 October 1991, in *Yearbook Commercial Arbitration* vol XVIII (A.J. van den Berg ed, Kluwer Law International 1993); *Société Fougerolle v Société Butec Engineering*, Cour de Cassation (1ère Ch Civ), 3 October 1984, in 2 J Int'l Arb 2 (1985); Arbitration Chamber of Paris, Award in Case No. 9246 of 8 March

acknowledgement of the New Law Merchant as a common core of legal systems. The latter claim (as discussed above, present already in the early *lex mercatoria* cases) can be perceived as a strategy, addressing the issue of legitimacy deficiencies of transnational rules, emphasized in their positivist critique. While not directly validated by the States, *lex mercatoria* is nevertheless grounded in their legal systems and discovered in practice by the means of comparative analysis.[81]

This line of reasoning appears, for example, in the decision of the English Court of Appeal in *Deutsche Schachtbau- und Tiefbohr GmbH v Rakoil*, where the argument, that principles applied by the ICC arbitrators were too uncertain, was not accepted. The court upheld that, in the absence of any limitations as to the choice of law introduced by the parties, the issue of determination of applicable rules was left fully to the discretion of the tribunal:

> the parties have left the proper law to be decided by the arbitrators and have not in terms confined the choice to national systems of law. I can see no basis for concluding that the arbitrators' choice of proper law – a common denominator of principles underlying the laws of the various nations governing contractual relations – is outwith the scope of the choice which the parties left to the arbitrators.[82]

Similarly, in an award in *Norsolor*, the ICC arbitral tribunal augmented its application of the *lex mercatoria* principle of good faith in international commercial relations by emphasizing that it is present as one of main trends observable in the convergence of national laws.[83]

The Dilemma of Legal Predictability

Such a perception of transnational principles – as the common core of domestic legal systems – underlies the restatement-type codification efforts, as seen in the UNIDROIT Principles. In arbitral practice it is consistent with frequent application of comparative analysis. As a result, some commentators have proposed a concept of the New Law Merchant not as a substantive body of rules, but rather as a method of adjudication, oriented purposively at determining the relevant, most universally shared standards. It would thus rely on 'deriving the substantive solution to the legal issue at hand (…) through a comparative law analysis which will enable the

---

1996, in *Yearbook Commercial Arbitration* vol XXII (A.J. van den Berg ed, Kluwer Law International 1997).

81 Jemielniak (n 23) 198.

82 *Deutsche Schachtbau- und Tiefbohr GmbH v Rakoil*, Court of Appeal decision of 24 March 1987, Lloyd's L Rep 2 (1987) 254.

83 *Pabalk Ticaret Limited Sirketi v Norsolor SA*, ICC Award No. 3131 of 26 October 1979, *Yearbook Commercial Arbitration* vol IX (P. Sanders ed, Kluwer Law International 1984) 109, 110.

arbitrators to apply the rule which is the most widely accepted.'[84] Whereas such a view of the *lex mercatoria* as an interpretative approach (and set of techniques) can be seen as reductionist, it also eliminates the criticism of *lex mercatoria*, referring to its fragmented, incomplete character, as inadequate.

This last point of critique has been, however, also addressed explicitly by arbitral case law. Fuzziness and indeterminacy of transnational rules have been accented in the ICC partial award in Case No. 7319 of 1992. The sole arbitrator stated that

> the failure of the parties to agree on the law governing the Agreement cannot ... be interpreted as an implied reference to some vague international legal or trade principles. Such reference must be made expressly and, if not expressly, then in an implied manner which gives reasonable certainty to the arbitrators or the courts, respectively, that the parties indeed agreed to submit their dispute to anational law or international trade principles, particularly considering the fact that such anational laws and principles, if not properly defined, are difficult if not impossible to assess.[85]

A remarkably limiting view of the scope of discretionary powers of the tribunal has thus been assumed, as the sole arbitrator suggests that a recourse to *lex mercatoria* is allowed only in case of an objectively ascertainable indication as to the intent of the parties in this regard.

Those reservations were also considered by the arbitral tribunal in *Compania Valenciana de Cementos Portland SA v Primary Coal Inc*, which reached a different conclusion:

> [i]n spite of the [fact that] principles of *lex mercatoria* are uncodified, they are gradually released from the practice and, notably, by an arbitral practice, which has found the support of national court. They have been thus confirmed as legal rules. In fact, they belong to the same category as national usages and customs, recognized as legal sources both in common law countries ... and in countries of Roman-Germanic tradition.[86]

As a result, the tribunal assumed that the transnational rules are not only sufficiently elaborated by adjudicatory practice and form a 'truly international' body of relevant principles, but also characterized them as the 'only possible solution' for the analysed controversy.

---

84 Gaillard (n 44) 224.

85 *French Manufacturer v Irish Distributor*, ICC Partial Award in Case No. 7319/1992, in *Yearbook Commercial Arbitration* vol XXIVa (A.J. van den Berg ed, Kluwer Law International 1999) 145.

86 *Compania Valenciana de Cementos Portland SA v Primary Coal Inc*, ICC Award No. 5953/1989, in *Yearbook Commercial Arbitration* vol XVI (A.J. van den Berg ed, Kluwer Law International 1991), English translation after López Rodríguez (n 7) 139.

The argument of the *lex mercatoria* as being too nebulous and fuzzy to be operative has often been invoked in jurisprudence and commentaries.[87] As Katherine L. Lynch remarks, from this perspective:

> *[l]ex mercatoria* rules are considered too vague and indistinct to constitute an objective legal system. It lacks the degree of clarity, objectivity, generality and universality required before a set of concepts, rules, standards, principles and institutions can be said to constitute a system of 'law'. Supporters of *lex mercatoria* argue, however, that if the law merchant is vague, what distinguishes it from other systems of law either national or international? The new *lex mercatoria*, it is argued, should aim at achieving clarity and coherence without sacrificing its inherent adaptability and flexibility.[88]

Indeed, the application of the new *lex mercatoria* principles has been perceived as an antidote to insufficiently distinct and ascertainable rules of domestic law already in its origins (as Joachim G. Frick remarks, it was the arbitrary character and indeterminacy of the law of Abu Dhabi as faced by the arbitrators, that led them to exclusion of this national system and the pioneering application of transnational principles instead[89]). In this approach, *lex mercatoria* does not introduce an element of legal uncertainty to arbitral decision-making but, on the contrary, alleviates it by a reference to universally known and commonly shared principles. Such a reference replaces the arguably often more unpredictable outcomes of the application of the domestic law, intermediated by the traditional conflict of laws analysis.

The flagship argument by Goldman, that the intrinsically supranational business transactions call for adequately supranational rules to regulate them, can be also invoked in this regard as referring to the issue of legal certainty in an international context. A similar line of reasoning has been adopted by the sole arbitrator who resolved the dispute stemming from a construction agreement between a US and a Belgian party, with Bulgaria stipulated as the place of performance, in Award No. 8385/1995.[90] The case was commented upon as a pioneering instance of piercing the corporate veil on the basis of *lex mercatoria*.[91]

---

87 Cf., for example, Mann, Michael Mustill (LJ), 'The New Lex Mercatoria: The First Twenty-Five Years' 4 Arb Int'l (1988) 86; Peter Schlosser, *Das Recht der internationalen privaten Schiedsgerichtsbarkeit* (Mohr Siebeck 1989) 141; Monica Kilian, 'CISG and the Problem with Common Law Jurisdictions' 10 J Transnat'l L & Pol'y (2000) 222.

88 Katherine L. Lynch, *The Forces of Economic Globalization: Challenges to the Regime of International Commercial Arbitration* (Kluwer Law International 2003) 321.

89 J.G. Frick, *Arbitration and Complex International Contracts: With Special Emphasis on the Determination of the Applicable Substantive Law and on the Adaptation of Contracts to Changed Circumstances* (Kluwer Law International 2001) 115.

90 ICC Award No. 8385/1995.

91 Philippe Fouchard et al., *Fouchard, Gaillard, Goldman on International Commercial Arbitration* (Kluwer Law International 1999) 822 n 201.

In this controversy, a strict application of the law of the state of New York, expressly indicated by the parties to the analysed contract, would have led to the awarding of triple punitive damages on the ground of the US 1970 Federal Racketeer Influence and Corrupt Organization Act. However, the sole arbitrator decided that – as such remedy was acknowledged as not available in civil law countries – the Belgian party could not have reasonably anticipated a recourse to it. As a consequence, the arbitrator abstained from applying the otherwise proper domestic provision and gave precedence to the value of certainty of the law, as

> in international commerce [it] is very important that legal rules produce foreseeable results, respond to the expectations of the parties and take account of the prevalent usages of the international marketplace. In such context it would be inappropriate to apply rules which solely respond to state interests.[92]

Additionally, the activity of arbitral tribunals in formulating and developing the body of the New Law Merchant over the last decades, as well as the codification efforts in different forms, have contributed to the consolidation of this set of rules and decreasing its indeterminacy. It is still worth reminding ourselves of Filip De Ly's observation that the higher appropriateness of transnational standards to the analysis of international transaction, or their 'better law' status in competition with domestic rules, should not be automatically assumed, but rather evaluated on a basis of the circumstances of a particular case.[93]

A similar stance is assumed by Frick, who emphasizes that the ascertaining of a status of a specific standard as a *lex mercatoria* rule of law (and thus its formal applicability to a case resolved by the means of arbitration) should be left to the discretion of the arbitrators and decided along with its implementation in the context of a particular case rather than *a priori* excluded.[94] While subscribing to the view that the possibility of applying transnational rules to the substance of the dispute (instead of relying solely on one national law) reflects the modern, pragmatic approach to arbitration,[95] he also articulates procedural framework conditions for legitimacy of such a choice.

In the case of lack of relevant, explicit choice of *lex mercatoria* by the parties, it can be applied if an implicit selection thereof can be determined or if the proper domestic law includes a reference to it. Otherwise, transnational rules can be applied if the conflict of laws analysis does not lead to any national legal system, or if the entirety of the circumstances of the case reveals a close 'intellectual connection' of the 'denationalized' transaction with *lex mercatoria*.[96]

---

92 After López Rodríguez (n 7) 127.

93 De Ly (n 11) 178.

94 Frick (n 89) 114–15.

95 Ibid. 116.

96 Ibid. 129.

Frick's list can be further supplemented by instances of *lex mercatoria* application, in which it is determined as proper law on the basis of the *voie directe* competence. While occasionally disputed by commentators,[97] this type of application of the New Law Merchant has occurred in arbitral practice. ICC Award No. 3540/1980,[98] rendered by a tribunal in Geneva, provides an early and widely commented upon, example of such reasoning. The tribunal, addressing a case between a Yugoslav and a French party, although authorized to *amiable composition*, nevertheless decided to apply conflict of laws rules it deemed appropriate in order to determine proper substantive law. Conflict of laws analysis, conducted under the rules of first Switzerland, and then France, did not however lead to conclusive and satisfactory results. As a consequence, the tribunal reasoned that, as the *voie directe* competence lay within the scope of its discretionary powers, it should determine the law applicable to the merits of the dispute by its direct decision and without mediating application of domestic private international laws.

The tribunal further argued that an exercise of the *voie directe* competence could lead it to establishing national law, substantive contractual norms, or general and common principles of laws as rules governing the agreement. The last option was chosen and explicitly phrased by the tribunal as *voie directe* for the application of *lex mercatoria*. However, the arbitrators decided that national legal orders should not be disregarded, and chose to apply transnational principles only insofar as they did not contradict Swiss and French relevant substantive norms.

This solution was later characterized by Werner Lorenz as a mere lip service ('*Lippenbekenntnis*') – a purely formal acknowledgement of the existence of the New Law Merchant. The actual ground for the award has been in fact found through comparative analysis, leading to establishing a 'comparative sum' of the two domestic legal systems.[99] It can be remarked that such an outcome of the process of ascertaining applicable rules did not indeed lead the interpreters to finding relevant *lex mercatoria* principles, understood as constituting an autonomous body of transnational rules. Those reservations would be, however, pointless if the alternative, reductionist concept of *lex mercatoria* (as a method of arbitral adjudication, based on comparative interpretation of domestic orders), as discussed above, was adopted.

The application of *lex mercatoria* in arbitral practice, involving very closely creative aspects of legal interpretation, be it as a sole substantive basis for the award or in connection with domestic (or domestic and international) rules, is

---

97 Cf., for example, Frank Vischer, 'The Relevance of the UNIDROIT Principles for Judges and Arbitrators in Disputes Arising out of International Contracts' 1 EJLR (1999) 204; Franco Ferrari and Stefan Kröll, *Conflict of Laws in International Arbitration* (Sellier 2011) 301–302.

98 ICC Award No. 3540/1980, in *Yearbook Commercial Arbitration* vol VII (P. Sanders ed, Kluwer Law International 1982) 124, 129.

99 Werner Lorenz, *Die Lex Mercatoria: eine internationale Rechtsquelle? Festschrift für Karl Neumayer* (Karl Neumayer and Werner Barfuss eds, Nomos 1985) 421.

thus performed. Various grounds for establishing transnational principles as rules applicable to the substance of the dispute further allow arbitrators to reach to the New Law Merchant with a notably wide discretion. As Andreas F. Lowenfeld observes, commenting on pragmatic approach of the arbitration practice towards *lex mercatoria*,

> [o]f course much has changed since [Justice Joseph] Story's time ... But the vision of 'general principles and doctrines of commercial jurisprudence', I would hope, retains its compelling character. Arbitrators do not make up the law as they go along and, contrary to popular view, most arbitrators do not look first of all for compromise. International arbitrators do seek to achieve just results within a legal framework, and that framework is by definition wider than the frontiers of any state.[100]

While actual significance of the *lex mercatoria* in arbitral decision-making is still an object of a dispute, a recourse to it remains an option or – rather – a whole range of options, allowing in some cases for issuing awards based exclusively on transnational rules, but also for fine-tuning the interpretation of domestic law.

100 Andreas F. Lowenfeld, 'Lex Mercatoria: An Arbitrator's View' *in Lex Mercatoria and Arbitration: A Discussion of the New Law Merchant* (Thomas E. Carbonneau ed, Transnational 1990) 91.

Chapter 9
Amiable Composition

Recourse to Extralegal Standards in Arbitration: *Amiable Composition* and Elements of Mediation

Amiable composition, as a competence which might be granted to arbitrators by the will of the parties, has a long history in international arbitral practice.[1] It has been acquired from domestic civil procedure regulations, developed in some continental legal systems since the nineteenth century. The origins of the notion of *amiable composition* can be traced back to the French 1804 Napoleonic Code and 1806 Code of Civil Procedure, which promoted conciliatory measures in private dispute resolution and aimed at preserving benign relationship between the parties.[2]

Such a basic understanding of this concept had been subsequently transferred and popularized in arbitration practice. The term, which has been traditionally translated literally as 'friendly compromise',[3] denotes an authority granted to an adjudicator to abstain from an application of the rules of law to the merits of the controversy and to decide the case on the grounds of fairness and equity (*amiable composition* is often combined with a competence to resolve the case *ex aequo et bono*, or from equity and conscience, and sometimes these two terms are treated as interchangeable[4]). The parties can anticipate that the resolution of their dispute, based on strict application of the rules of law, would lead to undesired, inadequate or unsatisfactory outcomes; in such a case they can empower the arbitrators to act as *amiables compositeurs* when needed.

As often emphasized, amiable composition should be distinguished from conciliation and mediation, as well as from the decision of the case on the basis of *lex mercatoria* principles. Even if empowered with competences to decide the case on the basis of equity, and in fact often actually willing to offer a solution satisfactory to both parties, the arbitrators still render the award independently from the parties' acceptance of it; once arbitral proceedings are commenced (and there is no successful attempt at settlement), their outcome no longer relies on the parties' consent.

---

1 E. Loquin, *L'Amiable composition en droit comparé et international: contribution à l'étude du non-droit dans l'arbitrage commercial* (Librairies techniques 1980).

2 W.L. Craig et al., *International Chamber of Commerce Arbitration* vol 1 (New York 1990) 310.

3 W.W. Park, 'Arbitration of International Contract Disputes' 39 Bus Law (1983) 1785.

4 Mauro Rubino-Sammartano, *International Arbitration Law and Practice* (Kluwer Law International 2001) 463.

On the other hand, the binding force of a result of conciliation or mediation processes is dependent on the agreement of the disputants to adhere to it, and hence these ADR procedures by definition require consensual collaboration for finding a compromising stance. It should still be remarked that, while formally clearly distinguishable on the basis of the source of the binding force of the outcome, *amiable composition* and conciliation/mediation techniques might turn out to be very close, if not identical, in practice. Moreover, as observed by René David, historically *amiable composition* was oriented at only offering the possible solution to the parties, not at compelling them to accept and observe it.[5] In its original version it was thus very close to the modern concept of conciliation, which Bruno Oppetit clearly defines as a process different from mediation. Whereas in the former a conciliator plays an active, managing role and proposes the final solution to the parties, mediation is characterized as more directly reliant on the continuous collaboration between the parties with the outcome created through a carefully worked out compromise.[6]

However, the boundary between mediation and conciliation becomes less clear when the facilitative mediation (the earliest form, characterized by the assisting role of the mediator and his or her abstention from offering advice, recommendations or opinions as to the possible outcome of the judicial resolution of the case) is distinguished from a more recent type, the evaluative mediation. In the latter, the legal positions of the parties (and not just their interests, preferences and needs) are being actively assessed by a mediator, who offers a proposed solution. The scope and character of the mediator's intervention in the process has been indeed characterized as the object of the most intense, ongoing debate, with growing significance of the evaluative form being sometimes treated as a departure from the original character of mediation, based on the parties' autonomy, preserved throughout the entire process.[7]

Due to the legal dimension strongly present in evaluative mediation, this form of ADR requires substantive legal knowledge applicable to the merits of the case, and the mediators, if they are not judges, are often practising attorneys. The direct presence of the parties is also not always necessary, as the discussion of the dispute takes place either between the mediator and the parties' counsel, or between mediator, counsel and the parties themselves. The closeness of this form of mediation to judicial practice is not accidental – it has been indicated that evaluative mediation historically evolved from, and is still strongly rooted in, the practice of settlement conferences, held by judges. As Leonard Riskin observes, the prospect of settlement lies at the core of evaluative mediation:

5 René David, *Arbitration in International Trade* (Kluwer Law & Taxation Publications 1985) 335.

6 B. Oppetit, *Théorie de l'arbitrage* (Presses universitaires de France 1998) 35.

7 E.A. Waldman, 'The Evaluative-Facilitative Debate in Mediation: Applying the Lens of Therapeutic Jurisprudence' 82 Marq L Rev (1998) 155–56.

> [t]he mediator who evaluates assumes that the participants want and need her to provide some guidance as to the appropriate grounds for settlement … Conversely, the mediator who facilitates assumes that the parties are intelligent, able to work with their counterparts, and capable of understanding their situations better than the mediator and, perhaps, better than their lawyers.[8]

Some authors also recognize a third (and newest) type of mediation – a transformative one. It is aimed at deep, mutual recognition of the other party's motivations and needs, as well as restoration of their relationship through a peaceful transformation achieved primarily by the parties, with a mediator playing a supportive role.[9] While there is undoubtedly growing interest in this form of dispute resolution in both the theory and practice of mediation, its applicability to legal disputes of a commercial nature seems so far still relatively limited.

Increasing popularity of evaluative mediation, its relatively formal (for an ADR method) character, its orientation at legal standards and its close relations with the courts' activity might be interpreted as the grounds for growing inclusion of its techniques into commercial arbitration practice as well. The need of parties for custom-tailored proceedings, when accompanied with an openness to the idea of settlement rather than confrontational procedure, might be addressed through a hybrid form of extrajudicial dispute resolution, such as med-arb or arb-med. The main point of critique of evaluative mediation – the risk of alienating the parties through a law-based solution proposed by a mediator, not forged by the disputants themselves – seems to lose much of its persuasive force when compared with a formal, binding character of an arbitral award, being rendered as an outcome of proceedings increasingly resembling litigation (see Chapter 5). Introduction of mediation (even evaluative mediation) components in the ICA proceedings arguably softens the adjudicatory, conclusive and external (not parties-driven) character of arbitration.

The problems with such a hybrid approach seem, however, worth consideration. The first issue seems to be that of competence: successful resolution of even numerous international commercial disputes through arbitration does not necessarily make an arbitrator similarly qualified to undertake the role of a mediator. The exercise of skills required from an arbitrator – in particular an ability to provide a neutrality of the procedure, including keeping a professional distance from the parties – might turn out to be disturbed if the same person is expected to get directly involved in seeking the final solution together with the parties as a mediator. The fact that an arbitral award is based on the rules of the law and does not have to be satisfactory for both parties (an arbitral case can be won or lost) also differentiates the role of an arbitrator from that of a mediator. It might be

8 L.L. Riskin, 'Understanding Mediators' Orientations, Strategies, and Techniques: A Grid for the Perplexed' 1 Harv Negot L Rev (1996) 24.

9 Cf. R.A.B. Bush and S.G. Pope, 'Changing the Quality of Conflict Interaction: The Principles and Practice of Transformative Mediation' 3 Pepp Disp Resol LJ (2002).

also particularly challenging for an arbitrator, after having formed an assessment of the case in the mediation phase, to keep a neutral position in the subsequent arbitration. The issues of neutrality and procedural fairness in the context of med-arb procedure have been an object of courts' decisions. In the US *Duke Group*,[10] as well as in the UK *Glencot v Barrett*,[11] it was upheld that just the fact of organizing private caucuses in the mediation phase can be interpreted as suggesting a bias in the med-arbitrator (although it was also decided that an objection on such basis may be an object of a waiver).

Finally, even most sincere mediation efforts in a combined, med-arb procedure might easily fail if the parties abstain from full participation and disclosure of relevant facts in an open and informal mediation procedure, while being aware that this information can be further used against them in the following arbitration part. In fact, the risk of being involved in a procedure in which the opponent is not necessarily participating *bona fide* should be taken into account. In med-arb the parties can be also particularly cautious about informing the mediator, who might be later called upon to arbitrate the same case, about the details of settlement proposals which they would consider accepting.[12]

On the other hand, the advantages of a hybrid procedure might be appealing to those parties who wish to possibly avoid the complications and formality, as well as the adversarial character of litigation or arbitration, while keeping an option of a smooth switch to it in case of a failure of the mediation phase. The disclosure of critical information in the mediation phase, even if it does not end with a settlement, might be perceived by the parties as beneficial, saving them time and effort in the following arbitration.[13] This is possible as long as the mediator/arbitrator enjoys the undeterred trust of both contestants – which arguably makes his or her role doubly demanding. The reluctance of arbitrators to undertake a role of a neutral in med-arb due to different procedural demands in two phases, and the resulting, increased risk of challenges on the basis of insufficient neutrality, can be also moderated by the use of contractual waiver clauses in the med-arb agreement (where the parties agree that it is within the discretion of the med-arbitrators to use confidential information gathered throughout the proceedings in the arbitration phase, and that they will abstain from attempts at undermining an award on this ground).[14]

Med-arb and arb-med can be also perceived as practical solutions in certain contexts. Inclusion of elements of mediation into adjudicatory proceedings

---

10 *Duke Group Ltd (in liq) v Alamain Investments Ltd*, SASC 275.

11 *Glencot Development and Design Ltd v Ben Barrett and Son (Contractors) Ltd* [2001], 17 Const LJ 336.

12 A.L. Limbury, 'Making Med-Arb Work' 9 ADR Bulletin (2007) 1.

13 D.C. Elliot, 'Med/Arb: Fraught with Danger or Ripe with Opportunity' 34 Alta L Rev (1995) 164.

14 Cf. M.M. Mironi, 'From Mediation to Settlement and from Settlement to Final Offer Arbitration: An Analysis of Transnational Business Dispute Mediation' 73 Arbitration: Journal of the Chartered Institute of Arbitrators (2007).

and the seeking of opportunities for settlement have been widely described as consistent with the East Asian approach to dispute resolution,[15] characterized by Junji Nakagawa as the 'conflict aversive culture of the region, where negotiated deals are preferred to formal dispute settlement'.[16] An option of a recourse to a non-adversarial way of handling the controversy might be in such cases appreciated.

Even when considered in the context of cultural or regional preferences, the practice of combining two types of dispute settlement procedure (and two different neutral roles by the same person in one case) has been sometimes treated with far-reaching reserve. Pierre Lalive, in his response to Tang Houzhi, while presenting the views of a 'Western European doctrine – or at least a "Swiss approach"',[17] advocates for clear delineation between arbitration, mediation and conciliation, and argues that:

> 'Combining' such different institutions may mean or involve various solutions or formulas, some of which may, in particular circumstances, be advantageous but are more often than not likely to create confusion and prove unprofitable … Suffice it to quote here one of the apt remarks of Mr. Carter who notes that 'Arbitration clauses alone offer myriad examples of inconsistency and other pathologies. The possibility for drafting chaos is multiplied when several mechanisms are integrated.'[18]

This critique of the use of hybrid methods of dispute resolution due to practicality and rationality concerns and restraint on the side of arbitrators in regard to mixing the roles, might be changing in the future, though. Along with the growing rates of commercial exchange between East Asia, the EU and the US, and the fast-increasing exposure of Western practitioners to regional standards, the ability to handle a case under the rules of procedure providing for an easy 'switch to mediation/conciliation' (such as Art. 45 of the 2012 CIETAC Rules) might become part of the competences required from a counsel or arbitrator operating in such an environment. It is worth noting that, for instance, it is estimated that as much as 20 to 30 per cent of all cases resolved by CIETAC are currently resolved by the means of arb-med,[19] with a vivid discussion following such cases as *Gao*

---

15 See, for example, David (n 5); S.J. Burton, 'Combining Conciliation with Arbitration of International Commercial Disputes' 18 Hastings Int'l & Comp L Rev (1994).

16 J. Nakagawa, 'No More Negotiated Deals?: Settlement of Trade and Investment Disputes in East Asia' 10 J Int'l Econ L (2007) 863.

17 Pierre Lalive, 'The Role of Arbitrators as Settlement Facilitators – A Swiss View' in *New Horizons in International Commercial Arbitration and Beyond* (A.J. van den Berg ed, Kluwer Law International 2005) 558.

18 Ibid. 558–59.

19 Neil Jamieson et al., 'Acting outside the Box – the Emerging Dispute Resolution Centres Developing Innovative Ways to Attract Business' at <legalweek.com> (2012).

Haiyan v Keeneye Holdings Ltd[20] (arbitrated in the People's Republic of China and sought to be enforced in Hong Kong, where the question of appearance of bias in arb-med as a basis for refusal of enforcement of the award on the ground of public policy had been considered).

Amiable Composition and Decision-Making *Ex Aequo et Bono*

As discussed above, despite sharp theoretical distinctions and the push of legal doctrine towards conceptual clarity, in practice acting as *amiable compositeur* may turn out to be very similar to conciliation or mediation attempts. This issue, as discussed above, has become increasingly important (and confusing), along with the growing saturation of ICA with elements of other methods of dispute resolution, especially in regional contexts. The difference, besides the binding, 'external' character of an award, lies also in the grounds for the decision. Whereas mediation and conciliation are characterized as driven primarily by a search for a possible compromise, *amiable composition* aims at a just and equitable solution of the controversy, consistent with the spirit of the law, even if not necessarily explicitly with its letter.

The scope of this term has been differently defined. In a *sensu stricto* version, *amiable composition* means decision-making based on the rules of law, from which the arbitrators may deviate if the considerations of equity so require. As Robert Briner remarks, this model has been traditionally associated with French legal doctrine and does not entitle an arbitrator to decide the case (directly) *ex aequo et bono*.[21] However, as Rene David observed in a 1946 article on frustration of contract under the French law,

> many commercial contracts contain in France a clause of submission to arbitration, which gives to the arbitrators the powers of *amiables compositeurs*. In this case arbitrators will be authorized according to French law to disregard rules of law and will be allowed to settle the case according to their conception of natural justice; they may of course do this by considering the change that has occurred in the attendant circumstances. It must be pointed out, nevertheless, that this does not commonly happen: *amiable composition* is stipulated in France, as a rule, not in order to allow, and still less to encourage, arbitrators to disregard rules of law, but essentially in order that their award should be final and that no appeal should be possible to the courts on the merits of such award.[22]

20 *Gao Haiyan v Keeneye Holdings Ltd*, 3 HKEC 514 (Hong Kong Court of First Instance).

21 R. Briner, *Special Considerations Which May Affect the Procedure (Interim Measures, Amiable Composition, Adaptation of Contracts, Agreed Settlements)* (Kluwer 1994) 355.

22 René David, 'Frustration of Contract in French Law' 28 J Comp Legis & Int'l L 3rd ser. (1946) 14.

Also in more recent French case law, this concept of *amiable composition* (as a power, explicitly conferred by the parties, allowing the arbitrators to abstain from strict application of the rules of law and to decide the case on the grounds of equity – *équité*) has been upheld.[23]

The narrow definition of *amiable composition*, as a competence resulting from an equity clause, had also been shared by early English case law, according to which it entitles an arbitrator to decide a case without being bound by 'strictness of the obligations' to follow the rules of law, yet not to ignore them entirely.[24] It is worth noting that, despite this evidence of relatively early adoption of the concept of *amiable composition* in England, Briner (after Stewart Boyd) comments on the traditionally cautious attitude and reluctance of the English courts and legal doctrine to recognize the validity of 'equity clauses', which has even led to discouraging the parties from including provisions of this type in their contracts. Courts' decisions in such cases as *David Taylor and Son Ltd v Barnett Trading Co*[25] and *Orion Compania Espanola de Seguros v Belfort Maatschappij voor Algemene Verzekgringeen*[26] expressed the standard of inadmissibility of decision-making *ex aequo et bono* in arbitration, based on the assumption that 'arbitrators cannot be allowed to apply some different criterion such as the views of the individual arbitrator or umpire on abstract justice or equitable principles'.[27] This averse approach to arbitration *ex aequo et bono* has, however, been moderated in the following decades, with legal doctrine gradually embracing the concept of contractual authorization for the arbitrators to depart from strict application of law, as long as the law itself permits it.[28] A widely discussed court's decision in *Eagle Star Insurance Co v Yuval Insurance Co*[29] marked the shift towards recognition of contracts including an equity clause as valid and enforceable.

In this context, the renowned American equity-friendly approach in arbitration is notable and has been characterized as closer to French tradition than to the English one (with some commentators stating that *amiable composition* might be used in arbitration in the US perhaps even more frequently than in France[30]). It has

---

23 Cf., for example, *Dame Krebs et autre v Milton Stern*, French Cour de Cassation, 1977 Rev Arb 269; *Intrafor Cofor et Subtec Middle East Company v M. Gagnant et consorts*, Cour d'appel de Paris, 1985 Rev Arb 299.

24 *Rolland v Cassidy* (1888) 13 AC 770. After Michael Kerr, '"Equity" Arbitration in England' 2 Amer Rev Int'l Arb (1991).

25 *David Taylor and Son Ltd v Barnett Trading Co* [1953] 1 WLR 562.

26 *Orion Compania Espanola de Seguros v Belfort Maatschappij voor Algemene Verzekgringeen* [1962] 2 Lloyd's L Rep 257.

27 Ibid. 264.

28 Cf. R.H. Christie, '*Amiable composition* in French and English Law' 58(4) Arb (1992).

29 *Eagle Star Insurance Co v Yuval Insurance Co* [1978] 1 Lloyd's L Rep 357.

30 Cf. K.S. Weinberg, 'Equity in International Arbitration: How Fair is Fair – A Study of Lex Mercatoria and Amiable Composition' 12 Boston U Int'l LJ (1994) 240.

been explained by the high saturation of American law with equity principles and the fact that their use in adjudication seems as natural for the American judges as it is for arbitrators.

In the *sensu stricto* variation, exercise of *amiable composition* powers has been thus characterized as an 'equity correction',[31] not a substitute for the rules of law in the process of arbitral decision-making. It is also emphasized that the departure from strict application of the rules of law is a competence of an arbitrator empowered as an *amiable compositeur*, not an obligation to be mandatorily fulfilled.[32] An alternative, wider definition of the concept of *amiable composition* includes competences for deciding a case *ex aequo et bono*, or on the grounds of '"equity", "fairness", "équité" and "Billigkeit"'[33] directly. Such a model seems to have been adopted in Switzerland, where the Federal Code on Private International Law of 18 December 1987 (CPIL), Art. 187, in regard to applicable law in arbitration, stipulates that the parties may authorize the arbitral tribunal to rule according to equity, without recourse to the rules of law.

Recent popularity of the wide concept of *amiable composition*, replacing application of substantive rules of law with decision-making based directly on equity, has led to the characterization of such contractual provisions as negative choice of law clauses.[34] The term, forwarded in the context of *amiable composition* by Karl-Heinz Böckstiegel, stems from the common intent of the parties not to make a reference to any legal system, but to vest in the arbitral tribunal powers to resolve the dispute on the grounds of fairness and justice.[35]

The main question is thus whether arbitrators, within their powers as *amiables compositeurs*, are entitled to skip the stage of application of substantive rules of law, determined as proper to the merits of the dispute. In the classic 'French' model, they are not: *amiable composition* is meant to be a safety valve, to be used in those cases where strict application of law would lead to unjust or inequitable outcomes. In its *sensu largo* variant, arbitrators empowered to act as *amiables compositeurs* may reach the decision without a formal consideration of the substantive law. Weinberg notes that arbitral decision-making can also refer to equity principles without an *amiable composition* authorization by the parties in those cases where an award is issued on the ground of application of the rules of such a domestic legal system that already by itself provides for equity considerations.[36]

---

31 Filip De Ly, *International Business Law and Lex Mercatoria* (North-Holland 1992) 124.

32 U. Scheuner, 'Decisions Ex Aequo et Bono by International Courts and Arbitral Tribunals' in *International Arbitration: Liber Amicorum for Martin Domke* (Martinus Nijhoff 1967) 275.

33 Briner (n 21) 355.

34 Cf. P. Devlin, *The Judge* (Oxford 1979) 92.

35 Karl-Heinz Böckstiegel, *Der Staat als Vertragspartner ausländischer Privatunternehmen* (Athenäum 1971) 249.

36 Weinberg (n 30) 232.

The consequences of authorizing the arbitrators to act as *amiables compositeurs* for their interpretive activity are very far-reaching and can be characterized as escapist, allowing for a retreat from the rigour of interpretive canons and directions. As Hong-Lin Yu observes, '[s]uch power not only enables arbitrators to deviate from the application of law and decide the case on the basis of what is fair and reasonable according to their personal sense of equity, but also allows arbitrators to avoid strict legal interpretation.'[37]

The limits of these discretionary powers can reach even further. Whereas a possibility of disregarding the rules of law is considered to be the essence of *amiable composition*, a separate question raised by some commentators is whether *amiables compositeurs* can also diverge from the terms of the parties' contract. The problem is whether an *amiable composition* clause entitles an arbitrator to *de facto* change the nature of legal relationship intended by the parties, as expressed in their agreement. This controversial issue has been addressed by authors representing a full range of opinions expressed in case law and literature – from a strict non-interventionist perspective to the proposals allowing for a moderate modifying activity, which would not affect the basic structure of the parties' rights and obligations, but would offer their interpretation oriented at the standards of fairness and equity. Even according to this latter, broad concept, *amiables compositeurs* are still considered not to be authorized to add ('create') any new rights or obligations to those provided for by the parties.[38]

Amiable Composition and *Lex Mercatoria*

When compared to *lex mercatoria*-based adjudication, *amiable composition* offers arbitrators considerably more freedom. A tribunal applying *lex mercatoria* to the merits of a case is obligated to determine the content of such principles, treated as rules of law. While the crucial role of arbitral case law in expressing, formulating and specifying the principles of autonomous law of the international trade is widely recognized (as discussed in the previous chapter), a pre-existence of such norms – even in a very rudimentary form, to be further developed in an award – is a logical precondition of this type of arbitral interpretive activity. The arbitrators, invoking *lex mercatoria*, are indeed obligated to apply the rules of law (albeit not associated with any domestic legal system) and, as a standard, they do not need a separate, explicit authorization by the parties to undertake such action; they act within the general limits of their discretionary powers.

In contrast, an arbitrator acting as an *amiable compositeur* is not bound by the existing state of the (rules of) law and can rely on his or her own sense of equity so as to either modify a possible outcome of the strict application of law to the case, or to decide the case directly. This particularly far-reaching character of the

37 H. Yu, *Amiable Composition – A Learning Curve*, 17 J Int'l Arb (2000) 80.

38 Craig et al. (n 2) 141.

amiable composition competence of an arbitrator, resulting in a power to alter the effect of the rules of law on the case, has led Weinberg to a conclusion that '[i]n effect, *amiable composition* refers to the structure of an arbitration, whereas *lex mercatoria* is a body of rules that might be applied in any arbitration'.[39]

While the first proposition in this dichotomy – that *amiable composition* denotes a particular, structural (or, perhaps, rather functional) aspect of arbitral decision-making does not seem controversial, the second one is unconditionally based on a concept of *lex mercatoria* as a substantive body of rules, recognized as uniform principles of international trade. It thus does not take into account an alternative concept of *lex mercatoria* as a method of arbitral adjudication, oriented at the use of comparative analysis so as to crystallize applicable rules common to different legal systems (see Chapter 8). If such a functional concept of *lex mercatoria* was to be theoretically recognized (or, at least, not excluded), the distinction proposed by Weinberg would not be operational, as both phenomena would have been defined through the specific delineation of the powers of arbitrators in regard to legal interpretation.

The difference, indeed grave, seems to lie elsewhere; not in the opposition of substantive/functional, but rather on the functional level, in the different orientation of arbitral inquiry. In case of *lex mercatoria* application, it aims at capturing the shared core of legal systems through comparative interpretation. A significant, creative aspect of this interpretation lies in recognition, extraction and specifying of the principles (often still general or not explicitly expressed) which, if performed thoroughly, requires detailed and complex studies, multiplying the efforts, sufficient in case of a straight application of rules of one domestic system. In *amiable composition* an arbitrator is relieved from such obligation and allowed to follow his or her sense of equity.[40]

It seems worth observing that the reasons for choosing contractually *lex mercatoria* or *amiable composition* as a basis for resolution of disputes have a tradition of being presented jointly. Michael Kerr, who recognizes four such rationales,[41] emphasizes the conciliatory character of such selection: an equity clause (as well as an explicit choice of *lex mercatoria*) serves the goal of overcoming divergences between legal approaches represented by the parties and their counsel, when coming from different legal systems. *Amiable composition* is thus used as an instrument of departure from legal differences on a substantive level, and opting for an anational standard instead – and as such can be perceived as a counterpart to compromising procedural solutions, analysed above. The definition and limits of *amiable composition* itself are, however, still embedded in national legal systems, which might delineate them to a different extent.[42]

39 Weinberg (n 30) 233.

40 Cf. T.E. Carbonneau, *Resolving Transnational Disputes Through International Arbitration: Sixth Sokol Colloquium* (University of Virgina Press 1984) 134.

41 Kerr (n 24).

42 Cf. Weinberg (n 30) 235ff.

Another possible, shared reason for choosing *lex mercatoria* or *amiable composition* is the wish of the parties to possibly preserve a long-lasting business relationship. Flexibility of the *amiable composition* mechanisms is in such cases perceived as endorsing such protection. A third rationale, proposed by Kerr, relates to the economy of the process: availability of an (arguably simpler) equity-based dispute resolution tool helps to tame quasi-litigious, adversarial endeavours of the parties' counsel and arbitrators, as well as to reduce costs of case management. The fourth argument is that of an amicable rather than a legally strict approach to the assessment of damages, which allows for relevant modification of rules, primarily meant for domestic purposes and less practical in the context of cross-border transactions.

Considered in the context of Kerr's arguments, the difference between deciding the case on the basis of *lex mercatoria* and *ex aequo et bono* seems to be *prima facie* rather one of degree than of character, with *amiable composition* allowing for even farther-reaching freedom and flexibility in deciding the case. In application of the New Law Merchant principles arbitrators are bound by the already-existing autonomous rules of international trade (even if these rules are vague and not expressed fully before the issuance of an award, the arbitrators are not supposed to create them out of thin air; they are also not entitled to disregard the already formulated and established principles). In comparison, *amiables compositeurs* enjoy a wider scope of discretionary powers, with a competence to decide the case by reaching beyond the limitations of the rules of law, both domestic and transnational.

This difference raises a question of the extent of the freedom of arbitrators acting as *amiables compositeurs*. The decision made by them ought to be confined to the limits of objectively verifiable fairness standards. As Manley O. Hudson remarks, the court resolving a case on equity grounds

> does not have a complete freedom of action. It cannot act capriciously and arbitrarily. To the extent that it goes outside the applicable law, or acts where no law is applicable, it must proceed upon objective considerations of what is fair and just. Such considerations depend, in large measure, upon the judges' personal appreciation, and yet the Court would not be justified in reaching a result which could not be explained on rational grounds.[43]

The difference between *amiable composition* and *lex mercatoria* decision-making thus lies also in the type of standard on which the decision is grounded. Another critical distinction is the source of these two competences: the powers to apply *lex mercatoria* are usually recognized as part of the general competence of the arbitrators to apply the rules of law they deem appropriate when no choice

---

43 M.O. Hudson, *The Permanent Court of International Justice, 1920–1942* (Macmillan 1943). Quoted after A.F. M. Maniruzzaman, 'The Arbitrator's Prudence in Lex Mercatoria: Amiable Composition and Ex Aequo Et Bono in Decision Making' 18 Mealey's Int'l Arb Rep (2003) 2.

of substantive law was made by the parties, and they do not require a separate, specific authorization. *Amiable composition*, on the contrary, is allowed only upon an explicit agreement of the parties, as can be seen, for example, in LCIA Rules Art. 22.4; ICC Arbitration Rules Art. 21.3; Stockholm Rules Art. 22(3); and HKIAC Administered Arbitration Rules, Art. 31.2.

Notably, the 2012 CIETAC Rules remain silent on the issue of admissibility and scope of *amiable composition*, analogically to the restrictive stance on the possibility of basing an award on the *lex mercatoria* principles. Article 47.1 of the CIETAC Rules provides that '[t]he arbitral tribunal shall independently and impartially render a fair and reasonable arbitral award based on the facts of the case and the terms of the contract, in accordance with the law, and with reference to international practices.'

The standard according to which the case is resolved is exclusively the law – no reference to the rules of law (interpreted as encompassing the *lex mercatoria* principles, as discussed in the preceding chapter) is made. *Lex mercatoria* can be then taken into account as long as it is consistent with international practices, although these two terms cannot be treated as synonymous. Moreover, the expression 'reference to international practices' denotes a possibility of application of such standards rather than a mandatory recourse to them. A departure from the wording adopted in the UNCITRAL Model Law, Art. 28(4) ('In all cases, the arbitral tribunal shall decide in accordance with the terms of the contract and shall take into account the usages of the trade applicable to the transaction'[44]) also seems to indicate a looser standard. This might be interpreted as consistent with what Chi Manjiao characterizes as historical reluctance of the Chinese arbitrators to applying *lex mercatoria* in case of lack of explicit choice by the parties, even though there are no definite legal obstacles to such determination.[45]

In this context, the accompanying lack of regulation on *amiable composition* in the CIETAC Rules can be seen as a deliberate exclusion of equity-based adjudication. Combined with a simultaneous, broad access to the conciliation mechanism by means of Art. 45, it signals preference for channelling a possibility of departure from strict application of the law to the merits of the case via the arb-med track.

As already stated, whereas an authorization to act as an *amiable compositeur* is generally considered to also encompass a possible *lex mercatoria* application,[46] the competence to adjudicate on the basis of *lex mercatoria*, common in modern rules

44 Cf. also HKIAC Rules, Art. 31.3; ICC Rules Art. 21.2. The LCIA Rules and Stockholm Rules do not contain an explicit reference to the usages of trade, but they provide for application of the rules of law (and not only law) to the merits of the case.

45 Chi Manjiao, '"The Iceberg Beneath the Water": The Hidden Discrimination against the Lex Mercatoria in Chinese Arbitration' 7 J Priv Int'l L (2011).

46 Some commentators expressed different views though, usually based on reluctance to recognize *lex mercatoria* as a possible ground for an award – cf. Mustill and Boyd's opinion, doubtful 'whether a Lex Mercatoria even exists, in the sense of an international commercial law divorced from any state law, or at least, that it exists in any sense useful for

of procedure of the major arbitral centres, does not entitle an arbitrator to perform *amiable composition* (which requires a specific, explicit agreement). David W. Rivkin also notes that, while exercising the *amiable composition* competence, arbitrators are not obligated to apply the *lex mercatoria* principles, but are entitled to do so as long as those principles are based on equity.[47] This distinction, while convincing, might nevertheless turn out to be blurred in adjudicatory practice, as the competence to apply *lex mercatoria* (including its non-equity-based rules) can also be currently drawn from the general provisions of the rules of procedure of most arbitral institutions, and not only from the specific *amiable composition* authorization.

Another possible source of confusion might be the fact of presence of rules providing for a recourse to equity in many domestic legal systems. If rules of this kind can be determined as *lex causae*, the resulting possibility of deciding the case on the grounds of fairness and equity will not be tantamount to *amiable composition* and will not require a separate authorization by the parties. As already observed by Filip De Ly in 1992:

> in many legal systems such as the Swiss, German and Dutch and to a lesser extent in French and Belgian law, the distinction between application of strict law and *amiable composition* has eroded due to the emergence of open-ended rules (*Generalklauseln, normes floues*). The law is therefore no longer as strict as it used to be and considerations of equity also are very important in its application. These developments may be seen in substantive law as well as in conflict of laws.[48]

As a result, the use of equity arguments in an award is no longer necessarily indicative of the accompanying will of the parties to extend the arbitrators' powers by granting an *amiable composition* competence (or, in case of lack of such authorization, of exceeding the limits of their powers).

The issue of distinguishing between *amiable composition* and *lex mercatoria*-based arbitral decision-making has been addressed by arbitral case law and related courts' decisions since the late 1970s. The courts' decisions in such cases as *Norsolor* and *Fougerolle*, recognizing validity of the reviewed awards, had also marked the emancipation of *lex mercatoria* as an autonomous basis for an arbitral award. Whereas *amiable composition* had been historically recognized as an option contractually available to the parties, the issue of the possibility of application of the *lex mercatoria* principles by arbitrators without an authorization to act as *amiables compositeurs* must have been separately expressed and clarified.

---

the solving of commercial disputes': M.J. Mustill and S.C. Boyd, *The Law and Practice of Commercial Arbitration in England* (Butterworths 1989) 81.

47 D.W. Rivkin, 'Enforceability of Arbitral Awards based on Lex Mercatoria' 9 Arb Int'l (1993) 71.

48 De Ly (n 31) 124.

In *Pabalk Ticaret Limited Sirketi v Norsolor SA*, both the French Cour de Cassation and the Austrian Supreme Court upheld an enforcement of an award despite the claims that the arbitrators exceeded their powers in deciding on damages on the grounds of equity without a proper authorization to act as *amiables compositeurs*. In its 1984 decision, the French Supreme Court thus shared the view of the Court of First Instance of Paris, which decided that the arbitrators

> had in conformity with Art. 13 of the Arbitration Rules of the ICC applied the law designated as the proper law by the rule of conflict which they deemed the most appropriate, which in this case was the general principles of obligations generally applicable to international commerce and that even if they had twice in their reasoning used the term 'equity', they had not decided as 'amiables compositeurs'.[49]

In its *Norsolor* decision, Cour de Cassation continued the line adopted earlier in *Fougerolle v Banque du Proche-Orient*,[50] where it found that general principles of international commerce are a source of law, as such they can be determined to be the rules of law governing the contract, and their application does not require a specific *amiable composition* authorization.

An opposite situation has been analysed by A.F.M. Maniruzzaman, who focuses on the influence of *amiable composition* upon the evolution of *lex mercatoria* (while also remarkably characterizing the distinction between these two methods as 'formalistic and artificial'[51]). Maniruzzaman considers situations in which arbitrators, acting as *amiables compositeurs*, develop *lex mercatoria* principles. He adopts as a starting point a well-known doctrinal assertion, discussed also in the preceding chapter, that the New Law Merchant in its current version is not a sufficiently consolidated and clear system of rules. He then further states that as

> [t]he method by which the arbitrator will arrive at the *lex mercatoria* can never be predetermined when the applicable lex is not clear cut or well established … In such a fluid situation of the *lex mercatoria* the arbitrator may arrive at *lex* via *amiable composition* and *ex aequo et bono*. Thus the arbitrator can develop the *lex mercatoria* by equity, fairness and natural justice principles which are not already part of the *lex mercatoria* but are made part of it by virtue of their appropriateness or suitability in the circumstances to reach a fair settlement of the dispute at his disposal.[52]

---

49 *Pabalk Ticaret Limited Sirketi v Norsolor SA* in *Yearbook Commercial Arbitration* vol XI (A.J. van den Berg ed, Kluwer Law International 1986), Cour de Cassation [Supreme Court] (First Civil Chamber) 485.

50 *Fougerolle v Banque du Proche-Orient*, 1982 Rev Arb 183 (Cour de Cassation).

51 Maniruzzaman (n 43) 4.

52 Ibid.

Further argumentation offered in this regard seems, however, unclear. The author advocates adaptability and flexibility of *lex mercatoria* formulated by the means of *amiable composition* supported by the 'arbitrator's prudence in the real life of trade and commerce',[53] yet it is not evident how exactly equity-based adjudication is related to the formulation of usages of international trade, or to the finding of the common core of contract law of different legal systems (as *lex mercatoria* has been traditionally defined). It seems possible to defend this position by pointing to the fact that many *lex mercatoria* principles are consistent with equity, for example with the concept of good faith in international commercial relations frequently invoked as permeating the New Law Merchant.

Such consistency is, however, first, not complete and total (there are also non-equitable *lex mercatoria* principles). Second, the concept of using *amiable composition* – the most individualized and based on the most subjective sense of fairness of all the methods of arbitral decision-making – seems rather stretched if it is to be a natural vehicle for formulating the most universal, objectively pre-existing and shared rules of law applicable in arbitration. The problem with distinguishing a 'regular', individual case-bound outcome of *amiable composition* from a formulation of a *lex mercatoria* rule by the means of equitable adjudication would arguably lead to an even more blurred image of the latter. As *lex mercatoria* does not need a particular arbitrators' competence enhancement any more to be applied in arbitration (as shown in the discussion of the *Norsolor* and *Fougerolle* cases), a possible argument of procedural rationality would be also void. The concerns of uncertainty of law and unpredictability of the results of arbitration are noticed by Maniruzzaman himself. Additionally, it can be remarked that significant efforts have been made in the past decades through arbitral case law and the private codifications movement to solidify the New Law Merchant and deprive it of its odium of particular nebulosity. In this context, an acceptance of a widespread use of *amiable composition* for the purpose of creative formulation of the *lex mercatoria* could be seen as a step back in solidification of this legal field.

Amiable Composition and Legal Certainty

The problem of predictability of the results of the process of dispute resolution, mentioned above, has often been discussed in the context of equity-based arbitration. For Weinberg, both the determination of *lex mercatoria* as *lex contractus* (or *lex causae*) and an authorization for arbitrators to act as *amiables compositeurs* are choices bearing a high risk of uncertainty of the result, which can be viewed, especially by the losing party, as 'arbitrary and capricious'.[54] It is worth noting that in regard to *lex mercatoria* exactly opposite arguments have been raised by other authors, who see the recourse to universal principles of international trade

53 Ibid.

54 Weinberg (n 30) 247.

as a potentially much more stable choice than reliance upon the determination and application of foreign domestic provisions.[55] Increased adequacy of the New Law Merchant for the circumstances of international commercial transactions (as compared to strictly national legal systems) has also been the object of discussion. A continuation of the stance advocated by Berthold Goldman,[56] it has been commented upon as enhancing rational expectations as to the possible outcome of a dispute arising in a cross-border business environment. For example, the issue of the predictability of law in an international context was addressed in the ICC Award No. 8385/1995, where the sole arbitrator reasoned that

> in international commerce it is very important that legal rules produce foreseeable results, respond to the expectations of the parties and take account of the prevalent usages of the international marketplace. In such context it would be inappropriate to apply rules which solely respond to state interests.[57]

Private codifications of the *lex mercatoria* rules (including such successful initiatives as the UNIDROIT Principles of International Commercial Contracts) have also been considered as significantly raising the level of certainty of standards applicable to international transactions (see Chapter 8).

It is rather *amiable composition* then, that seems more predestined to lead to uncertain results in dispute resolution. Its limited applicability, specifically restricted to the explicitly expressed will of the parties, can be seen as a sufficient precaution, though: it is only when the parties clearly wish the arbitrators to act as *amiables compositeurs* that they are entitled to undertake such a role. The relative unpredictability of the outcome of arbitration can be then interpreted as outweighed – in the opinion of the parties themselves – by other values, which *amiable composition* endorses. Among them are flexibility of procedural approach (particularly remarkable in the context of the growingly 'litigious', regular arbitration) and detachment from legalistic rigours in those cases where the parties would perceive them as an unnecessarily stiff corset to their relationship (where business approach prevails over legal concerns). Other arguments for *amiable composition* may include the following: avoidance of many antagonistic, adversarial aspects of arbitral procedure; a higher possibility of preservation of the amicable relationship between the parties who are not faced with court-like technicalities; evaluation of the parties' relationship through a standard that is truly anational and can be perceived as uncontroversial (with equity understood as an ethical common reason in international commerce); as well as highly individualized adaptability of the process of decision-making to the particularities of a case instead of application of general rules, not necessarily perceived as fully

55 Cf. Ana M. López Rodríguez, *Lex Mercatoria and Harmonization of Contract Law in the EU* (Djof 2003) 85.

56 Berthold Goldman, 'Lex Mercatoria' 3 Forum internationale (1983).

57 ICC Award No. 8385/1995, 124 J Droit Int'l (Clunet) 1061–73.

adequate by the parties. Finally, unlike in mediation, it is not a drive towards a compromise that guides the process – the case is evaluated against a standard (equity) and decided accordingly; the binding character of an award might be attractive for those parties that would like to avoid unnecessary exacerbation of their relations throughout the procedure, yet they wish for a definite, internationally recognized and easily enforceable resolution of their dispute.

The fact that equity-based arbitration – unlike mediation – offers a solution reached 'externally' (not by the parties themselves) might also in some cases enable the parties to distance themselves from the dispute and its solution (it might turn out to be psychologically easier to accept losing an arbitration case than to feel 'tricked into' unfavourable settlement reached through mediation, in which the parties are necessarily personally involved). Preservation of a long-term relationship between the contractors might be thus in some cases, paradoxically, more easily achieved through arbitration than via an ADR track. *Amiable composition* as the 'soft' version of arbitration would be then attractive for those contestants who are interested in flexibility and freedom from overly legalistic constraints, combined with a final outcome that is firm, final and based on justice considerations.

This last attribute (equity as an aspect of justice) corresponds with the concept of equity as an objectively verifiable standard, as advocated by Judge Hudson, quoted above. This doctrine was formulated in 1888 in a Canadian appeal case, *Rolland v Cassidy*, where the Earl of Selbourne remarked that arbitrators adjudicating on the grounds of equity are not entirely free in their decisions, as 'being amiables compositeurs, and not bound to proceed with strict form and regularity in everything, though they were, as their Lordships assume, bound to proceed according to the substantial rules of justice'.[58] This objective aspect, contrasted with resolution of the dispute on the basis of individual consciousness of the arbitrators, is more prominent in those legal systems in which *amiable composition* is clearly distinguished from decision-making *ex aequo et bono*. While the latter would invoke external standards of justice as a ground for the decision (as an alternative to a decision based on the rules of the law), *amiable composition* or contractual arbitration is understood as an authorization to settle the case, not to decide it. Mauro Rubino-Sammartano remarks that,

> [u]nder Italian law, a distinction is made between procedural arbitration (in which arbitrators reach a decision similar to a judge's decision) and contractual arbitration (or a mandate to settle) … Settling, not deciding, the dispute is the task of an arbitrator in the Italian *arbitrato irrituale*, and apparently in the *arbitraje informal* in Spain.[59]

Even in those jurisdictions, the equity-based arbitral decision-making raises doubts related to low predictability of the results. Indeed, the practical possibility of

58 *Rolland v Cassidy* (1888) 13 AC 770, 774.

59 Rubino-Sammartano (n 4) 471.

anticipating the outcomes of resolution of a dispute based on *amiable composition* is rather dubious, partially because of the fact that the ability of the parties to foresee an outcome and the exact character of potential controversies stemming from a contract is naturally highly limited. This trait is, however, not necessarily in conflict with the proclaimed, objective character of equity: while *amiable composition* is based on *a casu ad casum* decision-making, it is also meant to be free from arbitrariness and capriciousness and should be executed in accordance with a verifiable standard (a relevant *ex post* evaluation of an award should be possible). What this standard is, in Hudson's view, seems to be an intersubjective (rather than objective), socially accepted sense of fairness. Moreover, it can (and, arguably, should) be further contextualized as a sense of equity and fairness shared by average participants of legal relations of a particular kind. In the context of *amiable composition* in arbitration that would be international commercial contractors (or the fictional *societas mercatorum*), focused on specific aspects of equity, relevant and recurrent in an international business environment.

In practice, *amiable composition*, even when performed in good faith by an arbitrator with no appearance of bias, seems particularly susceptible to suspicions of him or her following individual inclinations and subjective preferences rather than applying a standard verifiable in a specialized, international context. It might also turn out that such a commonly accepted standard of reference is virtually impossible to be found in the rich and growingly diversified realm of international commerce where the 'international framework must fit a world where ethical values are not always shared'.[60] Analogically to the historical evolution of the concept of *lex mercatoria* – from a set of principles forwarded in the 'oil cases' in the 1950s and 1960s to rules developed through comparative analysis – *amiables compositeurs* must also face the problem of lack of a globally shared definition of equity. An arbitrator might then simply not have much choice but to seek the best available solution, which would be consistent with his or her own sense of fairness and justice, as well as possibly uncontroversial in the light of the circumstances of a particular case (with a regard to the connotations of the concept of fairness and justice in the parties' legal environments).

60 Craig et al. (n 2) 138.

Chapter 10
Public Order Considerations

Public Order – Concept and Contexts

A specific consideration, affecting the outcome of a process of legal interpretation in international commercial arbitration, is recourse to *ordre public*, understood as a transnational concept. A drive towards ensuring conformity of the adopted rendition of applicable rules with the demands of public international order has manifested itself in some arbitral awards to a modifying effect on the application of *lex causae*. In this sense, *ordre public international* can be seen as an interpretive directive, adopted in the practice of international commercial arbitration.

While present in the private international law regulations of some domestic legal systems, and indeed borrowed from national jurisprudence, in arbitration it is treated as a transnational principle of a presumably universal character. Its application is thus different from a domestic one, which aims at preserving specific public values, as seen through the lenses of the legal system of the adjudicating, national court (and is, as such, more territorially embedded in *lex fori,* even in regard to the international version of the concept, as discussed further in detail below). It should be also distinguished from national policies, taking the form of a domestic public order, the limits of applicability of which in arbitration are an object of a separate discussion.

The concept of public international order is also well established and widely commented upon in the literature of public international law, as one of the foundations of harmonious relations between States in a global context. The scope of public international order considerations, defined in the context of disputes of commercial character between private parties, is naturally different in character, as well as in content, from its public international law counterpart. Still, the discussion of implementation of such a modifying principle in a process of legal interpretation, vivid in public international case law and literature, can serve as a source of inspiration in determining the limits of discretionary powers of arbitrators and the consequences of application of a transnational version of this concept in ICA, oriented at private relations. It also affects arbitral legal interpretation of public international law instruments.

In the doctrine of public international law, the wording of Art. 53 of the Vienna Convention on the Law of Treaties (VCLT), referring to the 'community of states as a whole' in the context of peremptory norms of general international law (*jus cogens*), has led some authors to formulate a thesis ascribing to this community a growing, autonomous power of determination of 'fundamental rules based on public policy, values, or public order (ordre public)'.[1] The assumption of the superior status of such rules in the hierarchy of norms of public international law and their excessive application is nevertheless disputed, and lack of sufficient evidence supporting this claim in relevant case law and literature has also been criticized as destabilizing international legal order and undermining the credibility of international tribunals and commentators.[2]

Besides controversies related to the hierarchy of norms of public international law, the use of *ordre public* arguments in resolution of public international law disputes has also been treated with reserve due to the relative indeterminacy of this concept. The tension between advocates of flexibility of legal interpretation and ethical orientation of public international order-based arguments on one side and public international law textualists on the other has led to the formulation of different kinds of *caveats* in regard to interpretation of international treaties and conventions. As Gerald Fitzmaurice, representing legal textualist approach, remarked, in case of inconsistencies between the parties' intentions and public order goals, where the latter were allowed to supersede the former in the process of interpretation,

> [s]ince it is thus left to the adjudicator to decide not only whether there is such inconsistency but also what *are* the goals of public order (and of which public order) to be taken into account, it is evident that on this wideranging, indeed almost illimitable basis, the parties could never be sure how their treaty would be applied or whether it would be applied at all. The process would, in fact, confer on the 'decision-maker' a discretion of a kind altogether exceeding the normal limits of the judicial function, amounting rather to the exercise of an administrative role.[3]

Ordre public considerations are thus treated with reserve as vague and too arbitrarily determined – as Fitzmaurice suggests, potentially filled with any content befitting the adjudicators (Jean-Marc Sorel characterizes them also as 'short-lived and politically reversible'[4]). The predictability of interpretation is thus, from this perspective, inevitably compromised. Counterarguments to this approach, regarding legal uncertainty, point to the generally wide scope of discretion in construing treaties, based on the observation that the 'plain reality is that the interpreter of a broad international agreement is operating in a largely indeterminate setting'.[5] Analogically, the doctrine of interpretation of public international law

1 D. Shelton, 'Normative Hierarchy in International Law' 100 Am J Int'l L (2006) 291.

2 Ibid. 292.

3 G. Fitzmaurice, 'Vae Victis or Woe to the Negotiators – Your Treaty or Our Interpretation of It' 65 Am J Int'l L (1971) 369.

4 J.-M. Sorel, 'Some Questions about the Definition of Terrorism and the Fight against its Financing' 14 EJIL (2003) 371.

5 R.A. Falk, 'On Treaty Interpretation and the New Haven Approach: Achievements and Prospects' 8 Va J Int'l L (1967) 351.

agreements seems to have early embraced the realistic assumption that the activity of an adjudicator in this field always necessarily involves a process of selection from between competing visions of public order, the results of which will never be free from policy repercussions:

> [s]ince there can be no 'objective' or 'neutral' application in the sense of applications devoid of Policy consequences for the contending systems of public order, it is inescapable that the authoritative appliers of international agreements make a choice, however implicit in what they decide, about the kind of world public order … they would establish and maintain.[6]

In the doctrine of private international law the notion of public order as a modifying element in legal interpretation is well established and may appear in the form of either internal, State-specific public policy or as international public order, barring the application of foreign law or its consequences. Besides numerous domestic legal systems, the *ordre public* exception has also been adopted in international instruments, such as the EC 1980 Rome Convention on the Law Applicable to Contractual Obligations (Art. 16) and the subsequent Rome I Regulation 593/2008. According to Art. 21 of the latter: '[t]he application of a provision of the law of any country specified by this Regulation may be refused only if such application is manifestly incompatible with the public policy (*ordre public*) of the forum.'

The internal public order was, arguably, the earlier and more commonly applied version of the *ordre public* argument in private international law cases. It has been characterized as the fundamental principles of the domestic legal order of the State of the court resolving the case. Their application in a private international case prevents the adoption of an interpretation of proper, foreign law in a way that would be inconsistent with those fundamental norms. As a consequence, the *ordre public* argument has been characterized as a 'safety valve', protecting the consistency and integrity of adjudication in a given State, so as to avoid legal effects incompatible with most rudimentary rules of *legis fori*[7] (observable, for example, in family law cases with an international element, where the application of provisions on family life institutions not recognized by the legal system of forum might be prevented due to an *ordre public* defence). Analysed from the point of view of legal interpretation in an international commercial context, such modifying use of the public internal order argument can be thus perceived as enhancing the domestic particularities of legal interpretation and preserving the territorial orientation and fragmentation of the application of law, rather than its uniform rendition worldwide – as public policy of the forum prevails over foreign substantive law determined as *lex causae*.

---

6 Myres S. McDougal et al., *The Interpretation of International Agreements and World Public Order: Principles of Content and Procedure* (Martinus Nijhoff 1994) lxxiii.

7 Pavel Kalenský, *Trends of Private International Law* (Martinus Nijhoff 1971) 243.

Despite long and widespread tradition of the use of this concept in domestic adjudication in private international law cases, the limits of *ordre public international* (while perhaps free from many of the political connotations of its public international law counterpart) remain imprecise and open. The problems with exact definition of this concept have led French legal doctrine to the formulation of a general characteristic of public international order as a set of superior and inviolable values, combining such interests of general character as political, moral, social and economic ones – perceived as a field narrower than that of internal public order.[8] Also, in this variation, the argument of inconsistency of an otherwise applicable foreign rule with public international order is treated by the court as an exception, validating non-application of such rule.

As Adi Chen observes:

> [t]he content and composition of international public order run the full gamut of standards, values, considerations and policy. But these are not defined by statute. And to the best of my knowledge, no legislature ... has defined international public order, although they occasionally refer to it. The definition has been left to the courts. International public order does not have the obligatory force of normal legal precedent and no formal procedure is required to change it.[9]

It is, then, not only the current content of this concept that is relatively vague and has to ascertained on an *a casu ad casum* basis. It is also its adaptability to changed, global circumstances, which fluctuates over time, that makes this notion even more open and its impact onto legal interpretation increasingly uncertain.

Another important feature of the *ordre public international* argument in private international cases resolved by the domestic courts is its localized character: while the domestic connotation is more subtle than in case of internal public order, it is still reflecting the perception of rules fundamental for public order from the perspective of the legal system of the court resolving the case. As the French Cour de Cassation declared, the otherwise applicable provisions of foreign law, which are contrary to the 'French conception' of international public policy cannot be given effect in France.[10] Formerly, the doctrine of public international order has been formulated by the Court as all the principles of universal justice, to which French public opinion ascribes absolute, international value.[11]

---

8 M.L. Niboyet, *Droit international privé* (LGDJ 2007) 307.

9 Adi Chen, 'Conflict of Laws, Conflict of Mores and External Public Policy in Israel' in *Yearbook of Private International Law* vol 12 (2010) (Andrea Bonomi and Gian Paolo Romano eds, Sellier 2011) 545.

10 France, Cour de cassation, Chambre civile 1, 23 janvier 1979, 77-12825 ('les dispositions de la loi étrangère normalement compétente qui sont contraires à la conception française de l'ordre public international ne sauraient avoir d'efficacité en France').

11 France, Cour de cassation, Chambre civile 2, 25 mai 1948, Lautour.

The distinction between the scope of application of French conceptualizations of *ordre public interne* and *ordre public international* is based not on the character of the dispute (entirely domestic or containing an international component), but on a substantive system of rules determined to be the proper law of the case. While the former of the orders is considered binding 'when the legal relationship or transaction is governed by French law or otherwise centered in France',[12] the latter shall be applied to all cases resolved by French courts, including those that are governed by the rules other than the French law.[13]

Thomas G. Guedj remarks that giving effect to the *ordre public* exception requires a performance of a value judgement on the content of foreign law, determined as *lex causae.*[14] In practice, it takes a form of a remarkably far-reaching, soft standards-based intervention of an adjudicator into what would otherwise be a regular outcome of the process of legal interpretation. As a consequence, admissibility of this type of argument can be perceived as a manifestation of mistrust, or even, as Guedj further puts it, hostility towards the application of foreign law. This hostility is expressed in the conditions of what a court perceives as a clash between the competing legislative policies of the two domestic legal systems: that of the forum, and the one that has been determined as governing the case. This hostility is somewhat mitigated by the defensive character of the *ordre public* exception and its impact, traditionally assumed to be limited to a negative effect (derogation of foreign rules determined as proper law). An alternative doctrine, seeking broader effects of this exception (including positive ones), argued for by Paul Lerebours-Pigeonnière,[15] has not been followed by the mainstream of continental legal doctrine and case law.

This, however, does not alter the fact of far-reaching, interfering, corrective effects of *legis fori* over *lex causae* when the exception is being applied. Interpretation of substantive law in such cases is thus a two-layered one: the 'neutral' construction of relevant rules of foreign law is subsequently modified by the application of principles, considered by *lex fori* to belong to the sphere of public international order. It can also be possibly argued that the dominance of *lex fori* is ascertained also in the cases where the exception is not applied, due to its sole existence and possibility of use – as any interpretation of foreign *lex causae* is (potentially) performed through the lenses of the law of the forum, and with a regard to consistency of the former with public policy values sought by the latter.

---

12 George A. Bermann, 'Mandatory Rules of Law' in *International Arbitration* (F. Ferrari and S. Kroll eds, Sellier European Law 2010) 328.

13 A. Sheppard, 'Mandatory Rules in International Commercial Arbitration – an English Law Perspective' 18 Am Rev Int'l Arb (2007) 129.

14 T.G. Guedj, 'The Theory of the *Lois de Police*, a Functional Trend in Continental Private International Law – A Comparative Analysis with Modern American Theories' 39 Am J Comp L (1991) 667 fn 27.

15 Paul Lerebours-Pigeonnière, *Précis de droit international privé* (4th edn, Dalloz 1946).

The public policy values, fundamental for the legal system of the forum, have also been found as a single possible ground for overriding decisions based on extralegal standards: as Ole Lando noted in his 1985 review of the use of *lex mercatoria* in international arbitration, a number of Swiss and German commentators agreed on a possibility of setting aside an *ex aequo et bono* award only in a case when giving an effect to it would violate a principle of German public policy.[16] A similar view has been expressed by authors from other legal traditions, commenting further on practical implications for arbitrators acting as *amiables compositeurs*, who should not disregard substantive and procedural norms of public policy, arguably not only of *legis loci arbitri*, but also of the States, in which the enforcement of an award is likely to be sought.[17]

The issue of public order considerations in international commercial arbitration has two aspects. The first one is a regard, recommended for arbitrators to retain, for *ordre public* rules of the place of the potential award enforcement (as described above on the example of *amiables compositeurs*) due to what has been defined as an obligation of the tribunal to rendering an award that will be enforceable.[18] Pierre Mayer characterizes this duty by pointing out that,

> [a]lthough arbitrators are neither guardians of the public order nor invested by the State with the mission of applying its mandatory rules, they ought nevertheless have an incentive to do so out of a sense of duty to the survival of international arbitration as an institution ... They should consider that if they do not apply a mandatory rule of law, the award will in all likelihood be refused enforcement in the country which promulgated the rule.[19]

While these considerations can be seen as secondary and corrective to the main process of legal interpretation performed by the tribunal, they may strongly affect the final outcome of the decision-making process.

The second aspect is a concept of public international order as a transnational principle, administered within the process of arbitral decision-making and serving the function of an exception to the application of proper substantive law, comparable to its domestic conflict of laws counterpart. The difference lies in the lack of direct embedment of the ICA-related notion of *ordre public international* in the legal system of the place of arbitration. Unlike the domestic courts, which render decisions in the name of the State, arbitral tribunals do not bear the same

16 O. Lando, 'The Lex Mercatoria in International Commercial Arbitration' 34 ICLQ (1985) 757.

17 Cf. S. Jarvin, 'The Sources and Limits of the Arbitrator's Powers' 2 Arb Int'l (1986); W.W. Park, 'National Law and Commercial Justice: Safeguarding Procedural Integrity in International Arbitration' 63 Tul L Rev (1988) 648.

18 Cf. ICC Award No. 4132/1983.

19 Pierre Mayer, 'Mandatory Rules of Law in International Arbitration' 2 Arb Int'l (1986) 284.

kind of close relationship with *lex loci arbitri*, for legal and institutional, but also personal reasons. The arbitral tribunals, unlike the domestic courts, do not act as the organs of the State:[20] but also, due to the increasingly cosmopolitan character of ICA, arbitrators frequently are not primarily trained in the law of the place of arbitration. While they can be (more or less consciously) prone to fill the concept of public international order with preconceptions grounded in their own legal systems, these are not necessarily identical with the vision of *ordre public* promoted by *lex loci arbitri*.

The question of the scope of the concept of *ordre public* in arbitration was also raised in the context of discussions as to whether it is limited to substantive law issues only (in those cases where they are irreconcilable with public order principles), or whether it also encompasses the cases of misapplication of conflict of laws rules of the place of arbitration. The latter, leading to a determination of specific legal system, other than the presumable *lex causae*, as the proper law of the dispute, can significantly affect the outcome of the dispute resolution. An inclusive approach in this regard has been represented by several Swiss commentators, pointing to the parties being denied a hearing as to the content of their rights and obligations under the law that should have been applied by the tribunal.[21] Another situation, considered by Dutoit to be falling within the limits of a violation of *ordre public*, is a disregard of the parties' explicit choice of law governing their relationship.[22]

This view is not commonly shared by the doctrine of arbitration though, and the dominant perspective connects the violation of *ordre public* with the outcome of the case, understood, after Dasser,[23] as the

> decision on the merits, and not on the preliminary question about the applicable law ... When arbitrators reach a result that does not violate the fundamental moral convictions of a legal system, there is no violation of ordre public, regardless of whether they have applied the 'right' or the 'wrong' law.[24]

The perception of misapplication of conflict of laws rules as *per se* constituting a violation of public order, is thus rather exceptional, and the analysis focuses on consequences of the final decision as to the substance of the dispute, as seen in the light of fundamental principles of the legal order of the forum (where the award is sought to be set aside or enforced).

Functional and purposive arguments of arbitral autonomy and the consequent keeping of arbitral awards free from unnecessary, excessive judicial control

20 Bermann (n 12) 329.

21 Cf. Poudret, after J.G. Frick, *Arbitration and Complex International Contracts* (Kluwer Law International 2001) 135 fn 617.

22 Ibid. 135.

23 F. Dasser, *Internationale Schiedsgerichte und lex mercatoria* (Schulthess 1989) 284.

24 Frick (n 21) 135.

are further invoked to oppose broad interpretation of the *ordre public* concept. Moreover, along with wide discretionary powers attributed to arbitrators under most rules of procedure in regard to the determination of proper substantive law, the risk of actual violation of the conflict of laws rules seems rather marginal. Growing popularity of the *voie directe* competence (allowing arbitrators to apply to the merits of a dispute substantive law or rules of law they deem appropriate, without the intermediary stage of conflict of laws analysis[25]) indicates this tendency to an even further extent. Analogically, the enforcement regime of the New York Convention is also considered to encompass a narrow concept of *ordre public*, not allowing for a review of the selection of conflict of laws rules applied by the abitrators.[26]

Ordre Public Exception and Mandatory Rules of Law

The concept of public international order in arbitration is often analysed in the context of the doctrine of mandatory rules of law. As Andrew Barraclough and Jeff Waincymer explain:

> Mandatory rules are laws that purport to apply irrespective of a contract's proper law or the procedural regime selected by the parties. In this sense, whether they are 'mandatory' does not depend on whether they will ultimately end up applying via the relevant conflict of laws analysis, but only on how the law itself defines its sphere of application. Mandatory rules can reflect states' internal or international public policy, and generally protect economic, social or political interests. They can be either procedural, for example requiring due process, or substantive, such as certain tax, competition and import/export laws.[27]

According to this doctrine, *ordre public* represents a set of fundamental rules that should be classified as mandatory rules of law, as they cannot be disregarded in adjudication and successfully intervene into the final outcome of legal interpretation and decision-making performed by the court.

In international commercial arbitration, the problem of application of mandatory rules of law is considered to be ubiquitous, and estimated to occur in

---

25 Cf. Linda Silberman and Franco Ferrari, 'Getting to the Law Applicable to the Merits in International Arbitration and the Consequences of Getting it Wrong' in *Conflict of Laws in International Arbitration* (F. Ferrari and S. Kroll eds, Sellier 2010) 320.

26 Andreas Bucher, 'Das Kapitel 11 des IPR-Gesetzes uber die internationale Schiedsgerichtsbarkeit' in *Beiträge zum neuen IPR des Sachen-, Schuld- und Gesellschaftsrechts: Festschrift für Prof. Rudolf Moser* (I. Schwander ed, Schulthess 1987) 214.

27 A. Barraclough and J. Waincymer, 'Mandatory Rules of Law in International Commercial Arbitration' 6 Melb J Int'l L (2005) 206.

more than fifty per cent of all arbitration cases.[28] It is also particularly demanding, as the legal relationship in question cannot be confined within the limits of a single domestic legal system (it contains an international component), but also because an arbitral tribunal is not acting in the name of a State of forum as a domestic court does; that is, it does not owe the same kind of allegiance to the national system of the *legis loci arbitri*. Serge Lazareff goes as far as to characterize this specific position of an arbitrator as one of not having *lex fori*, and thus not being

> *a priori* linked to any national public policy except, of course, that of the *lex contractus*; therefore the very concept of a foreign law is unknown to him. It also will be extremely difficult for him to deviate from the will of the litigants, since the autonomy of the parties is a more important element before an arbitrator than before courts. Furthermore, he must always stay politically neutral.[29]

This statement, stemming from the concept of anational, floating arbitration, seems, however, to be too far-reaching. It is certain that mandatory rules of the law governing the agreement shall be applied to the merits of the dispute, irrespective of the explicit will of the parties or lack thereof in this regard (cf. for example ICC Award No. 6142[30]). The status of public policy rules in this context (analysed 'from within' the legal system to be applied to the merits of the dispute) is a complex issue in itself, as discussed earlier. What forms an additional tier of *ordre public* considerations in arbitration, are, however, enforcement concerns. As a result, l*ex fori* (*lex loci arbitri*) does not remain irrelevant in the process of rendering an award.

The considerations of the law of the place of arbitration are to be taken into account, primarily due to the territoriality principle permeating the legal framework of international arbitration, and in particular the New York Convention provisions. As further discussed below, it is the recognition and enforcement concerns under the Convention that additionally channel arbitral interpretation and decision-making, with regard to public order principles of the systems other than *lex contractus*.

As Barraclough and Waincymer observe, arbitrators in such cases face the challenge of deciding between conflicting interests of the parties and the State[31] (as the effects of the parties' explicit or tacit decision as to the law governing their relationship are to be modified due to application of the *ordre public* exception). Their task becomes even more intricate when they have to give priority to directives of one of the conflicting public orders over another, when

---

28 M. Blessing, 'Mandatory Rules of Law versus Party Autonomy in International Arbitration' 14 J Int'l Arb (1997) 24.

29 S. Lazareff, 'Mandatory Extraterritorial Application of National Law' 11 Arb Int'l (1995) 138.

30 ICC Award No. 6142 (Clunet) 1039, after Lazareff (n 29) 139.

31 Barraclough and Waincymer (n 27) 206.

there is more than one legal system involved, either on the level of interpretation and application of the provisions of proper law *per se*, or by taking into account *ordre public* considerations of the law of the place (or places) of anticipated enforcement.

The New York Convention regime provides, in Article V (2) (b), for the public policy exception to recognition and enforcement of an arbitral award. It has served as a basis for formulation of the doctrine of rendering an enforceable award as one of the rudimentary duties of an arbitrator, further adopted by domestic laws on arbitration, rules of procedure, codes of professional ethics, as well as arbitral case law.[32] As a consequence, arbitrators are commonly faced with the challenge of fulfilling double standards: those of the seat of arbitration (where the award can be sought to be set aside) and those of the assumed place of enforcement. These considerations are multiplied in those cases where the place of enforcement is hardly predictable, due to a complex, international character of the case, as well as the legal status and possible, aggregate structure of the parties and diversified locations in which they might hold their assets.[33] In this context, Barraclough and Waincymer assume, after Derains, that arbitrators should take into account enforcement issues only if the conceivable place or places of enforcement can be reasonably anticipated. Consequently, they further suggest an adoption of a pragmatic standard, based on an analysis of concentration of the assets of the parties:

> [i]f there are assets in multiple jurisdictions that could meet the award, and only one promulgates a mandatory rule, enforceability does not compel it to be considered. However, if mandatory rules of all those states purport to apply, then weight may be given to at least one. Which that is and whether it would ultimately be applied would depend on the methodology adopted to assess the applicability of mandatory rules. In this context, the tribunal would have to resolve the conflict between each relevant state and the parties, and also the conflict between the states competing for application of their laws.[34]

The public policy concerns, related to recognition and enforcement of an award, and based on the territoriality principle of the New York Convention, are further considered as potentially undermining the character of international arbitration as a neutral and autonomous forum – and changing it into an arena for clashing domestic approaches.[35]

32 Gunther J. Horvath, 'The Duty of the Tribunal to Render an Enforceable Award' 18(2) J Int'l Arb (2001) 135ff.

33 Lazareff (n 29) 140.

34 Barraclough and Waincymer (n 27) 216.

35 Cf. N. Voser, 'Mandatory Rules of Law as a Limitation on the Law Applicable in International Commercial Arbitration' 7 Am Rev Int'l Arb (1996) 335.

Arbitration and Transnational Public Policy

Problems with this aspect of arbitral interpretation of applicable rules have led some authors to insist upon genuinely international public policy concerns as the only ones that should be taken into account in arbitral decision-making, as only then would the international character of arbitration be preserved.[36] Such a solution has been advocated as enabling arbitration to avoid fragmentation and domestic orientation of its case law. Considered by Gaillard in the context of *lex mercatoria* application in arbitration, adoption of such orientation has been commented upon as enhancing anational trends in arbitration. It would also make much easier the task of interpretation and application of proper law (and its further filtering through domestic public policy rules of the systems of the place of arbitration and enforcement), faced by arbitrators, by eliminating unnecessary parochial influences.

The postulated, consistent adoption of such an approach on a global scale seems currently still problematic, due not only to the setting aside and enforcement concerns discussed above. It is also a matter of globally and regionally diversified institutional frameworks of arbitration that would make the implementation of such a uniform policy difficult. The proliferation of similar procedural standards might serve as an example: while existent to a certain extent, it is realized through concerted practice of the arbitral centres rather than via adoption of a common stance. As the history of the *voie directe* competence demonstrates, it is also stretched in time and not necessarily completely universal. An aspect of competition between arbitration centres seems to be another important factor here, with enforcement prospects being a key consideration for the parties seeking resolution of their controversy, and consequently for arbitrators and their institutions as well. The issue of substantive content of such uniform, international public policy (as opposed to domestic principles, grounded in national legal systems) is yet another problem, mirroring the discussion on the content of *lex mercatoria*. Finally, ubiquity of arbitration in commercial disputes, and the large number of cases combined with the individual interpretive preferences of arbitrators, adopted in resolution of particular controversies, would certainly make the postulated harmonization of standards additionally difficult in practice.

A strive towards adoption of international policy considerations in arbitral decision-making can nevertheless be observed in practice. This has led some commentators to consider whether there are sufficient grounds for seeking relevant, applicable principles of *ordre public international* not in domestic legal systems (as discussed above in the example of French law, and explored by jurisprudence

36 Emmanuel Gaillard, 'Thirty Years of Lex Mercatoria: Towards the Selective Application of Transnational Rules' 10 ICSID Rev (1995) 223.

on the ground of other legal systems as well[37]), but directly in instruments and customs of international law.[38]

As regards terminology issues, the concept of public international order seems indeed to bear strong connotations with the domestic context of private international law. As Pieter Sanders remarks: 'International public policy, according to a generally accepted doctrine, is confined to violations of really fundamental conceptions of legal order *in the country concerned*.'[39] Consequently, the terms 'transnational public policy' and 'transnational public order' are being used to denote those fundamental principles, that are globally recognized and shared by different legal systems, or, as Pierre Lalive characterizes it, an osmosis of the genuinely international public policy considerations of national legal orders.[40] Such a concept is consistent with the definition of public policy offered by the International Law Association at its sixty-ninth conference, where the general rapporteur Audley Sheppard observed that it encompasses the fundamental economic, legal, moral, political, religious and social standards of either a particular State or extranational community.[41] Martin Hunter and Gui Conde e Silva, who propose in this context the term 'supranational public policy', further observe that it is logically narrower in scope, but also more uniform and universal than its domestic counterparts.[42]

The existing procedural framework of arbitration leaves arbitrators with a significant amount of freedom to modify the performed legal interpretation through recourse to a truly international (or transnational – as opposed to domestic concepts of *ordre public international*) public order. This is uncontroversial in cases where parties have not selected applicable substantive law, and arbitrators can then resolve the case on the ground of such rules they determine as appropriate (including transnational public policy considerations). Furthermore, when the parties have authorize arbitrators to decide the case as *amiables compositeurs* or *ex aequo et bono*, application of *ordre public transnational* is also legitimized.

In those cases where parties have validly designated the law governing their relationship, the question whether arbitrators can (despite that choice) give priority

37 Cf. U. Kornblum, '"Ordre public transnational", "ordre public international" und "ordre public interne" im Recht der privaten Schiedsgerichtsbarkeit' in *Beiträge zum internationalen Verfahrensrecht und zur Schiedsgerichtsbarkeit: Festschrift für Heinrich Nagel* (W.J. Habschied and K.H. Schwab eds, Aschendorf 1987).

38 Bermann (n 12) 336ff.

39 Pieter Sanders, 'Commentary' in *Sixty Years of ICC Arbitration: A Look at the Future* (ICC Publishing 1984), after M. Hunter and G.C. e Silva, 'Transnational Public Policy and its Application in Investment Arbitrations' 4 J World Inv (2003) 367 (emphasis JJ).

40 Pierre Lalive, 'Transnational (or Truly International) Public Policy and International Arbitration' in *Comparative Arbitration Practice and Public Policy in Arbitration* (P. Sanders ed, Kluwer Law & Taxation Publishers 1987) 295–96.

41 Report of the sixty-ninth conference held in London 25–29 July 2000 (International Law Association 2000) 343–44.

42 Hunter and e Silva (n 39) 368.

to transnational public policy principles is, however, more controversial. The main argument forwarded against such a liberal concept of the limits of discretionary power of arbitrators is that of legal certainty and predictability of the outcomes of the dispute. Reliability of arbitral recognition and respect for the parties' choice of law is considered to be one of the key advantages of arbitration. According to Michael Pryles,

> To compromise this principle by permitting the arbitrators to have regard to transnational principles of public policy introduces an element of discretion which could do much to undermine the certainty which is so essential to international commerce.[43]

Another point raised in this context is the very nature of the role of an arbitrator and the question whether in resolution of commercial disputes he or she is legitimized to depart from the parties' explicit intent, in a manner analogous to that of a domestic judge, yet without sufficient embedment in a domestic legal system. This observation, combined with arguments on the insufficiently precise content of *ordre public transnational*, leads to a claim that the role of an arbitrator not constrained in its application by requirements of a national legal system would be thus much more creative than in the case of international public policy considerations (defined from within a particular legal system).

In the case of arbitration, a method of dispute resolution dependant directly upon the parties' agreement, the question of the discretionary powers of arbitrators, not explicitly or impliedly (through a recourse to relevant rules of the forum) covered by such agreement, remains indeed disputable. It can be addressed through invoking alternative concepts of legitimization of arbitration, accentuating its autonomy (or hybrid character); the issue of legal grounds for such activity seems, however, so far rather controversial. In practice this problem would arise in somewhat extreme interpretive situations when the applicable rules of proper law, selected by the parties, were obviously disregarded due to their irreconcilable conflict with *ordre public transnational* principles – and not just interpreted within their general, possible scope of application in the context of transnational public policy considerations. This would be the case when arbitrators wish to avoid an outcome that, albeit consistent with the applicable domestic rules, would be nevertheless obviously and severely irrational in the context of international commercial relations, and do not find any other ground for relevant modification of their interpretation.

The surrounding controversy reflects thus traditional reservations in regard to invoking *ordre public* arguments, expressed in 1824 by an English judge in *Richardson v Mellish*, who described public policy considerations as a 'very unruly horse, and when once you get astride it you never know where it will carry you. It may lead you from sound law. It is never argued at all, but when other

43 M. Pryles, 'Reflections on Transnational Public Policy' 24 J Int'l Arb (2007) 6.

points fail.'[44] The equine trope was further famously developed in *Enderby Town Football Club Ltd v The Football Association Ltd*, where the judge observed that 'with a good man in the saddle, the unruly horse can be kept in control. It can jump over obstacles'.[45]

Another practical issue is the determination of the scope and content of applicable transnational rules in the course of the interpretive process in a way that is not only sufficiently precise but also free from the domestic influences of an interpreter. A conflict between the attempt to move towards the distillation and application in international cases of universal public policy principles on one side, and the influence of the background of the adjudicator on the other has been captured in the 2006 Federal Swiss Supreme Court's decision in *X (SpA) v Y (Srl)*.[46] The Court recognized that the public policy exception is meant to serve as a 'safety valve', securing compliance with fundamental values, which should be ideally shared and endorsed by all States. It also noticed, however, that a

> Swiss judge, who does not live in a no man's land but in a country attached to a given civilization where certain values are privileged as opposed to others, is led to identify these principles with his own sensitivity and on the basis of the essential values shared by this civilisation; his is the Swiss component of the public policy reservation.[47]

While this tension is definitely less prominent in international arbitration, the question of the ability of arbitrators to abandon national influences in their understanding and implementation of *ordre public* remains material.

In the light of this doctrinal endorsement a question then arises as to whether the *ordre public transnational* considerations are indeed applied in arbitral decision-making and, further, whether arbitral case law itself contributes to the formulation and development of the doctrine of transnational legal order in a way comparable to its role in expressing the rules of the new *lex mercatoria*. Awards where arbitrators decided to make a recourse to transnational public policy principles are rather rare. These kinds of considerations seem to play a much more prominent role in investment arbitration, particularly in those cases where the parties are a foreign investor and a host country, with the latter usually perceived as being naturally inclined to invoke *ordre public* arguments (including those of transnational character) more frequently than private parties.

The considerations of transnational public policy have been, however, occasionally applied in commercial arbitration as well, in a manner generally consistent with the character of this exception as a 'safety valve' or a last resort

44 *Richardson v Mellish* (1824) 2 Bing. 228 [1824–34] All ER Rep 258.

45 *Enderby Town Football Club Ltd v The Football Association Ltd* [1971] Ch 591, 606.

46 *X (SpA.) v Y (Srl)*, ASA Bulletin, vol. 24 no. 3 (2006), 550–60 (Swiss Federal Supreme Court).

47 Ibid. 554.

argument in hard cases. One such case was a controversy between a Brazilian and an American party, related to a joint venture aimed at securing a supply of Brazilian raw materials to the US, and addressed by an ICC interim award 4695/1984.[48] The arbitral tribunal dealt with an argument of the Brazilian party, which sought to render the arbitration clause in the parties' agreement invalid on the ground of Art 153.4 of the Brazilian Constitution, which provided for a jurisdiction of Judicial Authorities over 'any infringement of individual right' that could not be excluded. This provision had been considered to form a part of deliberate Brazilian public policy, in accordance with this State's long-time abstention from joining the New York Convention regime (Brazil only became a party to the Convention in 2002).[49]

The arbitrators thus faced a problem of the parties' explicit will to find their disputes resolved by the means of international arbitration, being in manifest conflict with mandatory provisions of the *ordre public* character of the applicable law governing the arbitration agreement. The public policy of Brazil, protecting the jurisdiction of domestic courts to the practical exclusion of arbitration, was at the time of resolution of this dispute clear and consistent in regard to domestic relations, but also, arguably, international ones.

The tribunal nevertheless decided not to give priority to the mandatory principles of Brazilian public policy, as it found in turn those principles to be in conflict with relevant considerations of transnational *ordre public*, and applied the latter to the effect of confirming the validity of the arbitration clause. It adopted a stance that following the Brazilian *ordre public* principle in this regard would be an 'extreme and unacceptable proposition, particularly when applied to international commercial contracts',[50] further claiming that it would be also inconsistent with 'current practice in Brazil' (albeit an argumentation to the contrary could probably also have been offered). The tribunal used an argument of the prevailing nature of an international commercial custom, by stating that, as a result of a move towards securing a truly neutral and impartial forum for resolving cross-border commercial controversies, arbitration clauses

> have become an essential guarantee to ensure the flow of international trade and serve the needs of transnational businessmen … A country like Brazil, more and more involved in the fabric of international trade, both as an importer and as an exporter, not just of raw materials, but of manufactured products as well, cannot place itself in a position of 'splendid isolation', which would imperil the ability of its

---

48 Interim Award of November 1984 in Case No. 4695, in *Yearbook Commercial Arbitration* vol XI (A.J. van den Berg ed, Kluwer Law International 1986).

49 Cf. André de Albuquerque Cavalcanti Abbud, 'Fifty Years in Five? The Brazilian Approach to the New York Convention' in *Interpretation of Law in the Global World: From Particularism to a Universal Approach* (Joanna Jemielniak and Przemyslaw Miklaszewicz eds, Springer 2010) 279ff.

50 Interim Award of November 1984 in Case No. 4695, in *Yearbook Commercial Arbitration* (n 48) 156.

> businessmen to enter into international commercial agreements and the expansion of overseas commercial activities by business enterprises based in Brazil.[51]

In terms of interpretive strategy, the tribunal thus introduced an additional level of considerations to trump the explicit public policy (both internal and international) of Brazil in regard to arbitration. The award is the more notable, as the rule which the tribunal decided to disregard was also a part of the Brazilian constitutional order. Arbitrators thus decided to 'save' the arbitration clause at a cost of ignoring a constitutional provision of applicable law as well as (as can be argued) the international public policy of Brazil (observable in its decades-long reluctance to subscribe to the New York Convention regime) – and its legitimization to adopt such an interpretation can be disputed.

An argument that can be raised in this context is that of the source and scope of powers of private arbitrators, not only to decide not to apply a mandatory rule (and an *ordre public* principle) of the highest possible rank in the applicable legal system, but also to formulate resolute expectations as to a relevant 'course correction' by a State which, as they deemed, 'cannot place itself in a position of "splendid isolation"' when it would impede commercial activities of private actors. Another interesting aspect of the case was also the resulting clash of conflicting public policy principles rooted in different orders. While such a situation in general is, as discussed above, often considered in the context of different domestic legal systems connected with the case, in this award the domestic, explicit directive of public policy was confronted with what the tribunal endorsed as a transnational principle, grounded in international commercial custom.

Transnational public order considerations were also applied so as to avoid parochial implications of the proper law in ICC Case No. 8385/1995[52] between an American and a Belgian party. The case was notable as the sole arbitrator decided to ignore a provision of the legal system (the law of New York) explicitly chosen by the parties as governing their relationship. The American party was denied a triple damages claim, which it brought under the US Federal Racketeer Influenced and Corrupt Organization Act (RICO), despite this instrument being a part of the law of New York. The arbitrator decided that recognizing the access of a party to such a specifically punitive remedy, practically non-existent in civil law countries, would in this case contradict the principle of basic certainty of law. He argued that

> in international commerce [it] is very important that legal rules produce foreseeable results, respond to the expectations of the parties and take account of the prevalent usages of the international marketplace. In such context it would be inappropriate to apply rules which solely respond to state interests.[53]

51 Ibid. 156–57.

52 ICC Award No. 8385/1995.

53 After Ana M. López Rodríguez, *Lex Mercatoria and Harmonization of Contract Law in the EU* (Djof 2003) 127.

Protection of good faith of a party to an international contract was then, in the argumentation of the sole arbitrator, given priority over the application of proper domestic rules. Despite the explicit choice of law, made by professional, sophisticated parties, the sole arbitrator upheld that the Belgian party, acting in the context of international commercial relations, could not have reasonably expected the existence of a remedy of this kind being applicable to its contract. The considerations, which can be classified as ones of *ordre public transnational*, were combined in this 'cosmopolitan' award with a recourse to *lex mercatoria* principles (for which the sole arbitrator indeed saw this case as an 'ideal opportunity' to apply[54]).

Another example of the application of transnational public policy arguments in arbitral decision-making is ICC Award No. 8891/1998,[55] rendering null and void a contract providing for corruption of officials. In a note to this award Dominique Hascher observes that the arbitrators' decision reflects the conviction that the recognition of validity of such an agreement would manifestly contradict the rudimentary function of the tribunal, which is administration of justice – even if it is '*private justice*'.[56] After Pierre Lalive, Hascher acknowledges that the arbitration practice cannot deny the existence of public transnational policy, based on a broad (if not universal) consensus of the values shared by the international community. The recognition of *ordre public transnational* as a ground for an award is remarkably combined with a pronounced characterization of the arbitral adjudication as a system with an autonomous standing in the administration of justice, exceeding the limits of merely providing *a casu ad casum* services of dispute resolution for private parties.

The existing case law thus shows a trend towards making recourse to *ordre public transnational*, understood as a set of fundamental, extranational considerations, which not only might prevail over domestic public policy concerns, but even, as seen in the ICC interim Award 4695/1984, were given precedence over explicit provisions of the law of constitutional rank. A regard to transnational public order can be categorized as a 'last resort' corrective argument, employed in purposive legal interpretation in cases where a straightforward application of proper law would lead to results standing in open conflict with core values, affecting the commercial sphere, and shared by the international community. As it is a consideration with an axiological grounding, used to neutralize the consequences of otherwise applicable law, particular instances of its use can be an object of a dispute, and a question about sufficient universal legitimacy of a particular value, to which a recourse was made in the award, can be raised.

54 ICC Award No. 8385/1995, 1066.

55 ICC Award No. 8891/1998.

56 Dominique Hascher, 'Note to ICC Award No. 8891' J Droit Int'l (Clunet 2000) 1083.

Chapter 11
ICA: A Paradigmatic Change in Legal Interpretation?

International commercial arbitration is in many respects a unique legal phenomenon. Characterized among the historically most ancient forms of dispute resolution and preceding litigation, it remained scarcely used for centuries. Its revival in the twentieth century and its later, rapid expansion have been an object of increased attention from legal doctrine and its different theorizations. Arbitration has been characterized as a particularly efficient way of exercising party autonomy, increasingly endorsed by States along with loosening the girdle of judicial control. It has thus been approached as a fulfilment of the doctrine of States' possible non-intervention into the commercial sphere in the context of the overall transnationalization trends of commercial law.[1]

Furthermore, its growing popularity and eventually its unprecedented elevation to the status of the default method of resolution of international business disputes led to the theorizing of arbitration as an area of emergence of a transnational adjudicatory system, largely undisturbed by constraints of national legal orders – an anational system of dispute resolution overcoming the traditional constraints of necessary connection between the law and the State and eroding positivist conceptualizations of law and judicial authority as an emanation of the State. Arbitration was argued to be functioning as an anational system of dispute resolution – and further considered as a procedural and institutional mechanism for applying and developing substantive 'global law without a state'. Such representations opposed the traditional view, as expressed by Francis Mann:

> [n]o one has ever or anywhere been able to point to any provision or legal principle which would permit individuals to act outside the confines of a system of municipal law; even the idea of the autonomy of the parties exists only by virtue of a given system of municipal law and in different systems may have different characteristics and effects. Similarly, every arbitration is necessarily subject to the law of a given State. No private person has the right or the power to act on any level other than that of municipal law.[2]

---

1 Gralf-Peter Calliess et al., 'Transformations of Commercial Law: New Forms of Legal Certainty For Globalized Exchange Processes?' in *Transforming the Golden Age Nation State* (Palgrave Macmillan 2007) 101.

2 Francis A. Mann, 'Lex Facit Arbitrum' in *International Arbitration, Liber Amicorum for Martin Domke* (P. Sanders ed, Martinus Nijhoff 1967) 157.

The opposing conceptualizations of monolocal arbitration, always legitimized by a specific national legal order, and its representation as an autonomous, transnational system of adjudication, have been supplemented by a third, pluralistic approach, offering a new, multicentric perspective. The focus in this representation is shifted from a view 'from within' a legal order of the place, defining the limits for undertaking arbitration, to an 'international' outlook, which sees the source of legitimization of ICA in the consent of all domestic legal orders potentially interested in the award.[3] The advancing institutionalization of arbitration has further led some authors to offer its analysis from the perspective of consolidation of this sphere, including studies of its responsiveness to market mechanisms and competition. Institutional aspects of arbitration were also an object of interest of the critical stream in legal and social studies, approaching arbitration as an instrument of exercise of economic power on a regional and global scale.[4]

This array of diversified theoretical approaches, aimed at capturing the main features of modern commercial arbitration, reveals those functional aspects of ICA which are prominent in the context of legal discourse, and which at the same time escape complete categorization. One of them is the relationship between ICA and the State. Recognition that arbitration is viable due to original authorizations granted by particular States via their arbitration laws and through the accession to the New York Convention, manifested in a monolocal or pluralistic version, is consistent with the positivist theory of legitimization. At the same time, however, it does not expose the strong institutional network of ICA and its dominant position in the field of cross-border business disputes, which has lead to a large extent to the exclusion of domestic courts in this field. This specific position is observable in a high degree of procedural autonomy, anational character (with localization anchors under the New York Convention regime limited in practice to the recognition and enforcement considerations) and in the elimination of judicial control that would exceed those grounds. Even if the original legitimization of ICA stems from the States' will, its operations have over the decades become more and more self-sustainable. Julian M. Lew observes that 'international arbitration is emerging increasingly as a *sui iuris* institution, with its own character and standing, independent of a national legal system.'[5] Does this specific status of ICA, accompanied by relevant, theoretical conceptualizations and self-consciousness of the arbitration community, further translate onto a paradigmatic change of legal interpretation? Or is legal interpretation in ICA merely a recycling of methods already well known from the domestic setting?

3 Emmanuel Gaillard, *Legal Theory of International Arbitration* (Martinus Nijhoff 2010) 25.

4 Yves Dezalay and Bryant G. Garth, *Dealing in Virtue: International Commercial Arbitration and the Construction of a Transnational Legal Order* (University of Chicago Press 1996).

5 Julian D.M. Lew, 'Determination of Applicable Substantive Law' 25 Int'l Bus Law (1997).

The largely autonomously functioning, structural and institutional framework of arbitration determines – as discussed in this volume – the dynamic character of legal discourse. Demands for efficiency, combined with the competitive character of ICA, have to be reconciled with neutrality requirements. Accommodation of the frequently divergent procedural expectations of parties representing different legal traditions and approaches is performed through decisions undertaken by arbitrators within the scope of their discretionary powers. The challenge of keeping equal footing for both parties throughout the entire course of the proceedings is thus yet another factor that detaches exercised legal interpretation from the context of a single domestic legal order.

Another important factor influencing the legal discourse of arbitration is its present, relatively high level of saturation with formalized procedural standards. As discussed in Chapter 5, in some opinions, proceduralization of ICA is tantamount to abandoning its initial main advantage of being speedy, informal and easily adjustable to the needs of specific parties. Its coincidence with the 'American wave' in arbitration has also led some commentators to merge these two phenomena. While the increased participation of US parties, counsel and arbitrators in ICA proceedings might have served as a catalytic agent for some aspects of proceduralization, the 'colonization of arbitration by litigation' should not be – as argued in Chapter 5 – identified with its 'Americanization'. It rather marks a stage in the development and consolidation of arbitration which aims at responding to mass needs, as well as at being able to accommodate large, procedurally complex cases – in which established, detailed standards are helpful. On the other hand, this phenomenon has also been explicated as a symbolic token of the autonomization of ICA, which no longer needs a pragmatic legitimization, rooted in arbitration's contractual and amicable conceptualization. As proposed by Dezalay and Garth, ICA does not have to be presented as an informal, flexible alternative to litigation anymore; it can absorb and function in accordance with increased amounts of procedural standards, as it enjoys a sufficiently independent status already.

Present-day arbitration – emancipated, competition-driven, dispersed and polycentric – forms a dynamic structure with several dominant institutions of global or regional significance, a further, numerous set of smaller arbitral centres, and a kaleidoscopic landscape of ad hoc arbitrations. In all its diversity, it is also a flat structure, generally characterized by lack of appeal proceedings on the merits of the dispute (with all benefits and dangers connected with finality of awards in this regard[6]). As proposed above, it can be described as rhizomatic, in the sense offered by Deleuze and Guattari.[7] According to their characterization of the rhizome-like forms of discourse,

---

6 Cf. William H. Knull III and Noah D. Rubins, 'Betting the Form on International Arbitration: Is it Time to Offer an Appeal Option?' 11 Am Rev Int'l Arb (2000).

7 Gilles Deleuze and Félix Guattari, *A Thousand Plateaus: Capitalism and Schizophrenia* (Continuum International 2004).

> Not every trait in a rhizome is necessarily linked to a linguistic feature: semiotic chains of every nature are connected to very diverse modes of coding (biological, political, economic, etc.) that bring into play not only different regimes of signs but also states of things of differing status ... A semiotic chain is like a tuber agglomerating very diverse acts, not only linguistic ... There is no ideal speaker-listener, any more than there is a homogenous linguistic community. Language is, in Weinreich's words, 'an essentially heterogeneous reality'. There is no mother tongue, only a power takeover by a dominant language within a political multiplicity. Language stabilizes around a parish, a bishopric, a capital. It forms a bulb.[8]

Arbitrators operate on a plan where both the language of the proceedings and the substantive applicable law are not obvious; they have to be determined. They are also frequently resolving cases in a language that is not their native tongue, and according to law systems in which they have not been primarily trained. The patchwork structure of applicable rules (with regard to the regime of the place of anticipated enforcement, to public international order, to transnational principles and international customs and usages) resembles Deleuze and Guattari's characterization of heterogeneity and multiplicity as inherent features of a rhizomatic discourse. The imagery of an extremely efficiently driven, mobile war machine is contrasted by them with the linear, vertical logic of the State apparatus.[9]

The specific character of legal discourse in arbitration affects legal interpretation. The fast-aggregating, largely unpublished body of case law is nevertheless an object (and a tool) of cross-referencing and cross-fertilization of legal concepts, running – again, rhizomatically – across institutions. The awards rely largely on the application of domestic law to the merits of the dispute, but the rendition of proper law is exercised from a distanced, outsider perspective (even if arbitrators indeed apply their 'own' national law, this is not automatic, but an effect of relevant conflict of laws considerations, the rules of which have themselves to be established first; moreover, unlike domestic judges, arbitrators do not perform an official function as an adjudicatory arm of the State).

Furthermore, the standard of judicial non-intervention, as well as the virtual lack of appeal and judicial control on issues qualified as the substance of the dispute, result in the protection of the outcomes of interpretative activity of the arbitrators. An accompanying risk is the potentially dubious quality (or even a completely erroneous character) of awards, from which no recourse can be sought. As William Park observes:

> [e]fficient arbitration implicates a tension between the rival goals of finality and fairness. Freeing awards from judicial challenge promotes finality, while enhancing fairness calls for some measure of court supervision ... Finality in

8 Ibid. 7–8.

9 Ibid. 10.

> arbitration enhances the political and procedural neutrality that is compromised if the winner must re-litigate the case in a public forum. Without finality, parties to international business transactions may have no reliable alternative to the uncertainty of third country courts or the perceived bias of the other side's 'home-town justice'. Absent the possibility of binding arbitration, some transactions will remain unconsummated. Others will be concluded only at increased prices, to reflect the risk of potentially biased adjudication.[10]

As a result, Park argues, the demands of practice call for a reasonable compromise, ensuring an option of 'judicial review for the grosser forms of procedural injustice'[11] – yet not for scrutiny on the merits of the dispute. This standard remarkably augments the protected position of legal interpretation in arbitration, which can be an object of a doctrinal critique, but not of further review by an appeal to judicial authority.

The theory of a paradigmatic change in legal interpretation in arbitration seems to be supported not only by analysis of the framework conditions of legal discourse. It finds a grounding in the self-conscious approach of arbitrators, their awareness of the function they fulfil and of difference between it and the role of a domestic judge. A number of procedural choices affecting legal interpretation – from a 'technical' decision on the language of the proceedings to balancing different considerations in ascertaining proper conflict of laws rules, as well as substantive rules governing the dispute – require a deliberate decision in place of following an established procedural pattern of the domestic law of the court.

The hypothesis of a paradigmatic change is also further aided by the growing response from legal theory, offering systematic conceptualizations of commercial arbitration as a *sui generis* legal phenomenon As discussed above, it has been attempted in several ways to reconcile the recognition of the practical, global role of ICA and its far-reaching autonomy with the doctrine of sources of the law and legitimization of adjudicative authority. The distinct institutions and environment for non-institutional arbitrations; specific procedural framework; structural conditions of legal discourse in ICA; its intercultural character; and distinguishable, characteristic sets of interpretative considerations; as well as autonomous self-awareness of the arbitral community and relevant support from legal theory – these are all arguments that can be used to advocate the thesis.

The question is, however, whether legal discourse in arbitration is already an accomplished structural project, to be repeatedly realized in multiple concretizations in subsequent cases – or whether it is still a 'work in progress', characterized by dynamic shifts of accents in allocation of procedural and interpretative competences. Is arbitration in its current form already consolidated

10 William W. Park, 'Why Courts Review Arbitral Awards' in *Recht der Internationalen Wirtschaft und Streiterledigung im 21. Jahrhundert: Festschrift für Karl-Heinz Böckstiegel* (R. Briner, L.Y. Fortier, K.P. Berger and J. Bredow eds, Carl Heymanns 2001) 596.

11 Ibid. 596.

and congealed, and how deeply will the prospective changes in its landscape affect its structure, being primarily of economic and political rather than legal character?

The rudimentary, international framework for arbitration provided by the New York Convention, stable in terms of its content, and serving as a cornerstone of the processes of autonomization of ICA, has been gradually augmented in the last decades by subsequent accessions of particular States to its regime (including some notable latecomers as Brazil, Iran, or some of the central Asian countries).[12] Shifting trends in regional and global commerce will certainly further continue to affect the position of particular arbitration centres, which might translate into a growing or diminishing popularity of certain interpretative standards, such as broad or narrow recourse to transnational principles, or an easy and frequently used (or rather exceptionally sought) switch to hybrid proceedings and resignation from adjudication based on legal standards.

Loukas, Mistelis and Kröll characterize the demands of legal interpretation in ICA stating that

> [w]hile the arbitrators should look at the methods of interpretation of the chosen substantive law, the process of interpretation should be free from doctrinal formalism. International tribunals should take account of the fact that they are dealing with an international dispute and should interpret national law rules to reflect international practice and to give effect to the parties' intentions. Many arbitrators are from jurisdictions different to the applicable law and may have difficulty interpreting the law in accordance with that legal system itself. Although the applicable substantive law should be interpreted in its context tribunals have employed international standards in interpreting domestic or uniform law.[13]

Arbitration can be described as anational in the context of its largely established procedural and institutional autonomy and independence from judicial intervention and review on the merits of the dispute, but nonetheless not completely delocalized (mostly due to the significance of laws on arbitration of its place and to the recognition and enforcement considerations). Legal interpretation in ICA also extensively bases itself on application of domestic rules to the substance of the disputes. Arbitration's rhizomes may be ubiquitous, but they are not autarkic. In this sense, ICA differs from the mercatorist view, perceiving it as a flywheel in a self-sustaining 'law machine' of global commercial law: giving effect to self-referencing contracts and formulating transnational principles, binding parties without States' endorsement. While arbitration has undoubtedly played a crucial role in developing new *lex mercatoria*, its application and interpretation

12 Information on the status of the New York Convention available at <http://www.uncitral.org/uncitral/en/uncitral_texts/arbitration/NYConvention_status.html>.

13 Julian D.M. Lew et al., *Comparative International Commercial Arbitration* (Kluwer Law International/Aspen 2003) 444.

is just a fraction of all operations on the body of substantive rules undertaken by arbitrators. Moreover, transnational principles, when applied, are frequently treated as modifying considerations in construction of domestic rules – and not necessarily as an independent and sufficient ground for the award.

Lex mercatoria-based adjudication is also a type of arbitral decision-making where the creative character of legal interpretation is particularly prominent. Wide scope of discretionary powers of arbitrators can, however, also be seen in other methods of legal interpretation characteristic to ICA. Diversified ways of application of the comparative method may serve as an illustration of this phenomenon. As discussed in detail in Chapter 7, comparative analysis can be employed as an instrument for 'internationalization' of interpretation of applicable domestic law; as a source of analogy for explication of foreign legal concepts; or as a negative argument, used to rebut reasoning offered by the other party as inadequate and falsely attributing foreign meaning and context to the norms of applicable law.

In regard to *amiable composition*, if its widely shared definition as an authorization for arbitrators to depart from strict application of the rules of law is adopted, those rules, as argued in Chapter 9, should be first identified. As – in accordance with the semiotic perspective, adopted in this book – every textual cognition presupposes an interpretation, then legal interpretation, even if exercised in a very basic and preliminary form, is a necessary component of *amiable composition*; otherwise arbitrators would not know what they decide to depart from. As *amiable composition* is generally a competence and not a binding instruction, if the potentially applicable law was not determined and thus the interpretative (*sensu stricto*) aspect of decision-making was omitted, arbitrators would also not be able to make a fully informed decision on choosing the optimal way of deciding the case. While this actually might happen, such a practice seems hardly recommendable. Moreover, in the concept of *amiable composition* as 'equitable correction' to the interpretation of applicable law, an adoption of a conscious, interpretative approach is inevitable.

International commercial arbitration has been thus operating through a specific institutional setting and with a remarkable scope of adjudicatory and procedural autonomy, which has allowed it to grow from a relatively niche method of dispute resolution, controlled by national courts, to the globally successful, prevalent way of resolving cross-border business controversies. Many of those disputes have involved parties representing different legal, cultural and linguistic traditions; arbitral decision-making has also necessarily required an insight into more than a single domestic legal system as a source of rules relevant to the merits of the controversy. In this characteristic setting for legal discourse, arbitration has adopted, adjusted to a new context and reformulated different methods of legal interpretation, originally stemming from domestic adjudication, but reapplied with at least a change of accents in the arbitral setting.

This change of accents can be observed to a different degree in the case of particular methods. In comparative analysis, it is mostly its common character and extensive employment in arbitration that distinguishes it from the use in domestic practice. A specific case is the application of comparative method in a way oriented at extracting rules common to national orders interested in the case, pointed out as a particular form of *lex mercatoria*-based adjudication. *Amiable composition*, while invented on the domestic ground, has been quite marginal outside the arbitration context, whereas in ICA it is a widely recognized and strongly grounded in the existing procedural framework competence, which can be vested in arbitrators. Arguably, the content of this competence (and the demands its proper exercise poses) is also different, as equity in domestic contracts can be perceived differently from transnational equity, considered in the context of a cross-border transaction.

Similar reservations can be taken into account in relation to public order as a consideration in legal interpretation in ICA. Its transnational variation is a concern underscoring the international character of the analysed transaction and, as discussed in Chapter 10, the doctrine and practice of arbitration has been a forum where competing versions of this concept (a 'pure' transnational versus a domestically filtered one) have been presented. As explicitly formulated in the context of analysis of the ICC Award No. 8891/1998, recourse to *ordre public transnational* can be seen as an expression of the autonomization of arbitration and its assumption of the official function of administration of justice (reaching beyond its conceptualization as a sphere of private, market-oriented, case-specific services). On the other hand, the concerns of award enforcement under the New York Convention direct arbitrators to consider domestic public policy regards, being thus one of the points hooking arbitral adjudicatory practice on the national legal orders, and being seen as an emanation of the territoriality principle, constraining the concept of a 'floating' arbitration.

Finally, the *lex mercatoria*-based arbitral adjudication has often been indicated as an example of interpretive activity highly characteristic to arbitration. As discussed in detail in Chapter 8, it has also been the object of a theory proposing that *lex mercatoria* itself is not an independently existing body of substantive rules, but a method of arbitral adjudication which combines comparative and purposive legal interpretation so as to distil a common core of relevant rules, belonging to different legal orders. Such representation of the New Law Merchant is one of its presently forwarded theories, and current consolidation of the *lex mercatoria* principles, visible in restatement-type codifications and initiatives such as the 'creeping codification' and the CENTRAL database, offer strong arguments for its existence independent from the demands and scope of inquiry related to a particular case. Nevertheless, the theory of *lex mercatoria* as a 'substantive method of adjudication' in ICA exposes those types of cases where the difference between the sources of the law, or the object of legal interpretation, and the outcomes of interpretative processes have become blurred.

The issue of a paradigmatic change in legal interpretation in the context of ICA thus still awaits categorization. The structural framework of legal discourse of commercial arbitration, with its high level of autonomy, private origin, developed institutional and extra-institutional base, significant procedural independence and ad hoc composition of the adjudicating bodies, distinguishes it not only from domestic litigation, but also from existing international permanent courts and tribunals.

The accompanying self-awareness of professionals involved in arbitration – international arbitrators and counsel – makes them without doubt a part of what has been characterized by Niilo Kauppi and Mikael Rask Madsen as transnational power elites.[14] Indeed, Kauppi and Madsen draw inspiration from the observations of Dezalay and Garth and Pierre Bourdieu on the hybrid identity of lawyers involved in international arbitration, who are being characterized not as denationalized experts (devoid of their national training and cultural background), but as 'legal cosmocrats' with advanced transitory skills, displaying on various levels of their professional activity connections to national concepts and structures. They thus form a distinct social group which is neither completely domestic nor purely international and delocalized, 'but rather transnational and reliant, to varying degrees, on both national and international resources and capitals'.[15]

This characteristic of the professional culture of international arbitration is further affected by an increased participation by general practitioners, which has been accompanying successive waves of 'newcomers', and resulting from the changing regional dynamics in this field. This has added a new layer to the tension between the domestic and anational element in arbitration. However, the successful accommodation of the American wave by ICA, and its responsiveness, also demonstrate the mutually transformative power of the arbitration culture, able to absorb new trends but also to broaden the competences of involved specialists.

This distinct character of the adjudication practice in arbitration, accompanied by the self-consciousness of its actors in performing their professional roles, has been an object of interest for legal theorists as well. This has allowed for introduction of relevant conceptual representations of arbitration and arbitral legal discourse. In the sphere of methods of legal interpretation, the dual anchorage of arbitration is also observable. The prevalent recourse to the substantive domestic law in addressing the merits of the case is accompanied by application of the nationally acquired methods of interpretation. At the same time the transnational context of dispute resolution in ICA, including the main background of an interpreter (whose nationality might be other than that of the State of the applicable law), establishes an 'outsider' environment for operations on proper law. This is further augmented by those methods and canons of legal interpretation that have been developed in a way characteristic to ICA.

This distinct, hybrid character of legal discourse and legal interpretation in arbitration allows for supporting the thesis on a specific paradigm of legal interpretation in ICA. Development of this paradigm is, however, not revolutionary

14 Niilo Kauppi and Mikael Rask Madsen, *Transnational Power Elites: The New Professionals of Governance, Law and Security* (Routledge 2013).

15 Ibid. 5.

in the sense proposed by Kuhn,[16] but exercised through accumulation, recycling, reformulation and adaptation of already existing interpretative patterns, supplemented with new and original ones. Rather than being a creation of an entirely original system, it operates through a change of context, accents, interpretative priorities and hierarchies of typical considerations, with the use of discretionary powers exercised by arbitrators to a diversified extent in specific cases.

The paradigmatic shift in legal interpretation in ICA, even if introducing a collage of already known and new components, is irreducible to a mere recomposition of domestically acquired and applied methods.[17] The change is not only quantitative (in other words, observed in an increased frequency of use of particular interpretative tools, such as comparative analysis). It is also qualitative, with marked significance of purposive interpretation, employed with regard to a set of international and transnational considerations of different type, scale and force, from customs and usages of trade to *ordre public transnational*. As the transnational setting of arbitral legal discourse is well established, and the characteristic patterns of legal interpretation as well as the distinctive interpretative repertory in ICA can be ascertained, the call of Charisios, one of the characters in *Epitrepontes* (Men in Arbitration) – a classical Greek comedy by Menander – 'Let's all go inside now, and put everything to rights',[18] can be thus extensively answered.

16 Thomas Samuel Kuhn, *The Structure of Scientific Revolutions* (University of Chicago Press 1996).

17 Joanna Jemielniak and Przemysław Mikłaszewicz, 'Capturing the Change: Universalising Tendencies in Legal Interpretation' in *Interpretation of Law in the Global World: From Particularism to a Universal Approach* (Joanna Jemielniak and Przemysław Mikłaszewicz eds, Springer 2010) 17.

18 Sallie Goetsch, *Family Values, A Reconstruction of Menander's 'Epitrepontes' (Act I/IV)* (Warwick 1995).

Bibliography

Legal Cases and Associated Material

American Almond Products Co v Consolidated Pecan Sales (United States Court of Appeals, Second Circuit).

American Arbitration Association, Supplementary Procedures for Large, Complex Commercial Disputes (1 February 1993. Amended and effective 15 September 2005).

Arbitral Award No. 97/2002, International Arbitration Court of the Chamber of Commerce and Industry of the Russian Federation.

Arbitration Chamber of Paris, Award in Case No. 9246 of 8 March 1996, in *Yearbook Commercial Arbitration* vol XXII (A.J. van den Berg ed, Kluwer Law International 1997).

British Petroleum Co (Libya) Ltd (BP) v Government of the Libyan Arab Republic, Award of 10 October 1973.

Chromalloy Aeroservices Inc v The Arab Republic of Egypt (District Court of District of Columbia, July 1996), in *Yearbook Commercial Arbitration* vol XII (A.J. van den Berg ed, Kluwer Law International 1997).

Compania Valenciana de Cementos Portland SA v Primary Coal Inc, Cour de Cassation [Supreme Court] 22 October 1991, in *Yearbook Commercial Arbitration* vol XVIII (A.J. van den Berg ed, Kluwer Law International 1993).

Compania Valenciana de Cementos Portland SA v Primary Coal Inc, ICC Award No. 5953/1989, in *Yearbook Commercial Arbitration* vol XVI (A.J. van den Berg ed, Kluwer Law International 1991).

Dame Krebs et autre v Milton Stern, French Cour de Cassation, 1977 Revue de l'Arbitrage 269.

David Taylor and Son Ltd v Barnett Trading Co [1953] 1 WLR 562.

Deutsche Schachtbau- und Tiefbohr GmbH v Rakoil, Court of Appeal decision of 24 March 1987, Lloyd's Law Report 2(1987).

Duke Group Ltd (in liq) v Alamain Investments Ltd, South Australia Supreme Court 275.

Eagle Star Insurance Co v Yuval Insurance Co [1978] 1 Lloyd's Law Report 357.

Enderby Town Football Club Ltd v The Football Association Ltd [1971] Ch 591, 606.

Fougerolle v Banque du Proche-Orient, 1982 Revue de l'Arbitrage 183 (Cour de Cassation).

France, Cour de cassation, Chambre civile 1, 23 janvier 1979, 77-12825.

France, Cour de cassation, Chambre civile 2, 25 mai 1948, Lautour.

French Manufacturer v Irish Distributor, ICC Partial Award in Case No. 7319/1992, in *Yearbook Commercial Arbitration* vol XXIVa (A.J. van den Berg ed., Kluwer Law International 1999).

Gao Haiyan v Keeneye Holdings Ltd, 3 HKEC 514 (Hong Kong Court of First Instance).

Glencot Development and Design Ltd v Ben Barrett and Son (Contractors) Ltd [2001] 17 Construction Law Journal 336.

Government of Kuwait v American Independent Oil Company (AMINOIL), Award of 24 March 1982, 976.

ICC Award No. 3540/1980, in *Yearbook Commercial Arbitration* vol VII (P. Sanders ed, Kluwer Law International 1982), 124, 129.

ICC Award No. 4132/1983.

ICC Award No. 6142.

ICC Award No. 7518/1994, in *Collection of ICC Arbitral Awards, 1996–2000* § 4 (J.-J. Arnaldez ed, Kluwer Law International. 2003).

ICC Award No. 8385/1995, 124 Journal du droit international (Clunet) 1061–73.

ICC Award No. 8873/1997.

ICC Award No. 8891/1998.

Interim Award of November 1984 in Case No. 4695, in *Yearbook Commercial Arbitration* vol XI (A.J. van den Berg ed, Kluwer Law International 1986).

Intrafor Cofor et Subtec Middle East Company v M. Gagnant et consorts, Cour d'appel de Paris, 1985 Revue de l'Arbitrage 299.

Iran–US Claims Tribunal Partial Award of 14 July 1987 in Cases Nos 74, 76, 81, 150 (311–74/76/81/150-3), in *Yearbook Commercial Arbitration* vol XIII (A.J. van den Berg ed, Kluwer Law International 1988).

Libyan American Oil Company (LIAMCO) v Government of The Libyan Arab Republic, Award of 12 April 1977.

Marine Transit Corporation v Dreyfus, 284 US 263, 52 S Ct 166, 76 L Ed 282 (1932).

Oberster Gerichtshof (Supreme Court), 18 November 1982, in *Yearbook Commercial Arbitration* vol IX (P. Sanders ed, Kluwer Law International 1984), 159.

Office and Professional Employees Intern. Union, Local No. 471 v Brownsville General Hosp. (United States Court of Appeals, Third Circuit).

Orion Compania Espanola de Seguros v Belfort Maatschappij voor Algemene Verzekgringeen [1962] 2 Lloyd's Law Report 257.

Pabalk Ticaret Limited Sirketi v Norsolor SA, ICC Award No. 3131 of 26 October 1979, in *Yearbook Commercial Arbitration* vol IX (P. Sanders ed, Kluwer Law International 1984), 109, 110

Pabalk Ticaret Limited Sirketi v Norsolor SA, in *Yearbook Commercial Arbitration* vol XI (A.J. van den Berg ed, Kluwer Law International 1986) (Cour de Cassation [Supreme Court] (First Civil Chamber)).

Petroleum Development (Trucial Coast) Ltd v Sheikh of Abu Dhabi, 247.

Petroleum Development Ltd. v Sheikh of Abu Dhabi Ad Hoc Award, International Law Reports 18 (1951).
Protocol on Arbitration Clauses Signed at a Meeting of the Assembly of the League Of Nations Held on the Twenty-Fourth Day of September, Nineteen Hundred and Twenty-Three (1923 Geneva Protocol on Arbitration Clauses).
Richardson v Mellish (1824) 2 Bing. 228 [1824–34] All ER Rep 258.
Rolland v Cassidy (1888) 13 App. Cas. 770.
Sapphire International Petroleums v NIOC, International Law Reports 35 (1967).
Société Fougerolle v Société Butec Engineering, Cour de Cassation (1ère Ch Civ), 3 October 1984, Journal of International Arbitration 2/2(1985).
Softwood Lumber (Canada v United States of America), LCIA Case No. 81010 (2011).
Softwood Lumber (Canada v United States of America), LCIA Case No. 91312.
Texaco Overseas Petroleum Company and California Asiatic Oil Company (TOPCO) v The Government of The Libyan Arab Republic, Award of 19 January 1977.
UNCITRAL Notes on Organizing Arbitral Proceedings (*UNCITRAL Yearbook* vol XXVII 1996, pt 1), paras 11 to 54.
UNIDROIT Principles of International Commercial Contracts (International Institute for the Unification of Private Law (UNIDROIT) 1994).
UNIDROIT Principles of International Commercial Contracts (International Institute for the Unification of Private Law (UNIDROIT) 2004).
Volt Information Sciences Inc v Board of Trustees of Leland Stanford Junior University, 468 (Supreme Court of the United States).
X (SpA) v Y (SRL), ASA Bulletin, vol 24 no. 3 (2006), 550–60 (Swiss Federal Supreme Court).

Secondary Sources

'1958 – Convention on the Recognition and Enforcement of Foreign Arbitral Awards – the "New York" Convention', available at <http://www.uncitral.org/uncitral/en/uncitral_texts/arbitration/NYConvention_status.html>.
Abbud, André de Albuquerque Cavalcanti, 'Fifty Years in Five? The Brazilian Approach to the New York Convention' in *Interpretation of Law in the Global World: From Particularism to a Universal Approach* (Joanna Jemielniak and Przemyslaw Mikłaszewicz eds, Springer 2010).
Abu-Nimer, Mohammed, *Nonviolence and Peace Building in Islam: Theory and Practice* (University Press of Florida 2003).
Akaddaf, Fatima, 'Application of the United Nations Convention on Contracts for the International Sale of Goods (CISG) to Arab Islamic Countries: Is the CISG Compatible with Islamic Law Principles?' Spring Pace International Law Review (2001).

Aksen, Gerald, 'Ad Hoc Versus Institutional Arbitration' 2 ICC Bulletin (1991).

Aksen, Gerald, 'The Tribunal's Appointment' in *The Leading Arbitrators' Guide to International Arbitration* (Lawrence W. Newman and Richard D. Hill eds, Juris 2008).

Alfons, Claudia, *Recognition and Enforcement of Annulled Foreign Arbitral Awards: An Analysis of the Legal Framework and Its Interpretation in Case Law and Literature* (Peter Lang 2010).

Al-Hejailan, Salah, 'Mediation as a Means for Amicable Settlement of Disputes in Arab Countries', WIPO Conference on Meditation, available at <http://www.arbiter.wipo.int/events/conferences/1996/hejailan.html> (1996).

Alqurashi, Zeyad, 'Arbitration under the Islamic Sharia' 1 Oil, Gas and Energy Law Intelligence (2003).

Alter, Karen J., and Sophie Meunier, 'The Politics of International Regime Complexity' 7 Perspectives on Politics (2009).

Alvarez, Guillermo Aguillar, 'To What Extent do Arbitrators in International Cases Disregard the Bag and Baggage of National Systems?' in *International Dispute Resolution: Towards an International Arbitration Culture*, ICCA Congress series 8 (Seoul 1996) (A.J. van den Berg ed, Kluwer Law International 1996).

Amin, S.H., *Commercial Arbitration in Islamic and Iranian Law* (Vahid Publications 1988).

Anesa, Patrizia, 'Language and Power in Arbitration Proceedings: Insights into Theory and Practice' in *Discourse and Practice in International Commercial Arbitration: Issues, Challenges and Prospects* (Vijay Kumar Bhatia et al. eds, Ashgate 2012).

Ardener, Edwin, *Social Anthropology and Language* (Routledge 2004).

Arfazadeh, H., 'In the Shadow of the Unruly Horse: International Arbitration and the Public Policy Exception' 13 American Review of International Arbitration (2002).

Aristotle, *'Categories' and 'De interpretatione'* (J.L. Ackrill tr and ed, Clarendon Press 1963).

Aristotle, *The Categories* (E.M. Edghill tr, Kessinger 2004).

Arnold, Tom, *Alternative Dispute Resolution: How to Use It to Your Advantage. A Vocabulary of Alternative Dispute Resolution Procedures* (American Law Institute & American Bar Association 1996).

Asser, T.M.C., and Alphonse Pierre Octave Rivier, *Eléments de droit international privé ou du conflit des lois* (A. Rousseau 1884).

Austin, John, et al., *Lectures on Jurisprudence, or, The Philosophy of Positive Law* (3rd edn, John Murray 1869).

Balkin, Jack M., 'Being Just with Deconstruction' 3 Social and Legal Studies (1994).

Balkin, Jack M., 'Tradition, Betrayal, and the Politics of Deconstruction' 11 Cardozo Law Review (1989).

Balkin, Jack M., and Sanford Levinson, 'Legal Canons: An Introduction' in *Legal Canons* (Jack M. Balkin and Sanford Levinson eds, New York University Press 2000).

Balkin, Jack M., 'Deconstruction's Legal Career' 27 Cardozo Law Review (2005).

Barraclough, A., and J. Waincymer, 'Mandatory Rules of Law in International Commercial Arbitration' 6 Melbourne Journal of International Law (2005).

Barrett, Jerome T., et al., *A History of Alternative Dispute Resolution: The Story of a Political, Cultural, and Social Movement* (Jossey-Bass 2004).

Bell, Andrew S., *Forum Shopping and Venue in Transnational Litigation* (Oxford University Press. 2003).

Benson, Robert W., 'The Semiotic Web of the Law' in *Law and Semiotics* (Roberta Kevelson ed., Plenum 1987).

Benson, Robert W., 'The Semiotics of International Law: Interpretation of the ABM Treaty' 2 International Journal for the Semiotics of Law (1989).

Bentham, Jeremy, *'A Fragment on Government' and 'An Introduction to the Principles of Morals and Legislation'* (Blackwell 1967).

Berger, Klaus Peter, *The Creeping Codification of the Lex Mercatoria* (Kluwer Law International 1999).

Berger, Klaus Peter, 'Lex Mercatoria Online: The CENTRAL Transnational Law Database' (2002) <www. tldb. de>, 18 Arbitration International (2002).

Berger, Klaus Peter, 'The New Law Merchant and the Global Market Place – A Twenty-First-Century View of Transnational Commercial Law' in *The Practice of Transnational Law* (Klaus Peter Berger ed, Kluwer Law International 2001).

Berger, Klaus Peter, and Center for Transnational Law, *The Creeping Codification of the New Lex Mercatoria* (2nd edn, Kluwer Law International, sold and distributed in North, Central and South America by Aspen Publishers 2010).

Bergsten, Eric, 'The Americanization of International Arbitration' 18 Pace International Law Review (2006).

Berman, Harold J., and Colin Kaufman, 'Law of International Commercial Transactions (Lex Mercatoria)' 19 Harvard International Law Journal (1978).

Bermann, George A., 'Mandatory Rules of Law' in *International Arbitration* (F. Ferrari and S. Kroll eds, Sellier European Law 2010).

Bernstein, Lisa, 'Merchant Law in a Merchant Court: Rethinking the Code's Search for Immanent Business Norms' May University of Pennsylvania Law Review (1996).

Betti, Emilio, *Allgemeine Auslegungslehre als Methodik der Geisteswissenschaften* (Mohr-Siebeck 1967).

Bhatia, Vijay Kumar, et al., 'Concepts, Contexts and Procedures in Arbitration Discourse' in *Legal Discourse across Cultures and Systems* (V.K. Bhatia et al. eds, Hong Kong University Press 2008).

Bhatia, Vijay Kumar, et al., *Discourse and Practice in International Commercial Arbitration: Issues, Challenges and Prospects* (Ashgate 2012).

Blessing, Marc, 'Choice of Substantive Law in International Arbitration' 14 Journal of International Arbitration (1997).

Blessing, Marc, 'Mandatory Rules of Law versus Party Autonomy in International Arbitration' 14 Journal of International Arbitration (1997).

Block-Lieb, Susan, and Terence C. Halliday, 'Incrementalisms in Global Lawmaking' 32 Brooklyn Journal of International Law (2007).

Bloomfield, Leonard, *Language* (Holt, Rinehart & Winston 1933).

Böckstiegel, Karl-Heinz, *Der Staat als Vertragspartner ausländischer Privatunternehmen* (Athenäum 1971).

Bohman, James, *Public Deliberation: Pluralism, Complexity, and Democracy* (MIT Press 1996).

Bonell, Michael Joachim, 'Do We Need a Global Commercial Code?' 106 Dickinson Law Review (2001).

Bonell, Michael Joachim, *An International Restatement of Contract Law: The UNIDROIT Principles of International Commercial Contracts* (Martinus Nijhoff 2009).

Born, Gary, *International Commercial Arbitration* (Wolters Kluwer Law and Business, Kluwer Law International; sold and distributed in North, Central and South America by Aspen Publishers 2009).

Borris, Christian, 'The Reconciliation of Conflicts Between Common Law and Civil Law Principles in the Arbitration Process' in *Conflicting Legal Cultures in Commercial Arbitration: Old Issues and New Trends* (Stefan N. Frommel and Barry Alexander K. Rider eds, Kluwer Law International 1999).

Bourdieu, Pierre, 'Foreword' in *Dealing in Virtue: International Commercial Arbitration and the Construction of a Transnational Legal Order* (Yves Dezalay and Bryant G. Garth eds, University of Chicago Press 1996).

Bowden, Paul, 'L'interdiction de se contredire au détriment d'autrui (Estoppel) as a Substantive Transnational Rule in International Commercial Arbitration' in *Transnational Rules in International Commercial Arbitration* (Emmanuel Gaillard and Piero Bernardini eds, ICC Publishing and International Law Association 1993).

Briner, Robert, *Special Considerations Which May Affect the Procedure (Interim Measures, Amiable Composition, Adaptation of Contracts, Agreed Settlements)* (Kluwer 1994).

Broekman, Jan M., and Larry Catà Backer, *Lawyers Making Meaning* (Springer 2013).

Brower, Charles Nelson, 'Introduction' in *International Arbitration in the Twenty-First Century: Towards 'Judicialization' and Uniformity?: Twelfth Sokol Colloquium* (Richard B. Lillich and Charles Nelson Brower eds, Transnational Publishing 1994).

Brower, Charles Nelson, and Jeremy K. Sharpe, 'International Arbitration and the Islamic World: The Third Phase' 97 American Journal of International Law (2003).

Brunet, Edward J., and Charles B. Craver, *Alternative Dispute Resolution: The Advocate's Perspective* (Michie 1997).

Bryde Andersen, Mads, 'Pragmatism in Nordic Contract Law' in *Unification and Harmonization of International Commercial Law* (Morten M. Fogt ed, Kluwer Law International 2012).

Bucher, Andreas, 'Das Kapitel 11 des IPR-Gesetzes uber die internationale Schiedsgerichtsbarkeit' in *Beiträge zum neuen IPR des Sachen-, Schuld- und Gesellschaftsrechts: Festschrift für Prof. Rudolf Moser* (I. Schwander ed, Schulthess 1987).

Bühring-Uhle, Christian, et al., *Arbitration and Mediation in International Business* (2nd edn, Kluwer Law International; sold and distributed in North, Central and South America by Aspen Publishers 2006).

Burrell, G., and G. Morgan, *Social Paradigms and Organizational Analysis: Elements of the Sociology of Corporate Life* (Heinemann Educational 1979).

Burton, S.J., 'Combining Conciliation with Arbitration of International Commercial Disputes' 18 Hastings International and Comparative Law Review (1994).

Bush, R.A.B., and S.G. Pope, 'Changing the Quality of Conflict Interaction: The Principles and Practice of Transformative Mediation' 3 Peppardine Dispute Resolution Law Journal (2002).

Byrne, Olga K., 'A New Code of Ethics for Commercial Arbitrators: The Neutrality of Party-Appointed Arbitrators on a Tripartite Panel' 30 Fordham Urban Law Journal 1815(2002).

Calliess, Gralf-Peter, 'Reflexive Transnational Law: The Privatisation of Civil Law and the Civilisation of Private Law' 23 Zeitschrift für Rechtssoziologie (2002).

Calliess, Gralf-Peter, et al., 'Transformations of Commercial Law: New Forms of Legal Certainty for Globalized Exchange Processes?' in *Transforming the Golden Age Nation State* (Palgrave Macmillan 2007).

Carbonneau, Thomas E., *Resolving Transnational Disputes through International Arbitration: Sixth Sokol Colloquium* (University of Virginia Press 1984).

Carbonneau, Thomas E., 'The Remaking of Arbitration: Design and Destiny' in *Lex Mercatoria and Arbitration* (rev edn, Thomas E. Carbonneau ed, Juris 1998 [1990]).

Carbonneau, Thomas E., *Cases and Materials on the Law and Practice of Arbitration* (rev 2nd edn, Juris Publishing 2003).

Carter, James H., 'Dispute Resolution and International Agreements' in *International Commercial Arbitration: A Transnational Perspective* (2nd edn, Tibor Varady et al. eds, Thomson/West 2003; 4th edn 2009).

Chase, O., and J. Bruner, *Law, Culture, and Ritual: Disputing Systems in Cross-Cultural Context* (New York University Press 2005).

Chen, Adi, 'Conflict of Laws, Conflict of Mores and External Public Policy in Israel' in *2010 Yearbook of Private International Law*, vol 12 (2010) (Andrea Bonomi and Gian Paolo Romano eds, Sellier 2011).

Chernick, Richard, and Rufus Rhoades, 'How to Conduct a Complex Financial Arbitration: A Rapidly Evolving Process' 1440 Securities Arbitration 2004,

Corporate Law and Practice Course Handbook Series (Practising Law Institute 2004).

Cheshire, G.C., and P.M. North, *Cheshire's Private International Law* (Butterworths 1970).

Chomsky, Noam, *Knowledge of Language: Its Nature, Origin, and Use* (Praeger 1986).

Chomsky, Noam, *Syntactic Structures* (de Gruyter Mouton 2002).

Christie, R.H., '*Amiable composition* in French and English Law' 58(4) Arbitration (1992).

Clark, D.S., 'Nothing New in 2000 – Comparative Law in 1900 and Today' 75 Tulane Law Review (2000).

Coe, Jack J., *International Commercial Arbitration: American Principles and Practice in a Global Context* (Transnational Publishers 1997).

Cole, Sarah Rudolph, 'Managerial Litigants? The Overlooked Problem of Party Autonomy in Dispute Resolution' 51 Hastings Law Journal (2000).

Congrès international de droit comparé tenu à Paris du 31 juillet au 4 août 1900: procès-verbaux des séances et documents vol 1 (LGDJ 1905).

Cornu, Gérard, *Linguistique juridique* (2nd edn, Montchrestien 2000).

'Corporate Counsel Prefer AAA Rules, Fulbright Survey Finds' 60 Dispute Resolution Journal (2005–06).

Craig, William Laurence, et al., *International Chamber of Commerce Arbitration*, vol. 1 (Oceana Publications 1990).

Cremade, Bernardo M., and Steven L. Plehn, 'The New Lex Mercatoria and the Harmonization of the Laws of International Commercial Transactions' 2 Boston University International Law Journal (1984).

Curtin, Kenneth M., 'An Examination of Contractual Expansion and Limitation of Judicial Review of Arbitral Awards' 15 Ohio State Journal on Dispute Resolution (2000).

Cutler, A. Claire, *Private Power and Global Authority: Transnational Merchant Law in the Global Political Economy* (Cambridge University Press 2003).

Dasser, Felix, *Internationale Schiedsgerichte und Lex Mercatoria: Rechtsvergleichender Beitrag zur Diskussion ber ein nicht-staatliches Handelsrecht* (Schulthess 1989).

David, René, 'Frustration of Contract in French Law' 28 Journal of Comparative Legislation and International Law, 3rd series (1946).

David, René, 'Droit naturel et arbitrage' in *Natural Law and World Law: Essays to Commemorate the Sixtieth Birthday of Kotaro Tanaka* (Yuhikatu 1954).

David, René, *L'arbitrage dans le commerce international* (Economica 1982).

David, René, *Arbitration in International Trade* (Kluwer Law and Taxation Publications 1985).

David, René, and J.E.C. Brierley, *Major Legal Systems in the World Today: An Introduction to the Comparative Study of Law* (Free Press 1978).

De Carvalho, Evandro Menezes, *Semiotics of International Law: Trade and Translation*, Law and Philosophy series no. 91 (Springer 2010).

Degan, Vladimir uro, *Sources of International Law* (Martinus Nijhoff; sold and distributed in the US and Canada by Kluwer Law International 1997).

Delaume, Georges, 'The Proper Law of State Contracts and the Lex Mercatoria: A Reappraisal', 3 ICSID Review – Foreign Investment Law Journal (1988).

Deledalle, G., *Charles S. Peirce's Philosophy of Signs: Essays in Comparative Semiotics* (Indiana University Press 2000).

Deleuze, Gilles, and Félix Guattari, *A Thousand Plateaus: Capitalism and Schizophrenia* (Continuum International 2004).

De Ly, Filip, *International Business Law and Lex Mercatoria* (North-Holland 1992).

De Ly, Filip, 'Lex Mercatoria (New Law Merchant): Globalization and International Self-Regulation' 14 Diritto del Commercio Internazionale (2000).

De Ly, Filip, 'Lex Mercatoria (New Law Merchant): Globalisation and International Self-Regulation' in *Rules and Networks: The Legal Culture of Global Business Transactions* (Richard P. Appelbaum et al. eds, Hart 2001).

Derrida, Jacques, *Positions* (Alan Bass tr, University of Chicago Press 1981).

Derrida, Jacques, *Of Grammatology* (John Hopkins University Press 1998).

Derrida, Jacques, 'Plato's Pharmacy', in *Dissemination* (Continuum 2004).

Derrida, Jacques, '" Genesis and Structure" and Phenomenology' in *Writing and Difference* (2nd edn, Routledge 2001).

De Saussure, Ferdinand, *Course in General Linguistics* (Columbia University Press 2011).

De Seife, Rodolphe J.A., 'A Plea for the Creation of Commercial Courts' Spring New England Law Review (1982).

Devlin, P., *The Judge* (Oxford University Press 1979).

Dezalay, Yves, and Bryant G. Garth, 'Merchants of Law as Moral Entrepreneurs: Constructing International Justice from the Competition for Transnational Business Disputes' 29 Law and Society Review (1995).

Dezalay, Yves, and Bryant G. Garth, *Dealing in Virtue: International Commercial Arbitration and the Construction of a Transnational Legal Order* (University of Chicago Press 1996).

Dezalay, Yves, and Bryant G. Garth, 'Fussing about the Forum: Categories and Definitions as Stakes in a Professional Competition' 21 Law and Social Inquiry 285(1996).

Dolinger, Jacob, 'Application, Proof, and Interpretation of Foreign Law: A Comparative Study in Private International Law' 12 Arizona Journal of International and Comparative Law (1995).

Domke, Martin, et al., *Domke on Commercial Arbitration (The Law and Practice of Commercial Arbitration)* (3rd edn, Thomson/West 2003).

Douzinas, Costas, et al., *Postmodern Jurisprudence: The Law of Text in the Texts of Law* (Routledge 1991).

Drahozal, Christopher R., 'Commercial Norms, Commercial Codes, and International Commercial Arbitration' 33 Vanderbilt Journal of Transnational Law (2000).

Drahozal, Christopher R., 'New Experiences of International Arbitration in the United States' 54 American Journal of Comparative Law (2006).

Drahozal, Christopher R., and Richard W. Naimark, *Towards a Science of International Arbitration: Collected Empirical Research* (Kluwer Law International; sold and distributed in North, Central and South America by Aspen Publishers 2005).

Dworkin, Ronald, *Taking Rights Seriously* (Harvard University Press 1978).

Eco, Umberto, *Lector in fabula. Współdziałanie w interpretacji tekstów narracyjnych* (Piotr Salwa tr, Państwowy Instytut Wydawniczy 1994).

Eco, Umberto, *The Role of the Reader: Explorations in the Semiotics of Texts* (Indiana University Press 1979).

Eco, Umberto, *A Theory of Semiotics* (Indiana University Press 1979).

Eco, Umberto, *Semiotics and the Philosophy of Language* (Indiana University Press 1986).

'Efforts to Increase Use of Arbitration in Middle East' August World Arbitration and Mediation Report (1998).

El-Ahdab, Abdul Hamid, 'Enforcement of Arbitral Awards in the Arab Countries' 11 Arbitration International 2(1995).

El-Ahdab, Abdul Hamid, *Arbitration with the Arab Countries* (2nd edn, Kluwer Law International 1999).

Elliot, David C., 'Med/Arb: Fraught with Danger or Ripe with Opportunity' 34 Alberta Law Review (1995).

Elsing, Siegfried H., and John M. Townsend, 'Bridging the Common Law – Civil Law Divide in Arbitration', 670 International Business Litigation and Arbitration (Practising Law Institute 2002).

Enkishev, Ilya, 'Above the Law: Practical and Philosophical Implications of Contracting for Expanded Judicial Review' 3 Journal of American Arbitration (2004).

Epstein, J., 'The Use of Comparative Law in Commercial International Arbitration and Commercial Mediation' 75 Tulane Law Review (2000).

Eskridge, William N., et al., *Legislation and Statutory Interpretation* (Foundation Press 2000).

Falk, R.A., 'On Treaty Interpretation and the New Haven Approach: Achievements and Prospects' 8 Virginia Journal of International Law (1967).

Ferrari, Franco, and Stefan Kröll, *Conflict of Laws in International Arbitration* (Sellier 2011).

Fisch, Max H., 'Introduction to Writings of Charles S. Peirce' in *Writings of Charles S. Peirce: A Chronological Edition* (M.H. Fisch and C. Kloesel eds, Indiana University Press 1982–2000).

Fitzmaurice, G., 'Vae Victis or Woe to the Negotiators – Your Treaty or Our Interpretation of It' 65 American Journal of International Law (1971).

Fortier, L. Yves, 'The New, New Lex Mercatoria, or, Back to the Future' 17 Arbitration International (2001).

Foucault, Michel, *The Archaeology of Knowledge* (Routledge 2002).

Fouchard, Philippe, et al., *Fouchard, Gaillard, Goldman on International Commercial Arbitration* (Kluwer Law International 1999).

Franck, Thomas M., *The Structure of Impartiality: Examining the Riddle of One Law in a Fragmented World* (Macmillan 1968).

Frick, J.G., *Arbitration and Complex International Contracts: With Special Emphasis on the Determination of the Applicable Substantive Law and on the Adaptation of Contracts to Changed Circumstances* (Kluwer Law International 2001).

Friedland, Paul D., and Lucy Martinez, '"The UNCITRAL Arbitration Rules: A Commentary". By David D. Caron, Lee M. Caplan, and Matti Pellonpää. Book Review' 101 American Journal of International Law (2007).

Friedman, George H., 'Is Administered Arbitration Still Needed?' C976 American Law Institute – American Bar Association Continuing Legal Education. ALI-ABA Course of Study (1994).

Frommel, Monika, *Die Rezeption der Hermeneutik bei Karl Larenz und Josef Esser* (Rolf Gremer 1981).

Gadamer, Hans-Georg, *Truth and Method* (Continuum International 2004).

Gaillard, Emmanuel, 'Thirty Years of Lex Mercatoria: Towards the Selective Application of Transnational Rules' 10 ICSID Review (1995).

Gaillard, Emmanuel, 'Transnational Law: A Legal System or a Method of Decision Making?' 17 Arbitration International (2001).

Gaillard, Emmanuel, 'Du bon usage du droit comparé dans l'arbitrage international' 2 Revue de l'arbitrage (2005).

Gaillard, Emmanuel, 'Souveraineté et autonomie: réflexions sur les représentations de l'arbitrage international' 134 Journal du droit international 4(2007).

Gaillard, Emmanuel, *Legal Theory of International Arbitration* (Martinus Nijhoff 2010).

Gaillard, Emmanuel, and Hague Academy of International Law, *Aspects philosophiques du droit de l'arbitrage international* (Libraire Hachette 2008).

Gaitis, James M., 'Reexamining Finality: How to Revise Institutional Practice Rules to Allow for Reconsideration of Reasoned Arbitration Awards' 23 Alternatives to the High Cost of Litigation (2005).

Geertz, Clifford, 'Thick Description: Toward an Interpretive Theory of Culture' in *The Interpretation of Cultures* (Basic Books 1977).

Gilson, Ronald, 'Value Creation by Business Lawyers: Legal Skills and Asset Pricing' 94 Yale LJ (1984).

Givón, Talmy, 'Isomorphism in the Grammatical Code' in *Iconicity in Language* (Raffaele Simone ed, J. Benjamins 1995).

Gizbert-Studnicki, Tomasz, *Język prawny z perspektywy socjolingwistycznej* (Państwowe Wydawnictwo Naukowe, Oddział w Krakowie 1986).

Glenn, H.P., 'Comparative Law and Legal Practice: On Removing the Borders' 75 Tulane Law Review (2000).

Goetsch, Sallie, *Family Values, A Reconstruction of Menander's 'Epitrepontes' (Act I/IV)* (Warwick 1995).

Goldman, Berthold, 'Frontiers du droit et "lex mercatoria"' 9 Archives de philosophie du droit (1964).

Goldman, Berthold, 'Lex Mercatoria' 3 Forum internationale (1983).

Goode, R., 'The Role of the Lex Loci Arbitri in International Commercial Arbitration' 17 Arbitration International (2001).

Goodrich, Peter, *Languages of Law: From Logics of Memory to Nomadic Masks* (Weidenfeld & Nicolson 1990).

Greenberg, Simon, et al., *International Commercial Arbitration: An Asia–Pacific Perspective* (Cambridge University Press 2010).

Guedj, T.G., 'The Theory of the Lois de Police, a Functional Trend in Continental Private International Law – A Comparative Analysis with Modern American Theories' 39 American Journal of Comparative Law (1991).

Guglya, Leonila, 'The Interplay of International Dispute Resolution Mechanisms: The Softwood Lumber Controversy' 2 Journal of International Dispute Settlement (2011).

Gumperz, John J., and Jenny Cook-Gumperz, 'Studying Language, Culture, and Society: Sociolinguistics or Linguistic Anthropology?' 12 Journal of Sociolinguistics (2008).

Gutteridge, H.C., *Comparative Law: An Introduction to the Comparative Method of Legal Study and Research* (Cambridge University Press Archive 1971).

Habermas, Jürgen, *The Theory of Communicative Action* (Thomas McCarthy tr, Beacon Press 1984).

Halket, Thomas D., 'The Use of Technology in Arbitration: Ensuring the Future is Available to Both Parties' 81 Saint John's Law Review (2007).

Hart, Herbert Lionel Adolphus, *The Concept of Law* (with 'Postscript' ed. by P. Bulloch and J. Raz, Clarendon Press 1997).

Hascher, Dominique, 'Note to ICC Award No. 8891' Journal du droit international (Clunet 2000).

Heidegger, M., *Sein und Zeit* (Max Niemeyer 1977).

Helmer, Elena V., 'International Commercial Arbitration: Americanized, "Civilized," or Harmonized?' 19 Ohio State Journal on Dispute Resolution (2003).

Herrmann, Gerold, 'Does the World Need Additional Uniform Legislation on Arbitration?' in *Arbitration Insights: Twenty Years of the Annual Lecture of the School of International Arbitration* (International Arbitration Law Library 16) (Julian D.M. Lew and Loukas A. Mistelis eds, Kluwer Law International 2007).

Hisham, 'Abd al-Malik Ibn, and Muhammad Ibn Ishaq, *The Life of Muhammad: A Translation of Ishāq's 'Sīrat Rasūl Allāh'* (Alfred Guillaume tr, Oxford University Press 1955).

Hjelmslev, Louis, and Hans Jørgen Uldall, *Outline of Glossematics; A Study in the Methodology of the Humanities with Special Reference to Linguistics* (2nd edn, Nordisk Sprog- og Kulturforlag 1967).

Hoenig, James K., 'The Pros and Cons of Administered Arbitration' 49 Dispute Resolution Journal (1994).

Holtzmann, Howard M., 'Recent Work on Dispute Resolution by the United Nations Commission on International Trade Law' 5 ILSA Journal of International and Comparative Law (1999).

Horvath, Gunther J., 'The Duty of the Tribunal to Render an Enforceable Award' 18(2) Journal of International Arbitration (2001).

Howarth, Richard J., 'Lex Mercatoria: Can General Principles of Law Govern International Commercial Contracts' 10 Canterbury Law Review (2004).

Hudson, M.O., *The Permanent Court of International Justice, 1920–1942* (Macmillan 1943).

Hunter, M., and G.C. e Silva, 'Transnational Public Policy and its Application in Investment Arbitrations' 4 Journal of World Investment (2003).

Hymes, Dell H., 'Ethnography of Speaking' in *Readings in the Sociology of Language* (Joshua A. Fishman ed, de Gruyter 1968).

Hymes, Dell H., *Foundations in Sociolinguistics: An Ethnographic Approach* (University of Pennsylvania Press 1974).

'International Commercial Arbitration Practices: A Discourse Analytical Study. Project Background' available at <http://enweb.cityu.edu.hk/arbitrationpractice/background.html>.

Iwasaki, Kazuo, 'Selection of Situs: Criteria and Priorities' 2 Arbitration International 57(1986).

Jamieson, Neil, et al., 'Acting Outside the Box – the Emerging Dispute Resolution Centres Developing Innovative Ways to Attract Business' <www.legalweek.com> (2012).

Jarvin, S., 'The Sources and Limits of the Arbitrator's Powers' 2 Arbitration International (1986).

Jemielniak, Dariusz, 'Kultura – odkrywana czy konstruowana?' 2 Master of Business Administration (2002).

Jemielniak, Dariusz, 'Time as Symbolic Currency in Knowledge Work' 19 Information and Organization (2009).

Jemielniak, Joanna, 'Just Interpretation: The Status of Legal Reasoning in the Continental Legal Tradition' 15 International Journal for the Semiotics of Law (2002).

Jemielniak, Joanna, 'Legitimization Arguments in the Lex Mercatoria Cases' 18 International Journal for the Semiotics of Law (2005).

Jemielniak, Joanna, and Przemysław Mikłaszewicz, 'Capturing the Change: Universalising Tendencies in Legal Interpretation' in *Interpretation of Law in the Global World: From Particularism to a Universal Approach* (Joanna Jemielniak and Przemysław Mikłaszewicz eds, Springer 2010).

Jolivet, E., 'Access to Information and Awards' 22 Arbitration International (2010).

Jung, Carl Gustav, *The Archetypes and the Collective Unconscious* (R.F.C. Hull tr, Princeton University Press 1980).

Kalenský, Pavel, *Trends of Private International Law* (Martinus Nijhoff 1971).

Kaufmann, Arthur, 'Die Sprache als hermeneutischer Horizont der Geschichtlichkeit des Rechts' in *Rechtsphilosophie im Wandel: Stationem eines Weges* (Athenäum Verlag 1972).

Kaufmann, Arthur, *Analogie und 'Natur der Sache': zugleich ein Beitrag zur Lehre von Typus* (Decker & Müller 1982).

Kaufmann-Kohler, Gabrielle, 'The Governing Law: Fact or Law? – A Transnational Rule on Establishing its Contents' in *Best Practices in International Arbitration*, ASA Special Series no. 26 (Markus Wirth ed, ASA Swiss Arbitration Association 2006).

Kaufmann-Kohler, Gabrielle, 'Arbitral Precedent: Dream, Necessity or Excuse?' 23 Arbitration International (2007).

Kauppia, Niilo, and Mikael Rask Madsen, *Transnational Power Elites: The New Professionals of Governance, Law and Security* (Routledge 2013).

Kerameus, K.D., 'Comparative Law and Comparative Lawyers: Opening Remarks' 75 Tulane Law Review (2000).

Kerr, Michael, '"Equity" Arbitration in England' 2 American Review of International Arbitration (1991).

Kevelson, Roberta, *Charles S. Peirce's Method of Methods*, Foundations of Semiotics series 17 (John Benjamins 1987).

Kevelson, Roberta, 'Introduction to the First Round Table on Law and Semiotics' in *Law and Semiotics* (Roberta Kevelson ed, Plenum 1987).

Kevelson, Roberta, 'Legitimizing "Repugnancy" in Law: Peirce and Contradiction' 1 Law and Semiotics (Plenum 1987).

Khan, Almas, 'The Interaction between Shariah and International Law in Arbitration' 6 Chicago Journal of International Law (2006).

Kilian, Monica, 'CISG and the Problem with Common Law Jurisdictions' 10 Journal of Transnational Law and Policy (2000).

Kingwell, Mark, *A Civil Tongue: Justice, Dialogue, and the Politics of Pluralism* (Pennsylvania State University Press 1995).

Kjaer, Anne Lise, 'Recontextualization of Concepts in European Legal Discourse' in *Dialogue and Rhetoric* (Edda Weigand ed, J. Benjamins 2008).

Knull III, William H, and Rubins, Noah D., 'Betting the Farm on International Arbitration: Is It Time to Offer an Appeal Option?' 11 American Review of International Arbitration (2000).

Kolev, Boris, 'Lex Sportiva and Lex Mercatoria' 1 International Sports Law Journal (2008).

Komendziński, Tomasz, *Znak i jego ciągłość: semiotyka CS Peirce'a między precepcją i recepcją* (Wydawnictwo Uniwersytetu Mikołaja Kopernika 1996).

Kornblum, U., '"Ordre public transnational", "ordre public international" und "ordre public interne" im Recht der privaten Schiedsgerichtsbarkeit' in *Beiträge zum internationalen Verfahrensrecht und zur Schiedsgerichtsbarkeit: Festschrift für Heinrich Nagel* (W.J. Habschied and K.H. Schwab eds, Aschendorf 1987).

Kripke, Saul Aaron, *Wittgenstein on Rules and Private Language: An Elementary Exposition* (Harvard University Press 1982).

Kuhn, Thomas Samuel, *The Structure of Scientific Revolutions* (University of Chicago Press 1996).

Labov, William, *Sociolinguistic Patterns* (University of Pennsylvania Press 1972).

Laeuchli, Urs Martin, 'Civil and Common Law: Contrast and Synthesis in International Arbitration' 62 Dispute Resolution Journal (2007).

Lalive, Pierre, 'Enforcing Awards' in *Sixty Years of ICC Arbitration: A Look at the Future* (ICC Publishing 1984).

Lalive, Pierre, 'International Arbitration – Teaching and Research' in *Contemporary Problems in International Arbitration* (Julian D.M. Lew ed, Martinus Nijhoff 1987).

Lalive, Pierre, 'Transnational (or Truly International) Public Policy and International Arbitration' in *Comparative Arbitration Practice and Public Policy in Arbitration*, ICCA Congress Series 3 (Pieter Sanders ed, Kluwer Law & Taxation Publishers 1987).

Lalive, Pierre, 'The Internationalisation of International Arbitration: Some Observations' in *The Internationalisation of International Arbitration: The LCIA Centenary Conference* (Martin Hunter et al. eds, Graham Trotman/ Martinus Nijhoff 1995).

Lalive, Pierre, 'The Role of Arbitrators as Settlement Facilitators – A Swiss View' in *New Horizons in International Commercial Arbitration and Beyond* (A.J. van den Berg ed, Kluwer Law International 2005).

Lando, O., 'The Lex Mercatoria in International Commercial Arbitration' 34 International and Comparative Law Quarterly (1985).

Lazareff, S., 'Mandatory Extraterritorial Application of National Law' 11 Arbitration International (1995).

'LCIA to Publish Challenge Decisions' in Global Arbitration Review, 1 June 2006 (vol 1(3)), available at <http://www.globalarbitrationreview.com/journal/ article/16483/lcia-publish-challenge-decisions>.

Lemmon, E.J., 'On Sentences Verifiable by their Use' 22 Analysis (1962).

Lerebours-Pigeonnière, Paul, *Précis de droit international privé* (4th edn, Dalloz 1946).

Lévi-Strauss, Claude, *Tristes tropiques* (Penguin 1997).

Lew, Julian D.M., *Applicable Law in International Commercial Arbitration. A Study in Commercial Arbitration Awards* (Oceana Publications/Sijthoff & Noordhoff 1978).

Lew, Julian D.M., 'Determination of Applicable Substantive Law' 25 International Business Lawyer (1997).

Lew, Julian D.M., and Laurence Shore, 'International Commercial Arbitration: Harmonizing Cultural Differences' 54 Dispute Resolution Journal (1999).

Lew, Julian D.M., et al., *Comparative International Commercial Arbitration* (Kluwer Law International; sold and distributed in North, Central and South America by Aspen Publishers 2003).

Lieberman, Seth, 'Something's Rotten in the State of Party-Appointed Arbitration: Healing ADR's Black Eye that is "Nonneutral Neutrals"' 5 Cardozo Journal of Conflict Resolution (2004).

Lillich, Richard B., and Charles N. Brower, *International Arbitration in the Twenty-First Century: Towards 'Judicialization' and Uniformity?: Twelfth Sokol Colloquium* (Transnational Publishers 1994).

Limbury, A.L., 'Making Med-Arb Work' 9 ADR Bulletin (2007).

Lookofsky, Joseph, 'The Limits of Commercial Contract Freedom: Under the UNIDROIT Restatement and Danish Law' 46 American Journal of Comparative Law (1998).

López Rodríguez, Ana M., *Lex Mercatoria and Harmonization of Contract Law in the EU* (Djof 2003).

Loquin, E., *L'Amiable composition en droit comparé et international: contribution à l'étude du non-droit dans l'arbitrage commercial* (Librairies techniques 1980).

Lorenz, Werner, *Die Lex Mercatoria: eine internationale Rechtsquelle? Festschrift für Karl Neumayer zum 65 Geburtstag* (Karl Neumayer and Werner Barfuss eds, Nomos 1985).

Lowenfeld, Andreas F., 'Lex Mercatoria: An Arbitrator's View' in *Lex Mercatoria and Arbitration: A Discussion of the New Law Merchant* (Thomas E Carbonneau ed, Transnational 1990).

Lynch, Katherine L., *The Forces of Economic Globalization: Challenges to the Regime of International Commercial Arbitration* (Kluwer Law International 2003).

Lyotard, Jean-Francois, *The Postmodern Condition: A Report on Knowledge* (Geoff Bennington and Brian Massumi trs, University of Minnesota Press 1984).

MacCormick, D. Neil, and Robert S. Summers, *Interpreting Statutes: A Comparative Study* (Ashgate 1991).

McDougal, Myres S., et al., *The Interpretation of International Agreements and World Public Order: Principles of Content and Procedure* (Martinus Nijhoff 1994).

Macneil, Ian R., et al., *Federal Arbitration Law: Agreements, Awards, and Remedies under the Federal Arbitration Act* (Little, Brown 1994).

Maniruzzaman, Abdul F.M., 'Choice of Law in International Contracts – Some Fundamental Conflict of Laws Issues' 16 Journal of International Arbitration (1999).

Maniruzzaman, Abul F.M., 'The Lex Mercatoria and International Contracts: A Challenge For International Commercial Arbitration?' 14 American University International Law Review (1999).

Maniruzzaman, Abdul F.M., 'The Arbitrator's Prudence in Lex Mercatoria: Amiable Composition and Ex Aequo et Bono in Decision Making' 18 Mealey's International Arbitration Report (2003).

Manjiao, Chi, 'Application of the UNIDROIT Principles in China: Successes, Shortcomings and Implications' 15 Uniform Law Review (2010).

Manjiao, Chi, 'Are We Paper Tigers – The Limited Procedural Power of Arbitrators under Chinese Law' Dispute Resolution Journal (2011).

Manjiao, Chi, '"The Iceberg Beneath the Water": The Hidden Discrimination against the Lex Mercatoria in Chinese Arbitration' 7 Journal of Private International Law (2011).

Mann, Francis A., 'Lex Facit Arbitrum' in *International Arbitration, Liber Amicorum for Martin Domke* (Pieter Sanders ed, Martinus Nijhoff 1967).

Marty, Robert, *76 Definitions of the Sign by Charles Sanders Peirce Collected and Analyzed by Robert Marty*, Department of Mathematics, University of Perpignan, France.

Mayer, Pierre, 'Mandatory Rules of Law in International Arbitration' 2 Arbitration International (1986).

Mayer, Pierre, 'The UNIDROIT Principles in Contemporary Contract Practice' in *ICC Bulletin Special Supplement: UNIDROIT Principles of International Commercial Contracts – Reflections on their Use in International Arbitration* (2002).

Melis, Werner, 'Note to the Austrian Supreme Court Decision' in *Yearbook Commercial Arbitration* vol IX (P. Sanders ed, Kluwer Law International 1984).

Miller, Grady, *The Legal and Economic Basis of International Trade* (Quorum Books 1996).

Miller, Russell A., and Peer Zumbansen, 'Introduction – Comparative Law as Transnational Law' in *Comparative Law as Transnational Law: A Decade of the German Law Journal* (Russell A. Miller and Peer Zumbansen eds, Oxford University Press 2011).

Mironi, M.M., 'From Mediation to Settlement and from Settlement to Final Offer Arbitration: An Analysis of Transnational Business Dispute Mediation' 73 Arbitration: Journal of the Chartered Institute of Arbitrators (2007).

Mistelis, Loukas, 'International Arbitration – Trends and Challenges', paper presented at the *Preventing and Managing International Commercial Disputes* conference, Rome (2007).

Molineaux, Charles, 'Applicable Law in Arbitration' 1 Journal of World Investment (2000).

Monateri, Pier Giuseppe, 'Introduction' in *Methods of Comparative Law* (Pier Giuseppe Monateri ed, Edward Elgar 2012).

Montesquieu, Charles de Secondat, et al., *The Spirit of the Laws* (Cambridge University Press 1989).

Morek, Rafal, 'The Regulatory Framework for Online Dispute Resolution: A Critical View' 38 University of Toledo Law Review (2006).

Morris, Charles W., *Foundations of the Theory of Signs* (University of Chicago Press 1938).

Moses, Margaret L., *The Principles and Practice of International Commercial Arbitration* (2nd edn, Cambridge University Press 2012).
Mustill, Michael, LJ, 'The New Lex Mercatoria: The First Twenty-Five Years' 4 Arbitration International (1988).
Mustill, M.J., and S.C. Boyd, *The Law and Practice of Commercial Arbitration in England* (Butterworths 1989).
Naimark, Richard W., 'Building a Fact-Based Global Database: The Countdown' 20 Journal of International Arbitration (2003).
Nakagawa, J., 'No More Negotiated Deals?: Settlement of Trade and Investment Disputes in East Asia' 10 Journal of International Economic Law (2007).
Naón, Horacio A. Grigera, *Choice-of-Law Problems in International Commercial Arbitration* (Mohr Siebeck 1992).
Nariman, Fali S., 'The Spirit of Arbitration: The Tenth Annual Goff Lecture' 16 Arbitration International (2000).
Nestor, Ion, *Problems concerning the Application and Interpretation of Existing Multilateral Conventions on International Commercial Arbitration and Related Matters: Report by Ion Nestor (Romania), Special Rapporteur* (A/CN.9/64) (UNCITRAL 1972).
Newman, Lawrence W., 'International Arbitration – Unfinished Business' April New York Law Journal 1(2001).
Niboyet, M.L., *Droit international privé* (LGDJ 2007).
Nicholas, Geoff, and Constantine Partasides, 'LCIA Court Decisions on Challenges to Arbitrators: A Proposal to Publish' 23 Arbitration International 9(2007).
Nielsen, Laura, *The WTO, Animals, and PPMs* (Martinus Nijhoff 2007).
Ogilvie, Sheilagh, *Institutions and European Trade: Merchant Guilds, 1000–1800* (Cambridge University Press 2011).
Olsen, Henrik Palmer, and Stuart Toddington, *Architectures of Justice: Legal Theory and the Idea of Institutional Design* (Ashgate 2007).
Oppetit, B., *Théorie de l'arbitrage* (Presses universitaires de France 1998).
Park, William W., 'Arbitration of International Contract Disputes' 39 Business Lawyer (1983).
Park, William W., 'The Lex Loci Arbitri and International Commercial Arbitration' 32 International and Comparative Law Quarterly (1983).
Park, William W., 'National Law and Commercial Justice: Safeguarding Procedural Integrity in International Arbitration' 63 Tulane Law Review (1988).
Park, William W., 'Arbitration Avoids "Hometown Justice" Overseas (The NLJ Corporation Counsel Report of Multinational Corporations Dispute Resolutions)' May National Law Journal (1998).
Park, William W., 'Why Courts Review Arbitral Awards' in *Recht der internationalen Wirtschaft und Streiterledigung im 21. Jahrhundert – Festschrift für Karl-Heinz Böckstiegel* (R. Briner, L.Y. Fortier, K.P. Berger and J. Bredow eds, Carl Heymanns 2001).
Park, William W., *Arbitration of International Business Disputes: Studies in Law and Practice* (Oxford University Press 2006).

Park, William W., 'The Procedural Soft Law of International Arbitration' in *Pervasive Problems in International Arbitration* (Loukas A. Mistelis and Julian D.M. Lew eds, Kluwer Law International 2006).

Parker, Ian, *Discourse Dynamics: Critical Analysis for Social and Individual Psychology* (Taylor & Frances/Routledge 1992).

Parker, Kelly A., *The Continuity of Peirce's Thought* (Vanderbilt University Press 1998).

Paulsson, Jan, 'International Arbitration Is Not Arbitration' 4 Stockholm International Arbitration Review (2008).

Paulsson, Jan, and Georgios Petrochilos (eds), *Revision of the UNCITRAL Arbitration Rules. A Report* (informal report 2006), available at <http://www.uncitral.org/pdf/english/news/arbrules_report.pdf>.

Peirce, Charles Sanders, 'On a New List of Categories' 7 Proceedings of the American Academy of Arts and Sciences (1868).

Peirce, Charles Sanders, 'Logic, considered as Semeiotic' Manuscript L75 (1902), available at <http://www.espeirce.com/menu/library/bycsp/175/175.htm>.

Peirce, Charles Sanders, *Collected Papers (Vols 1–8)* (C. Hartshorne, P. Weiss and A.W. Burks eds, Harvard University Press 1931–35).

Peller, Gary, 'The Metaphysics of American Law' California Law Review (1985).

Petsche, Markus A., *The Growing Autonomy of International Commercial Arbitration* (Sellier European Law Publishers 2005).

Phillips, Nelson, and Cynthia Hardy, *Discourse Analysis: Investigating Processes of Social Construction*, Qualitative Research Methods 50 (Sage 2002).

Potter, Jonathan, and Margaret Wetherell, *Discourse and Social Psychology: Beyond Attitudes and Behaviour* (Sage 1987).

Pryles, M., 'Reflections on Transnational Public Policy' 24 Journal of International Arbitration (2007).

Puelinckx, A.H., 'Frustration, Hardship, Force Majeure, Imprévision, Wegfall der Geschäftsgrundlage, Unmöglichkeit, Changed Circumstances' 3 Journal of International Arbitration 47(1986).

Quine, Willard Van Orman, *Word and Object* (MIT Press 1964).

Rabault, Hugues, Granice wykładni sędziowskiej (B. Janicka tr, Wydawnictwo Naukowe Scholar 1997).

Rabault, Hugues, *L'interprétation des normes: l'objectivité de la méthode herméneutique* (Harmattan 1997).

Racine, Jean-Baptiste, 'Réflexions sur l'autonomie de l'arbitrage commercial international' 3 Revue de l'Arbitrage 305(2005).

Radhi, Hassan Ali, State Courts and Arbitration in the Gulf Cooperation Council (GCC) Countries' 3 ICC International Court of Arbitration Bulletin (1992).

Rashid, Syed Khalid, 'Alternative Dispute Resolution in the Context of Islamic Law' 8 Vindobona Journal of International Commercial Law and Arbitration (2004).

Redfern, Alan, and Martin Hunter, *Law and Practice of International Commercial Arbitration* (2nd edn 1991; 4th edn Sweet & Maxwell 2004).

Reisman, W. Michael, 'International Arbitration and Sovereignty' 18 Arbitration International 231(2002).

Reuben, Richard C., 'Process Purity and Innovation: A Response to Professors Stempel, Cole, and Drahozal' 8 Nevada Law Journal (2007).

Riskin, L.L., 'Understanding Mediators' Orientations, Strategies, and Techniques: A Grid for the Perplexed' 1 Harvard Negotiation Law Review (1996).

Rivkin, D.W., 'Enforceability of Arbitral Awards based on Lex Mercatoria' 9 Arbitration International (1993).

Rogers, Catherine A., 'Transparency in International Commercial Arbitration' 54 University of Kansas Law Review (2005).

Rorty, Richard, *Contingency, Irony, and Solidarity* (Cambridge University Press 1989).

Rubino-Sammartano, Mauro, *International Arbitration: Law and Practice* (Kluwer Law International 2001).

Saeed, Abdullah, *Islamic Banking and Interest: A Study of the Prohibition of Riba and its Contemporary Interpretation* (Brill 1996).

Saleh, Samir, *Commercial Arbitration in the Arab Middle East: A Study in Shari'a and Statute Law* (Graham & Trotman/International Chamber of Commerce 1984).

Sanders, Pieter, 'Commentary' in *Sixty Years of ICC Arbitration: A Look at the Future* (ICC Publishing 1984).

Scheuner, U., 'Decisions Ex Aequo et Bono by International Courts and Arbitral Tribunals' in *International Arbitration: Liber Amicorum for Martin Domke* (Martinus Nijhoff 1967).

Schlag, Pierre, '"Le Hors de Texte, C'est Moi": The Politics of Form and the Domestication of Deconstruction' 11 Cardozo Law Review (1990).

Schlag, Pierre, 'Clerks in the Maze' 91 Michigan Law Review (1993).

Schlosser, Peter, *Das Recht der internationalen privaten Schiedsgerichtsbarkeit* (Mohr Siebeck 1989).

Schwenzer, I., 'Force Majeure and Hardship in International Sales Contracts' 39 Victoria University of Wellington Law Review (2008).

Sebeok, Thomas A., 'The Semiotic Web: A Chronicle of Prejudices' 2 Bulletin of Literary Semiotics (1975).

Shelton, D., 'Normative Hierarchy in International Law' 100 American Journal of International Law (2006).

Sheppard, A., 'Mandatory Rules in International Commercial Arbitration – An English Law Perspective' 18 American Review of International Arbitration (2007).

'SIAC Comes of Age with the Record Case Filings' (19 February 2013), available at <http://www.siac.org.sg/index.php?option=com_contentandview=articleandid=420:siac-comes-of-age-with-the-record-case-fillingsandcatid=1:latest-newsandItemid=50>.

Silberman, Linda, and Franco Ferrari, 'Getting to the Law Applicable to the Merits in International Arbitration and the Consequences of Getting it Wrong' in *Conflict of Laws in International Arbitration* (F. Ferrari and S. Kroll eds, Sellier 2010).

Slate II, William K., 'Culture Connection in International Commercial Arbitration.' Speech delivered on 18 May 2004 at the 17th ICCA conference in Beijing, China, Aug–Oct 2004 Dispute Resolution Journal (2004).

Slate II, William K., et al., 'UNCITRAL (United Nations Commission on International Trade Law). Its Workings in International Arbitration and a New Model Conciliation Law' 6 Cardozo J Conf Res 1 (Fall 2004).

Smit, Hans, 'The Future of International Commercial Arbitration: A Single Transnational Institution?' 1986 Columbia Journal of Transnational Law (1986).

Smith, David M., and Roger W. Shuy, *Sociolinguistics in Cross-Cultural Analysis* (Georgetown University Press 1972).

Smith, William. D., 'Price Quadruples for Iranian Crude Oil at Auction' *New York Times* (12 December 1973).

Sorel, J.M., 'Some Questions about the Definition of Terrorism and the Fight against its Financing' 14 European Journal of International Law (2003).

Sourgens, F.G., 'Comparative Law as Rhetoric: An Analysis of the Use of Comparative Law in International Arbitration' 8 Peppardine Dispute Resolution Law Journal (2007).

Spencer, Glen H., 'Administered vs. Non-Administered Arbitration' 54 Dispute Resolution Journal (1999).

Steinberg, Lukas and Chen Yun, *New CIETAC Rules to Internationalize China Arbitration* (R & P China Lawyers 2012).

Stelmach, Jerzy, *Współczesna filozofia interpretacji prawniczej* (Wydział Prawa i Administracji Uniwersytetu Jagiellońskiego. 1995).

Stelmach, Jerzy, and Bartosz Brozek, *Methods of Legal Reasoning*, Law and Philosophy Library 78 (Springer. 2006).

Stipanowich, Thomas J., 'Rethinking American Arbitration' 63 Indiana Law Journal (1988).

Stromberg, Winston, 'Avoiding the Full Court Press: International Commercial Arbitration and Other Global Alternative Dispute Resolution Processes (III)' 40 Loyola of Los Angeles Law Review (2007).

Strong, S. I., 'Research in International Commercial Arbitration: Special Skills, Special Sources' 20 American Review of International Arbitration (2009).

Tao, Jingzhou, *Arbitration Law and Practice in China* (2nd edn, Kluwer Law International: sold and distributed in North, Central and South America by Aspen Publishers 2008).

Teubner, Gunther, *Autopoietic Law: A New Approach to Law and Society* (Walter de Gruyter 1988).

Teubner, Gunther, 'Global Bukowina: Legal Pluralism in the World Society' in *Global Law without a State* (Gunther Teubner ed., Dartmouth 1997).

Teubner, Gunther (ed), *Global Law without a State* (Dartmouth 1997).

Tod, Marcus Niebuhr, *International Arbitration amongst the Greeks in International Commercial Arbitration: A Transnational Perspective* (Tibor Varady et al. eds, Thomson/West 2003).

Toope, Stephen J., *Mixed International Arbitration* (Cambridge University Press/ Grotius Publications 1990).

Tushnet, Mark V., 'Perspectives on Critical Legal Studies' 52 George Washington Law Review (1983).

Ulmer, Nicolas C., 'A Comment on "The Americanization" of International Arbitration?' 16 Mealey's International Arbitration Report 24(2001).

Ungar, Kenneth T., 'The Enforcement of Arbitral Awards under UNCITRAL's Model Law on International Commercial Arbitration' 25 Columbia Journal of Transnational Law (1987).

Unger, Roberto Mangabeira, *What should Legal Analysis Become?* (Verso Books 1996).

Van Creveld, M., *The Rise and Decline of the State* (Cambridge University Press 1999).

Van den Berg, A.J., et al., *Arbitragerecht* (W.E.J. Tjeenk Willink 1988).

Van den Berg, Albert Jan, 'Consolidated Commentary on New York Convention (109 I. Arbitral Award: A-National Award)' in *Yearbook Commercial Arbitration* vol XXVIII (A.J. van den Berg ed, Kluwer Law International 2003).

Varady, Tibor, et al., *International Commercial Arbitration: A Transnational Perspective* (3rd edn, John J. Barcelo and A.T. von Mehren eds, Thomson/ West 2006).

Venzke, Ingo, *How Interpretation Makes International Law: On Semantic Change and Normative Twists* (Oxford University Press 2012).

Vermeule, A., *Judging under Uncertainty: An Institutional Theory of Legal Interpretation* (Harvard University Press 2006).

Vischer, Frank, 'The Relevance of the UNIDROIT Principles for Judges and Arbitrators in Disputes Arising out of International Contracts' 1 European Journal of Law Reform (1999).

Von Mehren, Arthur Taylor, and Eduardo Jiménez de Aréchaga, 'Final Report on Arbitration between States and Foreign Enterprises' 63 Annuaire de Institut de Droit International (1989).

Von Mehren, Arthur Taylor, and Eckart Gottschalk, *Adjudicatory Authority in Private International Law: A Comparative Study* (Martinus Nijhoff 2007).

Voser, N., 'Mandatory Rules of Law as a Limitation on the Law Applicable in International Commercial Arbitration' 7 American Review of International Arbitration (1996).

Wagner, Anne, 'Introduction: The (Ab)use of Language in Legal Discourse' 15 International Journal for the Semiotics of Law (2002).

Wagner, Anne, et al., *Interpretation, Law and the Construction of Meaning: Collected Papers on Legal Interpretation in Theory, Adjudication and Political Practice* (Springer 2006).

Wakim, Mark, 'Public Policy Concerns regarding Enforcement of Foreign International Arbitral Awards in the Middle East' 21 New York International Law Review (2008).

Waldman, E.A., 'The Evaluative-Facilitative Debate in Mediation: Applying the Lens of Therapeutic Jurisprudence' 82 Marquette Law Review (1998).

Ware, Stephen J., *Alternative Dispute Resolution* (West Group 2001).

Watson, A., *Legal Transplants: An Approach to Comparative Law* (University of Georgia Press 1993).

Watt, Horatia Muir, 'Further Terrains for Subversive Comparison: The Field of Global Governance and the Public/Private Divide' in *Methods of Comparative Law* (Pier Monateri ed, Edward Elgar 2012).

Weinberg, K.S., 'Equity in International Arbitration: How Fair is Fair – A Study of Lex Mercatoria and Amiable Composition' 12 Boston University International Law Journal (1994).

Werner, Jacques, 'Competition within the Arbitration Industry' June J Int'l Arb (1985).

Werner, Jacques, 'The Trade Explosion and Some Likely Effects on International Arbitration' June Journal of International Arbitration (1997).

Westlake, John, *International Law* (Cambridge University Press 1904).

Wolenski, Jan, 'Carnap's Metaphilosophy' in *Language, Truth and Knowledge: Contributions to the Philosophy of Rudolf Carnap* (Thomas Bonk ed, Springer 2003).

Wróblewski, Jerzy, 'Pragmatyczna jasność prawa' 4 Państwo i Prawo (1988).

Yergin, Daniel, *The Prize: The Epic Quest for Oil, Money, and Power* (Simon & Schuster 1991).

Yu, H., 'Amiable Composition – A Learning Curve' 17 Journal of International Arbitration (2000).

Zaccaria, Guiseppe, 'Analogy as Legal Reasoning. The Hermeneutic Foundation of the Analogical Procedure' in *Legal Knowledge and Analogy. Fragments of Legal Epistemology, Hermeneutics and Linguistics* (Patrick Nerhot ed, Kluwer Academic Publishers 1991).

Ziembiński, Zygmunt, *Szkice z metodologii szczegółowych nauk prawnych* (Państwowe Wydawnictwo Naukowe 1983).

Zirk-Sadowski, Marek, 'European Judicial Governance and Legal Philosophy' in *Between Complexity of Law and Lack of Order. Philosophy of Law in the Era of Globalization* (Bartosz Wojciechowski et al. eds, Toruń 2009).

Index

a casu ad casum 43, 143, 149, 155, 192, 209
a priori 142, 172, 201
Abu Dhabi 114, 161, 171
actors 5, 8, 47, 49, 57, 69, 128, 151, 219
ad hoc arbitration 2, 3, 5, 6, 7, 9, 73ff., 100, 142, 161, 213, 219
  costs 83
  data on 89
  discretionary powers 80
  and *lex mercatoria* 82
  and new technology 83
  procedural rules 75ff., 78
  and UNCITRAL Rules 75–7
adaptation 66, 93, 220
addressee 46
addressor 46
adjudication 22
  methods 17, 159
  private awards 86
adjudicators 31, 36, 133, 135, 175, 195, 197
  see also arbitrators
administered arbitration, *see* institutional arbitration
administration 73
administrative support 83, 102
ADR methods 16–19, 176, 177
adversarial model 108, 110
Africa 106, 117
agreements 14, 100, 120, 138, 146, 178
  public international 194–5
Aksen, Gerald 74
Algeria 116
Alqurashi, Z. 120
alternative dispute resolution *see* ADR methods
America 5, 6, 93, 94, 95–6
American Arbitration Association (AAA) 78, 79–80, 91
  growth of 89–90
  Rules 92
    Art. 16 79
    Art. 20 110
    Art. 28.2 166
amiable composition 4, 10, 29, 38, 42, 63, 64, 80, 81, 175–92, 198, 217, 218
  advantages of 185, 190–91
  and conciliation 175–6, 180, 184, 186
  criticism of 189, 192
  decision-making 180–83, 190, 192
  definitions of 181, 182
  flexibility of 185, 190, 191
  and *lex mercatoria* 162–3, 173, 183–9
  and mediation 175–6, 180, 191
  origins of 175
  sources of competence 186
  uncertainty of 189–92
amiable compositeurs 10, 64, 100, 163, 175, 180, 182ff., 192, 204
  competences 182–3, 186–7
  freedom of 185
  and Islamic law 119
  and uncertainty 190
analogy 38, 132, 133, 146, 151, 200, 217
anational arbitration 3, 14, 15, 22, 25, 28, 136, 139, 143, 144, 184, 201, 203, 211, 212, 216
Andenas, M. and Fairgrieve, D. 128
Andersen, M.B. 158
Anesa, P. 47
Anglo-American procedure 108ff., 111
annulment 99
anthropology 36, 45, 46, 57
appellate awards 86
applicable law 22, 27, 62, 63, 65–6, 67, 131, 143, 160ff.
Arabs 113, 117, 118
arb-med 17, 19, 43, 63, 177ff., 186

arbitral proceedings 47–8, 69, 130, 138
  bifurcation of 85
  cultural differences 106
  data on 89ff.
  arbitral tribunals 3, 5
  criticism of 5, 6
  see also tribunals
arbitration 1, 2, 42–3, 69
  and ADR 17–18
  antagonistic 132
  definitions of 15–16, 136
  history of 13–15, 95, 98
  Islamic 113–21
  limits of 6, 74
  and litigation 19–21
  see also ad hoc arbitration; institutional arbitration; international commercial arbitration (ICA); limited administration
arbitration centres 2, 3, 5, 215
  competition between 95, 203
  in Middle East 117–18
arbitration clauses 21, 34, 61, 93, 118, 131, 151
  enforceability of 140ff.
  and transnational public order 207–8
arbitrators 3, 4, 7, 16, 17, 23, 28, 67, 85, 107, 112, 133, 143, 178, 179, 180ff., 205, 215
  ad hoc 80, 82
  challenges to 88
  choice of law 63, 109
  and comparative method 129, 131, 132, 139–40, 146
  competences 23
  competition between 95
  discretion of 34, 38, 39, 48, 65, 79, 95, 143
    and *lex mercatoria* 167, 169, 170, 172ff., 183
    and oral hearings 110
    and public order 193, 205, 208
  expertise of 25
  facilities for 77–8, 82–3
  and interpretation 36
  and Islamic law 118, 119
  as judge 133ff.
  knowledge of 97, 98
  and location 139
  and mandatory rules 201
  and multicultural cases 103ff.
  neutrality of 16, 28, 30, 34, 43, 88, 103, 178, 201
  and public order 198, 205
  revocability of 14
  selection of 19, 43–4, 64, 77, 78, 80
    and Islam 116, 119
  training 3
  and transnational public order 204–5
  and Westphalian approach 142
  see also amiables compositeurs
Aristotle 40, 53, 126
Arnold, Tom 17
Asia 106, 117
Asser, Tobias 135
Austin, John L. 32, 150n.
Austria 163, 188
authority 31, 33, 34, 94, 128, 138, 143, 146, 175
  informal 87
authors 37, 53, 56, 57, 63, 69, 70
autonomization 33, 213, 216, 218
autonomy 7, 16, 24, 25, 43, 49, 67, 100, 105, 164, 212, 213, 215, 216
  in comparative method 141–6
  and *lex mercatoria* 149–50, 154, 163, 173
  limits 116
  and public order 193, 199, 209
awards 16, 21, 74, 118, 125, 136
  additional 86
  criticism of 214–15
  foreign 116
  interim 16
  institutional 82–5
    finality of 84ff.
    preliminary review 84, 85
    refusal of 84–5
    substantive control of 84, 85
  location of 23–4
  and public order 198
    transnational 206
  publication of 7, 16, 20
  reasoned 80
axiology 161, 209

Back, L.C. 51
Bahrain 114
Balkin, Jack M. 42
Balkin, Jack M. and Levinson, S. 47
Barraclough, A. and Waincymer, J. 200, 201, 202
being 38, 39
Beirut 118
Belgium 172, 187, 208
Benson, Robert 29, 56–61, 70
Bentham, Jeremy 54
Berger, Klaus P. 105, 153n., 157, 158
Bergsten, Eric 106
Bernstein, Lisa 98
Betti, Emilio 37
Bhatia, V. 21, 47
Bhatia, V.K. et al. 28, 69, 70
bias 10, 83, 103, 178, 180, 192, 215
binding force 14, 17, 86, 162, 176, 177, 191, 197
Blessing, M. 164, 165, 201n.
Block-Lieb, S. and Halliday, T.C. 116
Bloomfield, Leonard 45
Böckstiegel, Karl Heinz 182
bona fide 178
Bond, Stephen 112n.
Bonell, J. 82, 155
bootstrap argument 143
Borris, C. 105n.
Brazil 121, 207–8
Briner, R. 180, 181
Broekman, Jan M. 51
Brower, Charles N. 93n., 96, 97n., 113
Brower, C.N. and Sharpe, J.K. 113, 114, 115n., 116n., 118n.
Brunet, E.J. and Craver, CB. 99n.
Bühring-Uhle, Kirchhoff and Scherer 19
Bulgaria 171
Burrell, G. and Morgan, G. 36

Calliess, G-P. 152, 160
Canada 6
Candlin, C. 47, 69, 70
Cao, Deborah 54
Carbonneau, Thomas E. 25, 99n., 149n.
Carter, James H. 20
case law 2, 5, 7, 34, 57, 82, 99, 111, 135, 149ff., 158–60ff.
  and *amiable composition* 187–8
  and international public law 194
  and transnational public order 206ff.
case manager 83
CENTRAL database 82, 158, 218
certainty 28, 41, 97, 171, 189ff.
chains 2, 5, 7, 214
challenges 16
change 69, 90, 106, 116, 130, 137, 183, 196
  paradigmatic 212, 215, 218–20
  qualitative 220
  quantitative 220
channel 46
Charny and Trachtman 95
Chase, O. and Bruner, J. 29–30
Chen, Adi 196
Chernick, R. and Rhoades, R. 80n.
China 19, 31, 43, 90, 166, 180, 186
Chinese language 31
choices 60, 62–3, 73, 78, 81, 94, 96, 99, 101, 141, 161, 162, 172
  negative 182
Chomsky, Noam 45
Chromalloy Aeroservices v *the Arab Republic of Egypt* 162
CIETAC 90
CIETAC Rules 31, 62–3, 109–10, 112, 160, 166
    Art. 21.2 85
    Art. 33.1 79
    Art. 33.2 109
    Art. 33.3 110
    Art. 45 19, 179
    Art. 47.1 186
    Art. 47.2 62, 166
    Art.52 86
    Art. 71(1) 31
CISG 119n., 160, 164, 165, 171n.
civil law 6, 22, 69, 118, 119, 125, 134
  and experts 111
  and legal argument 111
  and procedural differences 105ff.
claim statements 107
closed texts 59, 60
codes 46, 50
codification 105, 156ff.
  'creeping' 158
  private 152

Coe, Jack J. 84
cognition 37, 53, 56
Coke, Lord 14
Cole, S.R. 99n.
collective approach 143
colonization 9, 17, 21, 27, 93, 94, 97, 213
commentaries 125
commerce 13, 28, 30, 149, 152, 157, 160
commercial disputes 14, 15, 17, 21ff., 43, 75
  Islamic 114
common commercial practice 168–9
common ground 94, 132
common law 6, 69, 85, 99, 125, 134
  and experts 111
  and legal argument 111
  and procedural differences 105ff.
  communication 2, 31, 32, 35, 68, 83
  and semiotics 56ff.
  and sociolinguistics 45, 46, 47, 48
community 104, 116, 143, 151, 153, 154, 193, 215
Compania Valenciana de Cementos Portland SA v Primary Coal Inc 170
comparative analysis 2, 6, 28, 61, 63, 97, 105, 125ff., 145–6, 155, 217–18, 220
  and autonomy 141–6
  and domestic law 130–31, 134
  functional nature of 126
  history 126, 127
  international growth of 128
  method 125–33
    and *lex mercatoria* 129, 130, 158, 159, 161, 169, 173, 184, 192
    paradox of 145
    uses of 129–30
  monolocal approach 133–7
  pluralist approach 137–41
comparative law 126ff., 129 *see also* comparative analysis
competences 125, 126, 143, 146
  and *amiable composition* 175, 181, 182, 184, 185ff.
  in hybrid forms 179
  and mediation 177
competition 5, 7, 30, 67, 93, 95–6, 100ff., 203
  regulatory 95, 101
completeness 7
complex cases 80, 87, 94
compromise 18, 107, 108, 110, 176, 180
conceptualization 27, 47, 55, 56, 105, 133ff., 149, 197, 211, 212, 213, 215, 218
  transnational 145
conciliation 16, 19, 120, 175–6, 180, 184, 186
concretizations 38, 45, 47, 48, 215
confidentiality 7, 20, 22, 43, 49
conflict of interests 88, 201–2
conflicts of laws 22, 23, 81, 128, 141, 143, 145, 146, 215
  analysis 62, 171, 172, 173
  comparative 126
  and public order 198–9
    violations 199–200
consensus 78, 82, 95, 104, 107, 112, 120, 141, 145, 176, 209
  Islamic 113, 120
consistency 101
context 28, 29, 31, 34, 36, 37, 46, 56, 69, 145, 193
contracts 7, 17, 21, 34, 78, 87, 93, 152, 155, 181, 182, 209
  Islamic 118
  limits 99
  model 155, 156
contractual clauses 34, 118, 152, 161, 181
control 16, 74, 84
  of awards 84, 85, 87
  judicial 84–5, 99–100
conventions 57, 59
convergence 101, 107, 111, 155
conversation 35
cooperation 78, 116, 117
Cornu, G. 58
corrections 86, 162, 166, 168, 182, 197, 198, 208, 217
cost-efficiency 20, 74, 78, 83, 102
costs 110, 112
counsel 4, 19, 24, 66, 90, 92, 102
  in civil law 108
  and common law 108–9

and comparative method 130, 132
and mediation 176
and multicultural cases 121
Cour de Cassation 168n., 181n., 188, 196
courts 5, 6, 7, 16, 29, 61, 99–100, 134, 141, 142, 177
Islamic 115
language of 65
CPR Rules 76
Art. 16.3 85
Rule 8.2 86
CPR Intentional Rules 76–7
Commentary 77
creativity 34, 37, 38, 39, 51, 54, 59, 60, 69, 173, 183, 184
Cremades, B.M. and Plehn, S.L. 34n.
critical legal studies (CLS) 41–2, 51
critique 41, 42, 54, 137, 159, 162, 165, 169, 177, 215
cross-border trade disputes 5, 30, 34, 67, 168
cross-examination 107, 109, 111
cultural context 2, 19, 28, 29, 32, 36, 56, 61, 94, 95, 129
and procedural differences 103–12
cultural differences 95
culture, arbitral 7
institutional 87
culture, human 55, 57, 58
customary law 104
customs 13, 34, 63, 67, 82, 104, 120, 137, 150ff., 159, 204, 207, 214, 220
Cutler, A.C. 153

Dasser, F. 199
data 3, 7, 89ff., 152, 218
David, René 15, 108n., 131, 145n., 176, 180
David, R. and Brierley, J.E.C. 126
David Taylor and Son Ltd v *Barnett Trading Co* 181
de facto 30, 141, 183
De Ly, Filip 152, 155, 172, 187
de novo review 99
decentralization 9, 133, 137
decision-making 38, 43, 97, 133, 198
in *amiable composition* 180–83, 190, 192
comparative 130, 131
decisions 16, 22
decoding 32
deconstruction 53 *see also* legal deconstructivism
Delaume, G. 105n.
delays 74
delegation 81
Deleuze, G. and Guattari, F. 7, 8, 213–14
delocalization 139, 140, 143, 144, 147
democracy 103
Derrida, Jacques 39, 40, 41
description 44, 45, 108
Deutsche Schachtbau- und Tiefbohr GmbH v Rakoil 169
developing countries 116, 117, 121
Dezalay, Y. and Garth, B.G. 30, 93, 95n., 96, 101, 212n., 213, 219
diachronic inquiry 126
dialogue 35, 36, 39, 44
Dilthey, Wilhelm 35, 37
disciplines 69, 127, 128
disclosure 43
discourse 1, 50, 61, 68
analysis 67ff.
democratic 103
professional 70
discovery 36, 37, 53, 60, 80, 106, 107, 129
discretionary powers 7, 23, 34, 38, 39, 42, 48, 61, 95, 107, 110, 112, 143, 185, 194, 200, 213, 217, 220
in ad hoc arbitration 80
and *amiable composition* 182
in institutional arbitration 79, 81
Islamic 119, 120
and *lex mercatoria* 167, 169, 170, 172ff.
limits 183, 193, 205
and med-arb 178
and public order 193, 205, 208
discursive process 1, 2, 8, 47, 51
dispositive motions 80
dispute resolution 13, 15, 136, 175
approaches to 18
diversity 39, 46, 58, 64, 88, 103ff., 126, 129, 160, 167, 203, 212ff.
document discovery 106, 107–8
documentary evidence 110

dogmatic scrutiny 2
Dolinger, Jacob 134–5
domestic arbitration 125
domestic courts 7, 20, 22, 29, 62, 96, 97, 146, 151, 158, 196, 198, 207, 212
  and comparative method 128
  and foreign law 64–5, 134, 141
  and review 100
domestic law 3, 4, 6, 14, 22, 28, 29, 33, 39, 49, 62, 63, 67, 80, 105, 133, 134, 212, 214, 216, 219
  and comparative method 127–8ff., 143
    contract laws 130
    foreign awards 139
    public order 140
  and equity 187
  and ICA 136, 147
  and *lex mercatoria* 150, 155ff., 159, 163ff., 167, 171ff.
  and public order 193, 195ff., 198, 201, 204, 206, 209
    French 197
domestic regulations 80, 101
domestic rules 216, 217
double standards 202
Drahozal, C.R. 90, 93n., 94, 96, 97ff., 101
Duke Group 178
Dworkin, Ronald 32
dynamic process 2, 7, 8, 27, 49, 51, 52, 54, 60, 112, 145, 154, 213, 215

Eagle Star Insurance Co v Yuval Insurance Co 181
early neutral evaluation 16
East Asia 5, 90, 112, 121, 179
EC 195
Eco, Umberto 50, 55, 56, 57, 59
efficiency 80, 93
Egypt 13, 153, 154, 162
Elsing, S.H. and Townsend, J.M. 106n., 107, 111
encyclopaedia 50, 51
Enderby Town Football Club Ltd v *The Football Association Ltd* 206
enforcement 25, 28, 33, 34, 39, 63, 64, 67, 84, 115, 116, 136ff., 141, 142, 146, 161, 180, 188, 212, 214, 216, 218
    arbitration clauses 140ff.
    concerns 201ff.
    and expanded review 100
    and public order 198
    refusal of 6
England 14, 65, 111, 135, 169, 181
Enkishev, I. 99n.
epistemology 35, 37, 38, 68
Epstein, J. 126n., 128
equal treatment 79
equity 99, 161, 163, 175, 181ff., 187
    clause 181, 182, 184
    correction 182
    principles 182
    value of 191, 192
errors 61
Esser, J. 37
estoppel 6
ethics 190, 192, 194, 202
EU law 131, 160, 179
Europe 17, 65, 104, 106, 111, 112, 115, 128, 153, 156, 160, 167
European Convention on International Commercial Arbitration (1961) 167
evaluation 3
evidence 108
    admissibility 24
    Islamic law 119
evolution 5, 6, 8, 9, 44, 45, 85, 94, 95, 98, 106, 112, 114, 121, 138, 144, 160, 192
ex aequo et bono 29, 38, 64, 80, 81, 100, 119, 164, 198, 204
    and *amiable composition* 175, 180ff., 191
    ex parte communication 83
expert determination 18
expert witnesses 111
expertise 80, 93, 98
expertise–arbitrage 16, 18
expressions 49, 50, 55, 61, 94, 160, 186
extra-legal factors 64

fact 65, 66, 70, 134
fairness 175, 178, 182, 183, 187, 189, 192
family law 195
Far East 19
Federal Arbitration Act (FAA) 99–100

fees 74
finality 84ff., 99
financial efficiency 74, 83
Fisch, Max 53
Fitzmaurice, Gerald 194
flexibility of 20, 25, 31, 49, 76, 90, 110, 121, 185, 190, 191, 194
  and convergence 112
  critique of 93
  and Islamic law 120
  threat to 97
floating arbitration 25, 28, 136, 143, 147, 201, 218
force majeure 130
foreign law 22, 24, 64–7, 126, 129, 132, 134–6
  awards 138
  and domestic courts 134, 141
  and public order 195, 197
formality 30, 41, 76, 94, 177, 178
formalization 15, 20, 78, 93, 97, 98, 100, 213
Fortier, Yves 157
forum 28, 29, 83, 102, 103, 121
forum shopping 3, 24, 141
Foucault, M. 68
Fougerolle 187, 188, 189
France 116, 134, 154, 167, 173, 196–7
  see also French law
Franck, Thomas M. 18
freedom 185, 204
freedom of contract 6, 7, 33, 150
French law 175, 180–81, 187, 188
  and public order 196–7
Freyhold and Gessner 152
Frick, J.G. 171, 172, 173, 199
Friedland, Paul D. and Martinez, Lucy 76
Friedman, George H. 79n., 80
frustration 130, 180
Fulbright and Jaworski 90
function 4, 9, 29, 30ff., 39, 126, 136, 145, 184, 199, 212
functus officio 85
fundamental principles 195, 204

Gadamer, Hans-Georg 35–6, 37, 56
Gaillard, Emmanuel 3, 105n., 133, 134, 137, 138n., 141ff., 203, 212n.
Gaitis, James M. 85n.
Gao Haiyan v Keeneye Holdings Ltd 180
Geertz, Clifford 55
general clauses 61
general legal practitioners 4, 49, 98, 99, 102, 121, 219
general principles 54, 112, 120, 129, 144, 157, 166, 174, 188
Geneva Convention (1927) 138
  Art. VII 167
Geneva Protocol on Arbitration Clauses (1923) 138
Germany 13, 35, 170, 187, 198
Gilson, R. 102n.
Gizbert-Studnicki, T. 44, 46, 47
Glencot v Barrett 178
Glenn, H. 127, 128, 129
global dynamics 1, 6
global leaders 3
global trade 93
globalization 28, 33, 96, 128, 145, 153, 154
Goldman, Berthold 104, 151n., 153n., 154, 190
good faith 6, 161, 163, 168, 169, 189, 192, 209
Goode, Roy 138–9, 141
Gotti, M. 47, 69, 70
Greece, ancient 13, 153
Greimas, A. 51
Grigera Naón, H.A. 154–5
Guedj, T.G. 197
Guglya, L. 7n.
guidelines 87–8, 152
Gulf Chambers of Commerce 117
Gutteridge, H.C. 126, 127

Habermas, J. 103
hard law 87, 104, 152
harmonization 5, 61, 106, 146, 152, 153, 155, 203
Hart, H.L.A. 32, 33
Hascher, D. 209
Hegel 36
Heidegger, M. 35, 37
Helmer, Elena V. 95–6, 106
'hermeneutic circle' 37
hermeneutics 1, 3, 35–9, 56

Herrmann, G. 93n.
hierarchy 34, 35, 40
history 40, 57, 58, 68, 126, 127, 153, 160ff.
Holtzmann, Howard M. 75
homogenization 106
Hong Kong International Arbitration Centre (HKIAC) 76, 90, 91, 101
  Rules:
    Art. 14.1 79
    Art.14.2 109
    Art. 31.2 186
Hong-Lin Yu 183
horizontal structures 7
Hoy, David 56
Hudson, Judge 191, 192
human culture 55
humanities 35, 37
Hunter, M. and e Silva, G.C. 204
Husserl 40
hybridity 17, 19, 63, 106, 147, 177–80, 216, 219
  criticism of 179
Hymes, D.H. 46

IBA Rules of Evidence 108, 110, 111
ICC 18, 79, 84, 91, 107, 156, 169
  Awards:
    No. 3131/1979 168
    No. 4695/1984 (interim) 207–8
    No. 6142 201
    No. 7319/1992 (partial) 170
    No. 7518/1994 167
    No. 8385/1995 171–2, 190, 208–9
    No. 8873/1997 167
    No. 8891/1998 (interim) 209, 218
  Rules:
    Art. 2(iii) 85
    Art. 13 188
    Art. 15 79
    Art. 20.6 109
    Art. 21.2 166
    Art. 21.3 186
    Art. 27 85
ideal 45, 50, 66, 103, 209, 214
'ideal speech conditions' 103
identities 69
ideology 68
impartiality 18, 143
inconsistency 37, 42, 54, 139, 179, 194, 196, 203, 207
INCOTERMS 156
independence 3, 10, 16, 19, 21, 94, 213
independent agencies 84
indeterminacy 32, 61, 156, 165, 170ff., 194
India 121
'informal justice' 5
informality 20, 87, 93
injustice 134
inquisitorial model 108, 110
insiders 34, 57, 140, 141
institutional arbitration 73, 77–87, 106, 142
  advantages of 77–8ff., 87
  awards 82–5
    review of 85, 86
  costs 83
  data on 89–92
  discretionary powers 79
  growth of 89–90
  and *lex mercatoria* 81, 82
  and litigation 80
  preference for 90, 92
  weaknesses 84
institutionalization 15, 27, 93, 212
institutions 2, 3, 5, 15, 20, 23, 30, 68, 73ff., 87, 105, 143, 162, 213, 215
  competition between 95, 203
  internal reviews 74, 85ff.
  rules of 75, 77–8, 136
integrity 69
intent 15, 31, 57, 130, 150, 182, 194
intentional design 31
interconnections 55, 61, 130, 131, 144, 160
interdiscursive cross-referencing 68
interim awards 85
interlocutory awards 85
internal control 85, 86
internal public order 195, 196, 208
international agreements 194–5
International Arbitration Act (2012) 90, 101
International Centre for Dispute Resolution 79

international commercial arbitration (ICA) 1, 20, 125, 128
antagonistic 132
autonomy 145, 212, 213, 215, 216
competition in 95–6, 100–102
consolidation of 5
critique of 129
and domestic law 3, 25, 28, 63, 136, 147
framework 3, 4, 27, 31, 33, 62, 95ff., 216
innovation in 1–2, 31
and interpretation 126ff., 212, 215ff., 217
popularity of 5, 6
and proper law 62–3
representations of 9, 133ff., 146, 212
scope of 6, 30
special nature of 212, 218–20
and States 14, 23ff., 33ff., 211, 212, 216
success of 15, 21ff., 33, 121
International Commission on Commercial Arbitration (ICCA) 75
international community 144, 145, 151, 209
International Congress of Comparative Law, Paris 126, 127
international courts 6, 7
international customs 63
International Institute for Conflict Prevention and Resolution 76
international law 104, 162, 166
and public order 193–4ff., 204
international trade 3, 4, 6, 13, 21, 29, 67, 137, 168
agreements 76
and equity 190
history 153
international treaties 87
internationalization 3, 112, 128, 130
interpretant 52, 53, 54, 67
interpreter 52, 57, 67
foreign language 64
interpretation 2, 126, 170, 173, 182, 217
comparative 126, 127, 130, 132
dynamic 60
habits of 4
limits of 59
and public order 193, 194ff.
semiotic 49ff., 54
sociolinguistic 47
see also legal interpretation
interpretative repertoires 68–9
interpretivism 37
investment treaty cases 76
Iran 119, 166
Iran–US Claims Tribunal 76, 109, 115, 166–7
irrevocability 86, 120
Islamic States 115–21, 160–61
and New York Convention 115, 116, 117
Iwasaki, K. 97n.

Japan Commercial Arbitration Association (JCAA) 91, 140
Jemielniak, D. 55n., 94n.
Jemelniak, J. 32n., 154n., 161n., 169n.
Jemielniak, J. and Miklaszewicz, P. 97, 128n., 207n., 220n.
judges 8, 16, 17, 23, 28, 29ff., 34, 41, 47, 57, 65ff., 97ff., 112, 205, 206, 214, 215
and comparative method 127, 133ff.
in different legal systems 108
and equity 182, 185
and foreign law 135
and mediation 176
judicial intervention 97, 142, 214, 216
judicial review 16, 84, 97, 99–100, 135, 215
expanded 99
judicialization 9, 21, 27, 93, 95, 96, 99
jurisdictions 25, 69, 101
jurisprudence 1, 6, 17
analytic 32
jury 17, 57, 135
justice 3, 20, 30, 97, 161, 182, 191, 196

Kaufmann, Arthur 37–8, 39
Kauffmann-Kohler, G. 15, 65, 147
Kauppi, N. and Madsen, M.R. 219
Kerameus, K.D. 127
Kerr, Michael 184
Kevelson, R. 50, 51, 53

Khan, Almas 118
Kjaer, A.L. 131
knowledge 7, 38, 47, 51, 67, 94, 176
  of arbitrators 97, 98
  sources of 154, 160
Kripke, Saul 45
Kuhn, Thomas 220
Kuwait v AMINOIL 115–16

Labov, William 45–6
labyrinth 55, 61
Lacan, Jacques 51
Laeuchli, U.M. 108n.
Lalive, Pierre 21, 97n., 112, 129, 131n., 179, 204, 209
Lando, Ole 198
language 24, 28, 31, 35, 38, 40, 44ff., 50, 61, 69, 214
  common 132
  domestic 65
  foreign 64
  indeterminacy of 32
  social function 5
Larenz, Karl 37
'last resort' 206, 209
Latin America 106, 117
law 1, 2, 3, 6, 15, 22, 31, 40–41, 65, 69, 186
  creation of 60
  and interpretation 37–8, 54, 58
  manifest disregard of 99
law of the seat 137–9
lawmaker 133, 134
law-making 6, 37, 60, 145, 153
lawyers 4, 70, 98, 219
  civil 107
  international 102
Lazareff, S. 201
LCIA 91, 110
LCIA Rules 100
  Art. 6 34
  Art. 14.2 79
  Art. 20.4 110
  Art. 22.4 186
  Art. 26.9 86
  Art. 27.3 86
LCIA tribunal 6, 16
Lebanon 116
legal argument 2, 130
  comparative 111–12, 130, 132
  deflection of 132
legal canons 47, 57
legal community 2, 3, 4
legal concepts 6, 130
  comparative 130–31ff.
  domestic 131
  foreign 132
legal culture 47, 104, 121
legal deconstructivism 39–44
legal discourse 31, 42–3, 44ff., 48, 213, 215, 219
  concept 49
  normative 59, 60
legal fiction 151, 155, 192
legal instruments 46, 47, 57, 61, 152
legal interpretation 1, 2, 3, 6, 27–31, 57, 97, 136–7, 211, 215, 217
  and *amiable composition* 183
  and foreign law 135
  and national/global context 28–9
  problems 64
  theories of 31–49
legal norms 34, 38, 58, 59
legal orders 30, 132ff., 137, 139ff., 146, 163, 194, 199, 204, 206, 212
legal positivism 1, 31–5, 54, 137, 149, 155, 212
  and ICA 33ff.
legal rendition 3, 7, 8, 9, 29, 31, 37, 56, 59, 61, 64, 67, 132, 193, 195, 214
legal scholars 98, 132
legal scholarship 128
legal semiotics 49, 51ff.
legal studies 1, 2
legal systems 34, 39, 53, 54, 56, 58, 61, 136, 150, 184, 212
  autonomous 141ff.
  choice of 63
  comparative 126
  procedural differences 105ff., 118ff.
legal text 46, 47, 57
legal theory 1, 2, 31ff., 37, 51, 53, 66–7, 126, 154, 215, 219
legal traditions 95, 102, 103ff.
legal training 3, 4
legalism 15

legis fori 195, 197
legis loci arbitri 198
legislation 101
legislators 46, 57
legitimacy 6, 30, 33, 35, 93, 94, 95, 129, 145, 150, 209
  deficit 155–6
  of *lex mercatoria* 151, 154, 159, 161, 169, 172
Lemmon, E.J. 32
lenses 57–8
Lerebours-Pigeonnière, P. 197
Lévi-Strauss, C. 40
Lew, J.M. 146, 154n., 212
Lew, Mistelis and Kröll 15, 18, 24n., 74n.
Lew and Shore 106–7, 112n.
lex causae 22, 23, 28, 34, 62, 63, 143, 146, 189, 193, 195
lex contractus 140, 141, 146, 189, 201
lex fori 6, 22, 23, 28, 62, 134, 135, 136, 137ff., 140, 193, 201
lex loci arbitri 23, 24, 80, 136, 137ff., 146, 199, 201
lex mercatoria 5, 13, 29, 34, 35, 36, 38, 62, 63, 67, 80ff., 99, 104–5, 144, 203, 209, 216, 217, 218
  and ad hoc arbitration 82
  and amiable composition 162–3, 173, 183–9
  and arbitral cases 149ff., 158–60ff.
  autonomy of 149–50, 153, 154, 163, 173
  and certainty 189–90
  choice of 81
  codification of 105
  criticism of 149–50, 155–6ff., 170, 171
  and comparative method 129, 130, 158, 159, 161, 169, 173, 184, 192
  corrective application of 166
  definition of 149
  and domestic law 150, 155ff., 159, 163ff., 171ff.
  history of 153, 160ff.
  and Islam 114, 160–61
  legitimacy of 151, 154, 159, 161, 169, 172
    deficit 155–6
  as method 159, 169–70, 173, 218
  rules 152, 155, 157ff.
    accessibility of 80
  sources of 154–8ff.
  transnational 152–3, 155ff.
  universal 104
  see also New Law Merchant
lex sportiva 149
liberal approach 6, 41, 101, 107, 111, 112, 143, 160, 167, 205
Libya 116
limited administration 84
limited trust 85
limits 99, 116, 119, 130, 131, 193, 196
linear models 2, 8
linguistic diversity 64
linguistic expressions 49
linguistics 44–5, 50
literature 30, 107, 126, 183, 193, 194
litigation 5, 15, 17, 18, 19–21, 22, 42, 69, 80, 93, 177
  American 94, 95, 107
  comparative 125, 130, 136
  see also colonization
'litigation bis' 21
localization 3, 5, 33, 36, 67, 134, 138ff.
logic 32, 37, 44
Logos 32, 39–40, 60
Lookofsky, J. 157
López Rodríguez, Ana M. 21, 82n., 93n., 105n., 150, 151n., 161n., 168
Lorenz, W. 173
Loukas, Mistelis and Kröll 216
Lowenfeld, A.F. 174
Lynch, K.L. 171

MacNeil, Ian R. et al. 85n.
'macro' 104
majoritarianism 145
manipulation 141
Maniruzzaman, Abdul 104, 188–9
Manjiao, Chi 166, 186
Mann, Francis A. 133–4, 211
Marine Transport Corporation v Dreyfus 14
maritime trade 13, 14
'mark of a mark' 53
market forces 2, 7, 8, 100, 129

Marty, Robert 52
Mayer, Pierre 137, 140, 163–4
meaning 1, 2, 31, 32, 50, 56, 66
meaning-making 40, 52, 53, 54, 55, 57, 60, 68, 69
med-arb 16, 17, 177–9
mediation 16, 18, 19, 113, 175–7, 180, 191
  evaluative 176–7
  facilitative 176
  transformative 177
mediators 17, 52, 176–7
  competences 177–8
medieval trade 13, 153
Melis, W. 163
Menkel-Meadow, C. 103
merchants 98, 114, 151, 153, 155, 161
merits of the case 3, 5, 15, 22, 28, 34, 36, 62, 67, 79ff., 102, 131, 134, 141, 150, 163, 166, 175, 182, 186, 219
  foreign 64
messages 46
meta-level 38, 58, 70
metaphors 7, 69, 106
Methodenlehre 37, 38
methods 2, 53, 54, 105, 125ff., 159, 169–70, 173, 217–18
'micro' 104
Middle East 117–18
Miller, R.A. and Zumbansen, P. 145
mini-trial 16
Mistelis, L. 20
Mitsubishi Motors Corp v Soler Chrysler-Plymouth Inc 140
mixed approaches 19 *see also* hybridity
model agreements 34
model contracts 155, 156
model laws 152
modification 10, 29, 34, 39, 77ff., 81, 85, 97, 105,
118, 131, 140, 183, 185, 193, 195, 197, 201, 204, 217
monistic concept 141
monolocal approach 9, 133–7, 212
Montesquieu 1, 8, 27, 31, 51, 60, 66, 126
Morris, Charles W. 49
Muhammad, Prophet 113, 120
multicultural cases 102, 103–21
multi-party disputes 77
Muslims 113, 116, 118ff.

NAFTA 76
Naimark, R.W. 89
Nakagawa, J. 179
Napoleonic Code 175
Nariman, Fali S. 17, 20, 93n., 94n.
narratives 7
national courts 3, 14, 15, 25, 28, 29, 96, 193
national law 80, 81, 82, 130, 150, 184
  and developing nations 117
  and comparative method 128, 131
  regulatory competition 101
  see also domestic law, national courts
nationality 131, 139
natural law 145
negative argument 132
negotiation 17, 18, 19
Nestor, Ion 117
networks 30, 31, 33, 42, 55, 57, 61, 117, 142, 143, 212
  normative 150
neutral listener arrangements 17
neutrality 3, 4, 5, 16, 25, 28, 29, 30, 43, 83, 178, 179, 213
  challenges to 88
  and comparative method 131
  and deconstruction 42
  problems of 24, 30, 64
    multicultural 103
new law 63
New Law Merchant 62, 63, 154ff.
  autonomy of 150, 154, 164
  and certainty 190
  codes 156–8
  criticism of 157, 188
  and comparative method 129, 130, 159
  conceptual difficulties of 105
  history of 153
  and Islam 114
  as method 159
  rules 81, 82
  and Western bias 104
New York Convention 3, 6, 22, 25, 28, 33, 43, 63, 74, 101, 136, 207, 212, 218

Art.5 84
Art. V(2)(b) 202
Art. VI 138
Art. VII 139
and developing countries 117, 121
and Islamic States 115, 116, 117
and law of the seat 138–9
and public order 200, 201, 202
New York State 172, 208
Newman, L.W. 96n.
Nielsen, Laura 61
non-binding arbitration 17, 87
non-linear process 2, 8
non-verbal signs 52
non-waivable cases 88
norms 60, 104, 173
comparative 126
international 104, 194
Norsolor 161–2, 162–3ff., 168, 169, 187, 188, 189

object 49, 52, 54, 55, 61, 66, 67ff.
objectives 78
objectivity 37, 60, 191, 192, 195
oil concessions 114, 115, 160–61
Olsen, H.P. and Toddington, S. 142
omissions 86
one-party approach 18
online arbitration 3, 139
ontology 37, 38, 39
opposites 40
opaqueness 7, 43
OPEC 114, 115
openness 54, 56, 160
Oppetit, B. 176
oral hearings 24, 109–11, 130
ordre public 63, 64, 193ff., 218
critique of 194–5
violation of 199, 204
see also public order; public policy
ordre public international 193, 196–8, 203–4
ordre public transnational 204ff.
ordinary language 32, 44
Organization of the Islamic Conference (OIC) 116
organizational culture 87
original 1, 40, 42, 64, 66, 136
Orion Compania Espanola de Seguros v Belfort Maatschappij voor Algemene Verzekgringeen 181
'others' 36, 37, 57
'ought' 38, 39
outsiders 3, 34, 57, 131, 142, 214, 219

Pabalk Ticaret Limited Sirketi v Norsolor see Norsolor
pacta sunt servanda principle 167
paradigmatic change 212, 215, 218–20
paraphrases 52
Park, William W. 87, 96n., 101n., 214–15
Parker, Ian 68
parole 45, 46, 47
partial awards 85
participants 2, 14, 19, 45, 46, 47, 57, 69, 70
participation 103, 106, 108ff., 149, 152, 157, 178, 192
parties 14, 15, 18, 19, 30, 33, 43, 62, 65–6, 73, 84, 94, 131, 138, 146
and *amiable composition* 175, 182, 183ff.
advantages of 190
choice of rules by 78, 81, 161, 162, 190
and foreign law 134, 135
and med-arb 178
and review 16, 99–100
party autonomy principle 100
paths 55
Paulsson, Jan 125
peers 987
Peirce, Charles 2, 49, 50, 51ff.
performativity 46, 55, 59
periodicals 95
Permanent Court of Arbitration 16
persuasive authority 5
petroleum 114, 115, 161
Petroleum Development Ltd v Sheikh of Abu Dhabi 161
Phillips, N. and Hardy, C. 68
philosophy 1, 36, 37, 39–40, 42, 50, 51, 127
analytical 32, 44
phonocentrism 40

place 14, 19, 25, 28, 31, 36, 63ff., 136, 138ff., 146
  and public order 198, 199, 201
Plato 41, 66
pluralism 129, 133, 137–41, 212
political context 29, 41, 42, 43
Pollock, Frederick 126
Portugal 168
positivism *see* legal positivism
post-structuralism 53, 56
postulates 37, 39, 53, 54, 56
Potter, Jonathan 69
power 18, 41, 42, 43, 48, 68
practices 68, 69, 203
pragmatics 46, 49, 50
pragmatism 21, 22, 51, 53, 110, 112, 149, 174, 202
precedent 112
predicate 52
predictability 22, 87, 94, 96, 134, 194
preliminary review 84, 85
preparation 83
prima facie 185
principles 5, 60, 104, 129, 155, 156ff., 182, 184
Principles of European Contract Law (PECL) 156, 157, 158
private agreements 100
private approach 3, 5, 6, 15, 28, 30, 33, 34, 35, 86, 89
  and judicial control 85
  and *lex mercatoria* 152, 153, 155
private institutions 67, 76
  discretionary powers 81
private international law 22, 62, 133, 134
  and public order 195, 204
private judging 17, 18
procedural approaches 4, 78, 108
procedural autonomy 67, 212
procedural rules 2, 5, 20, 22, 23, 24, 39, 90, 97, 112, 119, 149, 162, 166, 179
  and ad hoc arbitration 75
  choice of 73
  and comparative method 143, 146
  convergence of 101
  and institutional arbitration 77, 78ff.
procedural standards 75, 87, 96, 106, 120, 213
proceduralization 15, 213
procedural/substantive dualism 143–4, 146, 151
procedure 83, 84, 94, 96, 97, 143, 149
  comparative 126
  differences 105ff.
  difficulties 24
  Islamic 119–20
processualization 9, 30, 96, 97
professionalism 15, 69, 70, 94, 99, 106, 129, 144, 147, 219
profit 118
proper law 62–3, 66, 129, 130, 131, 134, 140, 143, 163, 173, 203, 209
propositions 32
provisional relief 80
psychoanalysis 43
psychology 57, 58
public international law 5, 6, 60–61
  and public order 193–5ff., 204
public order 10, 140, 193–209, 218
  concept 193–200, 205
  criticism of 194–6, 205–6
  and domestic law 193, 195ff., 198, 201, 204, 206, 209
    French 197
  exception 195ff.
    and mandatory rules 200–202
  international 193–7, 203ff.
  scope of 199–200, 205–6
  transnational 193, 198–9, 203–9
  violation of 199
  see also ordre public
public policy 29, 34, 36, 39, 84, 101, 119, 140, 162, 180, 194ff., 218
  definition of 204
  transnational 203ff.
  violations of 99, 199
  see also public order
purpose 57, 59, 159, 199

Qatar 116
quality control 84

Rabault, H. 59, 60
Racine, Jean-Baptiste 145

radical humanism 37
Rashid, S.K. 119, 120
readers 55, 56, 57, 59, 61
reading 36, 57
realism 51, 58
reality 68
reasoning 32, 41, 47, 66, 82, 111, 127
  comparative 130, 132–3
rebus sic stantibus 131
recognition 18, 21, 23, 25, 32, 33, 63, 67, 84, 115, 116, 138, 139, 142ff., 161ff., 181, 184, 201, 205, 209, 212, 216
  exception to 202
  global 35
  refusal of 6, 85
reconstruction 37, 38, 44, 56, 135
recontextualization 131
Redfern, Alan 73, 138
Redfern, A. and Hunter, M. 89, 138n., 143, 146n.
reductionism 33, 58, 130, 154, 160, 170, 173
reformulations 2, 52, 69, 217, 220
regional centres 5
regional cultures 19
regional instruments 156
regulations 145, 152, 160
  domestic 80
  institutional 97
regulatory framework 4, 31, 89, 96, 139, 152, 154ff.
reinterpretation 2, 54
relations 55, 177, 190
remedies 23
reproduction 31, 53, 56, 60, 68
research 2, 3, 36, 44, 45, 68, 89ff., 125, 126, 127, 134
resolution methods 18
resources 125
Reuben, R. 100
review 16, 20
  awards 84, 85
  internal 74, 85, 86
  see also judicial review
rhetorical devices 1, 2, 41, 42, 50, 66, 67, 89, 130, 132
rhizomatic structures 7–8, 42, 213–14, 216
Richardson v Mellish 205–6
right to be heard 79
rights 33
Riskin, L. 176–7
Rivkin, David W. 187
Rogers, Catherine A. 7n.
roles 47, 48, 59
Rolland v Cassidy 191
Roman law 153
Rome Convention on the Law Applicable to Contractual Obligations 195
Rorty, Richard 55
rules 2, 5, 15, 22ff., 24, 28, 29, 67, 75ff., 97, 101, 106, 131, 145, 166, 186, 217
  analysis of 32, 33
  choice of 73
  institutional 77, 78, 81ff., 136
  interpretation of 39, 67
  Islamic 119
  lex mercatoria 152, 155, 157ff., 173, 174
  linguistic rules 57
  manipulation of 141
  new 78
  pre-existent 73, 78
  substantive 151, 217
  transnational 97, 105, 145, 149, 152–3, 155ff.
  web of 61
  see also rules of law
rules of evidence 108, 109
rules of law 62, 64, 146
  and *amiable composition* 175, 180ff.
  mandatory 200–202
Russian Federation 164–5, 167

Saeed, Abdullah 118
Sanders, Pieter 204
Saudi Chamber of Commerce 117
Saussure, Ferdinand de 44–5, 51, 52, 56
scepticism 50, 94, 114, 117, 138, 149
scheduling 83
Schlag, Pierre 42, 67
Schleiermacher, F. 35, 36
science 35, 50, 51, 53, 54, 55, 126, 127
script 40, 41
seat 134, 202

law of the 137–9
Sebeok, Thomas A. 57
selectivity 84
self-consciousness 3, 212, 215, 219
self-control 85
self-legitimization 143, 144
self-reflexivity 68
self-referential system 145
self-regulation 151, 153
self-sustainability 145
semantic authority 7
semantics 49–50
semiosis 2, 52, 54, 55, 60, 61, 68, 69
semiotic web 57–61
semiotics 1, 2, 49–56ff., 64, 67, 68
definition of 49
generations 50, 57
inquiry 51
sensu largo 18, 29, 126, 157, 182
sensu strictu 17, 18, 57, 58, 70, 155, 160, 180, 182, 217
sentences 49, 50
settlement 177, 178
settlement conference 17
Shanghai 90, 112
Shari'a law 113, 116–21, 160
Shenzhen 90, 112
Sheppard, A. 204
shield 132
signifier–signified distinction 52
signs 2, 49, 52, 57, 8
Singapore (SIAC) 90, 91, 101–4, 112
skills 125, 219
Slate II, William K. 103
Smit, Hans 77–8, 80ff., 106
social construction 55, 68
social context 2, 28, 29, 42, 45, 46, 58, 104, 151
definition 47
social groups 151, 219
social interactions 68
social sciences 37
sociolinguistics 1, 44–9
definition of 46
sociology 36, 44, 57, 127
soft law 87–9, 97, 152, 156
Softwood Lumber 6
Sorel, Jean-Marc 194
soul 40
sources of law 34, 35, 67, 87, 111
lex mercatoria 154–8ff., 185–6
Sourgens, F.G. 129, 130, 131n., 132
sovereign will 31, 134, 138
Spain 167, 191
specialists 70, 97, 98, 99, 121
speech 40
Spencer, Glen H. 82n., 83, 84
standard contractual clauses 34
standardization 93, 94, 95, 97
standards 5, 99, 155, 177, 190, 191, 192
cultural differences 103, 106ff.
statements 65, 68, 104, 107, 108, 110, 112
States 14, 23, 24, 25, 28, 29, 30, 31, 33, 34, 35, 39, 84, 87, 94, 127, 138, 146, 150, 211, 212, 216
community of 143
decline of 128
languages 65
and legislation 101
and *lex mercatoria* 151, 152, 153, 160
and public order 193, 195, 198, 204, 208
statutory law 14
Steinberg and Yun 90n.
Stelmach, J. and Brózek, B. 37
Stipanowich, Thomas J. 74, 81n.
Stockholm Chamber of Commerce 90
SCC Rules 79, 86, 109, 186
Strong, S.I. 7, 125, 126
structuralism 53, 56
structure 2, 3, 5, 7–8, 44, 52, 184, 215
subject 18, 42, 52, 56
subject matter 98, 116, 166
subjectivity 37, 192, 195, 197
substantive law 3, 10, 22, 23, 63, 66, 102, 105, 112, 129, 131
in comparative analysis 143
foreign 134
Islamic 118
and place 140
and procedure 143–4, 146
and public order 197, 198ff.
substantive rules 23, 24, 28, 29, 79, 80, 82, 142, 144, 149, 152, 155, 159ff., 173, 197, 215, 217, 218
and *amiable composition* 182

subsumption 32
sui generis 3, 5, 10, 133, 141, 215
sui iuris 212
summary jury trial 17
supranational public policy 204
surveys 90, 92
Switzerland 173, 179, 187, 198, 199, 207
syllogistic models 2, 8, 27, 32, 39, 53, 60, 66
symbols 29, 40, 68, 94, 115, 213
synchronistic inquiry 126
syntactics 49, 50
systems 40, 41, 50, 145

techniques 16–18, 126, 159, 170
technology 22, 83
territoriality 22, 28, 138, 139, 202
Teubner, Gunther 35, 145, 149n., 151, 155
texts 31, 32, 36, 37, 42–3, 50, 55, 57, 68
  closed 59, 60
textualist approach 194
theory 41, 42, 50, 133, 143, 150, 154, 212
third parties 18, 19, 90
time efficiency 7, 78, 83, 94, 99, 110
tools 3
topic 46
trade associations 98, 99, 155
training 125, 129
transformation 54, 56, 177, 219
translation 40, 64, 65, 66
Trans-Lex Database 82
transnational approach 3, 6, 24, 29, 34, 63–4, 66, 67, 104, 117, 128, 133, 141ff., 165, 211, 212
  concept of 145
  limits of 143
  and public order 193, 198–9, 203–9
transnational rules 6, 97, 105, 149, 150, 158, 160, 166ff., 172ff., 206
  Indeterminacy of 170
transparency 7, 16, 43
  financial 83
treaties 61, 76, 87, 160, 193, 194
tribunals 28, 31, 62, 73, 130, 133, 136, 146, 160, 161, 172
  composition 138
  discretion of 79
  institutional 81
  and different cultures 103ff.
    oral hearings 109–10
  and public order 199
  seat of 134
truth 32, 36
two-party approach 18

UCP 156
UK 90, 128, 178
uncertainty 24, 99, 118, 127, 141, 150, 153, 169, 171, 189, 194, 208, 215
  and *amiable composition* 189–92
  linguistic 65
UNCITRAL Arbitration Rules 73, 74–7
  and ad hoc arbitration 75ff.
  and oral hearings 109
  revision of 77
  Art. 35.3 166
  UNCITRAL Model Law 23, 65, 80–82, 101, 116, 138, 163
  Art. 24(1) 109
  Art. 28 81, 82
  Art. 28(1) 81
  Art. 28(2) 81
  Art. 28(4) 81, 166, 186
  Art. 32(1) 85
  Art. 35(1) 62
UNCITRAL Notes 88
understanding 35, 36, 37, 38, 47
unforeseeable consequences 130
Ungar, Kenneth T. 117n.
Unger, Roberto M. 1
UNIDROIT Principles 105, 155, 156–8, 165, 190
  and comparative method 159
unilateralist approach 134–5, 136
United Nations 117
  see also CISG
United States 6, 14, 17, 51, 65, 90, 99–100, 106, 107, 115, 134, 162, 172, 178, 179
  antitrust laws 140–41
  and equity 181–2
  influence of 95–6
  and transnational public policy 207, 208
universalism 97, 104, 134, 135–6, 196, 206

unpredictability 141, 165, 171, 189, 190
and *amiable composition* 191–2
US Federal Rules of Civil Procedure 66
US Supreme Court 14, 100
usages of trade 98, 104, 105, 137, 166, 189
users 55
utterances 8, 50, 57, 58, 59, 69, 70

vagueness 61, 89, 155, 170, 171, 185, 194, 196
values 60, 64, 78, 116, 161–2, 190, 192, 193, 194, 196ff., 206, 209
van den Berg, A.J. 144, 151
Varady, Barcelo and von Mehren 18
Venzke, Ingo 6, 7
Vermeule, A. 127
vertical structures 8
Vienna Convention 61, 104, 193
Vienna Court of Appeal 163
Vienna Rules (VIAC) 79
Art. 19.1 109
Art. 20.1 79
violations 199, 204
voice 40
voie directe 5, 23, 39, 62, 79, 81, 101, 143, 173, 200, 203
Volt Information Sciences Inc v Board of Trustees of Leland Stanford Junior University 100
von Mehren, A. and Jiménez de Aréchaga, E. 14, 24

waivers 86, 88, 100, 178
Watson, A. 126n.
Watt, H.M. 128n., 129
webs 55, 57, 59, 61
Weinberg 182, 184, 189
Werner, Jacques 95, 98n., 100
Werner, Wouter 54
Western countries 39, 40, 104, 107, 114, 115, 116, 160, 161, 179
Westlake, John 104
Westphalian approach 9, 138, 139, 141ff., 146
and arbitrators 142
Wetherell, Margaret 69
will of the parties 19, 23, 100, 150, 163, 167, 187, 207
witnesses 47, 70, 107ff.
absence of 110
evidence 109
oral testimony 109ff.
statements 107, 110
Wittgenstein, L. 44, 45
writing 35, 40, 41
written submissions 49, 109, 110, 111, 130
and Islamic law 119

X (SpA.) v Y (Srl) 206

Zirk-Sadowski, M. 87
Zurich Court of Appeal 168

For Product Safety Concerns and Information please contact our EU
representative GPSR@taylorandfrancis.com
Taylor & Francis Verlag GmbH, Kaufingerstraße 24, 80331 München, Germany

www.ingramcontent.com/pod-product-compliance
Ingram Content Group UK Ltd.
Pitfield, Milton Keynes, MK11 3LW, UK
UKHW010957180926
475701UK00004B/420
* 9 7 8 0 3 6 7 6 0 0 9 7 6 *